GENDER, HONOR, AND CHARITY IN LATE RENAISSANCE FLORENCE

This book examines the important social role of charitable institutions for women and children in late Renaissance Florence. Wars, social unrest, disease, and growing economic inequality on the Italian peninsula displaced hundreds of thousands of families during this period. To handle the social crises generated by war, competition for social position, and the abandonment of children, a series of private and public initiatives expanded existing charitable institutions and founded new ones. Philip Gavitt's research reveals the important role played by lineage ideology among Florence's elites in the use and manipulation of these charitable institutions in the often futile pursuit of economic and social stability. Considering families of all social levels, he argues that the pursuit of family wealth and prestige often worked at cross-purposes with the survival of the very families it was supposed to preserve.

Philip Gavitt is Associate Professor and Chair of the Department of History at Saint Louis University and the founder of its Center for Medieval and Renaissance Studies. A recipient of several fellowships from the Fulbright-Hays Program, the American Council of Learned Societies, and the National Endowment for the Humanities, and both a former Fellow and visiting professor at the Harvard University Center for Italian Renaissance Studies (Villa I Tatti), he is the author of *Charity and Children in Renaissance Florence* (1990).

GENDER, HONOR, AND CHARITY IN LATE RENAISSANCE FLORENCE

PHILIP GAVITT

Saint Louis University

CAMBRIDGE
UNIVERSITY PRESS

CAMBRIDGE UNIVERSITY PRESS
Cambridge, New York, Melbourne, Madrid, Cape Town,
Singapore, São Paulo, Delhi, Tokyo, Mexico City

Cambridge University Press
32 Avenue of the Americas, New York, NY 10013-2473, USA

www.cambridge.org
Information on this title: www.cambridge.org/9781107002944

First published 2011

Printed in the United States of America

A catalog record for this publication is available from the British Library.

Library of Congress Cataloging in Publication data
Gavitt, Philip, 1950–
Gender, honor, and charity in late Renaissance Florence / Philip Gavitt.
p.   cm.
Includes bibliographical references and index.
ISBN 978-1-107-00294-4 (hardback)
1. Charities – Italy – Florence – History.   2. Family – Economic aspects – Italy –
Florence – History.   I. Title.
HV295.F5G38   2011
361.70945'5110903 1–dc22   2010042281

ISBN 978-1-107-00294-4 Hardback

To Terry

She was the youngest daughter of Prince — , a leading nobleman of Milan, who could count himself among the richest men of the city. But the high opinion he had of his title made him regard his resources as barely sufficient — actually inadequate, in fact — to support its dignity. His one thought was to preserve the family fortune at least at its present level, and to ensure that it would never be split up, as far as lay in his power. We are not told exactly how many children he had, but only that all the younger ones were destined to the religious life, so that his wealth could pass intact to the eldest son, whose fate it was to carry on the family name — in other words, to beget children, and then to torture them and himself in the same way that his father had done. The poor Signora was still hidden from view in her mother's womb when her future status was irrevocably fixed.

— Alessandro Manzoni, *The Betrothed*, trans. Bruce Penman
(London: Penguin, 1972), 175

"Gli italiani sono indisciplinati cronici, sembrano non comprendere che la libertà individuale si coniuga con quella collettiva, che le regole vanno rispettate." Se il ministro dei Lavori pubblici, Enrico Micheli, reagisce con un laico rimprovero al weekend con 51 vittime, il teologo ammonisce: "Se il carabiniere non vede, Dio vi guarda. Violare il codice della strada è peccato."

— *La Repubblica*, 21 July 1999

CONTENTS

ACKNOWLEDGMENTS

Long book projects seldom, if ever, come to completion without the assistance of institutions, colleagues, friends, and family – certainly, this is no exception. Fundamental to the support of this project have been the National Endowment for the Humanities, which provided two summer stipends and a yearlong fellowship for college teachers in 1996–7; the American Council of Learned Societies, in the summer of 1990; and the Harvard University Center for Italian Renaissance Studies (Villa I Tatti) and its director at that time, Walter Kaiser, who through the Leopold Schepp Foundation provided a fellowship in 1990–1, and again, quite generously, a visiting professorship in 1996–7. I wish especially to thank Patricia Rubin, the Villa I Tatti acting director that academic year, whose scholarly collaboration in particular on matters Vasarian and Borghinian was generous and invaluable, as was the assistance of Allen Grieco, Sara Matthews Grieco, Peggy Haynes, Julian Kliemann, and Michael Rocke. The Villa I Tatti seems to have a particular gift for bringing together scholars whose work is closely related, and I benefited from collaborations far too numerous to list here. One collaboration stands out, however, and that is the many useful and witty discussions with William Wallace, to which I always look forward in ways that only good friends can. For the Venetian references in the book, I thank the Gladys Krieble Delmas Foundation – its funding of another project inadvertently yielded documents of interest to this project as well.

Many Italian institutions and friends deserve thanks, such as the Archivio di Stato, the Biblioteca Nazionale Centrale, the Biblioteca Medicea Laurenziana, and the Biblioteca Moreniana in Florence. Obviously the most crucial institution for my research has been the archive of the Ospedale degli Innocenti. During the years of my research there, Franco Sartini and his family emerged as particularly welcoming and gentle spirits, as did Lucia Sandri, whose support, friendship, and scholarly collaboration have made my forays into the Innocenti archives a constant source of joy. Scholars can now also benefit from her dedication to the reorganization and digitization of the Innocenti's archival inventory. Of the many Italian scholars who were willing to discuss areas of mutual interest, Gustavo Bertoli, Carlo Corsini, Maria Fubini Leuzzi, Pietro Mozzato, Giuliano Pinto, Sergio Piva, and Pier Paolo Viazzo were all gracious hosts and colleagues.

The College of Arts and Sciences at Saint Louis University has generously supported my research with numerous Mellon grants and summer stipends. In addition, my colleagues in Saint Louis University's Department of History have also listened to my ideas with a keen and even occasionally sympathetic ear, especially Don Critchlow, Tom Madden, and Hal Parker; the executive committee of the department has been generous with departmental grants. Michal Rozbicki generously helped obtain copyright permission for the cover image from the National Museum in Posnan, Poland. Practically every graduate student in the department has helped in some way, but in particular Chris Lane's eye saved me from a potentially embarrassing omission, and a seminar discussion with Patrick O'Banion and Vincent Ryan considerably sharpened my thinking on the limits of the term "confessionalization." Eric and Julie Forster were wonderful companions, neither annoying nor crazy.

The support, goodwill, and even patronage of colleagues in the field was indispensable, especially from Renèe Baernstein, Karen-edis Barzman, Elizabeth Bernhardt, Judith Brown, Gene Brucker, William Connell, Jonathan Davies, Wietse de Boer, Konrad Eisenbichler, Felicia Else, Edward English, Angela Fritsen, Mayu Fujikawa, Richard Goldthwaite, John Henderson, Bill Kent, Dale Kent, David Kertzer, Julius Kirshner, Thomas Kuehn, Marion Leathers Kuntz, Carol Lansing, Thomas Mayer, Tony Molho, Reinhold Mueller, John Najemy, John Paoletti, David Peterson, Elizabeth Pilliod, Eve Sanders, Rick Scorza, Jutta Sperling, and Nicholas Terpstra. To the last two scholars I owe a special debt of gratitude. The late Marvin Becker's influence is, I hope, apparent – his absence is certainly deeply felt. I thank my editor at Cambridge University Press, Beatrice Rehl, as well as Emily Spangler, Brigitte Coulton, and James Dunn, for their patience and their tireless efforts during the production of this book. I beg forgiveness from any colleagues or friends inadvertently omitted; I thank all of them as well, retaining responsibility for any errors in the book that remain.

In addition to the Sartini family, I owe a great debt to the Italian families who provided shelter and often a good deal more: the late Paolo Poesio, and Carla Poesio, as well as Marino Zorzi and Rosella Mamoli-Zorzi. Finally, my own family has suffered mostly in silence while they waited for this project to finally come together. My sons, Brendan, Thomas, and Leo, have been staunch advocates, close friends, and loyal Italophiles. This book's dedication reflects gratitude beyond measure.

INTRODUCTION

I SAIAH BERLIN'S RECONSTRUCTION OF THE FABLE OF THE HEDGEHOG AND the fox, in which the former knows one big thing and the latter many little things, does of course admit the logical possibility of a species that knows one little thing. The fear of that possibility is at the center of this book, which began as an extension into the sixteenth century of the work I had begun with my first volume, *Charity and Children in Renaissance Florence.*[1] Further research into the hospital's archives and in the state archives of Florence began to reveal an institutional pattern that the Innocenti shared with many other charitable institutions during the sixteenth century: the subversion of its original charitable mission to receive orphans and foundlings by increasing attention to the limited choices female foundlings had to face when they reached marriageable age. Even if their destiny was not irrevocably fixed, they shared with the nun of Monza the consequences of an age in which the enforcement of the rule of patrilineal inheritance became less flexible and in which competition for inheritance seemed to leave both boys and girls with institutions rather than families as their last resort.

As a result, sixteenth- and seventeenth-century Tuscany (and, for that matter, much of Catholic Europe) can be described as a landscape consisting of self-enclosed charitable and conventual communities responding, much like the urban world at large, to a monastic vision of discipline. However, this book argues that the process of creating a disciplined urban civilization based on aristocratic values, the "civilizing" process, also created throughout northern Italy (at the very least) "cities of women" in the same sense that Augustine understood the community of Christian believers to be a city of God: one in which *cultura femminile* added a dimension of femininity to

---

[1] Philip Gavitt, *Charity and Children in Renaissance Florence: The Ospedale degli Innocenti, 1510–1536* (Ann Arbor: University of Michigan Press, 1990).

the larger humanist program of defining what it meant to be human. In this sense, what Constance Jordan has defined as "Renaissance feminism"[2] was not an attempt to carve out separate space or to subvert discourse, but an attempt, often undertaken by the male writers Jordan herself cites, to amplify both the definition of humanity and to add more ample descriptive categories to the world of nature. The larger project of redefinition was in many senses a neo-Aristotelian project: a sixteenth-century reappropriation of Aristotle to understand the relationship of femininity and feminine roles to discipline and to Christian upbringing. It is not without irony that this neo-Aristotelian project deliberately aimed to reinforce that same noble culture to which Manzoni's historical novel *I promessi sposi* (*The Betrothed*) alluded and which, in practical terms, continued to fill the terrestrial and institutionalized cities of women with more citizens.

Thus, one of the most absorbing difficulties of this project has been the unavoidable blurring of the distinction between gender history and institutional history. Indeed, there is now a plethora of authoritative studies on the history of gender and gender roles during medieval and early modern periods. In addition, the work of Michel Foucault has inspired among some historians extremely creative, even fertile, conceptions of the areas of intercourse between public and private life. In this one respect, Foucault, as well as those historians who have benefited from the discipline of anthropology, have rescued social history from the sort of schematic Marxism and epistemological pessimism that attempted to separate the lives of the individuals from the political and institutional structures with which, at the very least, they had to contend daily and personally, perhaps even more intrusively than the impersonal, bureaucratic, early modern state. Decentralized government, in other words, may have been a more powerful and coercive force in daily life precisely because it was based on personal bonds and jurisdictions that frequently overlapped. By consequence, even though historians are far away from what Fernand Braudel thought of as "total history," the blurring of public and private, of gender history and institutional history, suggests that the Enlightenment project envisioned by Vico and the French Enlightenment of the possibilities of a science of humankind is neither politically nor epistemologically incorrect. Indeed, Nancy Struever has been right to locate this project in the Italian Renaissance, the communitarian stance itself of which implies that the private self, the individual, defines the essence of humanity incompletely: that only confidence in social institutions and social

---

[2] Constance Jordan, *Renaissance Feminism: Literary Texts and Political Models* (Ithaca: Cornell University Press, 1990).

groups permits a full definition of "human." Humans, according to this early Renaissance model, derive their humanity from being in the divine image, a responsibility that implies individual action moderated by the associative *and* coercive nature of community and authority.

Although Burckhardt defined the major characteristic of the Italian Renaissance as individualism, the term works more easily for the sixteenth century than the fifteenth, not because men and women shed their associative bonds as the veil of corporatism was lifted but because the discovery of the individual is the discovery of the power to fashion actively the public self – the individual, in short, not the state "as a work of art." Here, then, is the key confusion engendered by Burckhardt's work: the confusion between individuality and privacy. Burckhardt's Renaissance individual was above all a public and a civic individual and an active individual. "God does not want to do all things, so as not to take away our free will or any part of that glory that belongs to us," argued Machiavelli, meaning that as for Aristotle, virtue consisted in repeated teleological action that approached perfection.[3] In this sense, to argue that the durability of corporative ties undermined Burckhardt's emphasis on the individual is to miss the larger link that Burckhardt himself made between the construction of the individual and the craftsmanship that went into making the state a work of art.[4]

Thus, the relationship of discipline to charity is at the center of this book. However, I wish to take great pains to define discipline, because Max Weber's concept of discipline in *Economy and Society* is that discipline is the vehicle for the "rationality and calculability of human conduct."[5] For Weber discipline consists of two parts: the routinization of human behavior through training combined with the "appeal to strong motives of an ethical character." Although Vittorio Frajese sees this as an ambiguity, it in fact has much in common with the classical and humanist paradigm of continued repetition of discrete virtuous acts that constitutes movement towards virtue itself. For Weber, for example, the defects of classical military discipline,

---

[3] Niccolò Machiavelli, *Opere*, ed. Mario Bonfantini, La Letteratura Italiana: Storia e Testi, vol. 29 (Milan/Naples: Riccardo Ricciardi, 1954), 84: "Dio non vuole far ogni cosa, per non ci tòrre el libero arbitrio e parte di quella gloria che tocca a noi." English translation from *The Prince*, trans. William Connell (New York: Bedford St. Martins, 2004), 121.

[4] See the judicious conclusion of John J. Martin, *Myths of Renaissance Individualism* (New York: Palgrave, 2006), 124–33, esp. 126: "Both Burckhardt's individualist self and Greenblatt's postmodern self are forms of anachronism."

[5] Vittorio Frajese, *Il popolo fanciullo: Silvio Antoniano e il sistema disciplinare della controriforma* (Milan: F. Angeli, 1987), 111–12, citing Max Weber, *Economy and Society: An Outline of Interpretive Sociology*, ed. Guenther Roth and Claus Wittich; trans. Ephraim Fischoff (Berkeley: University of California Press, 1978), 2:1149–50.

traces of which he discerned in Loyola's *Spiritual Exercises,* were that it provided only for routinized training and failed to make an ethical appeal. Key to more recent treatments of discipline is the individual's role and the autonomy in the face of institutions of social control. If external institutions provide the training and the routinization of virtues, what compels or moves individuals to heed or respond to the implicit ethical appeal? What kind of social contract, in other words, is implied, and to what extent does the school, the parish, or the educational institution work to impose disciplinary systems?

Indeed, the mention of social contract is centrally relevant to the question, especially when one remembers that for Rousseau, virtue, that concept so beloved to Renaissance humanism, "is nothing more than this conformity of the particular wills with the general will. . . . We ought not to confound negligence with moderation, or clemency with weakness. To be just, it is necessary to be severe; to permit vice, when one has the right and the power to suppress it, is to be oneself vicious." Rousseau's claim that of his contemporaries, he alone understood Machiavelli, finds vindication in this quotation. Bronowski and Mazlish are certainly correct to cite in the same breath Calvinism and Catholicism as the roots of Rousseau's severity but neglect to tie Calvin and Machiavelli together as products of Christian humanism, as Christianized and, in Calvin's case, confessionalized virtue.[6]

The origins of sixteenth-century discipline, in which the schoolmaster had a precisely defined moral as well as pedagogical role, undoubtedly find their roots in medieval conceptions of Aristotelian order. Their fusion with Renaissance humanism can certainly be detected in Valla as well as such fifteenth-century *trattatisti della famiglia* as Alberti, Palmieri, Rucellai, and Barbaro. Even before the wholesale embrace of the Aristotelian corpus in the mid-sixteenth century, the period from 1490 to 1520 in Florence was pivotal in working out the implications of order, discipline, and society. Machiavelli's *Discourses* (written sometime between 1515 and 1519) themselves praise the Egyptians, who despite their warm climate and fertile soil managed to fashion an entire society around military discipline. Even Livy's *History of Rome,* the primary text on which Machiavelli's *Discourses* constitute a gloss, laments how, "I would then have [the reader] trace the process of our moral decline, to watch, first, the sinking of the foundations of morality as the

[6] J. Bronowski and B. Mazlish, *The Western Intellectual Tradition* (New York: Harper, 1960), 302–3. Rousseau's admiration of Calvin is clear in *The Social Contract*; cf. Rousseau: *The Basic Political Writings,* trans. D. Cress (Indianapolis/Cambridge: Hackett Publishing, 1987), 164, n. 7. On Machiavelli, cf. the 1782 edition of *The Social Contract,* translated in Rousseau, *Basic Political Writings,* 183, n. 5.

old teaching was allowed to lapse, then the rapidly increasing disintegration, then the final collapse of the whole edifice, and the dark dawning of our modern day when we can neither endure our vices nor face the remedies needed to cure them." Robert Black, in his introduction to a collection of documents concerning pedagogy in Arezzo, also notes an important change that occurred in masters' hiring contracts at Arezzo in the period of the Savonarolan reforms in Florence: for the first time, these contracts specify that the moral character of masters must be beyond reproach, a development that ironically coincides with a growing preference for clerical rather than lay pedagogues.[7]

Thus, even in the late quattrocento, educational authorities began to forge links between political and religious discipline. Both Protestant and Catholic confessionalization contained the ambiguity implied in Weber's model: *The Spiritual Exercises*, for example, were exercises in noncoercive self-examination and self-discovery but governed and responded to the imperatives of coercion and conversion. In this respect, the coercive power of Church and State paradoxically amplified and extended individual repression but did so by mutual agreement between believer (or subject) and institution. Jean-Jacques Rousseau's previously mystifying paradox in *The Social Contract* that individuals who were unable to abide by the Social Contract had to be "forced to be free" is much more understandable in the light of early modern disciplinary systems. Rousseau had certainly not only read his Machiavelli but had understood him better than most: coercion and freedom of the will depended on one another.

Thus, I do not define discipline as Michel Foucault would define it – that is, as only the increasing encroachment of social and institutional order on the prerogatives and behavior of individuals. For Foucault, regimentation was the key to early modern pedagogy: power structures in schools reflected the vocabulary of military hierarchy. Indeed, this theme tends to run through French historiography in general and has much to say about the interests of French historians and their relationship to the state in the 1960s. Philippe Ariès, to take a prominent example, argued that the new "Renaissance" distinction between adult and child made things much worse for the child, who became confined and defined by increasingly coercive

---

[7] Machiavelli, *Discorsi* 1:1.4, in *Discourses on Livy*, trans. Harvey C. Mansfield and Nathan Tarcov (Chicago/London: University of Chicago Press, 1996), 9; Livy, *The Early History of Rome: Books I–V from The History of Rome from Its Foundation*, trans. Aubrey de Sélincourt (London: Penguin Books, 1960, repr. 1971), 34. On the moral language of schoolmasters' contracts, see Robert Black, *Studio e scuola in Arezzo durante il medioevo e Rinascimento* (Florence: Leo S. Olschki, 1996), 127.

educational institutions. Foucault's *Madness and Civilization* posits a similar "ideal" environment of the Middle Ages insofar as the mad wandered freely among the rest of us and only when they became the "lepers" of a more rationalistic age did they suffer the constraints of both physical and mental imprisonment.[8]

Yet it is certainly not wrong to see the genesis of the modern and even the totalitarian state in these developments. To argue that such development hardly constitutes progress in any meaningful sense of the term does not preclude the importance of tying the earlier to the later stages. Indeed, one might argue, harshness of the treatment of marginalized groups is inversely proportional to the actual effectiveness of the state. In a somewhat similar vein, as recent historians of discipline and confessionalization have argued, stable political orders are dependent on a highly developed sense of *civiltà*, a virtue appropriated by the aristocracy during the Renaissance and presumed in theory not to extend to other social groups until the Enlightenment. However, it is extremely important not to forget that the roots of *civiltà* are in Italian humanism, and in Italian civic humanism in particular. At stake here is the deliberate cultivation of self-discipline not in the sense of self-coercion or coercion by others but the kinder, gentler regime described in Erasmus's *Colloquies* as discipline through the republic of letters, discipline through appeal by positive reinforcement to the divine features of human nature – discipline, in short, appealing to "strong motives of an ethical character."[9] It is precisely because the prince's role is pedagogical that Erasmus pays so much attention to the education of Christian princes. Not very far apart in spirit is Machiavelli's *Prince*, whose study of classical example makes the prince fit to lead by example, and in particular to teach virtue by example.

In this sense, the present work is closer in spirit to the work of Norbert Elias, for whom the discipline of perfectibility linked the individual to the state in early humanist thought.[10] Virtue could be taught, and once again the

---

[8]   Philippe Ariès, *Centuries of Childhood: A Social History of Family Life* (New York: Vintage, 1962), 241–68; Michel Foucault, *Madness and Civilization: A History of Insanity in the Age of Reason*, trans. Richard Howard (London/New York: Routledge, 2001), 5.

[9]   Erasmus, *Colloquies*, translated and annotated by Craig R. Thompson (Toronto: University of Toronto Press, 1997), 1: 88–108, in *Desiderii Erasmi Roterodami opera omnia*, ed. J. Le Clerc (Leiden: Pieter van der Aa, 1703–06), 1: 648.

[10]   Norbert Elias, *The Civilizing Process: The History of Manners*, trans. Edmund Jephcott (Oxford: Blackwell, 1994), 42–178. Nonetheless, I am in agreement with both implicit and explicit critiques of Elias's work, such as those proffered by Dilwyn Knox, "Disciplina: The Monastic and Clerical Origin of European Civility," in *Renaissance Society and Culture: Essays in Honor of Eugene F. Rice, Jr.*, ed. John Monfasani and Ronald G. Musto (New York: Italica Press, 1991), 107–35, and by Hans-Peter Duerr, *Der Mythos vom Zivilisationsprozess* (5 vols., Frankfurt-am-Main: Suhrkamp, 1988–2002), esp. vol. 1, *Nacktheit und Scham*.

associative nature of teaching also provided the bonds that tied authorities to their subjects. Indeed, the closeness of "discipline" and "disciple" suggests not only totalitarian regimentation, but also correction. Correction concerned itself with the process of bringing the marginalized back from the edges and into the mainstream. This will appear a strange observation to those familiar with the increasing intolerance of early modern social policy toward the poor, especially the tendency of municipal regimes to throw them out of the city for begging and the increasing reluctance to provide direct subsidies indiscriminately. This will seem even a stranger position to take when one observes that it is precisely in the semantic hedging involved in modern-day "correctional centers" (that in fact function as warehouses in which any hope of correction has been abandoned) that permits the modern state to flourish in a much more totalitarian fashion than it otherwise might.

For this reason, it is important not to push the "kinder, gentler" aspects of discipline too far back into the past. Neither Machiavelli nor Erasmus would have been in the least inclined to diminish the importance of the pervasiveness of human evil nor the important role that secular authorities had in correcting it, by coercion if necessary. On both sides of the Catholic–Protestant confessional divide, Augustine's condemnation of the notion that infants were innocent found a sympathetic audience among moralists, and its implications were clear for household management. Discipline, according to the treatise printed by Silvio Antoniano for Carlo Borromeo in 1584, could not wait for the child to attain the age of reason but had to begin even in the crib.[11]

Moreover, the Tridentine Reformation appears to have marked some sort of divide, at least in Antoniano's work, from a liberal humanism (based on Quintilian and Plutarch) in which discipline was taught not by blows but by example and its imitation, to a harsher correctional regime that coincided with the expansion of ecclesiastical authority into matters that connected confessionalization to political obedience. Thus, Antoniano compared punishment in the family to punishment in a small city, in which the father assumed the role of magistrate, using the rod and the whip for the correction of children, "either for making them retreat from evil, or to change them for the better."[12] Further, where Machiavelli saw love and fear as a choice, Antoniano saw mixed love and fear as necessary for stable political order. More important, as Frajese points out, what was new about the Tridentine

---

[11] Silvio Antoniano, *Tre libri dell' educatione cristiana de' figliuoli* (Verona: Sebastiano delle Donne, 1584), 20.

[12] Ibid., 123v.

disciplinary system is that the family became the vehicle for confessional-ization and obedience.[13] Even so, the temptations and wiles of Satan were omnipresent. For this reason, Antoniano argued, in language reminiscent of Elizabethan notions of the body politic, education should be a cooperative project between Church and State:

> Finally it is important that between the temporal and spiritual governor there should be the greatest possible unity and concord, not only for education, but in any other matter relating to the public good. The secular governor should remember that he must minister and provide help to the ecclesiastical governor just as the left arm acts in unison with the right for the benefit of the entire body. The more that temporal government makes itself conform to the spiritual, and favors and promotes it, the more it will be useful for the conservation of the Republic. While the spiritual governor's task is to make a good Christian, in carrying out this task he necessarily makes a good citizen, which is just what the temporal governor claims to do. This happens because the Holy Roman Catholic Church, City of God, placed on a mountain, and consisting of all those baptized and regenerated in Christ, are citizens of a most holy City and most perfect Republic, of which the ancient philosophers could only dream. The same is absolutely true of the good citizen and nobleman. Therefore those who distinguish between things that are so closely tied together, are in serious error, when they think that good citizens can be had under other rules than those that define the good Christian.[14]

This passage combines virtually every element of the complex fabric of discipline, state-building, and confessionalization that was the culmination of post-Tridentine reflection on the relationship between reform and the *respublica Christiana*. Such a combination is hardly revolutionary, however. The connection between education and governance was the legacy of the polis. Even in practical terms discipline describes a process that in many north Italian centers had begun well before even the first session of the Council of Trent in 1545. In Florence, this sort of ideology drove Cosimo I to undertake reforms of charitable and conventual institutions simultaneously, to bring them into the orbit of territorial and institutional consolidation. This process and this passage reflect another important social development that was the outcome of fifteenth-century humanism and its fortunes under courts rather than republics: the equation of the *buon cittadino* and the *huomo da bene*. The

---

[13] V. Frajese, *Il popolo fanciullo*, 55; see also Adriano Prosperi, "Intellettuali e Chiesa all'inizio dell'età moderna," in *Storia d'Italia. Annali*, ed. Corrado Vivanti, vol. 4, *Intellettuali e potere* (Turin: Einaudi, 1981), 248.

[14] Silvio Antoniano, *Tre libri dell' edcuatione christiana*, 26a.

appropriation of Renaissance humanism by courtiers as a means of defining their status as elect nobility is a process that is a common element in the evolution of dialogues and treatises on domestic economics and education.[15] It is a process, moreover, closely aligned with changes in inheritance practice that tightened the enforcement of norms of patrilineal succession, norms that constituted another form of preserving definitions of nobility.

As coercive as sixteenth-century theories of noble discipline might be, they nonetheless had to distinguish between what was effective and what might be counterproductive. In this respect, it is important to make a distinction between charitable institutions and prisons. Indeed, the Council of Trent worked diligently to eradicate abuses through which women were forced into convents against their will.[16] Obviously, as Manzoni's example in this book's epigraph shows, coercion could take such subtle forms that young women might believe they were pursuing their own free will when they were being coerced (and convents did serve, as we shall see, as charitable institutions, in the sense that what family structure and property could not provide, even in aristocratic families institutions had to supplement). However, Sandra Cavallo's exemplary cautions in her study of Turin apply more broadly: not until the Enlightenment, that age of great faith in the unlimited powers of human reason, did secular authorities employ methods of confinement that were truly and effectively totalitarian.

Female foundlings, for the most part, faced such a hostile world by the mid-sixteenth century that hospital officials no longer allowed them to venture out into it. The fifteenth-century practice of sending small girls into household service had ceased by the 1530s, prohibited on the well-founded grounds that such girls, even at a very young age, were vulnerable to sexual exploitation.[17] The only legitimate alternatives, marriage and the conventual

---

[15] For this important point, see Daniela Frigo, *Il padre di famiglia: governo della casa e governo civile nella tradizione dell'<<Economica>> fra Cinque e Seicento* (Rome: Bulzoni, 1985), 34. Frigo persuasively argues that this process is signaled in the domestic literature beginning in about 1540, when Alessandro Piccolomini translated Xenophon and reinforced in 1552 with the publication of his own treatise addressed to the noble father of a newborn son.

[16] *Canons and Decrees of the Council of Trent*, Twenty-fifth Session, 17:228, cited in Anne Jacobson Schutte, "Legal Remedies for Forced Monachation in Early Modern Italy," in *Heresy, Culture, and Religion in Early Modern Italy*, ed. John Jeffries Martin (Kirksville MO: Sixteenth-Century Essays and Studies, 2006), 232 n3. On coerced monachation and patrician family strategy in Venice, see Jutta Sperling, *Convents and the Body Politic in Late Renaissance Venice* (Chicago/London: University of Chicago Press, 1999), 29–38, 301, n. 229.

[17] That the Innocenti's boys were also subject to sexual exploitation seems not to have concerned the guardians of the Innocenti. When the Ufficiali della Notte had begun to take an interest in sodomy, in the 1480s and 1490s, adolescent *fanciulli* of the Innocenti were frequently implicated. I thank Michael Rocke for this information. On patterns of child sexual abuse in Renaissance

life, became increasingly circumscribed by the inadequacy of the dowries the Innocenti offered. Until 1561, the Innocenti provided a dowry of 150 lire di piccioli, which was doubled to 300 lire di piccioli because

> up to today the number of girls of marriageable age has increased quite a bit, and seeing that little by little the number still multiplies, [it is clear that] an impossibly large census will result, causing great expense, and running counter to the major purpose of this institution.[18]

Even at three hundred lire, the Innocenti offered considerably less than the average artisan dowry of approximately eight hundred lire, so that not surprisingly, even this hard-won concession had little effect.

At least one testator, Giovanbattista di Ser Andrea di Cristoforo Nacchianti (who would later become bishop of Chioggia), in 1518 had already seen this as a sufficiently pressing problem that his will provided funds for the construction of a convent that would house the Innocenti's girls who could not marry nor find a place in one of the city's convents.[19] The first building contracts were signed and work begun in 1528 on renovating the houses that stood along the Via de' Fibbiai southward toward the monastery of Santa Maria degli Angeli. Another enlargement for the same purpose was undertaken in the 1540s, so that by the early 1570s, the Ospedale degli Innocenti finally had enough space to house its adolescent girls and its wet nurses separately. By the 1580s, nonetheless, the hospital's resident female population outgrew the debt-ridden institution's ability to support it, and women who had reached age thirty-six were transferred to the widows' asylum of Orbatello, which had been founded by a member of the Alberti family in the 1370s. As Richard Trexler has documented, the sixteenth century was an era of unprecedented expansion for the Orbatello as well. In Florence and Venice, as well as many other northern Italian cities, convents had always been refuges for the younger daughters of wealthy families anxious to preserve their shrinking patrimony.[20]

Florence, the reader is directed to his excellent study, *Forbidden Friendships: Homosexuality and Male Culture in Renaissance Florence* (New York and Oxford: Oxford University Press, 1996), 162–3.

[18] Archivio dell'Ospedale degli Innocenti (AOIF) Giornale L (XIII, 18) fol. 80v, 10 March 1560: "che essendo infino ad hoggi in questo nostro spedale cresciuto assai il numero delle fanciulle di età nubile; et vedendo che di mano in mano e multiplica tuttavia più: talche se ne viene a fare una ragunata insopportabile, con grande spesa, et contro le prime intentioni di questa casa; et considerando dell'altra parte la pocha dote et i cattivi riscontri, et la mala qualità dei tempi che è corsa, et corre, la quale oltre all'altre areca particular difficoltà di maritarle, o monacarle."

[19] Archivio di Stato di Firenze (ASF), Diplomatico, Spedale degli Innocenti, 22 February 1517.

[20] Richard Trexler, "A Widows' Asylum of the Renaissance: The Orbatello," in *Old Age in Pre-Industrial Society*, ed. Peter Stearns (New York: Holmes and Meier, 1982), 119–49. In Genoa, for example, Edoardo Grendi notes the increasing emphasis in municipal charity on the fate of young

In Florence, for example, there were thirty convents for nuns in 1470, and sixty-three by 1574. The average convent in 1478 housed thirty-three nuns; by 1552, that figure had more than doubled, to seventy-three nuns per convent.[21] In the 1560s, the problem of convents bursting at the seams with women who would rather have been elsewhere attracted the attention of the Council of Trent. The Tridentine reformers, slightly anticipated by Cosimo I's own reforms,[22] as well the Innocenti's own superintendent, Vincenzo Borghini, focused on minimum-age requirements and formal, written, contractual procedures of consent to ensure that girls in their late teens on the brink of entering convents actually had vocations. Equally intense was a new focus on restricting contact between nuns and the outside world, a focus that eventually worked to the financial disadvantage of convents and their individual nuns who had relied on the patronage of laymen and laywomen.[23] Indeed, Borghini served on a four-member commission begun by Cosimo to investigate Tuscan religious institutions between 1566 and 1569.[24] Among their findings was that hospitals such as San Paolo de' Convalescenti (the facade of which pays homage to Brunelleschi's Innocenti), were devoting more of their financial and other resources to housing older women than to the charitable purposes for which they had been built, a development in Italian charitable organization not confined to Florence.[25]

girls of marriageable age. See Edoardo Grendi, "Ideologia della carità e società indisciplinata: la costruzione del sistema assitenziale genovese (1470–1670)" in *Timore e carità: i poveri nell'Italia moderna*. Atti del convegno "Pauperismo e assistenza negli antichi stati italiani," Cremona, 28–30 marzo 1980, ed. G. Politi, M. Rosa, and F. della Paruta. (Cremona: Libreria del Convegno editrice, 1982), 67. On the Soderini and Medici families' rival patronage of the convent of Le Murate in Florence, see K. J. P. Lowe, "Patronage and Territoriality in Early Sixteenth-Century Florence," in *Renaissance Studies* 7.3 (1993): 258–71.

[21] Gabriella Zarri, "Monasteri femminili e città (secoli XV–XVIII)," in *Storia d'Italia* (Turin, Einaudi: 1986), 9: 363, citing Trexler, "Le célibat à la fin du moyen age," *Annales: Economies, Sociétés, Civilisations* 27 (1972): 1329–50. In the early 1570s, as the Florentine grand duchy attempted to address the problem, statistics provided by Vincenzio Borghini showed that in Florence, the average number of nuns per convent had risen to 76.9 in the city of Florence, and in the immediately surrounding area, rose to 84.4 nuns per convent. See Chapter 6, Table 6.1, for a more detailed enumeration.

[22] Sherrill Cohen, *The Evolution of Women's Asylums since 1500: from Refuges for Ex-prostitutes to Shelters for Battered Women* (New York/Oxford: Oxford University Press, 1992), 30–1.

[23] This point is made by S. Cohen, *Women's Asylums*, 31.

[24] Borghini's notes as part of this commission, as well as letters from disgruntled nuns, can be found in AOIF, Estranei (CXLIV, V), passim, as well as in ASF, *Segretario del Regio Diritto* 4893 and 4896, Biblioteca Nazionale Centrale di Firenze (BNCF) fondo Magliabechiano, Serie VIII, 1393, and Fondo Nazionale II. X. 138, and II. X. 73.

[25] In Genoa, for example, a medieval hospital that originally functioned as a hospital for the poor and infirm had excluded lepers and slaves by 1442. Just five years before, a testator left funds to Florence's Ospedale degli Innocenti to build an additional wing for young girls, Don Tomaso Doria added to the hospital in Genoa a wing for girls for whom the hospital could not find

Although the Ospedale degli Innocenti itself harbored at least seven hundred women of marriageable age and older in 1579, the year before some were transferred to the hospice of Orbatello, neither the foundling hospital itself nor convents were sufficient to deal with what contemporaries saw as a menacing social problem.[26] At least five Florentine foundations in the sixteenth century attempted to do what neither the Innocenti nor the Orbatello were doing with complete success. Two of these foundations, Santa Maria Vergine and S. Niccolò del Ceppo, began in the Oltrarno but later moved across the river and merged into a single institution. The latter of these two took in at its foundation eighteen "povere fanciulle abbandonate," who, once they reached their midteens, could choose to stay on in the service of the convent by taking more formal vows, accept a modest dowry if they had marriage prospects, or take on domestic service in the homes of the convent's wealthy benefactors.[27]

The foundation date of the Pietà is less easily established, but evidence for it begins to appear in 1554. Between 1559 and 1623, the Pietà took in 917 girls ranging in age from five to nineteen years of age, although admissions clustered around the ages of twelve and thirteen. Around 1590, yet another foundation, after taking up residence briefly near the Porta alla Croce settled into more permanent quarters in Via S. Gallo under the portico of the hospital of the Broccardi. This hospice for prepubescent and adolescent girls was dedicated to Saint Catherine of Alexandria and became known as the

outside placement. On the Genoese hospital, see Edoardo Grendi, "Ideologia della carità," 66. On the hospital of San Paolo, see Bernice Trexler, "Hospital Patients in Sixteenth-Century Florence: San Paolo 1567–68," in *Bulletin of the History of Medicine* 48 (1974): 41–59, and R. Goldthwaite and W. R. Rearick, "Michelozzo and the Ospedale di S. Paolo," *Mitteilungen des Kunsthistorischen Instituts in Florenz* 21 (1977): 221–306. Borghini's concerns can be found in AOIF Estranei (CXLIV, V) fol. 2r, undated. The census of 1562 shows that there were forty-two women and nine men resident, presumably as administrators and medical staff, at the hospital of San Paolo, which in 1567–68 admitted 364 patients. See B. Trexler, "Hospital Patients," 46, and Silvia Meloni-Trkulja, *I fiorentini nel 1562: descritione delle bocche della citttà et stato di Fiorenza fatto l'anno 1562* (Florence: Bruschi, 1991), 63v.

[26] For a chronologically broad overview, see Cohen, *Women's Asylums*, 13–37.

[27] For excellent detailed histories of these institutions in both Florence and Bologna, see Nicholas Terpstra, *Abandoned Children of the Italian Renaissance: Orphan Care in Florence and Bologna* (Baltimore: Johns Hopkins University Press, 2005). The 1562 census, published in S. Meloni-Trkulja, *I fiorentini nel 1562*, ix, records 645 girls resident in the city's conservatories, plus 1,048 at the Innocenti. The only institution listed for boys was the hospital of Bonifazio degli Abbandonati, which housed 95 boys. The census lists 552 boys resident at the Innocenti, and on fol. 191r gives the city's population as 59,216, divided into 8,726 households. The resulting mean household size of 6.8 persons per household is no doubt slightly inflated by counting each conservatory, monastery, and convent as a single household. For the statistics on the Innocenti, see Meloni-Trkulja, *I fiorentini nel 1562*, fol. 120r. I thank my former graduate student, Christopher Lane, for this last reference.

"monastero delle ruote" after the instrument of Catherine's martyrdom. Its site was presumably what is now the eastern terminus of the Via delle Ruote at Via S. Gallo.[28]

Virtually all of the statutes of these foundations described as their major institutional objective the prevention of girls wandering the streets "so that nothing bad will happen to them." This euphemism for prostitution is a phrase into which several centuries' fears for the safety of feminine honor are compressed. Sherrill Cohen has described and analyzed the proliferation of institutions such as houses for the *convertite* and the *malmaritate* in the sixteenth century designed, in her view, to address the problem of controlling female sexual behavior.[29] Although the Council of Trent succeeded in giving new and more effective force to this form of social control, the intensity of the problem of prostitution spurred the creation of institutions several decades before the Council of Trent.[30] By 1550, charitable institutions as well as convents succeeded in creating a class of women who would spend their entire lives under institutional care, from admission as infants to the Innocenti, then as hospital employees or nuns, or, after 1580, as inmates of the "widow's asylum" of Orbatello.

Just what proportion of the female population of Florence did these institutions assist? In a city of 59,557 persons in 1552, the percentage of women in convents has been estimated to be as high as 25 percent, to whom must be added the large number of Florentine women who were scattered throughout the dominion, especially in Prato.[31] Even the most conservative estimates place the percentage of women in Florentine convents at about 14 percent. That this was specifically a feminine issue is clear from the 1552 census: there were 45 feminine monastic institutions in Florence, housing 2,786 women, and only 15 male monastic institutions, housing 441 men.[32] The 1562 census shows 22 monasteries (and 1 orphanage) housing

---

[28] Both Daniela Lombardi and Nicholas Terpstra have noted that in the sixteenth and seventeenth centuries, as family strategy dictated concern with dowries and inheritance, Santa Caterina became something of a patron saint of adolescent girls. See Terpstra, *Abandoned Children of the Italian Renaissance*, 61, citing Daniela Lombardi, "Poveri a Firenze: Programmi e realizzazzioni della politica assistenziale dei Medici tra Cinque e Seicento," in Politi, Rosa, and della Paruta, eds., *Timore e carità*, 168, n. 12.

[29] S. Cohen, *Women's Asylums*, 38–60.

[30] Cohen, 17–20.

[31] R. Trexler "Le celibat a la fin du moyen age," *Annales: Economies, Sociétés, Civilisations* 27 (1972): 1329–50. For Prato, see Elena Fasano-Guarini, ed., *Prato: Storia di una città* (Florence: Le Monnier, 1986) 2: 851.

[32] D'Addario's figures, taken from Battara, *La popolazione di Firenze alla meta del '500* (Florence: Rinascimento del libro, 1935), 34, and from ASF *Miscellenea Medicea*, 304: 25 February 1551: "Manoscritto cartaceo contenente i dati del censimento ordinato da Cosimo I per Firenze,

748 men, and 57 institutions (including 5 conservatories) housing 4,664 women. This 1562 census also shows that about 645 females were confined in conservatories, which when added to the approximately 1,048 girls and women in the Innocenti, results in 1,693 women confined in institutions that were conventual in nature but not, strictly speaking, convents. The Innocenti by far had the greatest number of women. The next largest institution was the Orbatello, to whom inmates of the Innocenti were occasionally sent, and where, after 1580, every woman above age thirty-six had to repair if the Innocenti had not succeeded in finding an alternative arrangement. In 1562, the Orbatello housed 174 women. The hospital for abandoned girls in Borgo Ognissanti housed nearly the same number, while the hospital for abandoned girls of S. Niccolò e S. Maria del Ceppo housed 122 girls, about the same number housed by the refuge for converted prostitutes. The hospice for abandoned girls near the gate of San Piero Gattolino took in 64 girls, and the hospital of San Paolo housed 42 nuns. Rather striking is the fact that three of these institutions specialized in charity to girls abandoned before they had reached marriageable age. Thus, in the middle of 1562, convents and quasi-conventual institutions taken together housed 5,712 women, or an amount not quite one-fifth of the number of women in Florence, whereas in the early 1570s, Tuscan convents alone (excluding Siena) counted 10,522 residents.[33]

Cohen largely attributes to syphilis this early-sixteenth-century revival of the medieval imperative to convert prostitutes to a more restrained Christian life. Although this successfully explains the response in the form of institutions to segregate prostitutes, it leaves unanswered the question of whether prostitution itself grew as a major social problem or if an increase in moralism (as a result of Savonarola and his sixteenth-century followers, for example) simply enlarged or even exaggerated public perception of prostitution as a

portato a compimento a cura di Antonio di Filippo Giannetti, detto <<del Muccione>>" are much more conservative than Trexler's. For more detail, see D'Addario, *Aspetti della controriforma a Firenze*. Pubblicazioni dell'Archivio di Stato, (Rome: Ministero dell'Interno, 1972) 77: 392ff. For the population of hospitals and monasteries, see Meloni-Trkulja, *I fiorentini nel 1562*, ix–x. Figures for the Innocenti (552 male, 1,048 female) are not listed in the prefatory material but do appear on fol. 120r. The 1552 and 1562 censuses are important because they both list convents and the number of mouths in each one. Cf. D'Addario, *Aspetti*, 397. Note how much higher the population of females is – 6.3 times as high as the males. Or put another way, nearly 13 percent of Florentine women were in convents, not even counting the ones abandoned to foundling homes and hospices, which brings the figure to approximately 20 percent. This percentage is based on an estimated population for the city in 1562 of 59,216.

[33] Vincenzio Borghini's census of the early 1570s (see Chapter 6) counts 28 convents in the city proper, another 34 in the immediately surrounding countryside, and 117 in the rest of Tuscany, excluding Siena. See BNCF, Cod. Magl. Cl. VIII, 1393, fol. 97r–101r for Borghini's detailed report to Grand Duke Francesco I.

social problem. Moreover, as Michael Rocke has shown, the dangers to girls
in the early sixteenth century were real: between 1494 and 1515, over a third
of rape cases prosecuted by the Florentine courts involved girls between six
and twelve years of age.[34] Only a full examination of the state of the economy in the first decades of the sixteenth century, one of the few things
missing from Cohen's otherwise fine book, can provide a satisfactory answer
to the question.[35]

This issue is critical to determining whether these new institutions had
to respond to an actual increase in the number of women without visible
economic and social support, or whether perception gave authorities the
opportunity to cast their net wider within an existing but numerically static
population of women. If the former is the case, it raises disturbing questions
about why there should have been such a sudden increase in the first decades
of the sixteenth century in women forced outside conventional social roles.
Certainly the more general invocation of "gender ideology"[36] is powerless
to explain the specific historical circumstances of the early sixteenth century,
because "ideology" concerning the subordinate position of women in the
Mediterranean social order has been a historical constant. Nor is it wise to
forget Pierre Bourdieu's admonitions to balance the study of legal history
and the study of legal codes with the infinite variability of practice.[37]

These reminders are especially timely in matters of examining the relationship between "gender ideology" and inheritance practices. As accurate as
Manzoni's historical fiction of the nun of Monza's story is, however, it reinforces some stereotypes while forcing us to reexamine others. Both anthropologists and anthropologically inclined historians have portrayed Mediterranean Europe as dominated by partible inheritance and northern Europe
as the home of primogeniture. Yet clearly, by the early seventeenth century, in Manzoni's portrait, seigneurial families in northern Italy seem to

---

[34] Michael Rocke, "Gender and Sexual Culture in Renaissance Italy," in *Gender and Society in Renaissance Italy*, ed. Judith Brown and Robert Davis (London/New York: Longman, 1998), 150–70, at 162–3.

[35] For a comprehensive discussion of the Florentine economy, see Richard Goldthwaite, *The Economy of Renaissance Florence* (Baltimore: Johns Hopkins University Press, 2009), briefly summarized infra, Chapter 1.

[36] "Gender ideology" is an increasingly popular phrase misapplied, in my view, to the phenomena involving social attitudes concerning females in the Mediterranean world. For its use, see not only Cohen, *Women's Asylums*, 13–37 and passim, but also David Kertzer's article, "Gender Ideology and Infant Abandonment in Nineteenth-Century Italy," *Journal of Interdisciplinary History* 22 (1991): 1–25. For a fuller discussion of the issue, see infra, Chapter 2.

[37] Pierre Bourdieu, *Outlines of a Theory of Practice* (Cambridge, 1972); idem, "Les stratégies matrimoniales dans le système de reproduction," *Annales: Economies, Sociétés, Civilisations* 27 (1972): 1105–25.

have practiced primogeniture with a vengeance wreaked upon younger sons and daughters alike. James Banker and Thomas Kuehn, for example, have noted for Sansepolcro and Florence, respectively, that even as early as the fifteenth century, some daughters were renouncing their portions of inheritance, although it is not clear to what extent they did this of their own volition.[38]

This book argues that even the intensification and more frequent application of patrilineal rules of inheritance that began in the third quarter of the fourteenth century were insufficient to precipitate a crisis of abandonment in the fifteenth century. Only when the political, social, and economic crises of the first decades of the sixteenth century combined to threaten the unity of noble patrimonies did the Florentine patriciate rigidify an inheritance system increasingly at odds with social realities. Certainly symptoms of inheritance crisis had appeared much earlier, and it is surely more than coincidental that intensification of patrilineal inheritance in Florence after the plague of 1362–3 should begin a process of dowry inflation. In the late fourteenth and early fifteenth centuries, however, among a population recovering from the ravages of the Black Death only with difficulty, the Florentine state, with the creation of the Monte delle doti in 1425, encouraged marriage and reproduction by helping wealthy and middling families absorb the shock of dowry inflation.[39] By helping them in this manner, however, the existence of the Monte delle doti undoubtedly contributed to dowry inflation, which, although it rose slowly throughout the quattrocento, took off again in the early cinquecento. By the early sixteenth century, however, as wealthy families tightened inheritance rules to preserve what they at least perceived were shrinking patrimonies, it became increasingly difficult to include younger sons and daughters as full beneficiaries.

Judith Brown's work on the demographics of Florentine nunneries from the fifteenth to the eighteenth centuries also points to dowry inflation as the

---

[38] Thomas Kuehn, "Law, Death, and Heirs in the Renaissance: Repudiation of Inheritance in Florence," *Renaissance Quarterly* 45 (1992): 484–516, at 490–3. I thank James Banker for this reference.

[39] Anthony Molho, *Marriage Alliance in Late Medieval Florence* (Cambridge, MA: Harvard University Press, 1994); J. Kirshner and A. Molho, "The Dowry Fund and the Marriage Market in Early Quattrocento Florence," *Journal of Modern History* 50 (1978): 403–38; J. Kirshner, "Materials for a Gilded Cage: Non-Dotal Assets in Florence, 1300–1500," in *The Family in Italy from Antiquity to the Present*, ed. David Kertzer and Richard Saller (New Haven: Yale University Press, 1991), 184–207. Dowry inflation was substantial also in Venice in the late fourteenth century. See Donald Queller and Thomas F. Madden, "Father of the Bride: Fathers, Daughters, and Dowries in Late Medieval and Early Renaissance Venice," *Renaissance Quarterly* 46 (1993): 685–711, citing Dennis Romano, "San Giacomo dell'Orio: Parish Life in Fourteenth-Century Venice," (Ph.D. diss., Michigan State University, 1982), 130.

principal engine driving the explosive growth of female religious vocations in the early sixteenth century. In particular, as patrician families concentrated their economic resources on their eldest daughters, other daughters sought out conventual life in such numbers that the spaces for daughters of less wealthy families diminished, leading to the nearly simultaneous creation of several quasi-conventual institutions in the 1540s and 1550s.[40] Conversely, when the marriage market stabilized, as it did in the late sixteenth and early seventeenth centuries, the average age of first profession of vows increased, and by the mid-seventeenth century, the census at Florence's two largest convents had seriously diminished.[41]

Yet what, the astute reader is entitled to ask, did this have to do with foundlings? Granted, Florentine patricians with an excess of daughters or younger sons might seek space in the convent, but did they resort to foundling hospitals? Certainly during the fifteenth century, the Ospedale degli Innocenti openly and unconcernedly served the urban patriciate by taking in the illegitimate children of master-servant, master-slave relations. Moreover, the Innocenti continued to serve this group in the sixteenth century. Yet there is evidence, such as the case of the Antinori, of sons of Florentine patricians abandoned to the Innocenti. Costantino, for example, is described as the "figlio naturale" of Alessandro Antinori (1481–1557), who had been a merchant in exile in the 1520s in Lyons but who returned to Florence under the protection of Duke Alessandro de' Medici. Mona Gostanza, the "legitimate and natural" daughter of Landozzo degli Albizzi, was brought up in the Innocenti and served as the governess of its girls from 1511 to 1551. Similarly, Jacopo Nacchianti, "il vescovo nocentino," who lived at the Innocenti from approximately age nine until he joined the Dominican order at San Marco at the age of fifteen, was the legitimate son of Ser Andrea Nacchianti, the hospital's notary.

Such lingering questions have a direct bearing on the type of institution the Innocenti would become over the course of the sixteenth century. Historians of Catholic charity after the fifteenth century have seen all charitable institutions, including foundling hospitals, as responses to overwhelming need and social pressure, brought on by a combination of war, plague, population increases, and widespread unemployment. The vastly increased scale on which foundling hospitals operated after 1500, and their horrifying mortality rates, strongly suggest that poverty had become such an overwhelming social problem during the sixteenth century that foundling hospitals, if they

[40] Judith Brown, "Monache a Firenze all'inizio dell'età moderna. Un'analisi demografica," *Quaderni Storici* 85 (1994): 117–52, at 129.

[41] Ibid., 121.

had ever served the wealthy, had now become predominantly the preserve of poor families who abandoned out of sheer economic necessity. Indeed, more than one historian has described the entire system of foundling hospitals in Catholic Europe as a premodern form of birth control.[42]

Yet closer examination of these institutions and their constituents yields a more complex picture. Even in late-eighteenth-century France, Jean-Jacques Rousseau abandoned several of his own children to the foundling hospital because he thought it was best for them. Certainly the foundling hospital had become a solution to the problem of illegitimacy. We may doubt, however, that foundling hospitals were ever charitable institutions that exclusively served the poor. Clearly it is critical to determine what caused the increase in the frequency and scale of abandonment from the fifteenth century to the mid-sixteenth century.

This sudden increase in the abandonment of children to the Innocenti had a dramatic impact on the organization of care. A century earlier, demand for both labor and children was sufficiently high that the Innocenti placed out children of both sexes for apprenticeship, adoption, and household service at the age of six or seven.[43] By the mid-sixteenth century, children did not begin serving apprenticeships until age ten or even later, and getting children out of the hospital at all was becoming extremely difficult. Borghini's statistics from 1579 show that of 1,220 staff and children in the hospital, 968 were females, 733 of whom were of marriageable age or older. Indeed, a substantial proportion, 233, were women over age forty.[44] It is nonetheless important to make a clear distinction here between the inheritance crisis and the problems of overcrowding and placement. In other words, was the imbalance in gender ratios that Borghini's census noted due to a wide gender imbalance on admission? Or did male and female infants come in with roughly equal frequency, with males either dying more frequently, or, if they survived, being more likely to be adopted or apprenticed? Evidence for the fifteenth century (1445–85) shows that females comprised a steady 56 to 57 percent of admissions, with males predominating only during those years in which male baptisms greatly exceeded female baptisms. If the vast increase in the number of infants admitted to the Innocenti involved an inheritance crisis that affected girls more than it did boys, figures for the sixteenth century would have to be consistently higher for females than in

---

[42] See for example, Jean-Pierre Bardet, "La société et l'abandon," in *Enfance abandonée et société en Europe*, ed. Jean-Pierre Bardet (Rome: Ecole Française de Rome, 1991), 3–26, at 25.

[43] Gavitt, *Charity and Children*, 243–59.

[44] AOIF, Filza d'archivio (LXII, 30), fol. 491r–491v, 18 June 1579.

the fifteenth, and except for crisis years, in which admissions by gender evened out between the sexes, more girls were admitted than boys.

Regardless of which problem is the more critical one for the Innocenti itself, gender issues also shaped shifts in discourse about charity and its practice. This shift has been described as one to "Tridentine" or "post-Tridentine" charity, but in fact the link between charity and moral reform was a product of late-fifteenth- and early-sixteenth-century Catholic reform. Such reform came from both ecclesiastical and governmental sources. In Mantua, for example, Archbishop Gonzaga in 1494 founded a Congregazione de' Poveri, which was specifically forbidden to assist with alms "ruffians, prostitutes, and other such persons who live in notorious mortal sin." Moreover, only the non-able-bodied poor were allowed to beg, and they had to exhibit a certificate as they went about begging.[45] Clearly, Protestants had no monopoly on the sixteenth-century tendency to require a moral life as prerequisite to becoming a beneficiary of almsgiving.

In particular, as lay piety came to be perceived as contaminated with Nicodemism,[46] ecclesiastical authorities in Florence succeeded in taking greater control of the city's confraternities and more formal charitable enterprises.[47] In doing so, however, they had the full cooperation by the authorities of the grand duchy. Indeed, Cosimo's active intervention was yet another important way in which the political milieu of charity had changed over the course of the sixteenth century. During the fifteenth century, the Silk Guild took responsibility for the patronage and protection of the hospital. Although both guild and commune agreed that the hospital would on occasion require help from city government, the burden of initiative fell on the guild in petitioning for tax exemptions, special gabelles and tolls, and the hospital's participation in the city's program of funded debt.[48] Such petitions became increasingly frequent over the course of the fifteenth century, as the government of Florence lurched from one fiscal crisis to another and city officials entrusted with the hospital's customs revenues did not always use them to the institution's benefit. By the early sixteenth century, the role of city government had shifted from merely passive to overtly antagonistic, culminating in the seizure in 1529 of large tracts of the hospital's real estate.

[45] Roberto Navarrini and Carlo Marco Belfanti, "Il problema della povertà nel ducato di Mantova: aspetti istituzionali e problemi sociali (secoli XIV–XVI)," in G. Politi, M. Rosa, and F. della Peruta, eds. *Timore e Carita*, 134–5.

[46] See Eva Marie Jung, "On the Nature of Evangelism," in *Journal of the History of Ideas* 14 (1953): 529.

[47] Nicholas Terpstra, in *Abandoned Children of the Italian Renaissance*, 69, has noted that this trend appears to run counter to developments in Bologna.

[48] Gavitt, *Charity and Children*, 64–76.

Largely as a result of this devastation, in 1533 Grand Duke Alessandro de' Medici (1530–7) intervened personally to restore to the hospital its rightful patrimony and reserved to himself the right to nominate the hospital's superintendent. Alessandro's successor, Cosimo I, deprived the Silk Guild of its control over the hospital and transformed the office of superintendent into virtually another arm of government. Cosimo also initiated legislation to grant to the Innocenti rights over the creek bed of the Torrente Mugnone to provide speedier transportation of food from the countryside to the orphanage, and oversaw the convictions and punishment of wet nurses accused of fraud.

Scholarly interest in Tuscan state-formation is long-standing. Eric Cochrane's *Florence in the Forgotten Centuries* made both a convincing and an entertaining case for the interest of the Florentine grand dukes in making the state more rational, bureaucratic, and efficient. Litchfield, in *The Emergence of a Bureaucracy*, although careful not to assign the term "modern state" to anything earlier than the eighteenth-century duchy of Lorraine, undertook a study of social mobility and patronage that suggests the sixteenth- and seventeenth-century grand dukes were building at least a prototype of the modern state. Historians of charity such as Natalie Davis and Brian Pullan have made conscious links between municipal government in Venice and Lyons and the use of charity as a form of social harmony as well as social control. Despite the insistence of both Pullan and Davis that these two cities looked to Florence as a model for their charitable programs, one looks in vain for evidence that Florentine republican government provided charity as efficiently as its later, northern counterparts. That Florence had to await the grand duchy to become rational and bureaucratic may tell us something about the relative efficiency of republican and authoritarian governments.

Did grand ducal intervention, however, make Florentine charitable institutions run more smoothly?[49] A detailed examination of the case of the Innocenti suggests that Cosimo and Francesco were far better served by state control of charity than was the Innocenti. Moreover, the use of charitable institutions such as Santa Maria Nuova, the Monte di Pietà,[50] and

---

[49] Nicholas Terpstra, in *Abandoned Children of the Italian Renaissance*, 242, argues that "In Florence's form of coordinated decentralization more of the strings went back to Medici hands, which pulled and slackened them inconsistently and in pursuit of dynastic political goals." I am inclined to agree.

[50] For the Monte di Pietà, see Carol Bresnahan Menning, *Charity and the State in Late Renaissance Italy: The Monte di Pietà of Florence* (Ithaca: Cornell University Press, 1977), 2. The observations Professor Menning makes concerning the Monte di Pietà as part of Cosimo's "statecraft" apply with equal force to the Innocenti, as Chapter 1 will show.

the Innocenti as virtual organs of state finance suggests that the sixteenth-century Medici "pattern of control" was hardly a model of centralization.[51] State formation, in these terms, was surely the formation not of the modern, but of the "Renaissance" state: dynastic, decentralized, and, even by comparison to Valois or Tudor power, weak.[52]

Similarly, the relationship that is outlined in these pages between grand dukes Cosimo I and Francesco I and Vincenzio Borghini make it clear that sixteenth-century Medici government had little conception of the difference between the ceremonial and the practical aspects of government. This is, of course, a fortunate occurrence for the cultural historian, because the relationship between the arts and political patronage still very much governed the way government imparted political and cultural ideas to its subjects.

The career of the hospital's superintendent, Vincenzo Borghini, from 1552 to his death in 1580 is thus both an insight into the relationship between charity and attempted state formation and a window onto the larger cultural world of the Late Renaissance. Borghini, born in 1515, became a novice in Florence's major Benedictine establishment, the Badia Fiorentina.[53] Among his early teachers was Pier Vettori, who would later hold a chair in Greek at the Florentine *Studio*, with whom Borghini worked on translations of Sophocles and who delivered the eulogy at the funeral services Borghini had orchestrated for Cosimo's death in 1574.[54] At the Badia Fiorentina, Borghini held a series of offices – at age twenty, he became sacristan, then, at twenty-one, he was placed in charge of the infirmary. Made cellarer in the same year, he began teaching Latin two years later, in 1538.[55]

It is likely that Borghini first came to the notice of Cosimo I when he drafted a report to Ferdinand of Austria in 1546 on the state of the

---

[51] J. R. Hale, *Florence and the Medici: The Pattern of Control* (London: Thames and Hudson, 1977), 17–20, sees continuity in Medici leadership over some three centuries. Although I do not deny continuity, I would suggest, as does R. B. Litchfield, *Emergence of a Bureaucracy* (Princeton: Princeton University Press, 1986), 313, that modern state formation in Tuscany is an eighteenth-century phenomenon. Even in that case, geographic limitations are still severe.

[52] Even those historians, such as Arnaldo d'Addario, in *La formazione dello stato moderno da Cosimo il Vecchio a Cosimo I* (Lecce: Adriatica Editrice Salentina, 1976), who see Cosimo's aims and achievements in terms of "statecraft," base their arguments on Cosimo's *personal* involvement in almost every area of Florentine civic, economic, and cultural life. *Lo stato* as an abstraction, Machiavelli notwithstanding, does still not seem prominent in sixteenth-century Florence.

[53] For a study of the library of the Badia Fiorentina, drawn from documentation in the Vatican Library, see Rudolf Blum, *La biblioteca della Badia fiorentina e i codici di Antonio Corbinelli*, Studi e Testi vol. 155 (Vatican City: Biblioteca Apostolica Vaticana, 1951).

[54] *Dizionario biografico degli Italiani*, s.v. "Borghini, Vincenzo Maria." For a mention of Pier Vettori's funeral oration for Cosimo, see ASF Manoscritti 129, Memorie fiorentine, fol. 10v, 17 May 1574.

[55] Dizionario biografico degli Italiani, s.v. "Borghini, Vincenzo Maria."

hospital of Santa Maria Nuova, a report undertaken as part of Cosimo's general reforms of hospitals and monasteries. He was appointed in 1552 as *spedalingo* of the Innocenti; by 1561, the year in which Cosimo appointed him to reform the foundling hospital of Pisa, he was already an *operaio* of San Lorenzo.[56] In addition to these heavy responsibilities, Borghini was named a *luogotenente* of the Accademia del Disegno in 1563 and in 1567 was one of four members of a commission Cosimo appointed to oversee the reform of feminine monastic foundations.[57] His contributions to theories of the origins of the Tuscan language, as well as his contributions to more exacting philological and historiographical methodology,[58] nonetheless earned Borghini the enmity of future generations when his talents were applied to the unenviable task of making Boccaccio's *Decameron* acceptable to the post-Tridentine church.[59]

R obert Williams has shown how, in addition to these accomplishments, Borghini put his historiographical sophistication into the service of artistic excellence by intervening between the first and second editions of Vasari's *Lives of the Most Famous Painters, Sculptors, and Artists*, in which he did not neglect the opportunity to assign himself a major role in the apotheosis of Michelangelo described in Vasari's work. Borghini's ideas stood behind several major artistic projects of sixteenth-century Florentines: he devised the program for Francesco's *studiolo* in the Palazzo Vecchio, as well as the arrangements for Michelangelo's funeral in San Lorenzo in 1564 and the celebrations for the marriage of Cosimo's son, Francesco, to Giovanna of Austria in 1565.[60]

Indeed, Borghini's apparent centrality to the cultural and intellectual life of sixteenth-century Florence seems difficult to reconcile with his role as "the

---

[56] AOIF, Suppliche e sovrani rescritti (VI, 1), fol. 294r, 20 May 1561, and fol. 295r-v, 28 May 1561, contain two letters from the canons of San Lorenzo to Lelio Torelli and Cosimo outlining the quarrels between the Priors and the Canons of San Lorenzo, quarrels that had become embarrassingly public. The *Dizionario biografico degli Italiani*, s.v. "Borghini, Vincenzo Maria." identifies Borghini as an *operaio* of San Lorenzo in 1563, when Cosimo placed the headquarters of the new Accademia del Disegno in the Medici chapel at San Lorenzo and appointed Borghini as the Academy's first lieutenant.

[57] *Dizionario biografico degli Italiani*, s.v. "Borghini, Vincenzo Maria."

[58] Eric Cochrane, *Historians and Historiography in the Italian Renaissance* (Chicago: University of Chicago Press, 1981), 432.

[59] *Dizionario biografico degli Italiani*, s.v. "Borghini, Vincenzo Maria." On Borghini and Boccaccio, see also G. Lesca, "Vincenzo Borghini e il Decamerón," *Miscellanea storica della Val d'Elsa* 21 (1913): 246–63, as well as V. Branca, *Linee d'una storia della critica al Decamerón* (Florence, 1937), and Robert Williams, "Vincenzo Borghini and Vasari's 'Lives,'" (Ph.D. diss., Princeton University), 1988, 55–6.

[60] Loren Partridge and Randolph Starn, *Arts of Power: Three Halls of State in Renaissance Italy* (Berkeley: University of California Press, 1992), 192–9.

good prior" of Florence's largest and most beloved charitable institution, an institution in crisis without surcease throughout much of the sixteenth century. A well-reasoned, if superficial, analysis might well question how serious either Borghini's or Cosimo's commitment was to the plight of abandoned children. Either Borghini was an enormously energetic, effective, and talented administrator, who could run a complex institution and much of the grand ducal cultural apparatus simultaneously, or he was the beneficiary of a particularly prestigious bestowal of patronage on which the lives of a few thousand infants were secondary to the deliberate fashioning of an image of centralized, benevolent power.

Judging from the incessantly loud tone of complaint in Borghini's correspondence, it is not unreasonable to infer that on his appointment in 1552, he thought the administration of the Innocenti would consume a relatively small amount of time and energy and that his primary focus could still be scholarship and culture. Borghini had the misfortune of assuming the post only two years before Cosimo undertook war with Siena to expand his rule into all of Tuscany, with the result that the more seriously Borghini began to take his administrative responsibilities as superintendent, the more deaf Cosimo and his secretaries became to the needs of the Innocenti itself. Only in 1561, after Borghini had been superintendent for nine years, did Cosimo finally answer his pleas for more funds by donating a large parcel of land in the Maremma as a source of grain for the Innocenti.

Even more controversial for Borghini's contemporaries as well as his biographers, has been the question of his administrative skill. Francesco Settimanni's court history, for example, written in the eighteenth century but constructed as though it were a daily diary, allowed that Borghini might have been a great antiquarian and linguist, and even a better scholar, but as financial manager, he was "the worst, because he brought the Innocenti to ruin." Worse, he accused him of being a great *dissipatore*, who had inherited an institution that was on a sound administrative and financial footing and had undermined it by selling off huge chunks of real estate to meet current expenses. Settimanni's judgment has been accepted by virtually every historian of Florentine charity as well as by Borghini's biographers. Luigi Passerini's magisterial 1853 survey of Florentine charitable and educational institutions, for example, argues that Borghini's death at age sixty-five is at least partially attributable to his being undone by the shame and regret resulting from his maladroit administration. Only Gaetano Bruscoli, writing circa 1900, discounts Settimanni's judgment, and even Bruscoli was sufficiently influenced that he thought the Innocenti would have been better off had Borghini never left his cloistered sanctuary of philology and letters.

In the following pages, the reader will find both a more sympathetic account of Borghini's tenure, and a much wider assessment of his administration of the Ospedale degli Innocenti as a reflection of sixteenth-century Florentine social, political, intellectual, and cultural history. The book's approach owes a great deal not only to Pierre Bourdieu's distinction between legal norms and actual practice but also to his notions of inheritance strategy. Although it is certainly true, as Queller and Madden have noted,[61] that in Venice, at least, fatherly affection often trumped considerations of lineage, Florentine families nonetheless strategized not only to advance their social and economic position but also attempted to recoup the psychic and economic costs that such strategies incurred for more vulnerable family members. It must be said that clever as these strategies were, they were less often completely successful.

Chapter 1 examines the relationship between charity and statecraft in early modern Florence. In particular, it will reexamine the role of charity in the sixteenth-century grand duchy both from the point of view of the effectiveness of Cosimo's vision of the proper role of the state in solving social problems and from that of the place charitable institutions had in the centralization of the apparatus of state control. Chapter 1 also examines the financial structure and function of the Innocenti's depository, especially given that this forms such an integral part of the financial crisis that threw the Innocenti and the state together in such dramatic fashion in 1580. In addition, this chapter examines the role of charitable institutions in the economic development of the grand duchy and Cosimo's and Francesco's proto-mercantilism.

Chapter 2 explores the legal and cultural expectations that governed the matrix of gender and inheritance in late Renaissance Italian society. Chapter 3 examines the relationship of those norms to the actual practices and experiences of Tuscan families. Chapter 4 examines the dynamics of institutionalization and care for boys in Tuscan charitable institutions, and chapter 5 does the same for girls.

The effect of these new attitudes toward female recipients of charity in convents is treated in Chapter 6, as are the clearly emerging pattern of social control and physical confinement increasingly imposed by both Church and state on the lives of women. The chapter also examines the somewhat surprising effects of such confinement: a new recognition of feminine voices

---

[61] Pierre Bourdieu, *Outlines of a Theory of Practice*, trans. Richard Nice, Cambridge Studies in Social and Cultural Anthropology, vol. 16 (Cambridge: Cambridge University Press, 1977). Cf. D. Queller, and T. Madden, "Fathers of the Bride," 711.

and the new inclusion of women in the expanded scope of pedagogy. All of these developments, however, remain inexplicable without reference to the social and economic crises faced by Florentine and other Italian families at the beginning of the sixteenth century. These crises were always latent in highly patrilineal inheritance systems but were often countered by highly imaginative social policy to lessen their impact on society. Even in the best of times, however, these imaginative solutions did not counter the vulnerability of women who fell outside the normal grid of family and religious life. When inheritance and gender collided, when Italian society was faced with a poverty of imaginative solutions as well as physical poverty on a grander scale, these women would suffer first, and feel the impact most severely. As a result, they would become the sixteenth century's most visible social problem

CHARITY, DISCIPLINE, AND STATE-BUILDING IN CINQUECENTO FLORENCE

O N SUNDAY, 12 MARCH 1564, THE COFFIN CONTAINING THE BODY of Michelangelo, recently spirited out of Rome, was surreptitiously placed in the vault of the Florentine church of San Piero Maggiore, behind the altar that served as a meeting place for the Confraternity of the Assumption of the Virgin Mary. After dark, a small group of Michelangelo's most devoted followers once again carried the coffin through the streets of Florence. Although this small group of followers made every attempt to keep the preliminary funeral rites a secret, a crowd materialized around the pallbearers and torchbearers carrying the coffin to its destination, the Franciscan basilica of Santa Croce. By the time the coffin had been placed inside and the monks had blessed the body, such a crowd had suddenly found its way to the basilica that only with difficulty did the official mourners bring the coffin to the sacristy. There, as the crowd pressed around Don Vincenzio Borghini, forty-nine years old, the prior of the foundling hospital of the Innocenti, he tentatively opened up Michelangelo's coffin.[1] In Vasari's account:

> And then, when that was done, whereas he and all of us who were present were expecting to find that the body was already decomposed and spoilt (since Michelangelo had been dead twenty-five days, and twenty-two in

---

[1] No full-scale study of Vincenzio Borghini (1515–80) has been published since A. Legrenzi's *Vincenzo Borghini studio critico* (2 vols., Udine: Tip. D. del Bianco, 1910). Borghini's role in the foundation of the Accademia del Disegno is well known, as is his stature as historian, linguist, and historiographer for the grand duchy of Florence. His tenure as superintendent of Florence's largest charitable institution, which spanned the years 1552 to 1580, has received only cursory attention. For a brief biography, see *Dizionario biografico degli Italiani*, s.v. "Borghini, Vincenzo Maria."

This chapter is the revised version of a lecture delivered at the Harvard University Center for Italian Renaissance Studies (Villa I Tatti), Florence, Italy, in February 1991, and subsequently published as "Charity and State Building in Cinquecento Florence: Vincenzio Borghini as Administrator of the Ospedale degli Innocenti," in the *Journal of Modern History* 21 (1997): 230–70.

the coffin) on the contrary we found it perfect in every part and so free from any evil odor that we were tempted to believe that he was merely sunk in a sweet and quiet sleep. Not only were his features exactly the same as when he was alive (although touched with the pallor of death) but his limbs were clean and intact and his face and cheeks felt as if he had died only a few hours before.[2]

So it was that Giorgio Vasari and Vincenzio Borghini together, in formal language reminiscent of the translation of saints' relics, constructed the "divine Michelangelo."[3]

Borghini wished for secrecy in March 1564 to prepare yet more spectacular funeral rites to celebrate the apotheosis of Michelangelo in July.[4] An elaborate affair, this celebration involved preparations made over several

---

[footnote] J. R. Woodhouse has published numerous studies of Borghini's theories of language and his historiography; see, for example, "Vincenzio Borghini's view of Charlemagne's Empire," *Viator* 19 (1988): 355–75; idem, "Borghini's Theory of the Decay of Tuscan," *Studi Settecenteschi* 13 (1971): 100–15; idem, "Per un'edizione critica dei Pensieri e annotazioni di Vincenzio Borghini," *Lingua Nostra* 33 (June 1972): 39–45. See also Mario Pozzi, *Lingua e cultura del Cinquecento: Dolce, Aretino, Machiavelli, Guicciardini, Sarpi, Borghini* (Padua: Liviana, 1975), 91–356. Robert Williams's dissertation, "Vincenzo Borghini and Vasari's 'Lives'" (Ph.D. diss., Princeton University, 1988), provides much information on his relationship with Vasari, as does Patricia Rubin in *Giorgio Vasari: Art and History* (New Haven: Yale University Press, 1995), 187–230. On Borghini and history, see also Eric Cochrane, *Historians and Historiography in the Italian Renaissance*, 432ff, and Ann Moyer, "Historians and Antiquarians in Sixteenth-Century Florence," *Journal of the History of Ideas*, 64 (2003): 177–93. Anna Maria Testaverde Matteini has provided a useful inventory of Borghini's library in "La biblioteca erudita di Don Vincenzo Borghini," in *Firenze e la Toscana dei Medici nell'Europa del '500*, ed. C. Garfagnini (3 vols., Florence: Leo S. Olschki, 1983) 2: 611–43. See also, in the same set of essays, Alessandro d'Alessandro, "Vincenzo Borghini e gli Aramei: mito e storia nel principato Mediceo," 1: 133–55, for an evaluation of the relationship between Cosimo I's political program and Borghini's theories of language. An extensive although incomplete catalog of Borghini's correspondence can be found in Vincenzio Borghini, *Carteggio 1541–1580: Censimento*, ed. Daniela Francalanci and Franca Pellegrini (Florence: Accademia della Crusca, 1993). The first of a projected six volumes of his correspondence has been published under the care of Daniela Francalanci, Franca Pellegrini, and Eliana Carrara as *Il carteggio di Vincenzio Borghini* (Florence: Società per Edizioni Scelte, 2001). See also G. Belloni, Riccardo Drusi, and Artemisia Calcagni-Abrami, eds., *Vincenzio Borghini: filologia e invenzione nella Firenze di Cosimo I* (Florence: Leo S. Olschki, 2002).

[2] G. Vasari, *Lives of the Artists*, trans. G. Bull (2 vols. London: Penguin, 1965), 1: 436–8.

[3] Rudolf Wittkower and Margot Wittkower, *The Divine Michelangelo: The Florentine Academy's Homage on His Death in 1564: A facsimile edition of Esequie del Divino Michelagnolo Buonarroti, Florence 1564* (London: Phaidon, 1964), 9–18.

[4] Ibid. Preparing funeral ceremonies and memorial services seems to have been Borghini's particular domain and skill. Not only did he describe at length the funeral rites and decorations for deceased prioresses of the Hospital of the Innocenti, but also he prepared the funeral honors for Grand Duke Cosimo I in May 1574. See ASF Manoscritti 129, "Memorie Fiorentine regnante Don Francesco Medici granduca di Toscana," (1574–87), 4: 4r, 17 May 1574. These "memoirs" were compiled by Francesco Settimanni (1681–1763), whose less than sympathetic treatment of the Medici has been noted by Arnaldo D'Addario, *Aspetti della controriforma a Firenze*, 422.

days, which were orchestrated by Grand Duke Cosimo I as well as by the
institution cofounded by the grand duke and Borghini: the Accademia del
Disegno.[5] Just as Borghini constructed the settings for the funeral rites, so
it is probable that he constructed his own role in Michelangelo's apotheosis. Certainly Borghini intervened between the first and second editions of
Vasari's Lives to bring them up to Borghini's own exacting historical and
philological standards, which would have given him every opportunity to
re-create himself as he would appear to posterity in the pages of Vasari.[6]

This chapter has two major aims. The first is to evaluate the effectiveness
of Vincenzo Borghini's administration of the foundling hospital of the Innocenti. The second is to examine the relationship between sixteenth-century
charity and Italian city-states both by comparison to charitable institutions in
other Italian cities and through a case study of the Innocenti, the real estate
and finances of which Grand Dukes Cosimo I (1537–74) and Francesco I
(1574–87) appropriated in the larger service of state-building. The centrality of Borghini, the Innocenti, and the mid-sixteenth-century reforms of
other large-scale charitable institutions to Tuscan "state-formation" tends
to support a historiographical focus on the development of charitable and
educational institutions as critical nodes in systems of political and economic
power. What Norbert Elias described as the "civilizing process" has more
recently acquired important sociopolitical dimensions that emphasize the
internalization of discipline as prerequisite to the implicit consent involved
in the social contract.[7] Moreover, by leaving aside older and somewhat

[5] On the Accademia del Disegno, see Karen-edis Barzman, *The Florentine Academy and the Early
Modern State: The Discipline of Disegno* (Cambridge: Cambridge University Press, 2000). See also
Zygmunt Wazbinski, "La Cappella dei Medici e l'origine dell'Accademia del Disegno," in *Firenze
e la Toscana dei Medici nell'Europa del Cinquecento*, 54–69; idem, "La prima mostra dell'Accademia
del Disegno a Firenze," *Prospettiva* 14 (1978): 47–57.

[6] See Williams, "Vincenzo Borghini," 1–6, and passim, and Rubin, *Vasari*, 190–5. Borghini also
contributed to the first edition of 1550, according to the *Dizionario biografico degli Italiani*, s.v.
"Borghini, Vincenzo Maria."

[7] The importance of Italian humanism to the civilizing process is elaborated in Marvin Becker,
Civility and Society in Western Europe, 1300–1600 (Bloomington: Indiana University Press, 1989);
idem, *The Emergence of Civil Society in the Eighteenth Century: A Privileged Moment in the History
of England, Scotland, and France* (Bloomington: Indiana University Press, 1994). On the nature of
such a social contract, however, see Giorgio Chittolini, "Il privato, lo pubblico e lo stato," in
Origini dello stato: Processi di formazione statale in Italia fra medioevo ed età moderna, ed. A. Molho, G.
Chittolini, and P. Schiera (Bologna: Il Mulino, 1994), 553–90, at 565–6, and Roberto Bizzochi,
"Stato e/o potere: Una lettera a Giorgio Chittolini" in *Storia e politica*, 3 (1990): 55–64. Bizzochi in
particular argues that to understand the social contract in the way Locke and Rousseau understood
it presupposes the parties' mutual interest in the common good. Instead, in Bizzochi's view, it is
more useful to conceptualize the problem as one in which the so-called social contract does not so
much remedy the relationship of repression but codifies and extends it. The state, in other words,
cannot be separated from the praxis of power in the hands of individuals and groups. It is on this

anachronistic formulations of "absolutism" and "centralization," the study of charitable institutions in the sixteenth century provides access to how ties between elites and citizen-subjects were forged and reaffirmed.[8] Indeed, the close attention that the grand dukes of Florence, especially Cosimo I, paid to the Innocenti and to other charitable and religious institutions reflects a matrix of connections among charity, confessional discipline, *civiltà*, and public order. In this respect, Vincenzio Borghini's multiple roles as educator, ecclesiastical reformer, Medici courtier, and administrator of a large charitable institution assume coherence by placing him at the center of the connection among civility, discipline, and the foundations of European state-formation.[9]

At the time of his appointment as the Innocenti's superintendent in 1552, Borghini found a hospital that was both much larger and more complex than it had been a century earlier. Admissions to the Innocenti between 1450 and

basis also that notions of confessionalization and discipline have come under attack as neglecting what Charles H. Parker has called "the moral autonomy of church folk" (cf. idem, "The Moral Agency and Moral Autonomy of Church Folk in Post-Reformation Delft, 1520–1620," *Journal of Ecclesiastical History* 48 (1997): 44–70.

[8] See Elena Fasano-Guarini's excellent summary of Italian historiography concerning regional and territorial states: E. Fasano-Guarini, "Centro e periferia, accentramento e particolarismo: dicotomia o sustanza degli stati in età moderna," in *Origini dello stato*, ed. Chittolini, Molho, and Schiera, 147–76. See especially 147–59, where Fasano-Guarini describes Tuscan "state-formation" as a process involving changes over the *longue durée* and as a process in which strong central authority could coexist with a strong sense of local community, pluralism, and even enduring resistance. Replacing "centralization" with "systems of power" clarifies the relationship of smaller political and geographical entities to larger ones as well: see her "Un microcosmo in movimento (1494–1815)" in *Prato: storia di una città* (Florence: Le Monnier for the Comune di Prato, 1986) 2: 827–80. Important theoretical contributions (as well as their practical implications) can be found in S. R. Epstein, "Cities, Regions and the Late Medieval Crisis," *Past and Present* 109 (1991): 3–50, and idem, "Town and Country: Economy and Institutions in Late Medieval Italy," in *Economic History Review*, 46 (1993): 453–77.

[9] For excellent summaries of connections between discipline, confessionalization, self-discipline, and the state, see Paolo Prodi, ed., *Disciplina dell'anima, disciplina del corpo, e disciplina della società tra medioevo, ed età moderna*. Annali dell'Istituto storico italo- germanico, vol. 40 (Bologna: Il Mulino, 1994). Within this volume, see especially the masterly survey of German historiography on confessionalization, discipline, and the state by Wolfgang Reinhard, "Disciplinamento sociale, confessionalizzazione, modernizzazione: Un discorso storiographico," ibid., 101–23; Heinz Schilling, "Chiese confessionali e disciplinamento sociale: Un bilancio provvisorio della ricerca storica," ibid., 125–60. The relevance of Borghini's career as monastic reformer, which has yet to be treated, gains added importance in the context of the regulation of feminine monastic communities. See G. Zarri, "Disciplina regolare e pratica di coscienza: le virtù e i comportamenti sociali in comunità femminili (secc. XVI–XVIII)," ibid., 257–78. For a discussion of more secular instruments of social discipline, see Karl Härter, "Disciplinamento sociale e ordinanze di polizia nella prima età moderna," ibid., 635–58. Interest in notions of "order" is ubiquitous in documentation: Borghini in particular conceived of his administrative tasks as exercises in reducing and eliminating *disordine*.

1500 had averaged about 200 per year, with a peak in 1480 of nearly 400.[10] Unfortunately, we lack data for the years between 1485 and 1529, but it is clear that by 1530, the Innocenti was an institution working on a vastly different scale from that which its founders had envisioned. In the decade between 1530 and 1540, the hospital received 5,400 children, or an average of 540 a year; in years such as 1539, a year of particularly severe famine, admissions reached nearly a thousand per year.[11]

That this was not merely a function of a greater number of births is quite clear. Between 1445 and 1485, for example, only for two years, 1479 and 1480, did the percentage of admissions to the Ospedale degli Innocenti to baptisms in Florence exceed 10 percent (for 1479, the figure is 13.9 percent; for 1480, 11.0 percent). By contrast, the average for the years 1531–9 was 21.9 percent, and during the famine of 1539, the percentage of babies abandoned of those baptized reached 38.9 percent, proportions more consistent with the nineteenth century than with the early modern period.[12] Of these, 70 percent died before their first birthdays: in the year of the siege, infant mortality rose to nearly 90 percent. In the five years before Borghini was appointed, admissions ranged from 417 in 1547 to 884 in 1551, and then more than 600 (25.2 percent of baptisms) in 1552, with infant mortality rates consistently pushing 75 percent.[13] Before attempting to measure the motivations and importance of grand ducal policy concerning charity and state, some assessment of the character of economic changes during the first half of the sixteenth century must be undertaken. Borghini himself ascribed them to the "cattività dei tempi e degli huomini," by which he meant both

[10] Gavitt, *Charity and Children*, 209, for the years 1445–66. For the years 1467–85, see Gavitt, "Perchè non avea chi lo ghovernasse: Cultural Values, Family Resources and Abandonment in the Florence of Lorenzo de' Medici, 1467–85," in *Poor Women and Poor Children in the European Past*, ed. J. Henderson and R. Wall (London: Routledge, 1994), 65–93, at 66.

[11] AOIF, Suppliche e sovrani rescritti (VI, 1), fol. 140r, n.d., cited in Gavitt, "Charity and State Building," 239n.

[12] Statistics for baptisms are from M. Lastri, *Ricerche sull'antica e moderna popolazione della città di Firenze per mezzi dei registri del battistero di San Giovanni dal 1451 al 1774* (Florence: Gaetano Cambiagi, 1775), 34–45. Statistics for admissions are from AOIF Balie e bambini A–L (XVI, 1–11), 1445–85; for the years 1531–9, see Gaetano Bruscoli, *Lo Spedale di Santa Maria degli Innocenti dall sua fondazione ai nostri giorni* (Florence: E. Ariani, 1900), 268–70.

[13] AOIF, Balie e Bambini A–H (XVI, 15–22). See also Gaetano Bruscoli, *Lo Spedale*, 270. For statistics covering the years 1546 to 1552, see AOIF Suppliche e sovrani rescritti (VI, 1), fol. 465r, which gives the following figures (percentage of admissions to baptisms at San Giovanni in parentheses):

1547: 417 (15.7)	1550: 635 (25.1)
1548: 518 (20.9)	1551: 884 (37.3)
1549: 654 (27.9)	1552: 607 (25.2)

economic hardship and the rapacity of relatives who hoped to profit by seizing the inheritance of children whose parents had died.[14]

Putting aside for the moment the malice of men, an accurate assessment of the state of the Tuscan economy is no easy task. It is complicated by the extremely turbulent political and social climate that climaxed in the siege of Florence in 1529–30, followed by a severe famine in 1539 and another less severe famine in 1551. If the debate on the "Renaissance economy" seems to have run its course with regard to the quattrocento, with almost unanimous agreement that the decline in the wool industry was more than counterbalanced by spectacular successes in silk and banking, the late Laurentian period presents a more complex and confusing picture. Certainly in 1479–80, immediately after the Pazzi conspiracy, there is considerable evidence of episodic problems in the Florentine economy. Just as this period was marked by a sudden increase both in admissions to the Innocenti and in infant mortality, so, too, does Goldthwaite's wage and price series show that increasingly in the late quattrocento, the wages of construction workers were failing to keep up with the price of grain.

Yet such crises, although certainly severe, were not necessarily repeated throughout all sectors of the economy and do not necessarily add up to a portrait of overall economic decline. Indeed, even though distribution of wealth downward to the poorest sectors of society was limited, a relatively broad swath of workers and merchants kept the Florentine business climate relatively robust, responding especially well after 1540 to Duke Cosimo I's economic stimuli and relatively mild taxation. The cloth and banking industries in particular welcomed innovation. Like all premodern economies, the Florentine economy was certainly vulnerable to famine and economic downturns. Moreover, the economic data are far clearer about the relatively optimistic prospects that Florentine merchants and artisans enjoyed but are still murky concerning the plight of more marginal elements in society, although they do suggest that the "working poor" became much poorer in the sixteenth century.[15]

Apart from the chronic problems of war, which even in 1517 Benedetto Varchi's history of Florence noted had caused large numbers of homeless

[14] AOIF, Suppliche e sovrani rescritti (VI, 1), fol. 242v, 4 November 1553; AOIF, Suppliche e sovrani rescritti (VI, 1), fol. 442v, 14 February 1571. See also fol. 226r, n.d., all cited in Gavitt, "Charity and State Building," 239n.

[15] Richard Goldthwaite, *The Economy of Renaissance Florence*, 268–98, 468–83, 570–4, 601–7. See also Luca Molà, "Artigiani e brevetti nella Firenze del Cinquecento," in *La grande storia dell'artigianato*, vol. 3 of *Il Cinquecento*, ed. Franco Franceschi and Gloria Fossi (Florence: Giunti, 2000), 57–79.

children to wander the streets, the siege of 1529–30 imposed special hardships on both the population and charitable institutions. Both the Innocenti
and the hospital of Santa Maria Nuova had huge tracts of land seized and
expropriated. An acute shortage of wet nurses caused by their lack of access
to the city caused appallingly high rates of infant mortality, which even the
year after the siege remained at more than 75 percent. The pages of the Balie
and Bambini tell a grim tale indeed: entries of the names and descriptions of
children, instead of being followed by the documentation of their wet nursing, contain the record only of their premature deaths by starvation. Even
under less extreme circumstances, the memory of the siege may have been
the reason that, in the 1530s, the officials of the hospital began to write down
in cipher the names of parents they could identify rather than keeping them
completely anonymous, so that in an emergency, infants could be returned
to them. On 1 June 1535, for example, a boy by the name of Fortunato was
abandoned at birth. As a countersign, his parents had left

> a square of smooth purple knit cloth with a double-braided black silk sewn
> in. And behind it in sheepskin for a countersign in the shape of a fish
> written on the back, was "Fortunato on the first day of June."

At the bottom the scribe drew a picture of the countersign and identified the father, in cipher, as Charlo di Gherardo Buondelmonte from
Montepulciano.[16] The importance of identifying parents in code becomes
clearer from an entry two weeks later when another child, Benedetto, who
was admitted at the age of three months, came with a note attached to him
giving only his name, birth date, and a countersign. Nonetheless, the scribe
identified his parents as the daughter of Ser Andrea del Fioravante and the
son of Girolamo Panichi. "We sent him back to his mother because there
was no one here who could feed him."[17]

The famine of 1539 marked a crisis of subsistence that must have been
severe for Florentine families. Both the number and continuity of admissions
to the Innocenti between 1539 and 1540 represent a sharp contrast to the
preceding year. In 1538, the Innocenti admitted 468 children: 256 girls and
212 boys. In 1539, this jumped to 566 (319 girls and 247 boys), and in
1540 to 959 children (631 girls and 328 boys). Although the gender ratio
of admission in 1539 was close to what it had been earlier (54 percent to

[16] AOIF Balie e Bambini (XVI, 19) fol. 224r, 14 June 1535: "uno quadro di raso paghonazzo in
una maglietta infilato in chordellina dopia nera di seta. E driento v'era in charta pechora per
chontrassegnio a uso di pescie scritto drento 'adì primo di giugno Fortunato.'"

[17] AOIF Balie e Bambini (XVI, 19) fol. 232v, 14 June 1535 "essi rimandato alla madre perche non
ci era chi gli dessi la poppa."

TABLE 1.1. *Percentage of male newborns in the population of male children admitted under a year old and infant mortality among males admitted to the Ospedale degli Innocenti, 1531–41*

Cohort	%	N	Infant mortality per thousand
1531	50.2	111/221	778
1532	50	98/196	806
1533	59.5	135/227	714
1534	58	130/224	607
1535	64.6	137/212	542
1536	63.4	132/208	577
1537	58.5	106/181	597
1538	58.5	121/207	643
1539	49.7	111/223	664
1540	44.6	117/262	641
1541	63.8	113/177	678
TOTAL	56.1	1311/2336	650

Source: AOIF, Balie e Bambini A–H (XVI, filze 15–22).

43 percent in favor of girls), in 1540 the proportion of girls increased to 65.8 percent. Moreover, the proportion of newborns among girls admitted that year was extremely low, suggesting that more than ever the decision to abandon older girls was being made as a response to financial and subsistence crises. Even though a decrease in the proportion of newborns among males is also evident, it is equally clear that it was much more pronounced among females, suggesting that in times of economic crisis, they were more likely to be abandoned. Indeed, among the girls abandoned in 1540, fully one-quarter were older than a year, compared with only 5 percent in 1538. The comparable figures for males are 20 percent in 1540 and 2.3 percent in 1538 (see Tables 1.1–1.5).

In Rome, the two decades spanning the years 1555 to 1575 witnessed three famines: 1556–7, 1567, and 1569–70.[18] In Florence, abnormally high wheat prices, which usually indicate famine, occurred in 1533, 1539, 1551, 1554–7, 1563, and most of the first half of the 1590s.[19] Certainly by the early

[18] Paolo Simoncelli, "Note sul sistema assistenziale a Roma nel XVI secolo," in *Timore e carità*, ed. G. Politi, M. Rosa, and F. della Peruta, 137–56, at 143.

[19] Richard Goldthwaite, *The Building of Renaissance Florence: An Economic and Social History* (Baltimore: Johns Hopkins University Press, 1980), 439. The years cited are those between 1531 and 1599 when the daily wage of an unskilled worker could purchase less than one-fifth of a *staio* (bushel) of wheat. Goldthwaite's price series omits the following years: 1532, 1533–8, 1540, 1542–7, 1549–50, 1555, 1560, 1565–9, 1572–3, 1575–9, 1582–3, 1585–6, 1588–91, 1593–5, and 1597. At no time during the sixteenth century is it likely that the daily wage of a skilled worker could

TABLE 1.2. *Percentage of female newborns in population of female children admitted under a year old and infant mortality among females admitted to the Ospedale degli Innocenti, 1531–41*

Cohort	%	N	Infant mortality per thousand
1531	42.4	100/236	788
1532	53.7	132/246	752
1533	45.9	129/281	683
1534	50.0	130/260	608
1535	61.6	146/237	637
1536	71	147/207	571
1537	54.8	125/228	592
1538	56.8	138/243	564
1539	44.2	123/278	633
1540	32.3	152/471	648
1541	53.9	131/243	712
TOTAL	48.8	1453/2977	653

Source: AOIF, Balie e Bambini A–H (XVI, filze 15–22).

1570s, a looming banking crisis was already causing severe shortages of cash so that silk and wool manufacturers had considerable difficulty paying their workers.[20] In 1577, Francesco I revoked the Bigallo's authority to supervise and control begging because it was "too great an undertaking."[21]

This economic crisis also directly affected the Magistrato dei Pupilli: in 1550, this wards' court supervised thirty orphans; in 1560, thirty-three; but in 1570, nearly twice that many (fifty-five). The number of orphans under the care of this magistracy directly reflects the link between economics and inheritance: in 1591 and 1592, the two years following the pan-Italian famine of 1590, the number of orphans under the care of this magistracy nearly tripled, from 26 in 1590, to 68 in 1591, and 74 in 1592.[22]

purchase more than half a *staio* of wheat, whereas in forty-two of the hundred years comprising the fifteenth century, an unskilled worker's day wages would have been sufficient to buy half a *staio* or more of wheat. More recently, Goldthwaite has cautioned against drawing overly broad inferences from construction workers' wages about the performance of the Florentine economy in general, showing that cloth workers, particularly highly skilled wool weavers, earned wages well above those of men in the building trades. See idem, *The Economy of Renaissance Florence*, 570, 575–6.

[20] Carlo Cipolla, *Money in Sixteenth-Century Florence* (Berkeley/Los Angeles/London: University of California Press, 1989), 105–12.

[21] Daniela Lombardi, "Poveri a Firenze," 169, citing a letter from Francesco I to the Bigallo on 20 March 1576 in ASF, Pratica segreta 184, fol. 64r.

[22] Giulia Calvi, *Il contratto morale: Madre e figli nella Toscana moderna* (Bari: Laterza, 1994), 76–8.

TABLE I.3. *Child death rates (infants included) per thousand at the Ospedale degli Innocenti, 1531–41*

Cohort	Male	Female
1531	786	777
1532	830	817
1533	743	740
1534	712	737
1535	671	808
1536	698	748
1537	774	742
1538	830	777
1539	769	780
1540	759	792
1541	795	805
TOTAL	759	776

Source: AOIF, Balie e Bambini A-H (XVI, filze 15–22).

TABLE I.4. *Percentage of deaths by age at death in years: boys*

	−1	+1	+2	+3	+4	+5	Total
1531	85.1	7.9	4.0	3.0	0.0	0.0	100.0
1532	89.8	5.6	2.3	2.3	0.0	0.0	100.0
1533	86.2	6.4	3.2	1.6	1.6	1.0	100.0
1534	81.0	8.9	6.0	1.8	0.0	2.3	100.0
1535	78.2	11.6	4.1	3.4	4.1	2.7	100.0
1536	76.5	8.3	7.6	5.7	1.3	0.6	100.0
1537	75.0	6.9	11.8	2.8	2.8	0.7	100.0
1538	75.6	11.9	7.4	2.3	0.5	2.3	100.0
1539	78.0	12.6	4.7	0.5	0.5	3.7	100.0
1540	67.5	18.9	10.4	2.0	0.8	0.4	100.0
1541	79.5	10.6	3.3	3.3	0.7	2.6	100.0
TOTAL	79.1	10.3	5.8	2.5	0.9	1.4	100.0

TABLE I.5. *Percentage of deaths by age at death in years: girls*

	−1	+1	+2	+3	+4	+5	100.0
1531	81.9	10.6	1.8	1.8	1.3	2.6	100.0
1532	84.5	9.1	3.7	1.4	0.9	0.4	100.0
1533	84.2	4.8	7.0	2.2	0.5	1.3	100.0
1534	76.4	13.1	5.8	1.4	1.9	1.4	100.0
1535	76.3	10.6	6.1	1.5	2.0	3.5	100.0
1536	73.0	8.0	7.0	7.0	2.5	2.5	100.0
1537	75.4	13.5	6.1	2.2	1.1	1.7	100.0
1538	68.9	20.1	6.0	2.0	1.5	1.5	100.0
1539	70.7	19.7	6.0	2.0	0.8	0.8	100.0
1540	61.0	21.4	11.0	1.8	2.6	2.2	100.0
1541	77.2	12.6	6.5	3.2	0.5	0.0	100.0
TOTAL	73.9	13.9	6.6	2.5	1.4	1.7	100.0

Francesco I's revocation of the Bigallo's authority to supervise begging was not typical of the Medici response to the problem of poverty earlier in the century. In the early 1530s, for example, Duke Alessandro de' Medici acted swiftly to restore the patrimony of the Monte di Pietà that had been seized at the end of the previous decade and to replenish the treasuries of the hospitals of Santa Maria Nuova and the Innocenti.[23] The accession of Cosimo I in 1537 was eventually to bring not only an ad hoc response to specific problems but a grander design for the centralization of the city's charitable response that would form the foundation of the links between discipline and confessionalization. The stimulus for this reform, which began to take shape in 1541, was almost certainly the famine of 1539 and the enormous pressure it put on the city's institutions. In 1540, for example, the Innocenti's superintendent, Luca Alamanni, complained:

> This past year we have been extraordinarily oppressed with regard both to the amount of grain and with respect to the huge numbers of children who, because of the famine, have been left here . . . because everyone is just thrown in the hospital.[24]

In 1541, Cosimo, citing "the growth in the number of poor derelicts of every kind, multiplying daily," centralized the administration of the city's charitable agencies under the Buonomini di San Martino and put the care of all the city's children under a new magistracy, the Buonomini del Bigallo.[25] In particular, the reforms were undertaken as a way to augment the Bigallo's revenues and to place its administration under the guidance of the bishop of Assisi, messer Agnolo Marzi de' Medici, "and the other respectable Buonuomini proposed for its care and governance." The reform was motivated by a concern to see that "the fruits of the revenues of Santa Maria del Bigallo and of its annexed and subsidiary institutions are put to their usual pious uses, and chiefly in support of miserable persons, and that the aforesaid company and its related institutions should be united under the same regime as the said hospital and should be supervised with greater diligence than in the past."[26] As was typical of Cosimo's reforms, this decree promised greater and more reliable revenues in exchange for the surrender of institutional autonomy. In a decree several months later, Cosimo's concern was addressed less to newborns and more to slightly older children – specifically, "considering in

---

[23] D'Addario, La formazione dello stato moderno in Toscana, 172.

[24] AOIF, Suppliche e sovrani rescritti (VI, 1) fol. 140r, n.d.

[25] John Henderson, "Charity and Welfare in Early Modern Tuscany," in Health Care and Poor Relief in Counter-Reformation Europe, ed. Ole Peter Grell, Andrew Cunningham, and Jon Arrizabalaga (London/New York: Routledge, 1999), 63.

[26] D'Addario, Aspetti della controriforma, 464, document 73: ASF Senato del Quarantotto, 5, fols. 13v–15v.

what misery and calamity the poor children of three, five, and up to ten years of age, derelict and totally abandoned by their fathers, mothers, kinsmen, and every other human and spiritual authority."[27] This set of reforms also established the hospital of the Broccardi, set up specifically to take in abandoned and derelict boys, to be "brought up and instructed in reading and writing, and who, once they've reached the age of ten, were entrusted to some skilled tradesman."[28]

These reforms were acknowledged by a papal bull of Paul III on 18 July 1543, the routine nature of which belies important changes that had taken place in the relationship between church and state over the previous century. In particular, where a number of charitable institutions in the fifteenth century jealously guarded their lay status even as they were denominated "pious establishments," Cosimo's conception of reform placed all of the newly created and existing charitable institutions in the same category as monasteries and convents and subsumed all of these under the single rubric of religious reform. In one sense, he was merely confirming the structural similarities that had already existed between charitable and monastic discipline, but the critical difference was that these were now yoked together in the service of political and social discipline, underlining once again the important links recent historians have made between confessionalization and early modern state-formation.[29]

This does not mean that relations between the grand duke and the Holy See always went smoothly in terms of the oversight of religious institutions. Indeed, their very turbulence reinforces the point that Cosimo meant as far as humanly possible to bring local ecclesiastical administration under his control as well. This often placed him in the position of defending charitable institutions against attempts by the papacy to extract money from them. Both the hospitals of the Innocenti and Santa Maria Nuova, for example, appealed at various times for Cosimo's aid, and incidentally, both their *spedalinghi*, or administrators, by the 1550s were Cosimo's own appointees and beneficiaries of grand ducal patronage.[30] Conflict with the Camera Apostolica reinforced rather than undermined Cosimo's determination to bring charities and other religious houses under his disciplinary system.

Cosimo's concern to tie religious reform to his own disciplinary system is also clear in a letter of recommendation for a Venetian preacher written in

---

[27] ASF Diplomatico, Bigallo, 19 March 1542, cited in D'Addario, *Aspetti*, 468.

[28] D'Addario, *Aspetti*, 469.

[29] See n. 9.

[30] For an example of Cosimo's intervention in the Innocenti's behalf, when Borghini's alleged failure to pay a papal imposition put him in danger of excommunication, see ASF Archivio Mediceo del Principato 472A fol. 855r, 13 August 1558.

1560 by Lorenzo Pagni. This preacher, wrote Pagni, drew an audience "larger than any seen since the preaching of Savonarola." This Fra Gabriello had a great memory, much eloquence and sweetness in his preaching, boasted "good Greek and Latin letters, logic, and philosophy," and was also well grounded in theology and the Holy Scripture. Most important, in Lorenzo Pagni's view, Fra Gabriello's preaching had moved even those nobility who had not been exposed to much preaching to distribute alms to girls and abandoned boys, as well as to "hospitals, monasteries, and other pious places of this city."[31] Both Cosimo and Francesco asserted their rights to include even the appointment of chaplains within their network of patronage. In December 1564, for example, Francesco, as prince, asked Borghini to name a new maestro of the chapel of the Visitation at San Miniato fra le Torri, because the hospital had *jus patronato* over that particular chapel. Thus, clearly even if Francesco did not overtly nominate the *maestro di cappella*, he at least entrusted the nomination to someone within the network of patronage. Borghini complained that Ferrante Capponi, the auditor general of ecclesiastical jurisdiction, had deliberately misled his own patron concerning the ecclesiastical nature of the hospital, portraying it as a lay institution, the superintendent of which therefore did not have the power to nominate someone for the post. Borghini insisted on his right, subject to Francesco's written confirmation, to confer a benefice that was under the *jus patronato* of "this his house."[32]

Cosimo's reforms also extended to Florence's subject cities and territories. In Prato, for example, Cosimo centralized the various Ceppi (communal funds for charitable donations) and made them not only subject to more direct control but also instrumental in the extension of political and social control, appointing nine deputies to oversee them.[33] Moreover, the Buonomini del Bigallo were given authority over the entire Medicean state. Directors of hospitals had to account to the Buonomini for their revenues and expenditures and to turn over any excess to Florence.[34] The success

---

[31] ASF Mediceo del Principato 477 fol. 709r–710v, 27 March 1559: Letter from Lorenzo Pagni to Cosimo I. "Et ha hauto una audientia così grande, che da fra Girolamo in qua nissuno si ricorda che alcuno altro predicatore habbi mai hauta maggiore.... Ha grandissima memoria, molta eloquentia, et dolcezza nel predicare (buone lettere greche, et latine, logica, filosophia), et molto bene fondato nella teologia, et nella scrittura sacra.... Et per opera sua si sono fatte moltissime et grande elemosine alle fanciulle, et fanciulli abandonati, a' spedali, monasterii, et altri luoghi pii di questa città."

[32] AOIF Filze d'Archivio (LXII) 18 fol. 68r, 26 December 1564.

[33] Elena Fasano-Guarini, "Un microcosmo in movimento (1494–1815)," 866.

[34] John Henderson, "Charity and Welfare in Early Modern Tuscany," 64, citing ASF, Senato del Quarantotto, 5, fols. 13v–15v, 19 March 1542, and Luigi Passerini, *Storia degli stabilmenti di beneficenza ed istruzione elementare gratuita della città di Firenze* (Florence: LeMonnier, 1853), 27–31, 800.

of Cosimo's reform program is clear from a description by Giovanni Maria di Baccio Cecchi of several of the city's charitable organizations, which he specifically describes as magistracies: "Sommario de' Magistrati di Firenze secondo che si truovano questo anno 1562." In addition to documenting the charitable activities of sixteenth-century Florentines, this summary makes clear the evolution of charity from relatively autonomous organizations that benefited from state assistance to organizations that were fully functioning departments in Medici government.

The Buonomini di San Martino, for example, were expressly forbidden to hold real estate or other property; rather, the sizable donations that reached them, including "generous sums of money and grain" from the duke and duchess, had to be spent on aiding the *poveri vergognosi* and on secretly providing dowries for noble girls.[35] Cecchi's description notes that the company of the Misericordia del Bigallo (previously the Misericordia and the Bigallo had been two separate charitable organizations) spent its generous benefactions on providing offices for churches, maintaining hospitals, taking care of abandoned children and protecting their inheritances, collecting the former in hospital "under the custody of women who clean them and tutors who teach them."[36] The grand duke personally chose the six captains of the Misericordia del Bigallo.

In addition to providing hospitals for abandoned children, the Bigallo also worked to eliminate the large numbers of children begging homeless in the streets by keeping a count of them and legislating that all who knew whose children they were to return them to their homes, or to bring them directly to the Bigallo's officers, to keep them until their relatives came for them. Cecchi also noted that there were three separate congregations "which have particular care of abandoned girls, so that they do not wander the streets and fall prey to evil. He collected them in rooms specifically set aside for them, made sure they were watched over, and taught them to work and then married them off – and all [this activity] is supported through almsgiving."[37] Several other companies also ministered to poor girls and to *poveri vergognosi*.

Cosimo also assumed personal patronage of the city's youth confraternities, which engaged in the same sorts of activities described earlier: dressed so that their charity would remain anonymous, they distributed bread and provided dowries. In addition, Cecchi notes, Florence boasted more than sixty convents for women, which, in addition to their spiritual governors,

---

[35] D'Addario *Aspetti*, 402–4, citing Biblioteca Moreniana, Palagi, 246, Giovanni Maria di Baccio Cecchi, *Sommario de' Magistrati di Firenze secondo che si truovano questo anno 1562* fols. 41v–44r.

[36] D'Addario, *Aspetti*, 402–4:

[37] D'Addario, *Aspetti*, 404–5.

reported to a commission of four male citizens (of whom Vincenzio Borghini would be one from 1567 until his death in 1580). Cecchi pointedly
remarks that this group of citizens was not a holdover institution from earlier days but an innovation by Cosimo himself.[38] Finally, although Cecchi
only mentions this in passing, guilds were also considered magistracies and
therefore properly under the tutelage of Cosimo and the administration of
his religious reforms.[39]

An instructive example of Cosimo's approach to combining the power of
charity and state was his reform of the Conservatori della Legge. Initially a
republican institution, this magistracy was founded in 1429 and consisted of
eight men drawn from the greater guilds and two from the artisan corpora-
tions. During the fifteenth and early sixteenth centuries, the Conservatores
Legum (its Latin name) oversaw the lists of those nominated to communal
offices to make sure that the nominees were not ineligible because they
were too young, tax evaders, illegitimate, or convicted criminals who had
not made restitution. The "conservatores legum et ordinamentorum comu-
nis Florentie" also monitored the performance of magistrates in enforcing
legislation and brought to account those accused of malfeasance in office.[40]
At least one of this magistracy's functions, as it developed beginning in 1532
under the duchy, was to provide legal aid, including the appointment of
a public defender, for the poor. The legislation of 1532 also extended the
magistrates' authority to act as arbitrators in family and marital disputes. In
Benedetto Varchi's view, at least, these reforms were consolidated by legislation of 1533 and 1534 that detailed how this magistracy was to proceed,
specifying that its function was "properly . . . to serve the interests solely of
poor persons."[41]

It was also to this magistracy, even before the reforms of the late 1560s,
that the hospital's widows could turn to reclaim their dowries. Thus, in
1549, hospital officials petitioned the Conservatori della Legge on behalf
of Dorotea, una "figlia" of the hospital, to recover her dowry of 150 lire

---

[38] Cecchi, "Sommario," fol. 44r, cited in d'Addario, Aspetti, 405.

[39] Ibid.

[40] Arnaldo d'Addario, La formazione dello stato moderno in Toscana, 166. On the function of this
magistracy as a legal defense fund, see Giuseppe Pansini, "I conservatori di leggi e la difesa dei
poveri nelle cause civili durante il Principato Mediceo," in Studi di storia medievale e moderna per
Ernesto Sestan (Florence: Leo S. Olschki, 1980), 2:529–70.

[41] D'Addario, La formazione dello stato, 166, and, on 172, paraphrasing Varchi, Storia fiorentina
(Cologne [false imprint; actually printed at Augsburg], 1721), 526. Cf. Pansini, "Conservatori
di leggi," 532, citing "Ordinazioni fatte dalla repubblica fiorentina insieme con l'Excellentia del
Duca Alessandro de' Medici dichiarato capo della medesima" in L. Cantini, Legislazione toscana
raccolta e illustrata (32 vols., Florence: Pietro Fantosini, 1800–8) 2:14.

(126 in cash and 24 as *donora*), which had been tied up as rental property since her husband's death twenty years earlier.[42]

Cosimo's reforms, which spanned nine separate legislative initiatives between 1538 and 1573, were addressed first of all, as with so many other agencies, to the restructuring of the agency to make its officials more directly accountable to the grand duke. By 1562, this magistracy was sufficiently active that it met to hear cases at least twice, and sometimes three times, per week. The magistracy also added a fourth sitting on Tuesday mornings to hear "solely the cases of the poor and of the widows and wards."[43] Second, the reforms sought to reduce the expense and the waste of time that poor persons had to endure when the magistracy heard their cases, a problem that at least one anonymous source traced to the "understaffing, lack of diligence, and carelessness on the part of the procurators who commonly await them, poor persons being unable to rouse those who with more intelligence are supposed to be serving them."[44] Thus, in civil cases, the reforms prescribed a time limit of forty days (three months in certain cases) from the time the assessor first reported on the case, and although criminal cases had no time limits, magistrates were encouraged to "keep in mind to expedite them as soon as possible making sure that necessary depositions are made to uncover the truth with the least harm and expense to the plaintiff."[45]

Nonetheless, the 1568 reforms, comprehensive as they were, produced little change in the way the magistracy operated or in the inconveniences still visited on the poor. Indeed, many of the protections designed to protect the poor, such as the requirement that petitions be written and not heard only orally, multiplied the number of cases among those pretending to be poor, as well as associated paperwork and expenses, the burden of which fell on the actual poor. A particularly vocal critic noted as early as 1569 that every three or four months, the required paperwork now filled four 500-page volumes, whereas previously two volumes of 200 pages each had sufficed.[46] Moreover, even though the 1568 legislation had specified that a public defender was to be drawn by lot from the lawyers of the Palazzo del Podestà and of the Mercanzia, the legal expertise of nominees from the Podestà

[42] AOIF Giornale K (XIII, 17) fol. 157r, 15 June 1549.

[43] For example, by 1562, Cosimo chose the Conservatori personally. D'Addario, 478, citing Giovanni Maria di Baccio Cecchi, "Sommario de' Magistrati di Firenze secondo si truovano questo anno 1562" fol. 25v–26r. The 1562 legislation is reported by Pansini, citing Cantini, *Legislazione*, 4: 344, and ASF Magistrato supremo 4310, fols. 162r ff.

[44] Cf. ASF Pratica segreta 6, fol. 441r (undated and unsigned), cited in Pansini, "Conservatori," 537.

[45] ASF Magistrato Supremo 4312, fol. 27v, cited in d'Addario, 475.

[46] Pansini, "Conservatori," 546, citing ASF Pratica segreta 9, fols. 35r-v, 1 January 1568.

often did not transfer easily to the Mercanzia and vice versa, so that the poor were still often defended incompetently by inexperienced public defenders. Even worse, according to subsequent complaints, the Conservatori della Legge routinely extorted large sums of money or even sexual favors from women seeking the return of their dowries. After the early 1570s, no major innovations or reforms took place for more than a hundred years.[47]

Cosimo acted with similar solicitude but with more conspicuous success in the 1565 reforms of the Magistrato dei Pupilli, the magistracy charged with the responsibility of overseeing the distribution of inheritance for minors whose fathers had died intestate or without nominating a guardian or whose interests in the estate required protection. The magistracy also protected minor children or others who needed guardians in cases in which neither the mother nor any member of the family on the father's side declared an intention to accept guardianship and administer the inheritance, when multiple guardians encountered a conflict of interest with one another, or when a widow guardian decided to enter a second marriage. If her husband had died intestate, she had to petition for guardianship.[48]

The first extant statutory legislation dates from 1384, when the authorities in charge of the reduction of the public debt were authorized to become guardians of testaments. The legislation of 1388 expanded this authority to cover the inheritances of minors and widows. By 1393, this task had proved sufficiently onerous to require the creation of a separate magistracy consisting of six "popolari e guelfi" called the Ufficiali dei Pupilli e Adulti.[49] Nonetheless, the history of this institution continued to interweave with the intricacies of the public debt, probably because the liquid capital these estates made available was extremely useful for temporary reduction of the funded debt. The 1388 legislation provided that deposits of Pupilli in the Monte should earn interest of 5 percent, and when the Monte di Pietà was created over a century later, the deposits of wards were placed in that institution, creating the foundations for Cosimo I's comprehensive, if decentralized, fiscal system.[50]

---

[47] Pansini, "Conservatori," 551–7, citing ASF Pratica segreta 9, aff. 35, anonymous memos in November and December 1571, and ASF Miscellenea Medicea 370, n. 36.

[48] For an excellent and clear summary of this magistracy's responsibilities, see Giulia Calvi, *Il contratto morale*, 18–23. Cosimo's reforms can be found in ASF Archivio del Magistrato dei Pupilli del Principato 248. I have relied, however, on a printed edition of the new statutes published in 1575 by the Giunti in Florence, and for the text of the statutes from 1384–8, I have used Francesca Morandini, "Statuti e Ordinamenti dell'Ufficio dei Pupilli et adulti nel periodo della Repubblica fiorentina (1388–1534)" *Archivio Storico Italiano* 113 (1955): 522–51; 114 (1956): 92–117, and 115 (1957): 87–104.

[49] F. Morandini, "Statuti," *ASI* 113 (1955): 522.

[50] Morandini, "Statuti," *ASI* 113 (1955): 528–9.

Most interesting is that the original and the reformed statutes applied differently to boys and girls. Once boys reached the age of eighteen, they were no longer under the care and protection of the Pupilli.[51] The same rule applied to girls until 1478, except for a girl who married before she was eighteen came under the protection of her new husband. Starting in 1478, however, providing she remained unmarried, a girl entered the protection of the magistrates. This was enacted mainly to prevent relatives of girls who had died intestate from "allowing them to get old" and stay unmarried, thus obviating the need to disburse the dowries. The officials were enjoined to make all efforts to ensure that their female wards were married off as soon as possible.[52] Only if boys entered the religious life, however, did the magistracy withdraw its protection before they reached the age of eighteen[53] The magistracy offered protection to girls in other ways as well, housing them for short periods of times in *serbanza* in such convents as Sant'Agata and San Luca.[54]

From the beginning the statutes allowed the debt reduction officials to "constitute the dowries of girls and widows," in the case of the latter, coming to the defense of those who, like the traditional categories of orphans and minors, "commonly do not know how to speak or to argue their cases, but need to be supervised by others."[55] Although the statutes had always included widows as part of their charge, sometime between 1503 and 1531, the statutes specifically addressed the problem of their poverty and how it constituted an impediment to recovering their dowries:

> The most powerful and magnificent lords, considering that in the city and dominion of Florence there are many poor widows who have no one to represent them and can ill-afford to spend money on it, so that poverty should not be an impediment to recovering what is rightfully theirs, but so that they can have their property under their own care and governance and can recover chiefly their dowry with little expense, they provide and ordain that: . . . they can be accepted by the said officials and that said officials can be their judges in all their cases, active and passive, especially those concerning their dowries.[56]

[51] Ibid., *ASI*, 114 (1956): 100.

[52] Ibid., 102.

[53] *Riforma delli statuti degli Uficiali de' Pupilli, fatta il di 20 d'agosto 1565. Con l'aggiunte sino al presente anno 1575* (Florence: Giunti, 1575), 2v.

[54] Sharon T. Strocchia, "Taken into Custody: Girls and Convent Guardianship in Renaissance Florence," *Renaissance Studies* 17 (2003), 177–80, at 184–5.

[55] Morandini, "Statuti," *ASI*, 114 (1956): 112. Cf. also *ASI* 115 (1957): 87. Even as late as 1473, the magistracy was concerned to protect the estates of Pupilli from fraud that arose when dowries became involved: Cf. *ASI* 113 (1955): 550–1.

[56] The exact date is difficult to pinpoint. Morandini dates the redaction of the statutes to 1503. See Morandini, "Statuti," *ASI*, 115 (1957): 92.

Before widows could obtain access to such legal help, however, they first had to be declared "poor and powerless widows [*vedove povere et impotente*]" by the Mercanzia as well as by the officials of the Pupilli. The 1565 reforms only slightly amplified this definition of vulnerable widows "who, for the exaction of their dowries, or the legacies left to them by their husbands, or for some other reason are forced to sue and who ordinarily could not do so without intolerable expense and waste of time."[57]

The first reforms of the Pupilli under the Florentine duchy occurred under Alessandro in 1534. In particular, the officials of the Pupilli noted that plaintiffs (i.e., legal representatives of the wards) were only required to give an accounting of money they spent for their wards' inheritances once a year and that this often became a useful device for hiding from the wards themselves what was rightfully theirs. Consequently, the magistrates appointed a scribe to review every three months the accounts of wards who lived in the city, every six months for those who lived from three to ten miles away, and every eight months for those who lived more than ten miles outside the city walls.[58]

The wording of Cosimo's 1565 reforms noted, not without sensitivity, the careful balance required between two fundamentally conflicting roles of the magistracy: on one hand to provide protection by pursuing the well-being of minors and other persons placed under their care, "as every good father would do for his children," and on the other hand to judge impartially, "having only in mind God, and that the magistracy must be favorable to widows, minors, and other such persons, provided that it does not do injustice to others."[59] These reforms were much more expansive and specific concerning the classes of poor they served, extending the magistracy's protection to the deformed and even to "dissipators of estates" and "those who lead evil lives." Where under the republic, the Signori e Collegi determined just who the *mentecapti* were, under Cosimo's legislation, it fell to the grand duke and his lieutenant and councilors.[60] Moreover, in those cases in which it had often been the practice of the magistracy to delay accepting control over an inheritance that had a large number of debts and obligations in the often vain hope that a solvent heir would step forward and relieve the magistracy of its burdens, the reforms provided that such inheritances had to be accepted immediately so that the magistrates could collect from the debtors and pay

---

[57] *Riforma delli statuti degli Uficiali de' Pupilli*, 4r–4v.
[58] Morandini, "Statuti," *ASI* 115 (1957): 95.
[59] *Riforma delli statuti degli Uficiali de' Pupilli*, 7v.
[60] *Riforma delli statuti degli Uficiali de' Pupilli*, 3v4r.

off the creditors to keep further claims and interest charges from making the estate virtually unmanageable.[61]

Another salient feature of the 1565 reforms involved the extension of magistrates' authority from the city into the countryside. Each local official in the *contado* had to denounce in Florence the presence of orphans or adults who in their jurisdiction were "defenseless on account of not having testamentary or legal guardians, or someone willing to take on guardianship."[62] When a new local official took office, the Magistrato required him to come to Florence, "where he will be given notice of all the inheritances and names of the executors (*attori*) under this jurisdiction. He must then force said executors to give a full accounting of their administration at the end of May every year."[63] In this respect, the reforms were well intentioned but were hardly a match for the provincial elite involved in complex and multiple relationships with the magistracy's clients that virtually guaranteed conflicts of interest. Nor were provincial elites exempt from the same social pressures that pushed their urban counterparts to tighten inheritance rules to the disadvantage of younger daughters.[64]

This magistracy, which according to the 1565 reformed document supervised as many as twenty thousand inheritances, had large amounts of landed and liquid wealth in its possession at any one time, and thus it was often called on to shore up more precariously financed charitable initiatives. As early as 1497, for example, the newly established Monte di Pietà replaced the defunct Medici bank as the official depository of the Magistrato dei Pupilli, and the Pupilli's treasurer was also an official of the Monte di Pietà. Reform legislation of 1534 specified that such a connection was a matter both of fiscal prudence and charitable intent, "considering that the said monies are better off with the Monte di Pietà of the city of Florence and can serve the needy poor during the time that the officials of the Pupilli have no need of them."[65] Similarly, the Conservatori della Legge had close ties to the Magistrato dei Pupilli: indeed, their jurisdictions overlapped so that in 1568,

---

[61] Ibid., 3v.

[62] Ibid., 26rv.

[63] Ibid., 26v–27r.

[64] Giovanna Benadusi, *A Provincial Elite in Early Modern Tuscany: Family and Power in the Creation of the State* (Baltimore/London: Johns Hopkins University Press, 1996), 113–28.

[65] Morandini, "Statuti," *ASI* 115 (1957): 97. Cf. also Carol Bresnahan Menning, *Charity and State*, 258. In 1549, Cosimo's secretary, Lelio Torelli, ordered that the treasurers of the Pupilli and of the Mercanzia should place their deposits in the Monte di Pietà to make up for a shortfall in revenues. Cf. ASF Magistrato Supremo 1122, cited in Menning, *Charity and State*, 180n. For the requirement that officials of the Pupilli deposit sums in the Monte di Pietà, see Morandini, "Statuti," *ASI*, 115 (1957): 109.

Cosimo had to adopt new definitions of their respective powers to untangle them.[66] Cosimo I's exploitation of these already-existing connections seems typical enough of his use of charitable institutions in state-building: to take existing institutions and ties forged in the republican period and to exploit their new statutes as arms of government that could be used to weather temporary crises.[67] One must be cautious even about ascribing to Cosimo I the close ties that existed among such disparate government agencies as the Monte di Pietà and the Magistrato dei Pupilli. As Polizzotto has shown, these ties during the late republic, in the 1520s especially, were part of a charitable network that had come increasingly under the control and influence both of Savonarolans and the Dominicans at San Marco. Cosimo's religious reforms of the 1540s, including the temporary and brief expulsion of Dominican friars from San Marco in 1545, were enacted not only to chase away the demons of anti-Medici sentiment but also formed part of a much larger effort to subsume the links among charitable institutions under the rubric of discipline.[68]

Cosimo's most conspicuous success was the imposition of accountability and discipline, especially through the transformation of religious and charitable institutions to vital organs within the grand ducal bureaucracy. This is above all the importance of the reforms of the 1540s, which in other respects could hardly be considered innovative, but rather replicated structures that had come into being under successive fifteenth-century republican regimes. It is particularly noteworthy that sixteenth-century reforms articulated the role of the Conservatori della Legge as arbiters in family disputes, an intrusion of government that, even though hardly novel even in the

---

[66] Pansini, "Conservatori," 541.

[67] For the use of charitable institutions, especially the Ospedale degli Innocenti, as depositories, see the section below, "Deposit Banking at the Innocenti."

[68] Lorenzo Polizzotto, *The Elect Nation: The Savonarolan Movement in Florence 1494–1545* (Oxford: Clarendon Press, 1994), 435, notes the ferocity of Cosimo's organized campaign to discredit the Dominicans and San Marco: "While it lasted, hooligans disrupted religious functions, manhandled and insulted the friars, made indecent proposals to them, fondled novices and young boys in the convent's charge, and went through the motions of committing sodomy with one another whenever the friars walked in procession though the streets of Florence." As Polizzotto points out, the Savonarola that emerged from biographies after this period reconstructed him as less prophetic and more tranquil. The connection among Savonarola, charity, and children, however, persisted in personal ties long afterward. For example, Vincenzio Borghini, who may have crossed out his reference to Bishop Nacchianti as a former pupil of the Innocenti in order not to anger Cosimo or to remind him of Nacchianti's *brutta figura* at the Council of Trent, corresponded with Don Silvano Razzi, whose brother Serafino had written one of the "reconstructed" biographies. Don Silvano, whom Vasari mentioned as a close friend and who may have collaborated on the *Lives* either along with or independently from Borghini, included the Savonarolan Francesco Valori among the five biographies of illustrious men, biographies that were eventually published in 1602.

republic, foreshadows the interest in having such charitable institutions as the Ospedale dei Mendicanti to care for the *malmaritate*.

As superintendent of the Ospedale degli Innocenti, Borghini consistently sought Cosimo's and Francesco's assistance to address four major concerns: the heavy influx of admissions and the hospital's relationships with its wet nurses, the extension and refinement of humanist pedagogy for the hospital's boys, the honor and fate of the girls and women of the hospital, and pressing issues of finance and state-building. Although Borghini had singled out the sixteenth-century inheritance crisis as the cause of ever-rising numbers of admissions, he devoted most of his administrative energies to reviving the remedies proposed by his predecessor, Luca Alamanni. In particular, Borghini complained, as Alamanni had done, that smaller hospices throughout Tuscany dumped their charges onto the doorstep of the Innocenti. In his first major report to Cosimo in late 1553, Borghini reviewed Alamanni's recommendations to prohibit other hospitals from sending children to the Innocenti, to restrict admissions from outside Tuscany, and to change rules of inheritance to allow illegitimate children to inherit shares of patrimony equal to those of legitimate children.[69] Alamanni had also proposed restricting admission to illegitimate children, an expedient mentioned often throughout the sixteenth century but not adopted in most areas of northern Italy until the eighteenth century.[70] In addition, Alamanni had proposed closing the hospital's doors to children of concubines, a solution Borghini rejected as highly impractical given the difficulty of identifying such children.[71]

No less frustrating were Borghini's attempts to regulate fraud and abuse among the hospital's wet nurses, especially those in the countryside out of immediate reach of the hospital's supervision. Five months after becoming superintendent in 1552, Borghini extracted from Cosimo authority for the hospital's *operai* to proceed against wet nurses who defrauded the hospital. His predecessor had already managed to interest the Otto di Guardia in these sorts of cases, but the powers granted the *operai* made them nearly

---

[69] AOIF, Suppliche e sovrani rescritti (VI,1), fols. 244r-v, 4 November 1553. Cf. Gavitt, "Charity and State Building," 242n.

[70] The distinction between illegitimate and legitimate children was taken to extremes in eighteenth-century Turin, where city officials designated separate hospices for them. See Sandra Cavallo, "Bambini abbandonati e bambini 'in deposito' a Torino nel settecento," in *Enfance abandonnée et société en Europe, XIVe–XXe siècle*, Collection de l'Ecole Française de Rome, no. 140 (Rome: Ecole Française de Rome, 1991), 341–75. In Venice, the Hospital of the Pietà obtained a papal bull, dated 12 November 1548, condemning and excommunicating parents who abandoned legitimate or "natural" children when the resources of the family were sufficient to support them, as can be read on a plaque on the Pietà's exterior wall.

[71] AOIF, Suppliche e sovrani rescritti (VI, 1), fol. 244v, 4 November 1553.

an independent judicial system, allowing them to "punish, confine, and condemn such delinquents in whatever afflictive penalties of the body the *operai* shall deem such [malefactors] deserve."[72] As Borghini wrote in drafting the petition, "the majority of tiny infants abandoned to this hospital are sent to wet nurse in various and sundry places of the dominion."[73]

In 1579, Borghini provided a geographic breakdown: of 568 children at wet nurses, 518 were in towns either in the Mugello or the Casentino, which had for at least a century been the traditional places for the Innocenti to send its newborns to be nursed.[74] The various parishes of the *podesteria* of Castel San Niccolò di Casentino, especially Sant'Angelo, Ceticha, Garliano, and Montemignaio, accounted for a high proportion of the hospital's nurses.[75] The resulting microeconomy was, nonetheless, both fragile and deadly, without sufficient resources to support the heavy influx of children both from the Innocenti and from private families.[76] Because Tuscans traditionally did not nurse more than one child at a time, wet nurses would either have had to abandon their own children, arrange for wet nurses themselves (which would cancel any economic benefit), or continue to feed their own children at the expense of the Innocenti's.[77] Complicating all these factors was a high rate of pregnancy, so that a child scheduled to nurse for fourteen months often nursed only three or four.

Wet nurses who became pregnant or whose charges fell ill had to return the children to the hospital and, in the event of the death of an Innocenti

[72] AOIF, Suppliche e sovrani rescritti (VI, 1), fol. 143, n.d. The Otto di Guardia became interested in wet nurses and their husbands who continued to accept payments after the death of a child in their care, levying a fine of twenty-five soldi for any death not reported to the Innocenti within one month. On the power of the Otto di Guardia to punish, cf. AOIF, Suppliche e sovrani rescritti (VI, 1), fol. 648r, 14 March 1552.

[73] AOIF, Suppliche e sovrani rescritti (VI, 1), fol. 143, n.d See Gavitt, "Charity and State Building," 244n.

[74] AOIF, Filze d'Archivio (LXII, 30), fol. 491r-v, 18 June 1579. Cf. Gavitt, *Charity and Children*, 228.

[75] Ibid., 227.

[76] Nonetheless, the Innocenti employed most wet nurses only once, which suggests either that wet nursing constituted a source of supplementary income for rural families but not one on which they could depend or that most nurses turned to more lucrative employment with private families. The account books often contain instructions in the margins that payments should be directed to a third party, perhaps as repayment of a short-term loan. See Tomoko Takahashi, *Il Rinascimento dei trovatelli: il brefotrofio, la città, e le campagne nella Toscana del XV secolo* (Rome: Edizioni de Storia e Letteratura, 2003), 83–4.

[77] Christiane Klapisch-Zuber, "Genitori naturali e genitori del latte nella Firenze del Quattrocento," *Quaderni Storici* 44 (1980): 543–63, translated into English as "Blood Parents and Milk Parents: Wet Nursing in Florence, 1300–1530" in C. Klapisch-Zuber, *Women, Family, and Ritual in Renaissance Italy*, trans. Lydia Cochrane (Chicago: University of Chicago Press, 1985), 132–64. On wet-nursing only one child at a time, see ibid., 137.

child under their care had to notify the hospital and bring back a sworn oath from the village priest testifying to the cause of death.[78] Much more remunerative from the nurses' point of view, however, was to continue to collect payments from the hospital after the child had died.[79] Although the Innocenti attempted to reduce this kind of fraud by having the parish priest certify that the child was still alive before the wet nurse's husband could be paid, these "oaths" were conveniently lost, or, in the case of long-term frauds, the same oath was brought back each month. On those occasions, the Innocenti conducted surprise inspections in the countryside (about twice a year), but news always traveled faster than the inspectors themselves, giving the culprits time to borrow an infant from a neighbor.[80] This was the most prevalent form of fraud, and every so often the Innocenti incarcerated the wet nurse's husband in the *Stinche* (the Florentine debtor's prison) as an example.[81] Other wet nurses, when they became pregnant and ceased lactating, fed infants concoctions ranging from cow's milk and goat's milk, to bread soaked and mashed in water to look like milk.[82] Wet nurses also took advantage of the size and complexity of an institution such as the Innocenti by abandoning their own children to it and then becoming employed and paid as their own child's wet nurse:

> The wet nurses, who come daily for babies to the very same location where the hospital's babies are, because there is nowhere else to put them, often abandon their own children to the hospital, and then come [posing] as wet nurses to take them. They are given their own children because they have made a countersign for them, and recognize it, and in this way they get paid to nurse their own children. In order to obviate this problem, which is of some consequence, a room would need to be arranged where the wet nurses who come to pick up babies could stay without seeing the babies or being allowed inside the hospital.[83]

[78] Gavitt, *Charity and Children*, 231.

[79] AOIF, Suppliche e sovrani rescritti (VI, 1), fol. 143r, n.d.

[80] AOIF, Suppliche e sovrani rescritti (VI, 1), fol. 8or, n.d. See Gavitt, "Charity and State Building," 245n.

[81] AOIF, Balie e Bambini G (XVI, 7), fol. 67 left, 19 October 1467, 23 January 1468, cited in Gavitt, "Cultural Values," 82, 91n. Although, as Christiane Klapisch-Zuber has noted, wet nurses' husbands, and not the nurses themselves, usually engaged in negotiations and transactions concerning the wet nursing of the hospital's children, Takahashi, in *Il Rinascimento dei trovatelli*, 81, found that this masculine focus does not apply to wet nursing at the Innocenti. See Klapisch-Zuber, "Blood Parents and Milk Parents," 143.

[82] AOIF, Balie e Bambini G (XVI, 7), fol. 98 right, 19 February 1467. See also AOIF, Balie e Bambini G, (XVI,7), fol. 398 right, 26 January 1471. Cf. Gavitt, "Cultural Values" 82–3, 91n.

[83] AOIF, Suppliche e sovrani rescritti (VI, 2), fol. 152r, n.d. See Gavitt, "Charity and State Building," 246n.

If such frauds led hospital officials to grumble about "la malignità dei contadini," historical perspective suggests the poignancy of the fragile balance between family size and survival in rural areas.

Although most forms of wet-nurse fraud can be documented from the Innocenti's beginnings in the mid-fifteenth century, two features seem especially characteristic of the sixteenth century: being paid to nurse one's own child and the concern on the part of hospital officials to separate nurses from babies as well as from older female foundlings. The cleverness of the first strategy may mean that the ordinary poverty of families in the *contado* had shifted into severe economic crisis during the third quarter of the sixteenth century. Certainly, the frauds that Borghini described had their origins both in the chronic poverty of the countryside (especially the Casentino) and in the temporary crises of the sixteenth century.

Artistic Patronage and Economic Centralization

Borghini faced throughout his administration the more vexing problem of carrying out Cosimo's mandate to reduce the hospital's expenses when admissions persistently pressed it. Even before Borghini began his tenure, Cosimo had attempted to compensate for the ever-shrinking number of outside apprenticeships by hiring master craftsmen and artisans to teach directly within the hospital itself. He also instituted outside apprenticeships for boys to train under the Flemish tapestry masters he had lured to Florence. In addition to the hosiers, carpenters, gardeners, and painters that Cosimo had brought in, Francesco, in the late 1570s, introduced tapestry manufacture to the Innocenti, hoping to make it one of the many centers of production his predecessor had established throughout Tuscany. In a letter of November 1579, Borghini wrote to Francesco:

> I send as a gift to Your Highness a small tapestry that owes its beginning and execution to our children, without any outside help. I do not know how it will please Your Highness, but here it has garnered much satisfaction, as well as praise for Your Highness who introduced us to this skill.[84]

There remained, Borghini noted, only the minor matter of how to raise the funds to keep the enterprise alive. Indeed, by 1585, Borghini's successor,

---

[84] AOIF, Suppliche e sovrani rescritti (VI, 2), fol. 228r, 30 November 1579. Gavitt, "Charity and State Building," 260n.

Fra Niccolò Mazzi, (who was also Bianca Cappello's confessor), halted tapestry manufacture within the hospital altogether.[85]

Judith Brown has noted that Cosimo introduced the manufacture of tapestries as part of a sophisticated and complex political economy that encouraged the establishment of new industry to compete with the supremacy of the Netherlands.[86] Cosimo made guild leadership directly accountable to the organs of ducal bureaucracy and reorganized both the tax and fiscal systems of Florence to revitalize the silk industry.[87] In this respect, Brown has argued, Cosimo and his successors were virtual mercantilists, closer to Colbert and to Louis XIV in spirit than to their contemporaries. It would be a mistake, however, to view this Tuscan phenomenon in isolation. Milan, Mantua, and Venice, for example, witnessed state-sponsored expansion of textile industries in the middle decades of the sixteenth century, and in Venice, at least, inmates of hospitals were employed as sail makers.[88]

This conscious economic policy of state intervention brings us nearly full circle to Francesco Settimanni's entry for 1579. Under Borghini's tenure, Settimanni wrote, the hospital fell into ruin, "the Grand Duke [Francesco] having lifted from it all the money that had been collected by the good administration of Luca Alamanni, the Prior."[89] Indeed, Borghini's reports to Francesco show no lack of awareness or interest concerning the hospital's precarious financial state:

> The hospital of the Innocenti, as several times has been shown to Your Most Serene Highness, was found by me in very grave disorder, which has increased steadily so that [the hospital] will soon come to ruin if it is not assisted.[90]

---

[85] Bruscoli, *Lo Spedale*, 75–7. On tapestry production in mid-sixteenth-century Florence, see Candace Adelson, "Cosimo de' Medici and the Foundation of Tapestry Production in Florence," in *Firenze e la Toscana*, 3: 899–924.

[86] Judith Brown, "Concepts of Political Economy: Cosimo I de' Medici in a Comparative European Context" in *Firenze e la Toscana* 1: 279–93.

[87] Roberta Morelli, *La seta fiorentina nel cinquecento* (Milan: A Giuffrè, 1976), 13.

[88] On Venice, see Robert Davis, *Shipbuilders in the Venetian Arsenal: Workers and Workplace in the Preindustrial City*. Johns Hopkins University Studies in Historical and Political Science, 109th series, no. 1 (Baltimore: Johns Hopkins University Press, 1991), 107.

[89] ASF, Manoscritti 129, Memorie fiorentine, 4: 182v, 21 August 1579, cited in Gavitt, "Charity and State Building," 261n. For the definitive correction of Settimanni's view, see Maria Fubini-Leuzzi, "Le ricevute di Francesco de' Medici a Vincenzio Borghini. La contabilità separata dello spedalingo degli Innocenti," *Archivio Storico Italiano* 140 (2002): 353–67.

[90] AOIF, Suppliche e sovrani rescritti (VI, 2), fol. 105r, n.d., cited in Gavitt, "Charity and State Building," 261n.

In his final report, written in early 1575 to Francesco, Borghini wrote:

> [I write to you] in order to put on paper what I explained orally to Your Highness, and to provide a report of my tenure, and to hear your will. I came to the care of the hospital in February 1552 [= 1553 modern], so that up to now I have completed 22 years. In my first few days I gave a report to Grand Duke Cosimo concerning the state and needs of the hospital, which was as follows: that the hospital found itself in debt for 45,000 scudi.[91]

Thus, the key to the Innocenti's crushing burden of debt was the very assistance provided by both Cosimo and Francesco. Not only had Borghini warned Cosimo of the hospital's problems from the very first, but also his first report of 1553 outlined Cosimo's own strategies concerning the centrality of the grand ducal bureaucracy and of the grand duke himself to the success of the hospital:

> Without your help and protection, there would be no alternative but the very gravest ruin. But I hope in God and in the bounty of Your Excellency, who has promised me among his other thoughts to address his mind to thinking also to the need of these poor boys and truly innocent virgin girls. . . . This very great charity, perhaps without equal in the world, which can be said to be the mirror of Italy, to the honor of God, and the satisfaction of Your Excellency, shall be maintained and has been maintained up to now by the grace of God and the protection of Your Excellency.[92]

Cosimo's unhelpful reply to Borghini's elaborate, detailed report consisted of only a few lines: "We are writing to Messer Jacopo Polverini, that he alert the *Pratica* to the need and disorder of the hospital, and that he should examine the whole business backward and forward because expenditures must be reduced and revenues increased."[93]

Borghini later noted in the margins of this report that in 1554 war with Siena distracted Cosimo from the assistance he was to provide for the Innocenti, suggesting that when charitable institutions bartered their institutional autonomy for government assistance, the advantage weighed rather one-sidedly in favor of the state. In a later *rescritto*, Cosimo counseled that Borghini should "put your plans on paper, trust in God, and for our part,

---

[91] AOIF, Suppliche e sovrani rescritti (VI,1), fol. 554r, n.d. [*anno* 1575]. A later hand has written in the margin that this was Borghini's final report to Francesco. Although Borghini wrote a number of *suppliche* to Francesco, no full reports are extant after this one, written, as Borghini suggests, twenty-two years after he became prior in 1553.

[92] AOIF, Suppliche e sovrani rescritti (VI, 1), fol. 242v, 4 November 1553, cited in Gavitt, "Charity and State Building," 262n.

[93] AOIF, Suppliche e sovrani rescritti (VI, 1), fol. 244v, 4 November 1553, cited in Gavitt, "Charity and State Building," 262n.

we will not disappoint."[94] Borghini began a *supplica* to Cosimo that suggests how many other reminders he must have sent:

not to cause you [unnecessary] bother, but only to fulfill the duties of faithful service. . . . I must remind you that . . . for several years this hospital (as I know you are aware), has had a provisioning deficit of more than 3,000 *scudi*.[95]

This deficit made especially acute the problem of maintaining an adequate supply of grain, a problem exacerbated during the flood of 1557 when the Innocenti's own storehouse was "covered by water."[96] Despite these frequent reminders, not until 1561 did Cosimo finally act. His solution was to attempt to make the Innocenti's supply of grain entirely independent of outside provisioning, to which end he donated to the Innocenti sufficient land in the malaria-infested Maremma to sow two hundred *moggia* of grain. The land, Cosimo wrote optimistically,

touches the walls of this place [Grosseto], and they are very perfect plots. Unimpeded by marshes, they have only the small disadvantage of certain thistles that grow in that area, which would have to be rooted out, and then the land would have to be cleared.[97]

In Cosimo's estimation, the Innocenti could sow fifty *moggia* of grain per year at little cost and on terrain that was not only "perfetissimo" but also "vicinissimo." The Innocenti, as a sort of institutional sharecropper, would turn over half the grain to Cosimo and keep the other half for its own needs. Whatever Borghini's decision, wrote Cosimo in a final burst of unintended irony, "advise us soon, because time flies."[98]

Despite both Borghini's and Cosimo's optimism, however, ten years later Borghini wrote that these lands "will begin, one hopes, to turn a profit not too far into the future."[99] As late as 1578, Borghini's summary of revenues and expenditures showed that "Grosseto this year yielded no revenue," although in previous years it had shown "an annual return of around 700 florins (and with little expense it could increase some)."[100] Literary historian that he was,

---

[94] Ibid., fol. 442r, 14 February 1571, cited in Gavitt, "Charity and State Building," 262n.
[95] Ibid., fol. 271r, 4 November 1556, cited in Gavitt, "Charity and State Building," 263n.
[96] Ibid., fol. 273r, 8 November 1557, cited in Gavitt, "Charity and State Building," 263n.
[97] Ibid., fol. 286r, 10 February 1560, cited in Gavitt, "Charity and State Building," 263n.
[98] Ibid., fol. 286v, cited in Gavitt, "Charity and State Building," 263n.
[99] Ibid., fol. 444v, 1 February 1571, cited in Gavitt, "Charity and State Building," 263n.
[100] Ibid., fol. 519v, n.d., Entrata 1574–78, cited in Gavitt, "Charity and State Building," 263n.

Borghini could have undoubtedly paraphrased the unfortunate Pia: "Firenze mi fé, disfecemmi Maremma."[101]

By 1579, furor over the Innocenti's debts had reached such a pitch that Francesco ordered the formation of a nine-man commission to oversee the reform and reorganization of the Ospedale degli Innocenti.[102] Under Borghini, the hospital's debt had increased from 300,000 to more than 700,000 lire.[103] It is the structure of this debt, however, rather than the amount, that showed how dramatically charitable institutions had changed under the regime of the Medici grand dukes: more than 75 percent of the Innocenti's debt consisted of investors' deposits earning 5 percent interest.[104] As was true both for the Monte di Pietà and for the hospital of Santa Maria Nuova, the grand dukes as well as other major investors used Florence's principal charitable institutions as savings banks to whom they entrusted, among other things, funds for their daughters' dowries.

Deposit Banking at the Innocenti

Deposit banking at the Innocenti during the sixteenth century connected the hospital's finances to two important developments. First, the Innocenti, like many other Florentine institutions, provided a substitute for the declining municipal dowry fund. Founded in 1425 as a response to dowry inflation and concerns about the preservation of lineage, this fund, known as the Monte delle doti, permitted fathers to deposit sums for seven and a half or fifteen years. At the end of the term, if the daughter's marriage had been consummated, the father would receive the principal plus accrued interest to be used toward her dowry. If the daughter died before she could be

---

[101] Dante, *Purgatorio*, Canto V: "Ricorditi di me, che son la Pia; Siena mi fé, disfecemmi Maremma."

[102] For an indication of the anxiety caused by the Innocenti's deficit, see AOIF, Suppliche e sovrani rescritti (VI, 1), fol. 459r, 27 April 1579, Borghini to Francesco de' Medici. On the formation of the reform commission, see AOIF, Suppliche e sovrani rescritti (VI, 1), fol. 559r, 21 October 1580, cited in Gavitt, "Charity and State Building", 264n.

[103] ASF, Archivio Mediceo del Principato 724, fols. 307r-v, 18 June 1579, cited in Bruscoli, *Lo Spedale*, 268, for the figure of 101,500 scudi, roughly equivalent to 700,000 lire. For the 1552 figure of 300,000 lire, see AOIF, Suppliche e sovrani rescritti (VI, 1), fol. 554r, *anno* 1574, cited in Gavitt, "Charity and State Building." 264n. At the established rate of seven lire per scudo, the debt when Borghini began his tenure already stood at 280,000 lire, most of which, as Borghini indicated, was interest payable on deposits.

[104] ASF, Archivio Mediceo 724, fols. 307r-v, May 1579, cited in Bruscoli, *Lo Spedale*, 268–70. Of 101,500 scudi pledged both to principal and interest, 73,774 were pledged to 775 creditors with no conditions attached, with another 4,072 scudi pledged to creditors who had pledged them to dower 130 girls. Calculations similar to those in the Archivio di Stato can be found in AOIF, Suppliche e sovrani rescritti (VI, 2), fol. 59r, n.d. Cf. Settimanni's entry for August 1579 in ASF Manoscritti 129, Memorie fiorentine, 4: 182v.

married or before the expiration of the term, the full amount reverted to the communal treasury. In 1433, the terms of the dowry fund were changed to diminish the risk to investors and to allow for more flexible terms. By the beginning of the sixteenth century, however, the management of the fund made it more difficult for dowries to be paid entirely in cash or in a timely fashion, just at a time of particularly acute dowry inflation. As a result, investment in the fund went into decline, and Cosimo I's financial reforms, as in so many other aspects of ducal administration, put the fund more under the personal control of the duke to reward "clients and protégés."[105]

As had been true during the fifteenth century at Santa Maria Nuova, married women and widows entrusted their own cash and valuables to the Innocenti, in some cases to be used along with their property as sources of future annuity income. Although some 40 percent of deposits were made by men, in many cases, men also made provision in this fashion either for dowries for female members of their own family or entrusted sums to be used for charity involving the provision of dowries for indigent girls. Second, the evolution of the Innocenti's deposit bank in the 1540s into an interest-paying institution attracted the deposits of the grand duke and duchess, an activity that not only cemented the ties of patronage among Cosimo, Eleonora, and the hospital but that hoped to solve the hospital's chronic fiscal problems. Although deposit banking ultimately failed in the latter objective, it was, for better or worse, one of the initiatives maintaining the Innocenti's position in the orbit of court finance.

The Florentine practice of entrusting sums of money and valuables to religious and charitable institutions had long and numerous precedents. At least as early as the thirteenth century, for example, the Parte Guelfa regularly parked its sums with the monastery of the Servi, and other donors and patrons followed suit.[106] In 1464, the hospital of Santa Maria Nuova opened its first series of deposit account books, running until 1549 and containing the deposits of Botticelli, Michelangelo, and Leonardo da Vinci, among many others. What kept the operation at Santa Maria Nuova financially afloat until it stopped accepting deposits in 1553 was its loans at 12 to 14 percent to the commune, while paying only 5 to 8 percent on deposits. At the Innocenti, an entry in the hospital's long series of *ricordanze* shows that the Innocenti was accepting deposits at least as early as 1451, perhaps in response to the appointment of Messer Pacie as prior, who in his previous

---

[105] Molho, *Marriage Alliance*, 78. For an excellent summary of the dowry fund's history, see ibid., 27–79.

[106] Louisa Bulman, "Artistic Patronage at SS. Annunziata, ca. 1440–1520" (Ph.D. diss., University of London, 1971), pt. 1: 5.

employment as prior of Bonifazio's hospital, had accepted deposits there. In May 1451, a certain messer Abondo from Como had entrusted Messer Pacie with a deposit of fifty-five florins, which was split up among the silk guild, the Innocenti, and Bonifazio's hospital. In February 1452, the Medici bank entrusted the Innocenti with a deposit of 85 large florins from Archbishop Antoninus.[107]

These early deposits did not accrue interest, at least not for the Innocenti, and indeed did not always involve cash. In November 1461, the *operaio* Mariotto di Dinozzo di Stefano Lippi left a locked chest weighing twenty-two *libbre* (approximately 7.5 kg) containing finely worked silver, silk, and gold, "on deposit for safekeeping." The prior placed the chest in the room belonging to the female staff of the hospital. The chest was to be given back to Mariotto "whenever he shall request it."[108] In the event of Mariotto's death, the chest was to go to his wife, and if both he and his wife should die, to a person mentioned in Mariotto's private account books.[109]

Apart from these scattered fifteenth-century examples, there is no widespread evidence of interest-bearing deposits until 1543. In 1509, the Libro Segreto dei Depositi of the Innocenti, integrated by a later archivist into the general series of *ricordanze*, mentions a whole series of deposits, which, if they cover the entire scope of the depository's activity, suggest that until midcentury this was hardly a thriving operation.[110] What the Innocenti's early *depositeria* lacked in volume was more than balanced by the variety of purposes for which people did deposit money in the operation. In 1510, Ser Andrea Nacchianti left funds on deposit to buy a farm as security for expenses his son Giovanbattista (see Chapter 3) would incur as a ward of Francesco Petrucci, the Innocenti's *piagnone* superintendent.[111] In 1511, the Priori di Libertà ordered the Innocenti to return a deposit being held in trust for a ward of the Magistrato dei Pupilli.[112] In 1515, Petrucci also held a

---

[107] AOIF Entrata e Uscita (CXXII, 3), fol. 59v, 31 May 1451. For Antoninus's deposit, see Ibid., fol. 10r, 1 February 1451.

[108] AOIF Ricordanze A (XII, 1), fol. 62r, 17 November 1461: "Nel quale dice detto Mariotto c'erano alchuni vasselli e altre chose sottili d'ariento di seta oro di peso in tutto libre xxii il quale casoncello di detto Mariotto noi priore e chamarlingho e monna Smeralda [the supervisor of the *donne commesse e velate*] sopradetti abbiamo ricevuto in deposito per via di serbanza . . . e quello rendere al dicto Mariotto d'ogno sua richiesta e volonta liberamente come sua chosa."

[109] Ibid.

[110] Cf. Richard Goldthwaite, "Banking in Florence at the End of the Sixteenth Century," *Journal of European Economic History* 27 (1998): 471–536, at 513: "The fact that this ledger was kept open until 1545 indicates how modest the operation was." On deposit banking in general, see idem, *The Economy of Renaissance Florence*, 437–42, 468–76.

[111] AOIF Ricordanze (XII, 6), Libro segreto di dipositi, fol. 4r, 10 March 1509.

[112] AOIF Filza prima di depositi pagati (XXXIII, 1), fol. 15r, 15 January 1510.

deposit of 140 florins for another young "clerk," which was to be returned to him whenever he might ask for it during his life, but if it was still there at his death, it was to be given in support of the dowry of three girls from San Donnino whom he had identified.[113]

Charity in the form of women's dowries quite often came mixed with other obligations. Hence, again in 1515, Maestro Francesco di Iacopo Lapini left a deposit of 316 florins that he could use at will during his lifetime. Upon his death, the hospital was to set aside fifty gold florins to pay for a thousand masses for the dead and to give seven soldi as alms for the poor at each mass. The rest of the money was to be used for bequests to charitable institutions and women: forty gold florins to an anonymous woman, thirty florins to Giovanni Guido for his eldest daughter, twenty gold florins to the hospital for syphilitics, four hundred lire to the Innocenti to spend for its resident girls, and a hundred gold florins to Marietta, the daughter of Nicholaio and Margherita, his wife, to be paid when Marietta entered a convent or to invest for her in the dowry fund.[114] Deposits sometimes came with no specific charitable purpose in mind. In 1526, Lisabetta, the widow of Agnolo di Bernardo de' Bardi and the daughter of Antonio di Francesco di Bartolomeo Scala had her uncle deposit 150 gold florins at the Innocenti. The money came attached to the condition that she be considered the true and rightful owner of the deposit and that if she should die without reclaiming, it would become the property of the Innocenti. The only other responsibility the Innocenti had was to "pray to God for her and for her ancestors." In April 1529, however, Mona Lisabetta added both more funds and more conditions to this deposit, depositing 400 ducats with very specific purposes in mind. In this case, she set aside monies to support the marriage of girls on both sides of the family, although she apparently changed her mind and cancelled this second transaction the same day.[115]

Although the Innocenti safeguarded the deposit, Lisabetta had apparently decided not to entrust its administration entirely to the hospital in the event of her death but instead split up the 400 ducats between the Innocenti and the Buonomini di San Martino. To the latter she entrusted the dowry of one of the four daughters of Antonio di Gieri de' Bardi. Should none of them live to the age of marriage, the Buonomini were to use the money to marry *fanciulle nobili* to be identified by the Innocenti's prior. The other 200 florins were to go directly to the Innocenti, whom she instructed to

---

[113] AOIF Ricordanze (XII, 6), Libro segreto di dipositi, fol. 22r, 18 June 1515.

[114] Ibid., fol. 35r, 19 June 1515.

[115] Ibid., fol. 43r, 10 February 1525: "ssenza altro charicho salvo che pregare iddio per lei et per sua passati."

give 100 florins to the daughter of Giovanni Scala as dowry for a convent or for marriage, and the other hundred for the same purpose to one of the daughters of Bastiano di Francesco di Lanzilaglio de' Bardi.[116]

What is instructive about this example is that clearly the Innocenti's deposit account enabled Lisabetta de' Bardi to safeguard her discretionary money to use for the needs of girls in her natal family and girls from the family into which she had married. Indeed, when Gostanza, the daughter of Lisabetta's kinsman Giovanni di Bartolomeo Scala entered the convent of Santa Chiara in 1532, the Innocenti paid out the required part of the deposit in five installments, just as it had done in 1531 for Maria, the daughter of Antonio di Gieri de' Bardi. In addition, the Innocenti administered bequests of several barrels of good oil "harvested by the nuns of the convent of San Miniato of the order of Monte Uliveto to keep the lamp burning in front of the Most Holy Sacrament."[117]

The importance of such deposit banking operations as the Innocenti's to women in particular is clear from Lucia Sandri's statistical study of depositors. In 1572, women made up 54 percent of depositors; in 1578, 60 percent; and 53 percent in 1579. The majority of these female depositors were widows: 54, 42, and 57 percent for the same years, respectively. After widows, married women were the next most visible categories: they account for about 30 percent of deposits by women in general. Servant girls were also an important category, amounting to some 18 percent of the female depositors. This category may well have overlapped with the girls from the hospice of the Pietà (also depositors), because both groups came predominantly from the Mugello, the Tuscan Romagna, and the Casentino and were therefore most likely using the Innocenti's deposit bank as a haven for accumulating money for their dowries. Families in general certainly used such deposits to make provision for the daughters of members of the lineage who might fall on hard times and thus become more susceptible to the stain of dishonor.[118]

The interest that Duchess Eleonora of Toledo took in the hospital's deposit banking operation confirms the concern that ruling classes had for the potentially fallen of their own number. In October 1545, she deposited

---

[116] Ibid., fol. 44r–45r, 12 April 1529.

[117] Ibid., fol. 45r, 18 June 1529: "el nostro spedale sia obbligato darne ogni anno per anni cinquanta mezo barile d'olio buono riccholte alle monache del monastero nella consta di Sancto Miniato dell'ordine di Monte Oliveto per tenere aciesa ina lampina dinanzi al sacratissima sacramento."

[118] Lucia Sandri, "L'attività di banco dell'ospedale degli Innocenti di Firenze: don Vincenzio Borghini e la 'bancarotta' del 1579," in *L'uso del denaro: Patrimoni e amministrazione nei luoghi pii e negli enti ecclesiastici in Italia (secoli XV–XVIII)*, ed. Marina Garbellotti and Alessandro Pastore (Bologna: Il Mulino, 2001), 153–78.

100 scudi at the Innocenti to be paid to Gostanza, the daughter of Luigi Tosinghi, and to Lisabetta, daughter of Francesco di Orazio Rubini. As had Archbishop Buondelmonte, Cosimo's wife left the choice of beneficiaries up to the Innocenti's superintendent, with the stipulation that the funds were "for marrying needy, well-born and well-brought-up girls of good reputation."[119]

At some point – unfortunately the documents are undated and anonymous – the Innocenti sought and obtained several legal opinions concerning whether paying interest on deposits amounted to usury. The closest equivalent the first two legal opinions could find to the practice of accepting deposits was the situation of a merchant at the fair of Lyon, who loaned 100 scudi to someone with the agreement that he would be repaid at the next fair three months hence. In the intervening period, the money earned two scudi, yielding an effective annual interest rate of a little over 8 percent. This was clearly the situation mostly closely analogous to the practice of accepting deposits over the short term, and the first legal opinion supported its legality on the basis of *causa minoris damni*.[120]

The consilium also pointed out in more general terms that insofar as the depositor seeks not profit for himself but to help his indigent neighbor in such a way that the likelihood of profit is small, such a transaction is licit from the point of view of the lender.[121] Indeed, this closely follows the position of Thomas Aquinas in the *Summa* that it is licit to borrow even from a usurer to provide a subsidy for a poor neighbor.[122] Obviously charitable institutions that welcomed deposits to facilitate their own charitable work fit quite well into this category. More specifically, this consilium cited as a precedent for the Innocenti the Florentine Monte di Pietà, which could legitimately lend money at the rate of 7 percent on large loans to cover

---

[119] AOIF Ricordanze (XII, 6), Libro segreto di diposito, fol. 90r, 15 March 1543: "La illustrissima signora duchessa della città di Firenze de avere fino adì 15 di marzo 1543 scudi cento. . . . Se ne dispone sechondo che parà al nostro priore per li tenpi esistenti per maritare fanciulle bisognose be' nate e bene alevate e di buona fama."

[120] Accepting a return higher than the original principal was licit in canon law on a number of grounds, including this one, which means the risk of minor harm borne by the lender. For an excellent discussion of this issue, see J. T. Noonan, *The Scholastic Analysis of Usury* (Cambridge: Harvard University Press, 1957), 118–28, 249–56.

[121] AOIF Filze d'Archivio (LXII, 7) fol. 176r, n.d.

[122] St. Thomas Aquinas, *Summa Theologica*, trans. Fathers of the English Dominican Province (London: Burns, Oates & Washbourne, 1918), 330–40, reprinted in Roy C. Cave and Herbert H. Coulson, *A Source Book for Medieval Economic History* (Milwaukee: The Bruce Publishing Co., 1936; reprint ed., New York: Biblo and Tannen, 1965), 182.

salaries for its administrators when 5 percent would have sufficed for its other expenses.[123]

Because the Monte di Pietà seems not to have considered the notion of charging large lenders more interest to cover the losses incurred on loans to the poor until 1568, it seems likely that it was Vincenzio Borghini himself who had sought these legal opinions preliminary to his reorganization of the Innocenti's deposit banking system in the 1560s. The motives for his reorganization are quite clear in a letter of 1569: he "accepted a deposit and paid another out of it in such a way that the [hospital's] credit has been and is maintained. I have done everything with your participation."[124]

Cosimo's participation is evident indeed from the account books. Even in 1543, he had placed 3,000 gold ducats in the Innocenti's deposit bank, but this was relatively small scale by comparison to his cooperation in Borghini's project in the 1560s, when his son Francesco deposited 33,000 scudi from the Depositeria Generale for the Monte di Pietà. Moreover, by 1565, the grand duke's account was earning 5 percent interest, or about 1,650 scudi the first year, which the Innocenti paid out irregularly.[125]

Less clear is the mechanism by which Borghini hoped to finance this deposit banking operation. Unlike Santa Maria Nuova, the Innocenti did not lend money at higher rates of interest than it paid out to depositors, and there is evidence that Borghini used some of the deposit money to pay back interest he owed the Capponi bank on a market-rate loan. More important, during the late 1570s, when depositors lost confidence in the Innocenti and began a virtual "run on the bank," Borghini himself had ever more frequent recourse to loans from friends.[126]

By comparison with the grand sums of money left on deposit, the hospital's actual operating expenses were minor.[127] In 1578, Borghini estimated

[123] AOIF Filze d'Archivio (LXII, 7) fol. 176r, n.d. On the deliberations of the Monte di Pietà concerning charging differential interest rates, see Menning, *Charity and State*, 189–99, 206–7.

[124] AOIF Filze d'Archivio 18, fol. 95r, 24 October 1569: "mi sono ito rammantellando, pigliando un deposito et pagandone un'altro in modo che il credito si è mantenuto et mantiene et tutto ho fatto sempre con partecipazione di V. A."

[125] AOIF Miscellenea (CXLV, 8), fol. 2 right, 10 January 1568. See Maria Fubini-Leuzzi, "Le ricevute di Francesco de' Medici," 353–67 for a detailed analysis of these transactions.

[126] Cf. Sandri, "L'attività del Banco di Deposito." I wish to thank Richard Goldthwaite for raising this obviously crucial aspect of Borghini's deposit banking operation. Richard Goldthwaite, "Banking in Florence," 514; idem, *The Economy of Renaissance Florence*, 469.

[127] On the Monte di Pietà, see Carol Bresnahan Menning, "Loans and Favors, Kin and Clients: Cosimo de' Medici and the Monte di Pietà," *Journal of Modern History* 61 (1989): 487–511, at 493, and *Charity and State*, 262. On Santa Maria Nuova, see Marvin Becker, "Aspects of Lay Piety in Early Renaissance Florence," in *The Pursuit of Holiness in Late Medieval and Renaissance Religion*, ed. C. Trinkaus and H. A. Oberman (Leiden: E.J. Brill, 1974), 199. For a summary of

the hospital's annual expenses to be approximately 100,000 lire – some 40,000 lire more than its revenues.[128] Why, then, did both Borghini, and later, Settimanni, his severest critic, speak of the hospital's impending ruin? The broader answer lies in the tendency of Grand Dukes Cosimo and Francesco to assume patronage of virtually every institution – indeed, of virtually every undertaking – in the public life of sixteenth-century Florence. As the sixteenth century progressed, the line between private charity and public finance, perhaps never distinct in any case, became even more seriously blurred. Students of Cosimo's administration such as Anna Teicher have posed the question of how Cosimo managed to finance the war with Siena without raising taxes and have found the answer in Cosimo's ingenuity in creating and expanding access to sources of credit.[129] To these sources of credit one may now add the patrimony of major charitable institutions.

R. Burr Litchfield has charted the development of Cosimo's financial base from a household *depositeria* to a decentralized treasury of several *depositerie* from which Cosimo or Francesco could withdraw large sums of money at will.[130] The *ricordanze* of the Ospedale degli Innocenti, as well as other *libri di dipositi*, show that the Medici grand dukes exercised this privilege frequently, even during the term of Prior Luca Alamanni's "buona amministrazione."[131] The role of the Innocenti, like that of other major charitable institutions, developed naturally from its responsibilities as the administrator of large estates, retaining considerable sums of money to execute various obligations specified in wills. Indeed, not only had the Innocenti become part of the grand dukes' decentralized system of finance, but also became, in 1564, the

---

the Innocenti's operating expenses, see AOIF, Suppliche e sovrani rescritti (VI, 1), fol. 519v–520r, n.d., Entrata e Uscita, 1574–8.

[128] AOIF, Suppliche e sovrani rescritti (VI, 1), fol. 519v–520r, n.d., Entrata and Uscita, 1574–8.

[129] Anna Teicher, "Politics and Finance in the Age of Cosimo I: The Public and Private Face of Credit," in *Firenze e la Toscana de' Medici*, ed. C. Garfagnini, 2: 343–62. Indeed, such was Cosimo's reputation that when the Duke of Alva, resident in Brussels at the beginning of the revolt of the Netherlands, was in such dire financial straits that local merchants refused to extend him credit, he turned to Cosimo in April 1572 for a loan. Because Cosimo and the Spanish Crown were not on good terms, however, the request was "disowned" and the loan never used. See F. Braudel, *The Mediterranean and the Mediterranean World in the Age of Philip II*, trans. Sian Reynolds (2 vols., New York: Harper and Row, 1972), 1: 485. Nonetheless, in the next three years, the grand duchy would be swept up in the ill fortune of private banks that, with the exception of Genoese banks, took enormous losses as a result of the Castilian bankruptcy of 1575. See Braudel, 1: 511.

[130] R. Burr Litchfield, *Emergence of a Bureaucracy: The Florentine Patriciate, 1530–1790* (Princeton: Princeton University Press, 1986), 100–1.

[131] See, for example, AOIF, Ricordanze (XII, 6), Libro segreto di dipositi, fol. 73v, 25 June 1543. A separate set of accounts, series LXXIX, spans the years 1564–1799.

depository for funds collected in Florence for the building project of St. Peter's in Rome.[132]

For Cosimo and Francesco, the patrimony of such institutions as the Ospedale degli Innocenti, the Ospedale di Santa Maria Nuova, and the Monte di Pietà provided a convenient treasury both for military and diplomatic adventures and for the enormous sums spent on artistic patronage and its attendant glorification of the Medici regime. By bringing charity into their personal orbit, the Medici could both tighten their control over the state and gain access to credit without imposing excessive taxes.

Previous students of the sixteenth-century Tuscan grand duchy have seen in these efforts the formation of an increasingly absolutist, centralized state. I would argue, by contrast, that centralization is neither the result nor even the intention of these reforms. Certainly they do not fit the criteria of the impersonal and effective bureaucracy that constituted the ideal of the eighteenth-century early modern state. This is instead the establishment of a system of very personal rule, which looks efficiently centralized because geographically the amount of territory was relatively small compared with nation-states that emerged much later. Nonetheless, the lack of a coherent system of bureaucratic integration would have important consequences in the fiscal crises that beset both the regime and its associated charitable and financial institutions in the 1570s.

During a short term-economic boom beginning in the mid-1560s, Florentine banks loosened their customers' access to credit with the eventual result that when depositors needed to withdraw cash, *polizze* (checks) had to be drawn on other banks. By the late 1560s, Florentine wool and silk manufacturers even had trouble withdrawing sufficient cash to pay their workers, so that in 1568 and again in 1574, an ordinance was passed requiring banks to pay their creditors when asked to do so. Exacerbating an already precarious financial situation was Francesco I's perfectly laudable if ill-timed attempt to impose a rational, even scientific financial system based on silver rather than gold as the currency standard, a policy he imposed with what Carlo Cipolla implies was a devoted fanaticism. Unfortunately, the banking crisis could not be solved by decree, so that in 1580, "one does not find credit, there is no more cash, and nothing stirs anymore."[133]

---

[132] AOIF, Fabbrica di San Pietro in Roma (CXXX, filze 1–11), covering the years 1560–1692.

[133] Cipolla, *Money*, citing Giuliano de'Ricci, *Cronaca (1532–1606)*, ed. G. Sapori (Milan/Naples: Riccardo Ricciardi, 1972), 249, 307. Braudel, 1: 530–1 notes the increasing number of bank failures after 1570. Some of these, he argues, such as those in Venice and Naples, were caused by the unfortunate intervention of public authorities responding to the price rise of the sixteenth

The seeming intractability of the financial crisis of 1575–80 as well as the regime's ineffective response were, in fact, both local examples of far broader problems in the Spanish system, particularly within the fiscal administration of Philip II. As was true for Cosimo's regime, Philip II's royal administration also made insufficient distinctions between public and private. Both the continuing Habsburg military presence in the Mediterranean and, more directly, the insatiable demands of provisioning Spanish troops in the Low Countries, led to Philip II's second bankruptcy in 1575.[134]

Among Florentine bankers, particularly hard hit was the Ricci bank, which lost some of its grand ducal privileges in 1576, at which time all cash deposits had to be taken to the grand duke's *depositeria*. In effect, the grand ducal treasury was hoarding the cash supply and so severely restricting access to credit that satellite depositories, such as the Innocenti and the Monte di Pietà, as well as banks, were unable to provide cash on demand to depositors.[135] It seems reasonable, then, to suppose that when Settimanni referred to Grand Duke Francesco as having taken all the money that Borghini's predecessor had saved, the historian was referring to this government policy. Indeed, the general fiscal crisis that resulted in 1578 forced Francesco to flee to his villa at Poggio a Caiano.[136] Thus, it hardly mattered what kind of *economo* Borghini was, although his role in the transfer of sums to the Monte di Pietà shows him to have been both able and reliable. These transactions were perfectly legitimate, and it certainly did not help ducal finance that the norms established by the Council of Trent made future recourse to charitable institutions difficult, if not impossible.[137]

For certainly there is nothing in the recommendations of Francesco's nine-man commission, which issued its report in October 1580, that represents major criticism, whether implied or overt, of Borghini's administrative priorities.[138] Indeed, the commission confirmed a number of initiatives Borghini had already pursued, including the provision that the hospital's children "shall be given to those persons of good reputation and status, [who lead] an upright life, and who ask to be chosen to take in adoptive

century. Braudel, 1: 511, also notes that non-Genoese Italian merchants suffered disproportionately from the Castilian bankruptcy of 1575. See A. W. Lovett, "The Castilian Bankruptcy of 1575," *Historical Journal* 23 (1980): 899–911.

[134] On the lack of distinction between public and private finance in Florence, see Menning, *Charity and State*, 262. For Spain, see Lovett, "Castilian Bankruptcy," 903.

[135] Cipolla, *Money*, 110. Lovett, "Castilian Bankruptcy," 911, tentatively suggests that 1575 represented a "signal" of constricting credit on a European scale.

[136] Cipolla, *Money*, 112.

[137] Fubini-Leuzzi, "Le ricevute," 365–6.

[138] AOIF, Suppliche e sovrani rescritti (VI, 1), fols. 562r–564v, 21 October 1580.

children."[139] Boys whom the hospital could not place, however, were to be dismissed from the hospital once they had reached age eighteen.[140]

The commission also confirmed the two initiatives to which Borghini had devoted the most time and energy: the placement of the hospital's girls with noble families and the provision of the larger dowry of three hundred lire and clothes to girls who wished to marry. Those who wished to enter a convent received the same amount plus fifty lire "to buy a bed, given that they will not be accepted into the convent unless they have their own bed."[141] In addition, to reduce expenses, hospital officials were to dismiss women who had reached age thirty-six, but instead of sending them into the street, give each one thirty lire and all possible assistance in securing a place at the "widows'" asylum of Orbatello.[142] Those women who neither married nor became nuns between ages 18 and 36, were to be taught "every sort of trade and manual labor useful and suitable for the sustenance of human life, [and] . . . according to their age, the usual and necessary things they would have to do in private houses."[143]

This commission did suggest minor organizational reforms as another way to reduce costs. Recommending that the number of priests be reduced to five, the commission specified both the number and the duties of all other hospital personnel. More important, the commission recommended that "neither the hospital nor other officials acting on its behalf may receive on deposit, or on commission, any money of any person, collectivity, or place, without the express consent of His Most Serene Highness."[144] Although the hospital should retain the master butchers, hosiers, carpenters, and weavers, the authors of the report wrote that the hospital could not support the expense of the four painters that Borghini had lodged on the premises; indeed, their presence was a "cosa al tutto dannosa."[145] No extraneous persons, including wet nurses from the *contado* and their husbands, could stay at the hospital's expense. The report's authors also proposed that

> in order to get rid of the hospital's superfluous expenses and to make use of them, it was considered that it be proposed to Your Serene Highness,

---

[139] Ibid., fol. 563r, cited in Gavitt, "Charity and State Building," 267n. "Adoption" in this context was usually informal because legal adoption was rare in this period.

[140] Ibid., fol. 563v, cited in Gavitt, "Charity and State Building," 267n.

[141] Ibid.

[142] Richard Trexler, "Widows' Asylum," 139–42, notes the enormous influx of women from the Innocenti in 1580.

[143] AOIF, Suppliche e sovrani rescritti (VI, 1), fol. 564r-v, 21 October 1580, cited in Gavitt, "Charity and State Building," 268n.

[144] Ibid., fol. 564v, cited in Gavitt, "Charity and State Building," 268n.

[145] Ibid., fol. 562v.

if appropriate, to discontinue the practice of weaving tapestries at the said hospital, which we find to have been of no little harm, given that around 10 [extra] mouths to feed are employed in it, i.e., five young men and five boys. The utility derived from it is very little.[146]

This is the only section of the report to provoke Francesco's written comment, which approved the remainder of the report but insisted on the continued utility of tapestry weaving.[147]

Placed in the context of the development of state administration and Tridentine charity, Borghini's administration reflects hardships and pressures that afflicted most large northern Italian urban centers, the "Indian Summer" of the Italian economy notwithstanding. As was true in Milan, Mantua, Venice, Genoa, and Rome, Tridentine conceptions of charity in Florence stressed not only the duty of the state to assist but also the obligation of the poor to undertake conversion to a reformed life. In Florence particularly (although not exclusively), such conversion might take the form of service to the state, whether in the grand duke's galleys or in his tapestry workshops. To understand that Borghini was in some sense at the mercy of demographic and social forces beyond his control is less important as a vindication of Vincenzio Borghini's "kindly paternal care" than as a recognition that even at the end of the sixteenth century, the Medici principate was still far from Machiavelli's ideal of a state that could prosper despite the weaknesses (or, for that matter, despite the strengths) of its individual rulers.[148] Borghini, as well as the city's major charitable and financial institutions, was undermined by a grand ducal administration that pursued all-encompassing personal rule while confusing the hoarding of cash with bureaucratic centralization.[149] As was true with other north Italian states, the Medici principate, despite farsighted attempts to control the supply of grain and to make charity more discriminating and efficient, found itself periodically overwhelmed by crises of famine and social dislocation well into the seventeenth century. These

---

[146] Ibid., fols. 562v–563r, cited in Gavitt, "Charity and State Building," 269n.

[147] Ibid., fol. 563r.

[148] On the lack of fiscal centralization under Cosimo I, see Enrico Stumpo, "Finanze e ragion di stato nella prima Età moderna. Due modelli diversi: Piemonte e Toscana, Savoia e Medici," in *Finanze e ragion di Stato in Italia e Germania nella prima età moderna*, ed. A. Maddalena and H. Kellenbenz (Bologna: Il Mulino, 1984), 181–233, at 224.

[149] Cosimo's personal involvement in almost all areas of fiscal and governmental administration has given rise to the term, "lo stato patrimoniale" to describe the Medici regime in the middle of the sixteenth century. Thus, state-formation was not so much a linear and progressive development as it was a "tension between centripetal and centrifugal forces in the organization and administration of the state." See A. Molho, "Lo Stato e la finanza pubblica. Un'ipotesi basata sulla storia tardo medievale di Firenze" in *Origini dello stato*, ed. G. Chittolini, A. Molho, and P. Schiera, 225–80, at 266–7, 279.

crises generated a multiplicity of charitable institutions such as the Ospedale dei Mendicanti, founded in response to the crisis of 1619–22 to control begging but became rapidly transformed into an institution that assisted and reformed women.[150] More modern states in the eighteenth century would find such institutions serviceable as authorities successfully undertook more repressive regimens of political and social discipline.

[150] For an excellent survey of the history of the Ospedale dei Mendicanti, see Daniela Lombardi, *Povertà maschile, povertà femminile: L'Ospedale dei Mendicanti nella Firenze dei Medici* (Bologna: Il Mulino, 1986).

2

GENDER, LINEAGE IDEOLOGY, AND THE DEVELOPMENT OF A STATUS CULTURE

T HE FOLLOWING TWO CHAPTERS PLACE THE PROLIFERATION OF INSTI-
tutions to assist unmarried women in the sixteenth century in the
context of an inevitable tension and conflict between the prevailing inheritance system (as the material expression of medieval and early modern
lineage ideology) and the economic and demographic realities of fifteenth-
and sixteenth-century families. To use terminology borrowed from the social
sciences, the family and inheritance systems of sixteenth-century Italy, and
to an even greater extent, sixteenth-century Florence, were functional only
to the extent that they defined the norms for transmission of property from
one generation to another. Systems of inheritance defined in Roman law,
their resurgence in the twelfth century, and their codification in communal
statutes rested on assumptions that were too narrow to accommodate the
economic and social realities of the early modern Tuscan marriage market.
How successfully one could respond to such exigencies depended in part
on the flexibility of the system itself and in part on the creativity of those
who would circumvent it, as well as of those whom it served most successfully. Thus, this chapter first examines the relationship between gender and
lineage ideology in the development of a specifically and self-consciously
aristocratic culture in sixteenth-century Florence and argues that the primary force driving the developing status culture of consumption (and its
attendant social crises of abandonment) was not the ideology of gender but
the ideology of lineage. The following chapter then discusses the relationship between law and practice and specifically how, given the exigencies of
the law, families worked charitable institutions into their marital and lineage
strategies.

The Sixteenth-Century Inheritance Crisis

Gabriella Zarri's studies of convents in northern Italy suggest that the inheritance crisis – and more precisely, the dotal crisis in sixteenth-century Italy – had been nearly a century in the making.[1] Zarri notes that the proliferation of feminine monastic foundations was not a product of the mid-sixteenth century but of the mid- to late fifteenth. Zarri attributes this "explosion" partially to rapidly expanding population, in turn due to the economic expansion of the mid-quattrocento, and partially due to the acceleration of dowry inflation over the course of the fifteenth century. This combined with the tendency of ruling elites, beginning in the late fifteenth century, to award the family patrimony to the eldest son, a development Zarri associates with the growth of a more active commercial economy.[2] What was at stake was not the existence of norms governing the transmission of property, which had been part of the background of Roman law, but the increasing tendency throughout the later Middle Ages, especially in Florence, to interpret those norms in favor of patrilineality.

As dowries became inflated (a development that in Florence and Venice seems traceable to the aftermath of the Black Death in 1348), elite and non-elite families alike also tended to concentrate their dowry resources on the eldest, or at least most marriageable, daughters, leaving younger or less marriageable daughters to celibacy.[3] The later fifteenth century, with its accelerated dowry inflation and increased population, propelled the tendency to send daughters to convents (the dowries of which were typically much lower than those required for a respectable marriage). Only with the Italian wars of 1498–1530, however, did the nobility come under such pressure to preserve patrimony that some sons and daughters became an insuperable liability. As a mid-sixteenth-century Bolognese chronicler wrote:

> Thus those women, who for whatever praiseworthy reason cannot find a husband without having an immense dowry, [are almost as badly off] as foundlings, are sometimes forced by their fathers and brothers to enter with a pitiable fortune into convents, not to pray or bless the name of the Lord,

[1] See, however, Sperling, *Convents and the Body Politic*, 43, in which she notes that contemporary perceptions of a dotal crisis are inadequate to explain forced monachation. This dotal crisis, in turn, was merely a symptom of a deliberate, contradictory, and self-destructive strategy of the Venetian patriciate to maximize its fiscal resources and its commitment to notions of honorable perfection. For an elaboration of this point of view, which also supports the primacy of "lineage ideology," see Sperling, "The Paradox of Perfection: Reproducing the Body Politic in Late Renaissance Venice," *Comparative Studies in Society and History* 41 (1999): 3–32.

[2] Gabriella Zarri, "Monasteri femminili," 364.

[3] Zarri, "Monasteri femminili," 365.

but rather to blaspheme and curse the bodies and souls of their parents and relatives, and to bemoan to God that they had ever been born. And those holy houses built for the total devotion of chaste souls, are used as dumps and rubbish heaps for the refuse of families.[4]

Just as worthy of note as the "throwaway" imagery is that in the chronicler's mind there existed an automatic association between the practice of monachation and the practice of abandonment. Samuel Cohn's work on Siena notes the proliferation of nonmonastic charitable institutions for young girls and women during the sixteenth century, which in his view perhaps served as alternatives to convents that had become too crowded to admit more nuns or which had become "dilapidated repositories for famine." Cohn also suggests that for women who were charitable givers, these new institutions represented a form of giving that served the interests of female sociability and identity.[5]

The work of Isabelle Chabot also locates the origins of the inheritance crisis not only chronologically in the mid-fourteenth century but geographically in Florence. Chabot makes persuasive claims that patrilineal inheritance rules were enforced and practiced with greater vigor in Florence than in Venice. Chabot attributes this, inter alia, to the lack of male heirs directly after the Black Death and the tendency in the late fourteenth century to allow women to inherit directly, a tendency that the Florentine (by contrast to the Venetian) patriciate promptly and energetically acted to suppress. Thus, the roots of the crisis, the symptoms of which are so dramatically evident in the sixteenth century, consisted of tightened enforcement of patrilineal inheritance rules in practice in collision with the actual situations and needs of families. Chabot argues that Florentine statutory law was much firmer on these points than comparable collections of statutes from other towns in the late Middle Ages.[6]

Gender Ideology and Lineage

To what extent, then, were these developments a result of "gender ideology," and to what extent were issues of gender subsumed under the larger rubric of

[4] Zarri, "Monasteri femminili," 365–6, citing the anonymous *Ragionamento sopra le pompe della citta di Bologna; nel quale anco si discorre sopra le perle, i banchetti, et corsi che si fanno per la città*. The edition Zarri used contains no indication of the name of the printer or date of publication, but an edition was produced in Bologna, in S. Mamoli, in 1568.

[5] Samuel K. Cohn, Jr., *Death and Property in Siena, 1205–1800: Strategies for the Afterlife* (Baltimore: Johns Hopkins University Press, 1988), 201.

[6] Isabelle Chabot, "La dette des familles: Femmes, lignages, et patrimonies à Florence aux XIVe et XVe siècles" (Ph.D. diss., European University Institute, Florence, 1995), 280.

the demands of lineage? As far as the Florentine patriciate is concerned, does the constellation of discoverable attitudes add up to an "ideology"? Sherrill Cohen, for example, in attempting to explain the evolution of institutions of confinement for women during the sixteenth century, cites a convincing quantity of fifteenth-century texts, of which San Bernardino of Siena and the early humanists provide much of the material. The unspoken assumption is that gender ideology was "Mediterranean" and therefore immutable. The abundance of available sixteenth-century texts, however, suggests that "gender ideology" was susceptible to change. The precepts enunciated by these later texts are themselves revealing: as humanism served the Medici court and not the republic, the importance of the family as the rehearsal for full participation in civic life became overshadowed by the cultivation of civility more appropriate to the courtier than to the orator. Yet the continued importance of family ties and connections in the burgeoning Medici bureaucracy suggests that whatever form preparation for public life took, the family's institutional role in that public life was only transformed, not diminished.[7] Certainly an important feature of that transformation was a new emphasis placed on "discipline," defined in Torquato Tasso's *Il padre di famiglia* (1582) as the training that fathers gave to sons so that "the discipline of the city remains uniform."[8]

A traditional reading of the history of the Mediterranean premodern world suggests two separate but related sources of gender ideology: the Judeo-Christian-Islamic tradition and a more deeply embedded cultural matrix of Mediterranean "values," of which the Judeo-Christian-Islamic tradition is itself a part. Much of this concern with the unity of the Mediterranean is a result of increasing interdisciplinarity among the humanities and social sciences: in particular, the anthropological studies of the values of honor and shame have been read, often uncritically, back into the past.[9] According to such a reading, Mediterranean societies rigorously enforced a distinction between the public and private worlds, with the former the

---

[7] See, for example, Torquato Tasso's dialogue, *Il padre di Famiglia*, in *Dialoghi*, ed. Ezio Raimondi (Florence: G. C. Sansoni, 1958), 363, which strikes a nice balance between competing political models: sons should be raised in such a way that they will be both good citizens and useful to princes. For this their training should consist of business, letters, and war, and their education should engage their bodies and their intellects equally.

[8] Tasso, *Dialoghi*, 363.

[9] See S. Cohn's discussion in *The Cult of Remembrance and the Black Death: Six Renaissance Cities in Central Italy* (Baltimore: Johns Hopkins University Press, 1992), 308n, and his review of Peter Burke's *A Historical Anthropology of Early Modern Italy* (Cambridge: Cambridge University Press, 1987) in the *American Historical Review* 93 (1988): 1359–60.

province of men and the latter the domain of women. Although in its broadest outlines, such a distinction is valuable, it also tends to override important differences within the Mediterranean region and having once illuminated our understanding of gender relations in European society, now threatens to obscure it.[10]

This reading informs much of the history of early Christianity, for example, despite compelling evidence that several systems of religious belief that coexisted in the ancient Mediterranean world accorded varying degrees of autonomy and public roles to women. Christianity, in particular, far from unilaterally incorporating whatever these Mediterranean values were supposed to have been, actively opposed them in the sense that opportunities for conversion and teaching freed many wealthier Roman women from the oppressive constraints of arranged marriage. Moreover, as Christianity developed new forms of popular devotion during the Middle Ages, the Marian cult, with its emphasis on the chastity and honor of the virgin, flourished with as much vigor in northern Europe as it did in the Mediterranean. In the Middle Ages as well, not just monachation but also other forms of the Christian life offered an escape from the demands of noble marriage alliance.

Diane Hughes has offered a persuasive explanation of how the demands of noble marriage alliance resulted from what amounted to a judicial revolution in the eleventh and twelfth centuries. This judicial revolution coincided with the medieval revival of interest in antiquity and, more particularly, in the great digests of Justinian's sixth-century codification of Roman law and replaced the Germanic practice of brideprice with the resuscitation of the Roman institution of dowry.[11] This was a revolution that represented a subjugation of the ties of husbands, wives, and children to the solidarity of men expressed through the assertion of patrilineal inheritance. The right to inheritance that had been established for women during the early Middle Ages was replaced by the dowry, a form of compensation for the loss of the right to inherit property directly. As a combination of Roman and Lombard

---

[10] Anthropologists of the Mediterranean region have now challenged, successfully in my view, much of the one-dimensional nature of earlier views. See especially David Gilmore, ed., *Honor and Shame and the Unity of the Mediterranean* (Washington, DC: American Anthropological Association, 1987), 3–17. The same point is addressed in David Kertzer and Richard Saller, eds., *The Family in Italy* (New Haven: Yale University Press, 1991), 4–5, in their discussion of the advantages and limitations of the typological approaches of the Cambridge Group. In a sixteenth-century context, even though honor and shame clearly dominated gender relations and lineage ideology in both Florence and Venice, the implications of those values for the lives of women in each city were vastly different.

[11] Diane Hughes, "From Brideprice to Dowry in Mediterranean Europe" *Journal of Family History* 3 (1978): 262–96.

law, however, communal statutes in north-central Italy went even further by specifying that by virtue of the dowry, women were excluded from inheritance. The Florentine statutes of 1415 set the dowry at "reasonable and proper" according to the family's social level, but these statutes set no minimum threshold and certainly did not provide for any avenue of appeal or redress.[12]

The case of Umiliana de' Cerchi of Florence (ca. 1219–46) strongly suggests how the form that her sanctity took represented "disaffection" from noble lineage and noble values. For example, Umiliana tore off her head-band and shred part of her clothing to give to the poor, particularly rebellious actions given the importance of clothing to noble status. More important, Umiliana offered to give her dowry away if her husband would only repent and give the proceeds of his usury back to the poor. Although she was turned down in this offer, when it became clear she would not accept remarriage, her father engaged in some rather devious legal maneuvers to regain control of Umiliana's dowry, a pattern apparently not uncommon in saints' lives and no doubt intended to prevent the entire family patrimony from being given away to the poor. Unable to enter a convent, she became a Franciscan tertiary who lived in a tower under the care of her family, leaving only to go to mass and perform pious errands.[13]

Two important observations emerge from this saint's life. First, the writer of the *Vita*, Vito da Cortona, implies that a great part of Umiliana's sanctity is wrapped up in a rejection of values, a rejection normal human beings could not possibly have managed, such were the strength of these lineage ties and the role women were expected to play in supporting those ties. Indeed, lineage was more important as a binding and unifying idea than as a formal, legal institution, so that rupturing the network of kinship rent the very fabric of human society. Second, the topos of Umiliana being tricked out of her dowry resonates within the accounts of the lives of very early Christian female saints who provided for their families before renouncing their ties to the secular world. Her father's trickery, in other words, acts as a rhetorical device to reassure readers that sanctity need not result in financial and social ruin for the rest of the family. The success of this rhetorical device does not undermine its veracity – indeed, its veracity is central to its effectiveness. Moreover, the dualism of Cathar heretical ideas shares important characteristics with official accounts of feminine sanctity,

---

[12] Chabot, "La dette des familles," 84–5.
[13] The preceding discussion relies heavily on Carol Lansing, *The Florentine Magnates: Lineage and Faction in a Medieval Commune* (Princeton: Princeton University Press, 1991), 112–15.

suggesting once again that the attractiveness of these religious ideas lay in their potential for women to escape the claims of lineage solidarity.[14]

To read the fifteenth-century Florentine humanists on the role women played in the transmission of property is to understand the magnetism of these avenues of escape. The second book of Alberti's *I libri della famiglia*, written in 1433, counsels that

> The elders of the house and all of the family shall reject no daughter-in-law unless she is tainted with the breath of scandal or of bad reputation. Aside from that, let the man who will have to satisfy her satisfy himself. He should act as do wise heads of families before they acquire some property – they like to look it over several times before they actually sign a contract.[15]

Tempering the language of property, however, is Alberti's admonition in the same paragraph that marriage had two purposes for men of the Florentine patriciate: "to perpetuate himself in his children, and second, to have a steady and constant companion all his life."[16] Indeed, Alberti's interlocutors are at considerable pains to explain that a potential wife should be judged "not only by the charm and refinement of her face, but still more by the grace of her person and her aptitude for bearing and giving birth to many fine children." This dichotomy between the mind and the body parallels the dichotomy in gender roles even in determining the qualities of paternal and maternal love.[17] The love of fathers is an affection "rooted in the minds of fathers," whereas the love of mothers is rooted in their role both in giving birth and in breast-feeding. In Montaigne's essays, this distinction automatically makes the maternal role inferior, because its source is subject to the degradation of all instinctive life. In an earlier treatise written in 1425 by Giovanni Gherardo of Prato, however, maternal love is a source of superiority because of its closeness to nature.[18]

[14] Lansing's more recent study of Cathars in Orvieto suggests important qualifications, however. On the initial issue, see Lansing, *Florentine Magnates*, 125, and for the qualifications, see Lansing, *Power and Purity: The Cathar Heresy in Medieval Italy* (Oxford/New York: Oxford University Press 1998), 108–20, where she discusses Cathar challenges to "traditional" gender roles but in a context in which patrilineality, to the extent that it existed at all, was interpreted and practiced flexibly.

[15] Leon Battista Alberti, *I libri della famiglia*, ed. Cecil Grayson, in *Opere volgari* (3 vols., Bari: Laterza, 1960), 1:110. This and subsequent translations are those of R. N. Watkins, *The Family in Renaissance Florence* (Columbia: University of South Carolina Press, 1969), 115.

[16] Alberti, *I libri della famiglia*, 110.

[17] Ibid., 111.

[18] Alberti, *I libri della famiglia* (Turin: Einaudi, 1969), 33, 34, 46, cited in G. Calvi, *Il contratto morale*, 30. For Giovanni di Gherardo da Prato's discussion of maternal love, see Giovanni Gherardo da Prato, *Il Paradiso degli Alberti*, ed. A Lanza (Rome: Salerno, 1975), 179–84, cited in Christiane Klapisch-Zuber, *Women, Family, and Ritual*, 130.

If this is more a veneration of body than of mind, the skills that a wife must possess to run complex households efficiently are nonetheless valuable. Alberti's interlocutors make it clear that husbands must teach these skills and that women do not come by them naturally. *I libri della famiglia* paint a portrait of the young wife as a fragile, tremulous creature, filled with pangs of longing for her own mother's household, against which the only defense is the sense of accomplishment and pride that her husband's training can instill in her: "My wife certainly did turn into a perfect mother for my household. Partly this was the result of her particular nature and temperament, but mainly it was due to my instruction."[19] Moreover, Alberti's interlocutors insist on the rigid separation between public and private worlds:

> for, to tell the truth, it would hardly win us respect if our wife busied herself among the men in the marketplace, out in the public eye. It also seems somewhat demeaning to me to remain shut up in the house among women when I have manly things to do among men, fellow citizens and worthy and distinguished foreigners.[20]

John Najemy has argued that this dialogue in general, and the interventions of Giannozzo in particular, are a deliberate parody of Florentine patriarchal attitudes, inspired by Alberti's suspicion of the conscious link that the city's ruling elite made between authority in the family and authority in the state. Such a reading makes sense especially in light of Alberti's own position of familial exile – he was an illegitimate son seeking family identity from a father who did not bother to legitimate him. To read this section of *Della famiglia* as a simple misogynist tract is to miss the cost that patriarchal inflexibility inflicted on Alberti himself.[21]

Indeed, the revival of household "economics," although surely present in fourteenth-century *ricordanze*, was dignified by the use of classical models in Leonardo Bruni's translation and commentary on the pseudo-Aristotelian "Economics," written in 1422, eleven years before Alberti's *I libri della famiglia*. Although there were medieval translations of this work, notably Durand of Auvergne's medieval Latin version, Bruni's version gained wide currency both in Italy and in much of the rest of Europe.[22] Bruni's notes

[19] Alberti, *I libri della famiglia*, ed. Grayson, 218.

[20] Ibid., 216.

[21] John Najemy, "Giannozzo and His Elders: Alberti's Critique of Renaissance Patriarchy," in *Society and Individual in Renaissance Florence*, ed. William J. Connell (Berkeley/Los Angeles: University of California Press, 2002), 51–78.

[22] Gordon Griffiths, James Hankins, and David Thompson, eds., *The Humanism of Leonardo Bruni: Selected Texts* (Binghamton, N. Y.: Medieval and Renaissance Texts and Studies, 1987), 311, citing Josef Soudek, "Leonardo Bruni and His Public: A Statistical and Interpretive Study of His

to this treatise make clear, however, that where Hesiod's *Works and Days* implicitly compared oxen and women, "the one to produce food, the other children," modern translators needed to recognize that in Aristotle, "what is here said of the wife is a violent distortion of Hesiod. For Hesiod was thinking not of a wife but of a slave-girl. The person referred to as a woman, as the next verse makes clear, was not someone accepted in marriage, but obtained by purchase."[23]

Bruni's commentary on chapter 3 of the first book constitutes his defense of marriage – that it is natural. Pursuing the theme that marriage is a partnership, Bruni emphasized that the mutual cooperation of husband and wife points to a greater end: that of maintaining the good life of the household, which in turn makes possible the common wealth of a city. On the basis that marriage is a partnership, Bruni, anticipating Locke, argued that the relationship between man and wife is constrained by certain behavioral obligations on the husband's part. Such constraints do not apply to servants and children (again, Bruni "anticipates" Locke), over whom fathers have absolute power. Injury to wives, however, contravenes natural law.

That Alberti viewed men as superior to women is impossible to deny. That his tone is patronizing at best is partially due to his belief in the superiority of men but surely due in some measure to the age difference between husband and wife that was the norm in fifteenth-century Italian marriage.[24] Indeed, more than a century later, Torquato Tasso's 1582 dialogue, *Il padre di famiglia*, invokes this disparity in age between husband and wife as naturally advantageous not only "because a younger woman is better suited for procreation, but also, according to the testimony of Hesiod, because she can better receive and remember all the prescriptions of custom that he would like to impress upon her."[25] For Alberti, the relationship between men and women is envisioned not as that between masters and servants, for "a slave can bear threats and blows and perhaps not grow indignant if you shout at him." The paradigm is rather the relationship between a prince and his subjects, in which the prince's duty is not only to command obedience but also to educate in loving and compassionate wisdom. Thus, Alberti describes the relationship between a man and his wife in precisely the same terms that Machiavelli would describe the ideal attitude of the prince: "A wife, however, will obey you better from love than from fear. Any free spirit will

Annotated Latin Version of the ps.-Aristotelian *Economics*," *Studies in Medieval and Renaissance History* o.s. 5 (1968): 51–136 at 51ff.

[23] Griffiths, Hankins, and Thompson, eds., *The Humanism of Leonardo Bruni*, 311.

[24] C. Klapisch-Zuber, *Women, Family and Ritual*, 20.

[25] Tasso, *Dialoghi*, 355–6.

sooner set out to please you than to submit to you."[26] Both subjects and wives, then, behave better when rulers and husbands appeal to them on the basis of freedom rather than subjection. Indeed, precisely those same qualities will be necessary for women in their management of household servants, who should be admonished with gentleness of gesture and words, not as if women were "mountain girls who are used to calling each other from slope to slope."[27]

By contrast, Bruni's notes to the first chapter of the first book of the pseudo-Aristotelian "Economics" carefully delineate the boundaries between government of the family and government of the commonwealth.[28] The former is entirely private, the latter entirely public. Nonetheless, "the city is a multitude of households which possesses sufficient land and money to make a good life possible, and soon after this, he defines the household by pointing to its parts, saying that the parts of a household consist of human beings and possessions."[29] By households, Bruni points out, "Aristotle" meant families, to which land and wealth are added so that families can be self-sufficient. Indeed, this wealth permitted relationships of exchange that held cities together. As was true for San Bernardino of Siena and the canonists, Bruni held that the wealth of a community is defined as its *substantia*.[30]

What sustains the wealth of cities, then, is the wealth of households that constitute a city, so that once again, the central issue involved in the connection between family and city was not gender ideology but lineage ideology. Gender ideology was important but only as a subset of a lineage ideology that saw clearly that for a community to survive, its individual households must have the means to sustain wealth and patrimony:

> That the city is a multitude of households sufficiently well-supplied with land and money is evident, he says, from the fact that if these constituent parts be lacking, the society falls apart. That is to say without them the city cannot survive.[31]

Bruni's governing metaphor in this instance is the commercial partnership, the *societas*. "For the city is a certain kind of *societas*. . . . Men bound together are thus what constitutes a city."[32] Thus, the good father possesses four skills crucial to the increase and preservation of patrimony: acquisitiveness,

---

[26] Alberti, *I libri della famiglia*, 227.

[27] Ibid., 232.

[28] Griffiths, Hankins, and Thompson, eds., *The Humanism of Leonardo Bruni*, 307.

[29] Ibid., 308.

[30] San Bernardino of Siena, *Opera Omnia* (8 vols., Florence: Ad Claras Aquas, 1956), 4: 383.

[31] Griffith, Hankins, and Thompson, eds., *The Humanism of Leonardo Bruni*, 309.

[32] Ibid. Bruni cites a passage from Cicero's *De re publica* that defines a city as "councils and assemblies of men bound together under the law," which, although invoking a legal rather than a commercial

conservation, an understanding of the proper uses of wealth, and an appreciation of the enjoyment that wealth brings. One might legitimately infer that the management of female honor is therefore the management of patrimony, not, as is commonly believed, because women were property but because the loss of female honor threatened the integrity of the patrimony. In the pseudo-Aristotelian treatise's striking metaphor, the paterfamilias of a household where the honor of women had been compromised was put in the position of trying "to draw water with a sieve."[33]

In an entire treatise devoted to the family, Alberti paid scant attention to dowries and none to daughters, because so much of his familial humanism is concerned to prepare boys for careers in public life. When he did turn his attention to dowries, however, it was to illustrate with consummate clarity the gap between legal theory and domestic realities. Alberti's interlocutors described sympathetically the plight of the young husband whose in-laws were slow to pay the dowry: the in-laws keep promising to pay in installments, the final date of which recedes ever farther into the future. The young husband has obligations to entertain his in-laws but can hardly spoil the mood of banquets and parties by insisting on speedier payment. Should he await a more propitious time, he then faces pressure from his wife, to the point that ultimately the husband must choose between getting the dowry paid on time or his wife's affections. For this reason, Alberti advises, "the dowry should be precisely set, promptly paid, and not too high."[34] At the same time, however, Alberti did not view marriage as exclusively or even primarily for the transmission of property but for the bearing of children. Ultimately, good kinsmen are worth more than wealth: "Wealth is a fleeting and perishable thing, while kinsmen, if you think of them as such and treat them accordingly, remain kinsmen forever."[35]

Matteo Palmieri's *Della vita civile*, also written around 1430, at first seems more preoccupied with mothers' bodies and their generative capacities than with issues of kinship and wealth. Palmieri paid special attention to nutrition during pregnancy and differences in growth of the fetus according to gender. Being born head first was "natural"; being born feet first, however, was the first ominous sign of misfortune.[36] At the beginning of book 3, Palmieri placed this concern with childbearing in its larger context, which was not

---

metaphor, nonetheless conveys the sense that both a commercial and a political partnership involve contractual obligation. Cf. Cicero, *De re publica*, 1.41 and 6.13.

[33] Griffith, Hankins, and Thompson, eds., *The Humanism of Leonardo Bruni*, 316–17.

[34] Alberti, *I libri della famiglia*, 113.

[35] Alberti, *I libri della famiglia*, 115.

[36] Matteo Palmieri, *Della vita civile*, ed. Gino Belloni, Istituto Nazionale di Studi sul Rinascimento, Studi e Testi, vol. 7 (Florence: Sansoni, 1982), 22.

only the perpetuation of the family but of the republic. Indeed, for Palmieri, love of country and love of one's own children were the two greatest ties that bound, and they were closely connected. Of all the possible objects of our love, only republics and children invoke our desire for earthly immortality.[37] And at the end of book 3, Palmieri ranked human obligation in charity hierarchically: first to country, then to father and mother (equally), then children of one's own family, then spouses, then friends, then neighbors, then the entire city, then languages, and finally all of humankind "connected by a natural love."[38]

In book 4, however, Palmieri argued that of all human loves, matrimonial union is the most delightful, and its generative possibilities the compensation for the brief and uncertain duration of human life. "The principal usefulness expected from a woman are children and future generations. The wife is like the fertile ground, which receives the seed and multiplies it in good and abundant fruit."[39] Because the better the ground, the better the fruit, Palmieri advised great care in the choice of a wife, "whose greatest adornment is the modesty and honesty of a well-arranged and well-ordered life."[40] For Palmieri, the commandment "to forsake all others" applies equally to husband and wife, although it is the woman who needs most to obey this. Not only must she not "conjoin herself" with another man, she must avoid all suspicion that she is doing so. This failure is "the highest insult to honesty. It takes away love, ruptures the union, and brings with it uncertain ancestry of children, and [ruins] the reputation of families."[41]

This, then is the crux of traditional values of honor and shame in which "gender" ideology consists. Surely, therefore, it is more useful to think in terms of "lineage" ideology than "gender" ideology. True, responsibility seems to devolve more heavily on female behavior and appearance than on male. The underlying anxiety is not that female infidelity compromises virility, but that it compromises succession: "incertitudine de' figliuoli" and "famiglie infami" suggest that unruly sexual behavior threatened the economic and social matrix of dowry, land, and inheritance.[42] According to Palmieri, husbands also needed to preserve that same economic and social matrix by avoiding a dissolute life, both to protect their own dignity and

---

[37] Ibid., 103.
[38] Ibid., 146.
[39] Ibid., 157.
[40] Ibid.
[41] Ibid., 158.
[42] This is noted by Sarah Pomeroy for classical Athens as well. See Sarah Pomeroy, *Goddesses, Whores, Wives and Slaves: Women in Classical Antiquity* (New York: Schocken Books, 1975), 86.

to avoid the infamy of illegitimate children. Palmieri also, in accordance with traditionally "Mediterranean" values, advocated the rigid separation of private life (the domain of women) from public. However, even in household management women were to seek advice and consent from husbands and to follow their will as though it were law. At the same time, Palmieri argued, although ideally men will marry women who are "honest, and of the best habits," those who are less lucky should first seek to change their wife's behavior, and if all else fails, to suffer it patiently as Socrates suffered Xanthippe: "I learn at home to bear those injuries that are received outside."[43]

Palmieri treated the education of children as though they were all masculine, suggesting in particular that virtue and femininity were opposites. Adolescent boys, even on ceremonial occasions, were "to shun every feminine adornment . . . since [none of these] are prerequisite to virtue: it is girls who require delicate beauty."[44] Palmieri recalled the "gentle" but humiliating reproof administered by a Florentine schoolmaster to some of his delicately adorned male charges. The schoolmaster repeatedly asked the pupils if they were dressed up to take a wife and, after their repeated denials, concluded, "Then you want a husband."[45]

Not only feminine fashions tempted the wayward male adolescent, but so, too, did the passions themselves, passions that "tire the intellect and make men disordered." Unbridled happiness, Palmieri noted, caused the death of Policrata, "nobilissima femina." Diagora saw her three sons the victors in the Olympic games and "died of unbearable happiness in the midst of a very great crowd."[46] Indeed, in all Palmieri's negative examples of unbridled passions, women, such as the Roman mother whose grief was overwhelming when she heard of her son's death in battle against Hannibal, were unvaryingly the victims of passion. When men fall victim to passion, love of women is the cause. Hercules, "so vilely subsuming his own dignity," of course, was the prime example of even the most heroic virtue undone by illicit love when "for love he became a woman's servant," but there was also Samson, willing for love to risk not only himself but his subjects.[47] Indeed, "to grieve, or to fear some adverse circumstance, and to lament and cry like a woman, is completely contrary to the modesty of the wise man."[48] *Della vita civile* set

---

[43] Palmieri, 159–60.
[44] Ibid., 36.
[45] Ibid., 37.
[46] Ibid., 78.
[47] Ibid., 79.
[48] Ibid., 81.

up a moral dichotomy between active masculine virtue and passive feminine vice. After his discussion of friendship in book 4, he writes:

> With admiration are those men esteemed who do or say uncommon deeds beyond the common opinion of other men. Outstanding and unique deeds raise one's esteem and reputation, and make men praiseworthy and glorious; and by contrast, those things in which there is neither mind, virtue, nor vigor, but rather which consist of feminine lassitude, without effort, without industry, without commitment, are good neither for them nor for others.[49]

In all these examples, passion and passivity are linguistically equivalent: both involve a disengagement of the rational, active intellect swept away either by emotion or by lassitude.[50] Even the humanist praise of women concealed a greater concern with secondary attributes of the body rather than the primary substance, the mind, reflecting the importance of virginity, dowry, and generativity. Angelo Poliziano's letter to Cassandra Fedele, "a most learned Venetian Maiden," begins "O virgin ornament of Italy" (in imitation of Vergil's *Aeneid*) and makes no less than seven references to her maidenhood and virginity in a letter of approximately five hundred words. Suggesting that she may have already achieved a place equal to Pico's in Poliziano's pantheon of the learned, the poet describes her as the only maiden living who "handles a book instead of wool" and tells her that her position is "as rare, as new, as if violets took root amid ice, roses in snow, or lilies in frost." Such a compliment was double-edged, because it described Cassandra's learning as not only rare but also explicitly unnatural.[51]

Matteo Palmieri's remarks on virginity contrasted the marriage customs of the ancient Romans, who took the bride-to-be to her husband's marriage bed under cover of night, "because they said it was not fitting that the virgin about to shed her very noble status should be seen in public," with the more vulgar Florentine custom of parading the bride-to-be everywhere in fancy clothes "so that everyone was aware that soon she should no longer be a virgin."[52] Indeed, the theme of virginity and humanist scholarship spoke to the very core of Mediterranean concerns about female honor. Virgins

---

[49] Ibid., 170–1.

[50] On the Aristotelian foundations of these views, see Genevieve Lloyd, *The Man of Reason: "Male" and "Female" in Western Philosophy*, 2nd ed. (London: Routledge, 1993), 2–9, and Ian MacLean, *The Renaissance Notion of Woman* (Cambridge: Cambridge University Press, 1980), 28–46.

[51] Angelo Poliziano to Cassandra Fedele, letter of 1491, quoted in *Her Immaculate Hand*, ed. Margaret King and Albert Rabil (Binghamton, NY: Medieval and Renaissance Texts and Studies, 1983), 126–7.

[52] Palmieri, 114.

mediated between the world of men and the world of women, occupying a middle position in which, otherwise susceptible to the loss of honor, they could in some but always ambiguous fashion reclaim their honor through association with masculine traits.[53]

Other humanist epistolary writing to learned women, such as Gregorio Correr's letter to Cecilia in 1443, made clear that the matrix of scholarship and social roles was far different for women than for men. Where Leonardo Bruni offered a defense of marriage and its role in active, public life, Gregorio Correr kept marriage and public life sharply separate for women. Indeed, female scholarship and female virginity were as closely intertwined as in Poliziano's letter to Cassandra Fedele. Although Correr intended his letter to Cecilia to strengthen her resolve to enter a convent against her father's wishes, it is not unrepresentative of other treatises. Correr went farther than most, however. In his discussion of Cecilia's curriculum, he recommended that the secular, classical authors should be avoided in favor of devotional books on the order of the *Mirror of Simple Souls*.[54] Nonetheless, conventual life did not preclude secular scholarship: in sixteenth-century Florence, Suor Fiammetta Frescobaldi, a nun at the convent of San Jacopo a Ripoli, wrote "a history of the world."[55] Such examples became even more common in the sixteenth and early seventeenth centuries. Beatrice del Sera, a nun in Prato, wrote a play in the 1550s called *Amor di virtù*, and the plays of Raffaella de' Sernigi, Cherubina Venturelli, and Maria Clemente Ruoti were published in the late sixteenth and early seventeenth centuries.[56] Indeed, the index to a volume on women, manners, and discipline lists sixty-seven female writers, the vast majority of whom were Italian holy women in the sixteenth and

[53] Anton Blok, "Notes on the Concept of Virginity in Mediterranean Societies," in *Women and Men in Spiritual Culture, XIV–XVII Centuries: A Meeting of North and South*, ed. Elisja Schulte van Kessel (The Hague: Netherlands Government Printing Office, 1986), 27–33, cited in Gabriella Zarri, "Ursula and Catherine: The Marriage of Virgins in the Sixteenth Century," in *Creative Women in Medieval and Early Modern Italy*, ed. E. A Matter and John Coakley (Philadelphia: University of Pennsylvania Press, 1994), 237–78, at 270n. See also Jane Schneider, "Of Vigilance and Virgins: Honour, Shame and Access to Resources in Mediterranean Societies" *Ethnology* 9 (1971): 1–24, and Sherry Ortner, "The Virgin and the State," *Feminist Studies* 4.3 (1978): 19–35.

[54] Gregorio Correr to Cecilia Gonzaga, letter of 1443, in ed. King and Rabil, *Her Immaculate Hand*, 101.

[55] Sherrill Cohen, *The Evolution of Women's Asylums*, 29. See Giovanna Pierattini, "Suor Fiammetta Frescobaldi: Cronista del monastero di Sant'Iacopo a Ripoli in Firenze (1523–1586)," *Memorie Domenicane*, 56 (1939): 101–268. I thank K. J. P. Lowe of the University of London for this reference. See her *Nuns' Chronicles and Convent Culture in Renaissance and Counter-Reformation Italy* (Cambridge/New York: Cambridge University Press, 2003).

[56] Elissa B. Weaver, "Suor Maria Clemente Ruoti, Playwright and Academician," in ed. Coakely and Matter, *Creative Women*, 281–96, at 281.

seventeenth centuries.[57] The musical careers of such nuns as Lucrezia Orsina Vizzana, Claudia Rusca, Chiara Margarita Cozzolani, and Isabella Tomasi have come to light through excellent monographs as well as important shorter studies.[58]

Lineage and the Development of a Status Culture

Alessandro Piccolomini's major work on the family, *De la institutione di tutta la vita del huomo nobile, e in città libera, Libri X in Lingua Toscana* (first edition, Venice, 1542) addressed to the Sienese noblewoman Laudomia Forteguerri, devoted several chapters in the ninth book to the relationship between the experience of human and divine love, weaving his discussion into a more general consideration of the marital bond and its relationship to nobility, government, and the role of order in society. Piccolomini's subtitle proclaimed his intention to treat the themes of cultivation of noble *civiltà* and humanist values "Peripateticamente e Platonicamente." In particular, Piccolomini found Aristotle's descriptions of the growth of states from single burgeoning families who build more houses to accommodate their excess children, into clusters of houses, neighborhoods, and cities, a powerful explanatory model for the connection between the lineage ideology of old, noble, families, and the viability of city-states.

For Piccolomini, as for Machiavelli, the exclusivity practiced by the Venetian patriciate was the key to defining and maintaining collective nobility:

> Therefore the Venetian Lords are on their guard to make sure that nobility is built up very clearly, step by step, with very great difficulty, indeed, so it is almost impossible to get into the ranks. They are extremely consistent in not giving their families noble status, or the title of Gentleman to just anyone. Thus their nobility does not come from anywhere except its own, legitimate and native succession of blood, and this applies equally to men and women. Therefore those who take as a wife an ignoble woman,

---

[57] Gabriella Zarri, ed., *Donna, disciplina, creanza cristiana dal xv al xvii secolo: studi e testi a stampa* (Rome: Edizioni di Storia e letteratura, 1996), 763.

[58] Cf. Craig Monson, *Disembodied Voices: Music and Culture in an Early Modern Italian Convent* (Berkeley and Los Angeles: University of California Press, 1995), 17–55, on Lodovica Vizzana, and Robert L. Kendrick, *Celestial Sirens: Nuns and Their Music in Early Modern Milan* (Oxford: Clarendon Press/New York: Oxford University Press, 1996), 104–5 and passim. For shorter studies, see also C. A. Monson, "Elena Malvezzi's Keyboard Manuscript: A New Sixteenth-Century Source," *Early Music History*, 9 (1989): 73–128; Elissa Weaver, "Spiritual Fun: A Study of Sixteenth-Century Tuscan Convent Theatre," in *Women in the Middle Ages*, ed. Mary Beth Rose (Syracuse, NY: Syracuse University Press, 1986), 173–206; Beatrice del Sera, *Amor di virtù: Commedia in cinque atti*, ed. E. Weaver (Ravenna: Longo, 1990).

believing that she will still produce noble children, are only fooling themselves . . . [in the woman's family also] there should be among the ancestors
persons who engaged in a very honorable calling, or science, who are illustrious and famous.[59]

Piccolomini's definition of nobility serves multiple social functions as well
as explaining much of what was certainly a pan-Italian strategy on the part
of aspiring aristocratic families. The strategy formed part of a clear-cut
ideology of lineage that concentrated the family's resources on the daughter
who could be most successfully married to other noble families, partially
accounting for the proliferation of women's institutions, both religious and
charitable, that dominated the sixteenth-century Italian landscape.

Marital considerations occupy the final sections of the treatise, which treat
household organization and management. Piccolomini deliberately post-
poned discussion of marriage until the young nobleman had been immersed
for twelve years in studying the moral sciences. The Sienese philosopher
described the marital bond as a joint venture characterized by the "obligation of nature, for the passing down of property through generations, for
the maintenance of the nobility of your lineage, and finally for the preservation of your republic."[60] Like the authors of humanist treatises of the
previous century who had relied on Xenophon and the pseudo-Aristotelian
Economics, Piccolomini stressed the importance of the rational and intellectual faculties that raised marriage beyond the level of the propagation
of the species and the guarantee of personal immortality.[61] However, where
Alberti in the fifteenth century had been concerned with the preservation of
household and lineage, Piccolomini stressed the preservation of the *nobility*
of one's family.

Within the family, Platonic conceptions of friendship and their elaboration in the Peripatetic tradition, based on separate kinds of inequality,
corresponded to the three traditional forms of government: monarchy, aristocracy, and the popular state:

To the republic, finally, which commonly considers the poor and the rich,
the law-abiding and the criminal, is opposed the popular state, which only
the poor, the vile, and the low exalt and honor. Governments [monarchy,
aristocracy, and the popular state] resemble those regimes found in a house.
Thus the rule of the father over the son resembles monarchy, which when

---

[59] Alessandro Piccolomini, *De la institutione di tutta la vita del huomo nobile, e in città libera, Libri X in
Lingua Toscana* (Florence: apud Hieronymum Scotum, 1543), 145r.

[60] Piccolomini, *Institutione di tutta la vita*, 242r.

[61] Ibid., 242v.

corrupted degenerated into tyranny as happened among the Persians. The principate of the husband over the wife is like an aristocracy, which through the insolence of the husband can degenerate into oligarchy. Finally, the republic is like the relationship among brothers, which when corrupted degenerates into popular government.[62]

This is strikingly similar to Machiavelli's discussion in *The Discourses* (I.2) of how the three existing forms of government each have their own virtues but which, when corrupted, inevitably lead monarchs to tyranny, aristocrats to the arrogance of the few, and citizens to a disordered popular government.[63] Both authors have a common source in Aristotle's *Politics*, but Piccolomini's more direct reliance on Aristotle led him to draw an explicit connection between familial bonds, household organization, and the state.

Piccolomini's discussion of love, however, was a complex and difficult one. He had no difficulty seeing how Plato and Aristotle agreed on issues of friendship, but in his discussion of love, Piccolomini distinguished between the purely Platonic love that can exist between two noble souls who become lovers, at least spiritually, and the love that exists between husband and wife, which serves entirely different ends. Truly divine love in a Platonic sense was impossible, because the limitations of our bodies always present an obstacle to perfect union. Only divine love is constant, even though humans have a partial share in it, just as mortal beings have a partial share of immortality.

The lovers' gaze became for Piccolomini the locus of the primacy that Plato accorded the eye. In guarding against deception, for example, the gaze was the best guide, because much more than the spoken word the gaze exposed the secrets of the heart: "the eyes are therefore the most noble part of the man, and they make manifest their nobility when one looks into the eyes of the beloved."[64] Thus, the perfect union of souls begins with the hearing of sweet words, progresses to the glances that reveal the hearts' secrets, and reaches the ultimate perfection of the transformation of two minds into one, a blessed state "much superior to all other mortal sweetness."[65]

Although Piccolomini retracted his formerly held opinion as meant only for comic effect, which he had expressed two years earlier in his dialogue *Raffaela, ouer creanza delle donne,* that love and marriage were incompatible, he made clear in the economics portion of the treatise that the love a husband

[62] Ibid., 189v–190r.

[63] Machiavelli, *The Prince: With Selections from the Discourses,* trans. Daniel Donno (New York: Bantam, 1966, repr. 1981), 92.

[64] Piccolomini, *Institutione di tutta la vita,* 212v.

[65] Ibid., 213r–213v.

bears his wife is in a different category from Platonic love altogether.[66] Married love is, first of all, a relationship of unequals, expressed not least in the inequality of the husband's and wife's age. Where the husband ideally married at age thirty, his consort should be between eighteen and twenty, or at the most, twenty-five. This not only made the noble woman he married more susceptible to instruction but also more suitable for bearing healthy and worthy noble children.[67] The unintended consequences of this prescribed marriage strategy were, of course, the high percentage of widows in the population and a considerable number of children from prior marriages who both hindered their mother's prospects of remarriage and who were more likely to be homeless. Within the household, women disproportionately bore the burden of maintaining its confessional and pedagogical integrity. For this reason, second only to the nobility of the woman's family was the importance of her own upbringing in ensuring the proper performance of her tasks during the early years of child rearing.

> because it is from nowhere else than education, good or bad, that either the infamous or honored life of man proceeds. Therefore it is necessary that a girl by all the forces of heaven be inclined, or to be more precise, encouraged to behave well, for if her parents maintain a less than honest life, she will seek to imitate them, especially in those brutish and, principally, venereal acts on which bodily pleasure depends, which more than any other emotion are extremely powerful in the young.... Watch out very carefully, therefore, and with all your ingenuity make sure that whoever you take as a wife is not only nobly born, but above all brought up at home with great modesty and honesty, and raised with the fear of God.[68]

The chronological inequality of husband and wife also dictated the husband's particular obligation to treat his wife well when she first entered her husband's house. Once again, lineage ideology preceded gender ideology, for the young bride felt out of place not only because of her age and inexperience but also because she faced the "novelty of your house, and of her new family, and by the fresh memory of the house she has just left, which is no longer hers."[69]

For Piccolomini, however, even this inequality is, in Aristotelian terminology, purely secondary and reflected a necessary division of labor within the household: the greater strength of the man is not ordained in nature to the disadvantage of women but for the smooth running of the household,

---

[66] Ibid., 228r.
[67] Ibid., 245v
[68] Ibid., 246v.
[69] Ibid., 247v. On the woman as a transitory guest in her husband's household, cf. Christiane Klapisch-Zuber, *Women, Family and Ritual*, 74.

just as "we do not say that the left hand, being weaker than the right, is inferior to the right."[70] Men use their physical strength and ingenuity to acquire
the wealth necessary to keep the household going and use their abilities to
maintain the wealth that has been acquired. In both cases, maintenance of
social and economic station is the minimum standard, the increase of wealth
the goal:

> The first kind of conservation does not belong to the woman, because it is
> connected with acquiring, and so belongs to the man. To his governance
> belongs buying, selling, pledging, loaning, disposing of, and similar con-
> tracts. . . . Of these things [acquired], once they are brought into the house
> the prudent woman, with all diligence must tell the father of the family
> where she has put everything.[71]

The division of labor also corresponded to private and public gender roles –
specifically the work of women to pursue both domestic and pedagogical duties to free men for the pursuit of "civil affairs and the pursuit of
knowledge."[72] If this implied her duty to obey, her reward was to be free of
the "efforts, travails, and impediments that comprise the transactions of the
public world and which surround men everywhere, such as letters, arms,
magistrates, lawsuits, jealousies, rebellions, enemies, hate, rancor, and infinite other such perturbations."[73] For all these reasons, pertaining both to
good order and to emotional sustenance, the father maintained with his wife
and family the authority of "neither a tyrannical nor a popular government,
but of an aristocratic government, as Aristotle would have it. Therefore
he should know that his wife is neither subject nor servant, but rather a
companion."[74]

Indeed, the woman's good management eventually maintained the order
and discipline at the center of household and estate management. The husband brought home the materials and wealth necessary for maintaining the
family's social station and determined where those foods and materials should
go. The wife merely placed those things in their appropriate places, a more
exalted duty than it might first appear. The rhetorical demands of decorum
and fit extended, then, to the most mundane details of the household. In
this respect, Piccolomini differed little from Alberti a century earlier, when

---

[70] Piccolomini, *Institutione di tutta la vita*, 261r.

[71] Ibid., 256–256v.

[72] Ibid., 249. Cf. Paula Findlen, *Possessing Nature: Museums, Collecting, and Scientific Culture in Early
Modern Italy* (Berkeley/Los Angeles: University of California Press, 1994), 99, on collecting as a
material basis for making social distinctions.

[73] Piccolomini, *Institutione di tutta la vita*, 249v.

[74] Piccolomini, *Institutione di tutta la vita*, 260v.

an interlocutor in the dialogue explained how, after his wife's "first pangs of longing for her mother had begun to fade," he had shown his new bride

> around the whole house. I explained that the loft was the place for grain and the stores of wine and wood were kept in the cellar. I showed her where things needed for the table were kept, and so on throughout the whole house. At the end there were no household goods of which my wife had not learned the place and the purpose.[75]

Yet in the sixteenth century, Piccolomini concocted from these mundane household details nothing less than an ode to order in which he finally unified the peripatetic and Platonic promised by his loquacious title and that drew an explicit connection between the order of the well-regulated household and, following Xenophon, the order of the militarily disciplined state:

> Order, therefore, is truly what we say: the form and perfection of all things. And if it is true, as others say, that the world is a living organism, as we are, without doubt it is order itself which is its soul, and ought to be esteemed. . . . Does it not suffice only that I tell you that the beauty of anything whatsoever is none other than that ordered division and proportion of its parts, not only among themselves, but with everything else? This is not merely the beauty of a beautiful woman, but the beauty that is in the sweetness of harmony, or the beauty that is in the strength of a well-disciplined army.[76]

This exaltation of order and discipline within both the family and the state resulted in the convergence of familial and institutional social pressures. Just as good order required aristocratic attempt to preserve lineages (even as such codes of behavior often undermined that goal), so did political order require institutions to house anomalous casualties of the rigidity of the inheritance grid.

Tasso's *Il padre di famiglia* marks the completion of the process of gentrifying domestic advice. Unlike the urban setting of Alberti's dialogue, the setting of Tasso's is self-consciously and elaborately rural. Although the interlocutors are careful to stress that all of the values of urbanity and *civiltà* have

---

[75] Alberti, 218. Although Alberti's interlocutor quite happily demonstrates to his bride where the linens, jewels, and valuables are kept, he deliberately withholds from her the diaries and account books of his own family, blatantly excluding her from his own lineage even though she has barely recovered from her pangs of separation from her own natal family.

[76] Piccolomini, *Institutione di tutta la vita*, 257v–258r. For the corresponding passage in Xenophon, see Xenophon, *Oeconomicus: A Social and Historical Commentary*, trans. Sarah B. Pomeroy (Oxford: Clarendon Press, 1994), viii, 4–10, 148–51.

been transplanted from the city to the resplendent country estate where the encounter takes place, Tasso's dialogue evokes the bucolic world of classical estate management. The immediate association in the reader's mind, then, was not between the family and the vicissitudes of urban politics but between the family and the management of its landed patrimony. The bounty of the *signore*'s table was the first and most important evidence of his qualifications as a *buon padre di famiglia,* a phrase still widely used in Italian car hire contracts and tenants' leases to indicate the care required in protecting the owner's property from damage. Tasso's dialogue, however, made an extremely careful distinction between women and property. The attention of the family father "extends to two things, persons and property. With persons, the father has three roles to play: husband, father, and lord." Property has two purposes: "conservation and increase." This division of care corresponds to rational and irrational, with the care of persons the nobler art because it deals with the rational, the care of property less so because it is irrational. Wives and even children therefore fall into the category of the rational.

A virtually contemporary Milanese treatise by Silvio Antoniano makes a similar distinction when it argues, based on Aristotle, that

> the free man commands the slave in a different way than does the male the female, or the man the boy, and they all possess the parts of the soul, but possess them in a different manner. The slave does not possess the deliberative faculty in all its fullness; the woman does possess it but without authority, and the child possesses it but it is not yet developed.[77]

Thus, for Antoniano, the subservience of the wife was based not on her irrationality, because she possessed "the deliberative faculty" in precisely the same degree as the man, but on her lack of authority to employ it.

Tasso noted that wives were properly called "consorts" because the husband's and the wife's fate are conjoined for better or for worse.[78] More particularly, the relationship of husband to wife was that of mind to body, and if this at first glance seems to reflect the common view that emphasized the corporeality of the woman as distinguished from the intellect of the man, for Tasso this also symbolized the indissolubility of marriage: "just as once the knot is untied that ties the mind with the body, it does not seem that the soul can be joined with any other body." Ideally, therefore, even at the death of one partner, a second marriage should not follow.[79]

---

[77] Antoniano, *Tre libri dell'educatione de' figliuoli,* 126r, cited in Frajese, 51. The author thanks Prof. Wietse de Boer for this reference.

[78] Tasso, *Dialoghi,* 353.

[79] Ibid., 354.

For Tasso, however, law and custom both provide for a second marriage, especially if there has been no issue from the first, that is, if the second marriage is motivated by the desire for succession, "a desire natural to all rational creatures." In terms of actual Florentine succession practices, this is very much a double-edged exception, hinted at in the next sentence, where Tasso writes that "nonetheless, happier are they who have tied only one matrimonial knot in their lifetime."[80] Florentine succession practices did legitimize second marriages, but because the legitimization hinged on the desire for succession, an implicit if unspoken disapproval attached to second marriages if the first marriage had already produced heirs. And indeed, Florentine statutory law had no official way of neutralizing conflicts that arose from the successorial rights of children from two marriages, except to privilege the rights of children of the second marriage and to nullify the rights of children of the first. This is perhaps both the most central and the most striking way in which lineage ideology, as expressed in statutory prescription and testamentary praxis, came into conflict with prevailing demographic and cultural patterns. Given the culturally sanctioned age difference at marriage among Florentine couples, the likelihood that a married woman would become a widow was high, and unless a first husband had made sufficient provisions in a will and had sufficient resources to make good on them, a second marriage became both a necessity for survival and a severe strain on the prevailing system of distributing family resources.[81]

Tasso's dialogue proposed a companionate model of marriage. The relationship between mind and body was not the relationship implied between husband and wife. The obedience that wives owe to their husbands "is not in the way the servant obeys the lord or the body the mind." In a clear association between the discipline required for the survival of the state and the governing of the family, Tasso portrayed the ideal form of marital obedience as that which the citizen owes to the state and its laws or its magistrates. If this placed the wife in a subordinate position, it also implied a value equal to that of citizenship (based on the reasonable nature of human beings) and the obligation of the husband to govern with prudence. Moreover, the complementarity of roles also required that spouses be of more or less equal social standing, "just as when oxen are yoked together they work more effectively when they are the same size." This emphasis on the importance of social equality also had an important subtext of preserving the noble social status of the family and of setting those with noble status apart from those of lesser

---

[80] Ibid.
[81] Chabot, "La dette des familles," 223.

condition and is commonplace in other sixteenth-century dialogues as well, such as those of Silvio Antoniano.[82]

Nonetheless, virtue was gendered: male virtues were prudence, strength, and generosity; female virtues were modesty and a sense of shame. At the same time, if a sense of shame was not one of the manly virtues, men nonetheless do well to restrain their libido when away from home, a restraint that also gives the wife a reputation for chastity.[83] Here the older topos of the unrestrained passions of women was itself restrained and modified by Tasso's observation that for "the woman, by nature libidinous and inclined to the pleasures of Venus no less than man," only a sense of shame, love for the husband, and fear keeps her behavior in check. Yet in a gloss on Aristotle, Tasso argues that shame is not worthy of praise in a man, but very praiseworthy in a woman. As is true with many of this treatise's predecessors, Tasso's dialogue concerned itself with the honor of women precisely because women were placed in charge of conserving the patrimony and material resources of the family. For Alberti, for example, the role of the woman's stewardship of household and land was to prevent those sudden shifts in material fortune that so quickly brought families to ruin. Because compromising the honor of women compromised succession, women were vulnerable not only because of their gender but also because their position as stewards of property and honor constituted double jeopardy.[84]

Tasso's treatise represents one important shift away from its quattrocento predecessors insofar as it adds to the burden of educating the young for civil society the freight of forming a cultural style of nobility.[85] In that sense, the shift that Carlo Ginzburg has noted for Europe in general, from a model in which cultural and intellectual resources circulated between the bottom and top rungs of the social hierarchy to one in which aristocratic and noble values increasingly defined an urbane and intellectual culture set apart from popular culture, is a shift reflected both in these later treatises on the household economy as well as in the immense popularity of courtesy books. Paradoxically, there is an extremely close relationship, as Ginzburg has noted, between the development of printing and a relatively widespread diffusion of aristocratic and noble values as exclusive of those who do not

---

[82] Tasso, *Dialoghi*, 355. Tasso does provide a manual for handling situations in which a man has a lesser social status than his wife. See Jordan, 148n. On Silvio Antoniano and others, see Frigo 114, 127–8n, citing Antoniano, 39.

[83] Tasso, 357.

[84] Tasso, 357. On Alberti, see Jordan, 47.

[85] Frigo, 103–22, esp. 107.

share them.[86] Printing codified distinctions into an elaborate set of rules for making such distinctions. Where Huizinga saw a sort of baroque elaboration of chivalrous codes that no longer corresponded to the order of civil society, I would argue, on the contrary, that life successfully imitated art – that these aristocratic codes came to create a more clearly defined social hierarchy.[87]

Nonetheless, when courtesy books and treatises on the household economy codified the values of urbanity and the civilizing process, they did not, as Hans Baron has characterized late quattrocento humanism under Lorenzo de' Medici, advocate a retreat into the contemplative life and the abandonment of public life. Quite the contrary. The cinquecento and seicento witnessed the fusion of noble educative discipline into the formation of civil society at large, and the religious formation of noble values was a second important step in the formation of the body politic.

Certainly, few treatises reveal as starkly the new vision of discipline and social order as Cardinal Silvio Antoniano's *Dell'educazione cristiana de' figliuoli libri III*, which argues that

The poor must remain content with their condition and not be jealous of the rich. . . . In this life the condition of the poor is better than that of the rich, because the most excellent things of nature such as the light of the sun, the breathing of healthy fresh air, of life, health, strength, and other such things, the poor enjoy no less, indeed, rather more than the rich. And the poor should not think that the rich undertake less effort, because the rich are responsible for preserving public peace, maintaining justice, defending the poor so that they are not oppressed by the more powerful, and providing material support. The poor must be grateful for this and remember it, rendering love, obedience, and loyalty to the rich.[88]

---

[86] C. Ginzburg, *The Cheese and the Worms: The Cosmos of a Sixteenth-Century Miller* (New York: Viking Penguin, 1982) xxiv–xxv, 125–6. Of the vast literature on printing, the reader is referred especially to Elizabeth Eisenstein, *The Printing Press as an Agent of Change* (2 vols., Cambridge: Cambridge University Press, 1979). Eisenstein argues (1:361n), although cautiously, that in England, at least, printing even in the sixteenth century aimed at "the middling sort" but also notes that printing reinforced the distinction already latent in manuscripts between those who had access to Latin culture and those who did not. See idem, "The Advent of Printing and the Problem of the Renaissance," *Past and Present* 45 (1969): 19–89, at 66–8; Walter Ong, *Ramus, Method, and the Decay of Dialogue: From the Art of Discourse to the Art of Reason* (Cambridge: Harvard University Press, 1958, repr. 1983), 75–98; Natalie Zemon Davis, "Printing and the People," in *Society and Culture in Early Modern France* (Stanford: Stanford University Press, 1975), 189–226.

[87] J. Huizinga, *The Autumn of the Middle Ages*, trans. Rodney Payton and Ulrich Mammitzsch (Chicago: University of Chicago Press, 1996), 61–125. On the codification of noble values into a mental universe, see Frigo, 9.

[88] Silvio Antoniano, *Dell'educazione cristiana de' figliuoli libri III* (Cremona: C. Diaconi, 1609), 500, cited in Frigo, 125n.

In short, the relationship between rich and poor, nonnoble and noble, is one of patronage and discipline, and it is not at all irrelevant that the practice of having the inmates of charitable institutions pray for their benefactors became widespread, not only in Tuscany but throughout Italy, in the later cinquecento.

How the demands of discipline played themselves out in Tuscan charity is the subject of later chapters. It is now time to consider how lineage ideology expressed itself in law, especially communal statues, and how individuals used charitable institutions to implement broader family strategies to fulfill as well as evade the harsh demands generated by the collision of law and practice.

3

LAW AND THE MAJESTY OF PRACTICE

HISTORIANS AND ANTHROPOLOGISTS OF THE MEDITERRANEAN WORLD have, for a long time, assumed that a strictly patriarchal model governed gender relations and that this model was fixed geographically over the entire Mediterranean world and chronologically from the Homeric age to the nineteenth century. More recent research, however, suggests that equality of property rights between men and women was not a progressive trend but a discontinuous series of advance and retreat.[1] By the late Roman empire, for example, women exercised considerable autonomy and independence concerning property rights, even though in theory these were vested in the male head of household.[2] The use of the *fideicommissum* (a testamentary restriction on alienation of property) during the Roman Empire as a legal instrument to keep the patrimony together was often undermined in practice by the specific exigencies of families that did not conform to the ideal structural model. In more modern examples, even areas with strict rules concerning the ideal transmission of property to the eldest son conformed to the ideal pattern in barely one-third of cases.[3]

Moreover, the use of the *fideicommissum* did not automatically imply a wish to entail patrimony in perpetuity: indeed, Roman law had forbidden "in perpetuity" clauses altogether in the transmission of property.[4] In the classical age, the infamous *patria potestas*, which theoretically prevented a son from owning property during his father's lifetime unless the son had been

---

[1] David Kertzer and Richard Saller, eds., *The Family in Italy from Antiquity to the Present* (New Haven: Yale University Press, 1991), 13–14.

[2] Kertzer and Saller, *Family in Italy*, 13.

[3] Richard P. Saller, "Roman Heirship Strategies in Principle and in Practice," in *Family in Italy*, 26–47, at 35, citing R. Sieder and M. Mitterauer, "The Reconstruction of the Family Life Course: Theoretical Problems and Empirical Results," in *Family Forms in Historic Europe*, ed. R. Wall, J. Robin, and P. Laslett (Cambridge: Cambridge University Press, 1983), 309–46, at 312.

[4] Saller, "Roman Heirship Strategies," 45.

emancipated, affected less than half of males of marriageable age because their fathers were no longer living.[5] This chapter argues that similar discontinuities between law and practice governed the experience of sixteenth-century Tuscan families and that such families used both traditional charitable institutions and religious institutions as part of their broader family strategies to cope with the demands of dowry and honor.

Law: Dowry and Inheritance

The dowry and female honor were closely linked in Mediterranean gender ideology and legal theory, even though dowerless marriages were possible, if rare.[6] In particular, both the construction of female honor and the institution of dowry served the larger function of marriage as an economic institution for the transmission of property and the preservation of families and their wealth through several generations.[7] The dowry, too, was a guarantee enforced by payment that, by excluding women from equal shares in an inheritance, provided greater assurance that the patrimony would remain undivided and allowed the continuity of succession through the patriline.[8]

[5] Saller, "Roman Heirship Strategies," 38. For an important opposing view to Saller's, however, see Yan Thomas, "The Division of the Sexes in Roman Law" in *From Ancient Goddesses to Christian Saints*, ed. Pauline Schmitt Pantel, vol. 1 of *A History of Women in the West,* ed. Georges Duby and Michele Perrot (Cambridge/London: Belknap Press of Harvard University Press, 1992), 83–137, at 90–5.

[6] On dowerless marriages in classical antiquity, see Pomeroy, *Goddesses, Whores, Wives and Slaves*, 63; on the association between dowry and honor, see Julius Kirshner, *Pursuing Honor while Avoiding Sin* (Milan: A Giuffrè, 1978).

[7] Family preservation was a sufficient motive for fifteenth-century Florentines to misrepresent the ages of their daughters in the 1427 Catasto in hopes of getting a more advantageous match. See Molho, "Deception and Marriage Strategy in Renaissance Florence: The Case of Women's Ages," *Renaissance Quarterly* 41 (1988): 193–217 and idem, *Marriage Alliance*, 11–12. Nonetheless, the traditions of Roman civil law and of canon law that governed it often had to be renegotiated through statutory modification and legal precedent. There is some evidence, moreover, that by the mid-sixteenth century, contemporaries were growing weary of the centrality of dowry: cf. Michelangelo's letter to his nephew Lionardo in *Il Carteggio di Michelangelo,* ed. P. Barocchi and R. Ristori (5 vols., Florence: Studio per Edizioni Scelte, 1965–83), 4:375, in which he advises Lionardo not to place as much emphasis on dowry as on the personal qualities of a future spouse. I thank William E. Wallace for this reference, cited in his "'The Greatest Ass in the World': Michelangelo as Writer," 2006, Geske Lecture for the Hixson-Lied College of Fine and Performing Arts, University of Nebraska – Lincoln (Lincoln: Hixson-Lied College of Fine and Performing Arts, 2006), 25. This was echoed by the Milanese moralist Silvio Antoniano in 1584.

[8] The following discussion relies heavily on Thomas Kuehn, "Some Ambiguities of Female Inheritance Ideology in the Renaissance," *Continuity and Change* 2 (1987): 11–36, reprinted in Kuehn, *Law, Family and Women: Toward a Legal Anthropology of Renaissance Italy* (Chicago/London: University of Chicago Press, 1991), 238–57. For an example of dowry as central to the preservation of agnatic masculine ties, see the statute of Trent cited in Kuehn, *Law, Family, and Women*, 239.

The dowry, in other words, especially as it evolved after the reintroduction of Roman Law into the medieval West, acted in theory as compensation to women for their exclusion from inheritance and from all further claims on the estate of her natal family, although as a widow she could still claim their support if she returned to them.[9]

Don Silvano Razzi's treatise on charity, for example, published in 1576, delineated clearly and precisely the property relationships between husbands and wives. Under normal circumstances, he argued, wives had no more right to disburse charity from the conjugal estate than nuns had to distribute patrimony of convents. In both cases, one cannot give what one does not have, and wives had no property of their own in precisely the same way that nuns had given over all private ownership to the convent. However, Razzi argued, women were free to give alms from any property of their own that they had brought to the marriage, so long as they did so moderately, so as not to impoverish their husbands. Although husbands and wives were equal in the act of matrimony, concerning property, the husband always held authority over the wife. This is clearly not the same as saying that women could not own property, and it is an important distinction, but from a practical point of view, the aim was to exclude women from the control of property already in the male line.[10]

In Thomas Kuehn's view, ideology concerning this function of dowry did not rigidly govern law or practice. Indeed, Kuehn notes that *ius commune*, the body of common law transmitted through the opinions and advice of jurists in both canon and civil law, was itself flexible in the interpretation of just how excluded women had to be to preserve agnatic succession – much more flexible than were late medieval communal statutes, especially in Tuscany. Although in theory marriage and dowry symbolized the relaxation of the bride's father's *patria potestas* and its transmission to the new husband, in practice fathers remained concerned after their daughters' marriages to look after their welfare or to use their "former" power to negotiate arrangements in their family's favor.[11] Communal legislation, moreover, did not

---

[9] Much recent scholarship has focused on the Florentine statutes of 1415 that governed intestacy and succession. Although rules governing intestacy also generally influenced rules of succession when a will actually existed, such rules had some, if not much, flexibility when it came to actual cases. For a clear and intelligent discussion of fifteenth-century inheritance practice in Florence, see Ann Crabb (2000), *The Strozzi of Florence: Widowhood and Family Solidarity in the Renaissance* (Ann Arbor: University of Michigan Press), 35–41.

[10] Silvano Razzi, *Trattato dell'opere di misericordia e corporali, e spirituali* (Florence: Bartolomeo Sermartelli, 1576), 66.

[11] Thomas Kuehn, "Person and Gender in the Laws," in *Gender and Society*, ed. J. Brown and R. C. Davis 87–106, at 93. See also Kuehn, "Women, Family, and *Patria Potestas* in Late Medieval

take exclusion from inheritance by reason of dowry as chiseled in concrete but modified legal precedent according to both the advice of such jurists as Bartolo di Sassoferrato and the demands of practice.[12]

The five cases Kuehn examines, taken from Alessandro Bencivenni's commentary on the 1415 communal statues of Florence, make clear that in practice, as opposed to theory, the dowry did not quiet a woman's claims either to inheritance or to further redress. This was especially true when statute failed to cover all the possible permutations of familial relations.[13] In such cases, commentators eschewed statutory interpretations favorable to the male line if the interests of cognates were thereby prejudiced.[14] Kuehn's research paints a portrait of male testators in patrician families who attempted to use the norms of agnatic succession embodied in Roman law to preserve the integrity of family honor and patrimony but who were sometimes opposed by women and the claims of their relatives. Although these were a minority of cases, they were statistically significant, so that in practice jurists interpreted the law to stifle too rigid an application of patrilineal inheritance rules.

Isabelle Chabot, however, drawing from a much broader sample of testaments and interpreting them in the light of the evolution of statutory law from 1325 to 1415, paints a much less equivocal portrait of the way in which the dowry, in Kuehn's words, "broadened [a woman's] dependence as a woman on support coming from property controlled by a man."[15] Even the cases in which Florentine testators were unusually generous in providing for women are classic cases of exceptions that prove the rule. Women were much more likely to be given control over property when there were no male heirs, and in cases in which male heirs became a possibility after the testament was drawn up, wills were often quickly changed to draw the inheritance back into the male line.

As Chabot has pointed out, in Florence even the generous annuities offered to widows in exchange for guardianship of their minor male heirs were more directed toward safeguarding the patrimony of the patriline than toward the material comfort of widows.[16] Further, even though Giulia Calvi,

---

Florence," *Tijdschrift voor Rechtsgeschiedenis* 49 (1981): 127–47, reprinted in Kuehn, *Law Family and Women*, 197–211. On dowries and family strategy, see also Donald Queller and Thomas F. Madden, "Father of the Bride: Fathers, Daughters, and Dowries in Late Medieval and Early Renaissance Venice," *Renaissance Quarterly* 46 (1993): 685–711.

[12] Kuehn, *Law, Family, and Women,* 241–4.

[13] In such cases, common law typically provided a broader interpretation of female inheritance rights, according to Kuehn, *Law, Family, and Women,* 245, because, in the consilium of Nello di San Gimignano "common law . . . makes no distinction between cognates and agnates."

[14] Kuehn, *Law, Family and Women,* 250.

[15] Ibid., 243.

[16] Chabot, "La dette des familles," 247–50.

who has studied the magistracy of wards (Magistrato dei Pupilli) from the mid-sixteenth century forward, argues that this magistracy gave women considerable freedom in terms of the guardianship of their sons and their sons' patrimony, this did not extend to remarriage. Indeed, argues Calvi, it was precisely the mother's exclusion from the inheritance grid that made it safe to entrust guardianship of children and their estates to widows. Her exalted status was, in effect, a tribute to her powerlessness. Once a widow remarried and deferred guardianship to the Magistrato dei Pupilli, she was legally dead: in no event could she become guardian to her children a second time.[17] Indeed, one of the primary functions of the Magistrato dei Pupilli was not so much the guardianship of orphans as the guardianship of lineage or, even more precisely, to provide assistance to those left behind in the inexorable march of the system of patrilineal inheritance.[18]

These aims were hardly mutually exclusive, as the case that Giulia Calvi cites from 1590 demonstrates. In that particular case, Settimia, the daughter of Count Nicola Orsino, on the verge of remarriage, had, by virtue of her husband's will, been appointed guardian of two minor children. Her cognate relative, Giovan Battista Simoncelli, broke into her house with several armed men and proceeded to take inventory, on the pretext that Settimia, from what he had heard, had already remarried, thus instantly losing claim to her dowry and her first husband's estate. The local *podestà* turned a blind eye and ordered that the inventory be completed. The count turned to the Magistrato dei Pupilli and sought redress against the decision of the local *podestà*, both on the grounds of lineage to make sure that the family patrimony was not lost and to make sure that Settimia was not deprived of her guardianship of the two minor children.

This case illustrates, in fact, the weakness of the prevailing inheritance system, because even though her husband had attempted to appoint her guardian in his will, and even though her father intervened in her defense, the Simoncelli family was still able to recruit the local *podestà* to the cause of seizing Settimia's property. Only the Magistrato dei Pupilli, which deferred prosecution of the Simoncelli to the criminal magistrates and reunited Settimia with her goods and guardianship, prevented what otherwise would

---

[17] Calvi, *Il contratto morale*, 19. Calvi's argument that evidence from the Magistrato dei Pupilli supports the optimistic view of the effect of the dotal system on women is more convincing for women of aristocratic families than for those without access to considerable familial resources. For a concise summary of Calvi's argument, see ibid., 25–8.

[18] Caroline Fisher, "The State as Surrogate Father: State Guardianship in Renaissance Florence, 1368–1532" (Ph.D. diss., Brandeis University, 2003), 27: "An examination of state guardianship within the context of governmental initiatives enacted between the Black Death of 1348 and the 1434 downfall of the oligarchical regime responsible for those initiatives shows how state guardianship fit into a more general governmental program to support lineages."

have been a bitter and irreconcilable struggle between two powerful patrilineal claims to property.[19]

Certainly Giovanni Morelli argued in his *Ricordi* that it was better to leave
an inheritance in the hands of the officials of the Pupilli than in the power of
women.[20] Paradoxically, the Venetian experience both in law and practice
would have further served to justify Morelli's concerns. In Venice, when
women by statute were much freer to dispose of their property through
inheritance than they were in Florence, they tended to do so in ways that
"undermine[d] . . . the wealth of patrilineal families," leaving property and
dotal assets to women "on the basis of affection rather than strict kinship."[21]

This relative freedom concerning female testation in Venice may well
also explain why Queller and Madden have argued that Pierre Bourdieu's
model of "gaming strategy," in which each "player" develops strategies to
maximize his or her family's advantages in the marriage market, does not adequately describe the behavior of Venetian fathers. Indeed in Venice, fathers
contributed a minority share of most women's dotal assets, and nonpater-
nal sources (taken cumulatively), especially those of women, contributed a
majority share, which itself fueled Venetian dowry inflation.[22] Thus, if statutory law uniformly enunciated the principle that the *exclusio propter dotem*
was a compensation for the loss of inheritance, the alleged unity of the
Mediterranean world completely falls apart in north-central Italy. In Turin,
for example, the statutes of 1360, following Lombard law, prescribed partible
inheritance and contained no provision specifically excluding women from
inheriting property.[23] The same held true for the 1407 statutes of Savigliano
and the 1347 statutes of Parma. By contrast, in the same region, the statutes
of Chieti (1313) and Cuneo (1380) prescribed that children from the first
marriage received two-thirds of the maternal dowry, whereas in Cremona
they received three-quarters.[24]

If the proliferation of feminine monastic foundations does have any relationship both to dowry inflation and to changes in inheritance practice, then

---

[19] Calvi, *Il contratto morale*, 81–4.

[20] Chabot, "La dette des familles," 249n., citing Giovanni di Pagolo Morelli, *Ricordi*, ed. Vittorio
Branca, (Florence: Le Monnier, 1956), 216.

[21] See Jordan, *Renaissance Feminism*, 42, citing Stanley Chojnacki, "Dowries and Kinsmen in Early
Renaissance Venice," *Journal of Interdisciplinary History*, 5 (1975): 571–600, reprinted in *Women
in Medieval Society*, ed. Susan M. Stuard (Philadelphia: University of Pennsylvania Press, 1976),
173–98.

[22] Queller and Madden, "Father of the Bride," 688, 693–9.

[23] Sandra Cavallo, *Charity and Power in Early Modern Italy: Benefactors and Their Motives in Turin,
1541–1789* (Cambridge/New York: Cambridge University Press, 1995), 173.

[24] Chabot, "La dette des familles," 280, n. 24, citing Franco Niccolai, *La formazione del diritto
successorio negli statuti comunali del territorio lombardo-tosco* (Milan: A. Giuffrè, 1940): 172–3, 175,
182, 190. For similarly nuanced coverage of statutes, see Kuehn, "Person and Gender," 94–5.

one might reasonably expect both dowry inflation and changes in inheritance practice to become noticeable in the middle of the fifteenth century. Certainly as early as the late trecento, dowry inflation was a sufficiently pressing problem that testators addressed it more frequently in their wills in Siena, whereas in Venice the senate attempted unsuccessfully to address the same problem with legislation.[25] As suggested earlier, the connection between dowry inflation and inheritance practice was stronger in Florence in the early sixteenth than in the early fifteenth century.

There is no doubt that at least two superintendents of Florence's foundling hospital of the Innocenti during the mid-sixteenth century saw the preponderance of females in the institution as directly related to inheritance. In 1572, for example, Vincenzio Borghini argued that the financial strain on the Innocenti caused by the influx of girls, as well as the enormous number of lawsuits it had to fight could be greatly reduced if the grand duke would enact legislation declaring that children who were abandoned to the Innocenti did not thereby lose their inheritances and that the hospital should be free to exercise complete legal authority over the assets of its foundlings:

> A short time ago, certain people near Bibbiena, after the father of a little girl who had some property had died, sent her here. The moment I heard about it, I had the property seized, because it seemed to me that it belonged to that little girl and to the hospital that had become her father and that had taken her in, and not to those wretched relatives. And finding some way to fix these ugly and wicked situations, I think, would be considered a pious and exemplary deed. I am certain that there is more than one case of this kind that has come our way, in which they have too many children, so they send us the surplus, and usually we get the girls, whom they throw away as though they were puppies. I don't know how justice can be served when these little children are disinherited and deprived of their portion. Not so long ago another case arose which we knew about because it involved a relative's dispute brought to the wards' court, but which otherwise we would not have heard of. It would seem a good idea for Your Excellency to be able to put a stop to this lack of conscience and lack of charity on the part of these bad fathers and relatives so as not to make the hospital a meat market.[26]

---

[25] Samuel K. Cohn, Jr., *Death and Property in Siena*, 28. A similar concern with the escalating cost of dowries animated Venetian parenthood. See Madden and Queller, "Father of the Bride," 688, and Chojnacki, "Dowries and Kinsmen," 571–2. In 1420, the Venetian Senate placed a limit of 1,600 ducats on patrician dowries, which by 1500 or so it had to raise to 3,000 ducats.

[26] AOIF Suppliche e sovrani rescritti (VI, 1,) fol 442v, 14 February 1571: "et poco fa, certi verso Bibbiena, essendo morto il padre d'una puttina che havea certi beni, La mandorono qui. Prima havutone notitia, n'ho fatto pigliar la tenuta, parendomi dovere che e sieno di quella creatura et dello spedale che è divenuto suo padre et l'ha ricevuta per figliuola et La tiene, et no[sic] di que' parenti sciagurati . . . Et il riparare a' questi simili modi brutti et scellerati, crederci che fusse

By the mid-sixteenth century in Bologna as well, the commentator Giovanni Boccadiferro placed dowry inflation at the center of his argument for female reclusion. Without convents, Boccadiferro argued, and given the excess of females and the high cost of dowering them, a father might otherwise be forced to have his daughter marry down for inability to supply a dowry.[27]

Indeed, even within marriage, historians of women argue, the institution of the dowry systematically enforced the subservience of women.[28] When this line of reasoning is taken to an extreme, the dowry system is represented as legitimizing the equivalence between women and property, making brides-to-be mere pawns to be exchanged for the larger pieces of property and social status that marriage alliance made possible. It is difficult, nonetheless, to understand why the institution of dowry makes women property to any greater extent than bridewealth does for men. Furthermore, the dowry placed women at the center of the most important economic transaction of a patrician family's life cycle: marriage. More important, even though the dowry in such a strictly patriarchal setting as Florence reverted to the wife's male relatives in case she became a widow, among wealthier families, it provided an opportunity to support the possibility of remarriage or monachation.

As Florentine families patched together marriage strategies in the face of dowry inflation, increasingly they tended to restrict the number of daughters offered in marriage. Indeed, these families faced a dotal crisis in late-fifteenth- and early-sixteenth-century Florence, in which dowry inflation was fueled by the very existence of the Monte delle doti itself. This also had the effect of causing the position of women vis-à-vis their families' finances to deteriorate even further, because "an increasing amount of real estate was being tied up in entails and was inalienable; it was therefore accessible only with great difficulty to wives and their heirs."[29]

---

opera santa et molto esemplare. Sono certi che questo caso ci è anche più d'una volta venuto alle mani, che, perche uno o gli altri suo figli habbino quel più, ce ne mandono parte, et massime si sono femine: et quanto è in loro, come se fossero cagniuoli, gli getton via. Ne so come sia giusto che questi poverini sieno così privati et diredati della portion loro. E non è molto che un simil caso se . . . a Pupilli che per gara nata fra essi parenti venne a luci che altrimente non si sapeva mai. Il porci quel riparo che paresse conveniente a V. A. S. raffrenerebbe La poca conscientia et nessuna charità di questi catti[vi] padri et parenti et non si farebbe dello spedale bottega."

[27] Cited in Zarri, "Monasteri femminili," 362.

[28] See Pierre Bourdieu, "Les stratégies matrimoniales dans le système de reproduction," *Annales: Economies, Sociétés, Civilisations* 22 (1972): 1105–27. For a useful corrective to that view, see Queller and Madden, "Father of the Bride," 685. On the institution of dowry, see Diane Hughes, "From Brideprice to Dowry," as well as J. Goody and S. Tambiah, *Bridewealth and Dowry* (Cambridge, England, 1973).

[29] Molho, *Marriage Alliance*, 324.

Thus, when one looks at the cycle of a wealthy household, the addition of sons did not often result in the diminution of patrimony for each one, but the addition of daughters brought with it no comparable elasticity of the part of the family fortune reserved for their dowries. Testators therefore often restricted the distribution of dowries by leaving four hundred florins if there was one surviving daughter, reduced to three hundred florins each for two, and a maximum of six hundred florins to cover all the daughters if they numbered three or more.[30]

Nor could Florentine women necessarily count on the dowry to support the burdens of widowhood. Although the *confessio dotis*, the final notarial act that succeeded the *sposalizio* and the *instrumentum matrimonialis*, in theory gave women strong juridical protection in the event that they became widowed, in practice the paperwork, according to the prescriptions of Florentine moralists and diarists, belonged among the private papers to which only husbands and their sons should have access. In 1364, for example, a petition to the priors complained of "the great number of widows" whose dowry paperwork could not be found, leaving them "reduced to begging and exposed to dishonor." As a solution, the resulting legislation gave testamentary clauses concerning the dowry the same juridical force as the *confessio dotis*.[31] Over the course of the fifteenth century, Florentine families increasingly had recourse to guarantors to pledge that the dowry would be restored in the event the husband predeceased the wife.[32]

All of this is to say that dowry, far from providing unconditional support to systems of patrilineal inheritance, both supported and undermined them. Although the dowry was designed to give men complete control over the transmission of lineage property, it also implicitly recognized the existence of feminine property that was both separate and juridically autonomous.

---

[30] This particularly striking example, which is found in the February 1415 will of Geri di Antonio Geri, is cited in Chabot, "La dette des familles," 87, and can be found in ASF Notarile Antecosiminiano 10519, fol. 88v–90r, 21 February 1414: "Item iure infrascripte reliquit et legauit filiabus suis feminis legiptimis et naturalibus nascitur ex se et ex quacque eius uxore legiptime si fuerit una tantum pro ea dotanda florenos quadringentos auri/ si vero fuerunt duo trecentos auri pro qualibet earum si vera fuerint plurimum flor. sexcentus auri inter omnes."

[31] ASF Provvisioni Registri, 51, fol. 97v–98r, 9 January 1363, cited in Chabot, "La dette des familles," 112n: "Quod propter pestem mortalitatis que in millesimo trecentesimo quadragesimo octauo fuit et propter pestem che fuit de proximo inbreuiature notorum ciuitatis comitatus et districtus Florentie necquiuerunt et necquerent reperiri propter quod quam plures mulieres cum dotibus remanserunt destitute et indotate et eas recuperire non possunt quia non reperiuntur talia dotalia infrascripta et ob dicta eam mendicare cogunt et non possunt se nec suas filias trahere ad honorem nisis ad deappositus remedio succuratur."

[32] Chabot, "La dette des familles," 112–24, notes that the percentage of husbands acting as sole guarantors of restitution of the dowry declined from 40 percent before 1350 to 12.5 percent in 1520.

If such property was separate and autonomous, it could be transmitted, and thus undermined the very male control it was supposed to serve. Moreover, the more the institution of dowry served to conserve patrimony within the male line, the greater burden it placed on families to provide a large dowry for marriage, a smaller dowry for the convent, or some other means of support for which the system of inheritance made no provision.[33]

For less wealthy families, dowry inflation may have put the marriage of daughters out of financial reach, and there is especially strong evidence that by about 1530, monachation of younger daughters was becoming an established pattern even among the Florentine ruling elite: Molho's study of the dowry fund shows that from 1425 to 1499, 3.6 percent of women enrolled in the dowry fund took religious vows. That figure increased to 15.5 percent between 1500 and 1520, and to 28.2 percent after 1530. Moreover, because mortality rates for girls enrolled in the fund appear to have declined dramatically, this not only suggests a surplus of girls in the marriage market (because girls married at an earlier age than boys) but can be linked to a decline in the percentage of girls getting married (from 80 percent in the fifteenth century to 61.8 percent after 1530). Thus, "it was primarily the balance between marriages and religious vocations that was shifting in the opening decades of the sixteenth century."[34]

In Prato, these trends affected a surprisingly large proportion of the population: some 18 percent of the female citizen population in the sixteenth century could be found in existing convents and newer foundations, a population, moreover, not largely indigenous to Prato but of Florentine origin.[35] Although the continuing vitality of Savonarolan piety may have played some role in this transformation, a shift in the nature of the marriage market is a more likely explanation, a shift occasioned by dowry inflation that became especially acute and severe in the opening decades of the sixteenth century. From the last quarter of the fifteenth through the first quarter of the sixteenth century, the average size of dowries listed in the dowry fund increased from 1,430 to 1,852 florins. By comparison with the second quarter of the fifteenth century, the size of dowries by the 1520s had practically doubled.[36] Similar dowry inflation could be observed in Florentine *libri di famiglia* in which the average dowry, which had risen only from 925 to 954 florins from 1400 to 1499, suddenly rose to 1,388 florins between 1500 and 1520.[37]

---

[33] Chabot, "La dette des familles," 6.
[34] Molho, *Marriage Alliance*, 306–7.
[35] Elena Fasano-Guarini, ed., *Un microcosmo in movimento (1494–1815)*, 840.
[36] Molho, *Marriage Alliance*, 310.
[37] Chabot, "La dette des familles," 103.

Economic and social crises may also have played some role in decisions families made to commit their daughters to the religious life, for between 1525 and 1560, peaks in the percentage of women taking religious vows coincided with major dislocation. The first sharp increase occurred just after the siege of Florence in 1529–30, followed by a slightly higher peak around the time of the 1539 famine. Rates dropped off sharply again until Cosimo began his war of conquest with Siena in 1554, and between 1557 and 1558, more than 70 percent of girls enrolled in the dowry fund chose a religious profession.[38] This was a temporary phenomenon, however, that can be closely correlated with the price of grain. The two highest peaks, 1539 and 1558, coincide with the two periods that saw the lowest purchasing power of wages during the sixteenth century.[39]

It is also during precisely those times that hospital officials noticed sharp increases in the proportion of legitimate children admitted to the Innocenti and that often coincide with the foundation of new institutions to assist particularly needy girls.[40] If in Florence this phenomenon seems to have begun earlier than elsewhere and to have provided fewer options, by the end of the sixteenth century, it was widespread throughout many Italian cities, according to Silvio Antoniano's treatise on the Christian education of children. Although one might argue that Antoniano's clerical status is an unreliable guide to the everyday practices of lay families, bishops, both before and after the Council of Trent, heard dozens of cases of matrimonial difficulty, and often quite intimate details of the problems that beset conjugal life. Moreover, Antoniano's distrust of the conspicuous consumption involved in dowries seems to have been shared among at least some of the late-sixteenth-century Italian patriciate.[41]

Antoniano's work, which was published for the first time in 1584 and was by all accounts the most widely read treatise in late-sixteenth-century Italy on household and family life, took to task husbands who sought marriage partners not on the basis of their innate goodness and inclination to lead a good Christian life but because they brought a large dowry to the marriage. Such husbands, thought Antoniano, were more interested in bringing home a prostitute or a commodity than in finding a good Christian wife. These

---

[38] Molho, *Marriage Alliance*, 305.

[39] Molho, *Marriage Alliance,* 305; Richard Goldthwaite, *The Building of Renaissance* Florence, 436–9.

[40] For an example involving the Innocenti, see AOIF Filze d'Archivio (LXII) 31, fol. 19r, 7 January 1592.

[41] Cases of matrimonial dissatisfaction more often came under the purview of ecclesiastical than civil courts, unless such disputes involved marital property. See Joanne Ferraro, *Marriage Wars in Late Renaissance Venice*, Studies in the History of Sexuality (Oxford: Oxford University Press, 2001), 5–10. For an example of the decline of the importance of dowry, see n. 7 to this chapter.

men ran the risks inherent in any marriage where wealth and position were unequal – "the bigger the sea, the more violent the tempest" – which to Antoniano meant that when a woman with an enormous dowry married a much less wealthy man, both partners were likely to find the resulting inequality intolerable and a source of constant marital friction. "A rich enough dowry the wife brings who is dowered with humility, a sense of shame, modesty, sobriety, tranquillity and care for her own family."[42]

To Antoniano the sort of excess display to which sumptuary legislation was properly addressed was intimately connected to dowry inflation. Inflated dowries provided a false excuse for display and pomp, "which have increased so much in marriage celebrations, in clothes, in other precious ornaments, as well as in the number of slaves and servants, cooks and carriages," so that families were financially ruined. Such display, and the dowry inflation of which display was merely a symptom, betokened the potential breakdown of important hierarchical distinctions, because "every female citizen in ornaments looks like a noble lady." Despite the sumptuary laws in force, Antoniano complained, no one objects, and as each generation tries to outdo its neighbor and its predecessors, these evils increase over time and are therefore more difficult to cure.[43] At the center of Antoniano's treatise was a concern for order, and inflated dowries and excess display, in his view, were the occasion for most of the seven deadly sins to sow social and political chaos, exacerbated by the likelihood that noble families, and indirectly the state, were vulnerable to ruin.

Certainly in Antoniano's view, dowry inflation placed young women from noble families at risk in the marriage market, and therefore in danger of being consigned to institutions. Single women and especially widows were even less well protected among lower economic strata, especially if they were at the mercy of rapacious kinsmen.[44] Moreover, practical barriers to remarriage often made convents or other forms of total institutionalization the only honorable alternative.[45] Husbands often stipulated in their wills that wives could accede to their portion of the legacy only if they stayed unmarried, chaste, and holy. Even women at all social levels who faced no such restrictions found it difficult to remarry, and would-be husbands were reluctant to take on and support a widow's children and face the conflicting

---

[42] Silvio Antoniano, *Tre libri dell'educatione christiana dei figliuoli*, 14r.
[43] Ibid., 15r–15v.
[44] Cohen, *Women's Asylums*, 27.
[45] Much of the following discussion relies on Cohen, *Women's Asylums*, 27–8. On the plight of widows in fifteenth-century Tuscany, see Isabelle Chabot, "Widowhood and Poverty in Late Medieval Florence," *Continuity and Change* 3 (1988): 291–311.

claims to patrimony. Florence's statutes of 1415, in fact, completely excluded the claims of children from a first marriage to inheritance, part of a larger overall strategy among Florentine elite families to concentrate wealth and patrimony in the male line.[46]

As a result, women who did remarry gave up their children to their husband's family, to an institution, or, failing provision for that, to the care of the officials of the Pupilli. The Pupilli statutes of 1473 complained that widows who initially hoped to live with their children took control of their estates and then sued in court for their dowries, grossly underestimating the value of their children's estates to complete a successful petition, and then remarried with the dowry, leaving their children with a severely depleted estate.[47] Moreover, women frequently cited remarriage as a cause of child abandonment. Claims not pursued by the former husband's family or the new husband might be taken up eagerly by the widow's family, especially if she had not been emancipated – and emancipation became an ever receding possibility over the course of the fifteenth century.[48] Taken together, these situations suggest a variety of responses to dilemmas over dowry and inheritance, and it is to this variety of responses in Tuscany, and the involvement of institutions in those responses, that I now turn.

The Majesty of Practice

The difficulties of arranging inheritance to cope with the conflicting demands of the law, the testament, and the situation of the family itself, suggest that not in every case did families favor the eldest son, even if the will itself specified him as the heir. The wills of Ser Andrea di Cristoforo Nacchianti and of his son Giovanbattista provide an interesting case in point. Ser Andrea Nacchianti was a prosperous Florentine notary, one of three brothers in what, numerically at least, was a large extended family. In his last will and testament, drawn up shortly before his death in 1510, he put his only son Giovanbattista, seven years old, under the tutelage of three guardians and appointed him as universal heir. During the seven years that elapsed between his father's

---

[46] *Statuta populi et communis Florentiae: publica auctoritate, collecta, castigata et praeposita anno salutis MCCCCXV* (Fribourg: Michaelem Kluch, 1778–83), 222–3: "Qualiter succedatur in dotem uxoris premortue," cited in Chabot, "La dette des familles," 159, makes clear that the surviving husband and his sons of the most recent marriage had precedence over both sons and daughters from a first marriage.

[47] Francesca Morandini, *Statuti et ordinamenti dell'Ufficio de' pupilli et adulti nel periodo della Repubblica fiorentina (1388–1534)*, part 1: *Archivio Storico Italiano* 113 (1955): 550.

[48] Cohen, *Women's Asylums*, 27. On emancipation, see Thomas Kuehn, *Emancipation in Late Medieval Florence* (New Brunswick, NJ: Rutgers University Press, 1982), 90–6.

death and his own decision to join the Dominican order, Giovanbattista was resident at the Ospedale degli Innocenti.

The will of the elder Nacchianti, Ser Andrea, drawn up 19 February 1510, noted that he had kept Antonia, his wife's daughter from her earlier marriage to Ser Bartolomeo di Lorenzo (interestingly, also a Florentine notary), in his house and fed her and clothed her for about eight years, and that half his wife's dowry was to be used to continue the said maintenance. Andrea's heirs were strictly forbidden to interfere in any way with this arrangement.

Moreover, Andrea left an amount for the maintenance of his own wife Mona Dianora, which she was to receive only if she remained a widow, pursued an upright life, and lived with her son Giovanbattista after Andrea's death. Notwithstanding this, however, Giovanbattista, despite his privileged position as universal heir, and the provision made for him in his father's testament, ended up for six years in the Innocenti under the guardianship of its superintendent, Francesco Petrucci. In March 1510, Ser Andrea died, and a deposit was left to the Innocenti "for the needs of his son Giovanbattista." The funds for Giovanbattista's maintenance came from his executors' purchase of a farm for 915 florins, the security for which was given as a deposit to the hospital of Santa Maria Nuova.[49] On 12 May 1510, Mona Dianora, now Andrea's widow, had Francesco Petrucci, Antonio Sassolini, and Francesco di Lese Magalotti appointed as Giovanbattista's guardians.[50] According to Giovanbattista's will, drawn up when he was only fifteen so he could leave his estate to the Innocenti and join the Dominicans at San Marco, his father's will had left many obligations and debts. Moreover, because half of his mother's dowry went to Antonia, Giovanbattista "spent some time" at the Innocenti and had a debt of his own to satisfy to the hospital and to his tutors "for the expenses involved in feeding me."[51]

---

[49] AOIF Estranei Debitori, Creditori, e Richordi (CXLIV, 634), fol. 41 left, 12 May 1509: "Lo spedale di Santa Maria degli Innocenti di Firenze dee dare fl. duegentto venttinove s. L. d. in oro et y sei s. dieci e quali sono appresso al detto spedale overo spedalingho di detto sotto di x di marzo 1510 [sic] prossimo passato descritti in ser Andrea di Cristofano Nachianti sotto detto dì per seghuirne la voglia di Giovanbatista suo figliuolo." The corresponding *ricordanze* entry makes clear that the deposit is for Andrea's son, Giovanbattista: AOIF Ricordanze (XII, 6) Libro segreto di dipositi, fol. 4r, 10 March 1509: "Ser Andrea Nachianti de avere per insino adì 10 di marzo 1509 fl. dugento ventinove y sei s. 10 . . . per bisogno di Giovanbatista suo figliuolo." For evidence of the role of Santa Maria Nuova and of the farm used as collateral, see AOIF Estranei Debitori, Creditori, e Richordi (CXLIV, 634), fol. 67 right, 1 August 1511: "El podere questo adì primo d'aghosto si chomperò da ser Antonio di ser Jachopo da san Chasciano de avere ogi questo di sopra detto fl. noveciento quindici di sugielo.. che sttieno per sichurtà di Giovanbattista de ser Andrea Nachianti chome a pieno per detta chartta si vede in tutto fl. 915."

[50] ASF Archivio notarile antecosiminiano 16279 fol. 7r2–75v, 76r, 86r–86v, 12 May 1510.

[51] ASF Diplomatico, Ospedale degli Innocenti, 22 February 1517: "condidit testamentum per quod uoluit quod dimidia dotis dicte domine Dianore deueniat in domine Antonie et sit ipsius antonie

Lest this case seem to illustrate only the ways in which families could circumvent the statutes, several important caveats must be offered. First, only a small portion of Andrea's estate benefited his wife and wife's daughter from the first marriage. Indeed, only by dividing his wife's dowry in half could Andrea support Antonia at all, and even then only at the short-term expense of Giovanbattista. If anything, this case illustrates that when it came to minors, both girls *and* boys had to suffer to keep inheritance within the patriline. Second, once minority was overcome, the boy still inherited, and the girl, if she stayed unmarried and did not enter a convent, was at best a continued burden on the family. In theory, the inheritance system as represented by Andrea's will contained possible solutions to its own contradictions. The solutions were fragile at best, however, and an estate burdened with too much debt could easily force a minor child of either sex into institutional care.

Certainly a striking example of how Florentines had to provide for daughters from a first marriage, and how they viewed such arrangements, occurs in another act of family generosity undertaken by Ser Andrea Nacchianti in May 1500:

> I record this day, 6 May 1500, Maddalena, my daughter and wife of Giovanni Guidacci, came to the villa with her daughter, Papera, from her husband, Lionardo Mazzei. She commended her daughter to me and I turn commended her to Maddalena my wife. And seeing that she [Papera] is in need, I am happy to help the said girl as much as I can. And concerning what I spend on her, I want it understood that my heirs may never at any time try to extract anything from her, so that God might concede to me his grace that I stay healthy so I can help her and do her this favor that I recognize as a worthy charity.[52]

As he would do later in his last will and testament for Mona Antonia, Nacchianti also specified here that his heirs were not to attempt to extract

prout in dicto testamento disponitur. . . . Et considerans in hereditatem patris sui remansisse multa bona immobilia et multa nomina debitis et qualiter alique ex dictis debitis sunt tales a quibus ipse testator non intendit quod ab eis fiat exactio sed uoluit quod illi debitis habeantur pro cancellatis nomina quorum significauit et conmisit in secreto venerabili patri fratri Matteo Iacobi fratri Sancti Dominici di Fesulis."

[52] Ibid., fol. 123r, 6 May 1500: "Ricordo chome questo dì 6 di maggio La Maddalena mia figluola donna di Giovanni Guidacci venendo in villa meno seco la Papera sua figlioula di Lionardo Mazzei suo primo marito: et rachomandomela et così la raccomando alla Madalena mia donna. Et veduto il bisogno di quella sono contento d'aiutare detta fanciulla in quello potrò et di quello sspendesse in lei non intendo che mia heredi mai ne possino per alcuno tempo adomandare alchuna cosa che iddio mi conceda grazia stia sano acciò possi aiutarla et farle questo bene che cognosco è buona limosina."

reimbursement, which would undermine the charitable nature of his enterprise. The wording of this *ricordanze* entry is telling, underscoring as it does the homeless status even of granddaughters and that the testator undertook the project out of charity and need rather than out of a sense of family obligation. That even Nacchianti, whose wealth was not inconsiderable, pledged to help her "as much as I can," and that he viewed this as a charity case, also suggests just how vulnerable daughters from a first marriage were in families who were less wealthy or whose patriarchs were less giving – hence, the greater likelihood that a daughter from the first marriage might end up in a foundling home. Even in this *ricordanze*, it is clear that neither Andrea's nor his wife's assent was automatic but undertaken only after discussion and deliberation. The specific prohibition against extracting reimbursement also suggests that in the absence of such a prohibition, daughters of first marriages were routinely dunned for the expenses caused by their mother's desire to remarry.

Nonetheless, Papera was able to marry, much to Ser Andrea's delight, but it does not appear that helping her in any way he could involved a contribution to her dowry. Although Nacchianti was certainly willing to make whatever arrangements he could to make sure Papera was honorably married, she was clearly at a disadvantage on the marriage market. Moreover, Ser Andrea's resentment toward the Mazzei concerning Papera is evident: "not even the whole shop would be worth what I have spent on her nor would it ever be possible to satisfy what she has had from me living in my house and being fed at my expense."[53]

Her dowry was two hundred florins that had been invested for her in the Monte, but in Ser Andrea's eyes, Lorenzo da Prato was a disastrous potential bridegroom. First, although it was the duty of Lorenzo's family to pay for the dinner expenses associated with the celebration of the marriage, Ser Andrea, through Lorenzo's "ignorance" of custom, had to foot the bill of forty lire himself. Then Lorenzo further aggravated Ser Andrea by failing to acknowledge receipt of the dowry, so Ser Andrea retaliated by holding back the *donora* until Lorenzo da Prato had "done his duty." Indeed, as long as the *donora* was still in Florence, there Papera had to remain as well. This had the desired effect: Lorenzo acknowledged receipt of the dowry and *donora*, and Papera and her clothes went to Prato. Ser Andrea's *ricordanze* thus

---

[53] Ibid., fol. 144v, December 1508: "Se mi observera tale promessa sarà al debito suo che in su detta Papera o speso tanto che tutta decta bottega non lo vale et egli tenuti alimentati in casa mia et di quello anno avuto del mio non potrebbono mai satisfare."

reveal that whatever good his charity toward his granddaughter might have done for his soul, his finances did not suffer it gladly.[54]

This sort of treatment stands out even more strikingly when compared with Ser Andrea's treatment of a son his wife brought with her from her first marriage. Because at this point Andrea had no heirs in the direct male line (Giovanbattista had not yet been born), there was no issue of conflicting inheritance, but the sense that this young man was not received with great warmth comes through in Ser Andrea's notation:

> Here I will record that I, Ser Andrea, having taken for my wife Maddalena di Bartolomeo Angiolini, as one can see in this book on page 97, and then on 24 May she went to my villa in Pian di Ripoli and stayed there until the 20th of June. She brought with her Baccio her son from her first marriage and kept him here at my expense. And then he returned to Florence and continually stayed and is still staying in my house at my expense. And he is going to a shop to learn [a trade]. I made a record of it here because it is my intention to ask him to reimburse me for my expenses while he was here, because when I took Maddalena for my wife the agreement was that I did not want him in my house, and since he is there I intend that he should pay his way as I see fit.[55]

Nine months later, nonetheless, Baccio was still in the house largely because of the good offices of his mother. Ser Andrea's *ricordanze* make clear that he relented only reluctantly to make her happy and that he extracted a price for his consent:

> I record on this day the 27th of February 1491 that Baccio, son of Maddalena and her first husband Cristofano, brought into the house a quilt and an old bedcover which my wife said were his that he brought from the

---

[54] On the bride's non-dotal assets, see Julius Kirshner, "Materials for a Gilded Cage," 184–207, esp. at 193. For Nacchianti's complaints about his expenses, see AOIF Estranei (CXLIV, 633), fol. 144v, December 1508: "Di poi appresandosi il tempo di menar detta Papera a marito detto Lorenzo suo marito venne a Firenze et steti lui et suoi frategli et parenti in casa mia et quivi la meno a tutte mie spese che mi costorono dette spese piu di y40 che detto Lorenzo non fece dal canto suo quello susci et e consueto a me tocchò a suplire alla sua ignoranza che allui e suoi parenti di Firenze e di Prato e a Mazzei e Guidacci io ebbi a ffare e coniunti."

[55] AOIF Estranei (CXLIV, 633) fol. 99r: "Qui farò ricordo ch'avendo io ser Andrea tolto per donna la Madalena di Bartollomeo Angiolini come si vede in questo @ 97 di poi adi 24 di maggio lei andò in villa mia di Piano di Ripoli et stettivi insino adì 20 di giugno et seco menò Baccio suo figliuolo del primo matrimonio et tennelo quivi a mie spese et così di poi tornò a Firenze e continualmente s'e stato e sta in casa mia a mie spese. Et va a bottega a imparare o nne facto qui ricordo perche è mia intenzione del tempo stara in casa mia di domandargli le spese che quando tolsi per donna detta Madalena. E patti farono che io non lo volevo in casa essendovi intendevo a domandare le spese seconde a me paresse."

house of Mona Angelica, the sister, because she had given them to him
to keep. He [Baccio] wanted to sell this quilt and bedcover to provide for
his clothing. I, to comfort my wife, was happy to take it from him and
because in the guild it fetched sixteen lire I was happy to credit him with
eighteen. And here below I will make a note of what he will get from me
for the said account.

Clearly Ser Andrea's hostility was at war with his generosity, because not
only did he credit Baccio with two lire more than he actually got for the
items sold, he also bought 22 lire worth of clothes for him without even
mentioning that this was beyond the original amount credited.[56]

Yet to compare all these examples is instructive because the inability of
daughters or granddaughters from a first marriage to support themselves
added another dimension to the difficulty of finding a place for them in the
extended household. From a male child of a first marriage, one could at least
require that he be self-supporting. By contrast, a daughter or a granddaughter
was not merely inconvenient but also an economic liability to the second
husband and his family, to the point that helping her was an act of charity
well beyond the normal routine of family obligation.

Families of lesser status did have the option of having their female children
employed elsewhere as domestic servants, and thus, Ser Andrea found himself
bargaining with mothers of young girls, as happened in early February 1492
when Ginevra came to stay with the Nacchianti as a servant. Her mother,
a widow, wanted her to stay eight years, at the end of which, providing the
girl's service was satisfactory, her mother would receive a hundred lire. Ser
Andrea, however, only wanted to give her eighty, and, moreover, to treat her
according to her performance. This arrangement suggests yet another way in
which a parent without resources might avoid the possibility of abandoning
a female child, and heartless as it may seem that the child should work while
her mother collected the money, the fact that she collected only at the end
of the eight years suggests that this might have been one way of putting
together a meager dowry or a supplement to a dowry.[57] For some reason

---

[56] Ibid., fol. 100r, 27 February 1491: "Ricordo chome adì 27 febraio 1491 Baccio figliuolo della
Madalena mia donna che fu figliuolo del di[sic] Cristofano suo primo marito recò in casa uno
coltrone et una sargia vecchii: le quali la Madalena mia donna disse erano suoi che gli recò da
casa mona Angelica sua sorella perche gle'l'aveva dato in serbanza volea vendere questo coltrone
et sargia per vestersi. Et io a conforti di decta mia donna fui contento torgli et perche nell'arte
se ne trovava y.xvi io fui contento contarcegli y xviii e qui dapie faro ricordo di quello ara da me
per decto conto _____ fl. y. 18" [at bottom of page is what he actually spent in clothes: y 22 s. 11
d. 4].

[57] On the relationship between late marriage for female domestic servants and dowry accumulation
in the seventeenth and eighteenth centuries, see Angela Arru, "Il matrimonio tardivo dei servi e

Ginevra did not last long, but the following year, when Ser Andrea hired Marietta, a girl "about eight or nine years old," as a servant for a term of ten years, the record makes explicit that the hundred lire was meant as a dowry for her to be married when the ten years had elapsed. If she left before then, her salary was at Ser Andrea's discretion.[58] In this respect, too, when the hospital sent out girls with the expectation of an eventual dowry, the institution was very much in line with the practices of the families from which these girls had come.

Families from the countryside also seem to have imagined domestic servitude as a viable alternative to abandonment when a mother remarried. Thus, the household of the silk merchant Tommaso Banchozzi, whose own family circumstances are discussed later in the chapter, took in a twelve-year-old girl, Fiore, whose father had died and who came from the main chain of the Apennines beyond Serravalle. Tommaso Banchozzi took her in for twelve years as his household servant, at the end of which he promised to give her seventy lire and in the meantime to provide clothes and shoes.

> It was my intention and will to do this even though I didn't make a note of it at the time, because she does not have a father, and that day [10 August 1514] she was sent to me here at home by a woman from the Val di Nievole who had sent her. She had fled from her relatives' house because she was dying of hunger. Her mother had remarried and the girl was in stockings and nude so that only with some effort was she able to cover up her flesh. Since none of her relatives showed up I was unable to put anything in writing, so here below I will make a note of everything I spend on her. On 25 June 1515 one of her brothers, the father's cousin was here, and he said he would come back to make a record but he never came back.[59]

delle serve," *Quaderni Storici* 23 (1988): 469–96, and for the 1400s, see Christiane Klapisch-Zuber, "Women Servants in Florence," in *Women and Work in Pre-industrial Europe* ed. Barbara Hanawalt (Bloomington: Indiana University Press, 1986), 56–80, at 68. For notice of a servant's contract, see AOIF Estranei (CXLIV, 633) fol. 99v, 1 February 1491: "Ricordo chome oggi questo dì primo di febraio 1491 la ginevra figliuola fu [left blank in original] venne a stare in casa nostra la quale menò la madre sua chiamata mona [left blank in original] disse voleva stesse anni otto a servire et forniti detti octo anni portandosi bene et servendo per detto tempo disse detta sua madre voleva avesse y cento e io volevo darle y. 80. La rimesse a me e secondo e sua portamenti io la tractero ch'iddio le conceda grazia facci bene."

[58] AOIF Estranei (CXLIV, 633) fol. 104r, 1 August 1493: "Ricordo farò qui da pie di quello spendero nella Marietta di . . . la quale a stare in casa pel mezzo di sua madre o lla a tenere anni x che s'intendono cominciati adì primo d'agosto 1493 et in fine de' detti anni x a avere y100 per maritarla avendo detto tempo d'anni 10 et partendosi prima disse fusse a mia discretione. La decta fanciulla è d'età d'anni 8 o nove in circha verano senza panni et con una camicia cattiva."

[59] AOIF Estranei (CXLIV, 89) fol. 18v, 18 February 1514: "Richordo questo dì 10 d'aghosto 1514 per insino adì 18 di febraio io tolsi la fiore d'anni dodici o in circha figliuola fu di Ventura di Valdinievole che stava alla chasa vochata alla magione di la da Serravalle la quale fare tolsi per

Thus, if wealthy families had to scramble to cover the problems caused by remarriage, for children of poorer families, the consequences could be devastating. In this particular case, it certainly left the twelve-year-old Fiore vulnerable to severe economic exploitation. Seventy lire for twelve years of work would still not have sufficed even for a peasant dowry.

In the Nacchianti family, boys could also be badly affected by the nebulous family status that resulted from their mother's remarriage. Cristofano di Lionardo Mazzei, Ser Andrea's grandson by his daughter's first marriage, was the family's resident juvenile delinquent. In May 1507, while Mona Gostanza, Mona Papera (Papera was the granddaughter "charity case"), and Ser Andrea were at home in his villa, Mona Maddalena, Andrea's second wife, was persuaded to leave the villa by the news that Cristofano had taken ill at the shop. While Papera and Gostanza were drying their hair, Cristofano arrived, and in Andrea's words: "his malady was that he had come to rob us." He forced open two large strongboxes of silver and jewels and fled to Montevarchi. Cristofano's family, in the meantime, were no help in tracking down their errant relative, so that when he finally reappeared in Florence two weeks later and was confronted about the theft, he said that he had sold everything to a fine cloth dealer and to an anonymous man from Bologna. However, "I believe he is lying through his teeth and rather that the woman he keeps got them, even though he denies it."[60] Nonetheless, Ser Andrea, extracting promises of a reformed life from his wayward grandson, bought him a horse, lent him ten ducats, and wrote him a letter of recommendation so he could go to Ancona and settle down to work there as a merchant, sealing all these good intentions with notarized contracts that Andrea would be repaid for all he had lent and that had been stolen from him.

Cristofano, however, got only as far as Montevarchi. He came back to Florence saying he had spent all the money and that he needed another six ducats, which Ser Andrea lent him, again with a promissory note drawn up in front of witnesses. On the next attempt to send him to Ancona, Ser

---

serva per tenerlla anni dodici e di poi darlle y. settanta e in questo tempo chalzarlla e vestirlla e a detto tempo dalle e sopradetti panni si trovera a suo dosso. E chosi e mia intentione e volonta di fare e io non o fatto una scrittura perche ella non a padre e questo dì detto mi fu menata qui a casa da una donna che ll'aueua menata di Valdinievole che s'era fugita da zio per che si moriva di fame e sua madre s'era rimaritata è in chaza e ignuda che a faticha poteva richoprire la charne e perche non c'e chapitato mai nessuno di sua io non o potuto farne scrittura ma que da pie io schriverò tutto quello ispenderò per indosso per detta Fiore e per suo chonto. E adì 25 di giugno 1515 ci fu uno suo fratello chugino del padre e detta fiore e disse tornarebbe a fare la scritta e non è tornato."

[60] AOIF Estranei (CXLIV, 633) fol. 136r, 5 May 1507: "Credo menta per la gola et credo piutosto che la femina che lui a tenuto di queste cose abbi avuto benchè lui lo neghi."

Andrea received word from his workers at Bagno a Ripoli that Cristofano had returned and once again was in need of help and shelter. This time Ser Andrea refused to help him or even speak with him, although he did send a new shirt and pair of shoes, swearing all the while that Cristofano would never be allowed to return to his villa, his shop, or his home in Florence. Nonetheless, Cristofano apologized, saying he had been robbed, and stayed at the hospital of Santa Maria Nuova to "serve the infirm at no charge."[61] Whatever reforms this might have produced in his character were certainly not immediately evident: he worked at several shops, including one owned by Ser Cristofano di Taddeo Nacchianti, continuing to sell things Ser Andrea had given him, and only when Mona Smeralda di Giovanni Mazzei died, leaving part of her inheritance to him, was Ser Andrea successful in filing a claim against the estate and recovering his money.[62]

Andrea was much more generous, however, with the "good" Cristofano, son of Andrea's cousin Taddeo Nacchianti, who was sent in 1488 to the household of Andrea and Maddalena as a boy to learn how to read. Andrea's generosity was not in the least ambivalent. When in 1495 Andrea sent off Cristofano to the *studio* in Pisa to get his degree in civil law, he both gave him money to buy books and lent him books from his extensive collection. It was not only family ties with his cousin that cemented this relationship: when Cristofano came back from studying civil law in March 1498 and once again stayed with Andrea, Andrea faithfully recorded all the expenses involved in clothing and books so that Taddeo would pay him back.[63] Nonetheless, the difference in treatment remains clear between sons in the direct male line and those who were not – so much the better, in either case, if, unlike daughters, they could pay their own way. The same more generous treatment was accorded to another Cristofano in the Nacchianti family, Cristofano di Piero Nacchianti, when he came to stay with Ser Andrea on 24 March 1498 so that he could

> go to the shop and learn and may it please God that he be in good health and that he learn and do well. I am recording my expenses for him because

[61] Ibid., fol. 136r, 5 May 1507: "s'era botato di stare a Sancta Maria Nuova a servire gl'infermi di decto spedale [per] amore dei lo ricesti e operai che lo spedalingo di detto spedale quello accetto piaccia a Dio da portale via di volere et fare bene abi efecto."

[62] On Cristofano selling what Andrea gave him, see ibid., fol. 141v, n.d., but on or before 13 August 1505. For the final restitution, see ibid., fol. 143r, August 1508.

[63] Ibid., fol. 89r, 2 May 1488: "Cristofano figliuolo di Taddeo venne a stare meco in Firenze a casa mia per studiare che Idio gli conceda grazia imparai et provenghi a buono commodo et a buona fine et facci honore alla casa nostra." See also fol. 114v, 2 November 1495, which indicates that Cristofano di Taddeo Nacchianti was studying civil law at the *studio* in Pisa using civil law books borrowed from Andrea.

his father wrote me that I should write what I spent on him so he can make good on it and repay me.[64]

Other families dealt with children from a first marriage by employing different strategies. The silk merchant Tommaso di Francesco Banchozzi recalled autobiographically in 1508 how on 8 November 1487 his mother had remarried, bringing her dowry of nearly 1,300 florins into her new alliance with Giovanbattista Quaratesi. On 17 November, Tommaso came to stay in his mother's and stepfather's house at Giovanbattista Quaratesi's expense, but on 16 February, "he kicked me out and did not want me to stay in the house any longer as appears in his *ricordanze*. I got from his house a couple of shirt rags and this and that."[65]

His sister appears to have been equally affected, because Tommaso forged a compromise with her that whatever property they might acquire or inherit, they were to use in common. This was one way in which brothers might protect sisters from being disenfranchised altogether, and perhaps a similar arrangement had obtained between Giovanbattista Nacchianti and his sister.[66] That this sort of family protection could endure for some time is clear from several other entries in the same *ricordanze*.[67] In this case, Tommaso's mother had made some provision from her dowry to invest in the Monte Comune, for on 24 May 1511, Tommaso made an agreement with his sister in which she transferred the interest she had in the Monte shares from their mother's dowry to Tommaso, so that Tommaso was able to buy them and use them to support his sister.[68] Two years later, on 27 April 1513, after Tommaso had married, his sister Francesca came to stay with him, as he makes clear, at his expense. She stayed five months with him as well as at the convent of the Candeli for two months. Finally, Francesca was sent to stay at the family villa so that she could live from the revenues produced by the property.[69]

---

[64] Ibid., fol. 118v, 24 March 1497: "Oggi questo dì 24 di marzo 1497 Cristofano di Piero di Francesco Nacchianti mio bisnipote venne a stare in firenze a casa mia acciò andasse a bottegha et imparasse che piaccia a Dio sia in buono punto et che lui impari et faci bene. Farò ricordo di quello spenderò in lui che mi scrisse Piero suo padre di quello spendesse farmegli buoni et rendermegli."

[65] AOIF Estranei (CXLIV, 89) fol. 2v, 2 February 1508/9: "Ricordo ogi questo dì 2 di febraio 1508 chome per insino adì 17 di novembre 1487 io Tomaso di Francesco Banchozzi andai a stare in chasa di Giovanbatista Quaratesi marito di mia madre e mio patrigno el quale mi venne in chasa a sua spese per insino adì 16 di febraio 1487 e in detto dì mi chaciò via e non mi volle più in chasa chome appare a libro suo richordanze chon dua stracci di chamicia e questo e quello chavai di chasa sua."

[66] Ibid., fol. 2v, 2 February 1508.

[67] Ibid., 2 February 1508.

[68] Ibid., fol. 10v, 24 May 1511.

[69] Ibid., fol. 14v, 27 April 1513, and 1 September 1513.

This case suggests, first of all, that families often used deposits in charitable and financial institutions as ways to support their unmarried daughters. In Francesca's case, coming as she did from a wealthy family, the convent served as only a temporary arrangement until a more satisfactory placement could be made with the help of the family's available land. Most important, this means that land was sought so avidly not just as part of the estate of the heirs of the patriline but was also acquired to support family members left out of the inheritance grid. Thus, competition for land was not so much the cause of the inheritance crisis but rather the means to alleviate it. Families, convents, monasteries, and charitable institutions were not mutually exclusive alternatives but formed a continuum, or an arsenal, perhaps, of strategies that families could employ on behalf of their more vulnerable members.

The *ricordanze* of an early-sixteenth-century barber-surgeon suggest that in some cases, the charity of those who were not burdened by large numbers of daughters offered various forms of charity to those who were. Maestro Baccio di Lodovico Alberighi, who during his lifetime was hired to draw blood at various convents and monasteries throughout the city, as well as for the women of the hospital of Santa Maria Nuova, made it a practice, even though he was married himself, to make deposits in the dowry fund for other men's daughters. In early January 1545, for example, he invested 178 florins in the Monte at 7 percent as a deposit of fifty florins for each of four girls whose fathers had died: Maria and Giuletta, both daughters of the late Giovanni d' Antonio, a tanner, and Brigida, daughter of the late Francesco di Michele Guardi from Figline (each of whom got fifty florins), as well as Diamante, daughter of the late Antonio di Francesco, a cooper (who received an investment of twenty-eight florins).[70]

Not all this charitable generosity was necessarily directed toward girls whose fathers had died. Later that year, Maestro Baccio spent another three hundred florins for dowries for two daughters of Simone di Guidantonio Mezetti, a broker in Rome. One daughter received an investment of two hundred florins; the other received one hundred florins in the Monte at 7 percent.[71] In 1548, this generous doctor disbursed another 575 florins for investment in the 7-percent Monte for several girls, some of whom received an initial investment of one hundred florins each, some fifty, and some twenty-five.[72]

---

[70] AOIF Estranei (CXLIV, 22) Ricordanze di Maestro Baccio di Lodovico Alberighi, fol. 29v, 8 January 1544.

[71] Ibid., fol. 31r, n.d.

[72] Ibid., fol. 33r-v, 19 September 1548.

TABLE 3.1. *Dowry investments made by Maestro Baccio Alberighi, 1548*

Recipient	Father's name and occupation (if known)	Amount
Lisabetta Gineura	Pagolo di Gregorio di Cristofano	fl. 100
Agnoletta Maria	G[i]ovanbattista Palagi	fl. 100
Lucretia Cilia	Domenicho di Lucha di Domenicho Pulciati	fl. 100
Gentile	Lionardo di Luigi Palmieri decto Ciufanza	fl. 100
Lisabetta	Romolo di Vangelista botaio (Cooper)	fl. 25
Angiela	Romolo di Vangelista botaio	fl. 25
Madalena	Romolo di Vangelista botaio	fl. 25
Lucretia	Romolo di Vangelista botaio	fl. 25
Margarita	Tomaso di Bartoleme sapolaio (soap merchant)	fl. 25

Source: AOIF Estranei (CXLIV, 22) Ricordanze di Maestro Baccio di Lodovico Alberighi, fol. 33r–33v, 19 September 1548.

The pattern of this informal network of Maestro Baccio Alberighi's charity also deserves comment. The surviving fathers of the recipients were barbers, coopers, and other tradesmen who needed assistance to augment the dowries they were already offering (Table 3.1). This is certainly true for Gentile Palmieri, and in other cases, the amounts involved were so small that they would not have been nearly sufficient for an entire dowry. At the same time, networks of business association and neighborhood patronage were decisive factors in Maestro Baccio's solicitude, and they reflect his other activities as well. He rented out several shops, for example, to barbers, coopers, and others who were likely to be involved with him as suppliers or recipients of medications, soap, and surgical instruments.[73] Although Maestro Baccio Alberighi was hardly at the top of the social scale, his *ricordanze* detail an impressive amount of landed wealth. He bought several farms and often rented them out and was sufficiently wealthy to have a villa on which he spent considerable sums.[74]

Having access to or control of landed wealth, however, did not preclude the use of charitable institutions, even if the Innocenti's superintendents lamented the way the Innocenti was often used to exclude daughters from inheritance. As in the case of Giovanbattista Nacchianti, a testator or the guardians of an estate, rather than or in addition to leaving cold cash in deposit to benefit a ward of the hospital, might assign the income from an estate to serve as maintenance or dowry. As a case from 1540 shows, for example, the relationship between families and charitable institutions was a complex one in which the institution assisted in the execution

[73] Ibid., fol. 12r, 13 March 1530; ibid., fol. 29r, 1 January 1544.
[74] Ibid., fol. 35r, *anno* 1549.

of family strategies intended to mitigate the effects of the inheritance grid.

Rafaello di Piero Paccetti and his infant sister Nannina were classic cases of children whose father had died, although they do not exactly fit the classic pattern described earlier. Rafaello was the eighteen-year-old son from his father's first marriage, and Nannina his daughter from his second marriage to Elisabetta. Before Piero Paccetti died, he arranged in his testament to pay back his second wife's dowry from the sale of his possessions. Whatever was left after the dowry was returned was to be split between Rafaello and Nannina. This amounted to a farm and 589 florins in Monte credits. Rafaello turned over his portion both so that the proceeds from this land and the interest from these credits could be used for the feeding and upbringing of Nannina and so that they could be used for her dowry. If she died before reaching the age of marriage, the property and Monte credits were to go to the hospital.[75]

This was precisely the arrangement that the Innocenti's superintendent, Luca Alamanni, had proposed as the rule for families who abandoned legitimate children to the Innocenti – that they should bring their portions with them, a rule that he hoped would deter families from using the hospital as a rubbish heap for inconvenient heirs or heiresses. Much as American nursing homes demand the impoverishment of patients so they can qualify for Medicaid payments, so did Alamanni imagine that inheritance portions would become a source of revenue and security for paying the expenses of abandoned children. Moreover, Alamanni proposed that whoever should notify the hospital of such inheritances would receive 10 percent of their value as a reward.[76] Although such a plan was never formally approved by the grand dukes, Luca Alamanni was sufficiently determined that he sought legal advice concerning "whether the children of the hospital can accede to an inheritance and if they die without children the inheritance may go to the hospital."[77]

There are other indications that testators saw inheritance and hospital as complementary, not mutually exclusive, alternatives. In 1531, Antonio di Giovanni del Papa left a farm in Greve to the Innocenti, with the stipulation that his former servant, Cosa, should be maintained either on the farm itself or, if that was not possible, that she should be taken in by the Innocenti and supported either from the farm's income or from whatever profit might be

---

[75] AOIF Filze d'Archivio (LXII, 9) fol. 387r, 20 August 1540.

[76] AOIF Suppliche e sovrani rescritti (VI, 1) fol. 259r, n.d.

[77] AOIF Filze d'Archivio (LXII, 7) fol. 180r n.d.: "Consiglio di Messer Domenico Bonsi se e figliuoli dello spedale succedino nelle heredità e se morendo quelli senza figliuoli lo spedale sia herede."

realized from its sale.[78] In 1577, an orphan by the name of Maria inherited a piece of land and two *staia* of grain per year for her maintenance, a provision that her mother had made in her will rather than entrusting her care to relatives. If in such cases children were abandoned to hold together the family patrimony, in this case at least the mother attempted to provide for the daughter she had abandoned, even if the land from which she was supposed to be nourished was of little value. The paternal uncle, although willing to intercede to a certain extent, did not relieve the hospital of Maria's care.[79]

The importance of the Innocenti as a depository, the major cause of its financial woes in the later sixteenth century, is closely tied to the deliberate way in which even wealthy testators involved the institution in their personal, financial, and other family strategies. In 1570, Bartolomeo di Zanobi Carnesecchi, who had served with Vincenzio Borghini as one of Cosimo's commissioners for convents, left to the Innocenti a chest with 1,181 florins in it. A quarter of this sum was to go to the Buonomini of the *poveri vergognosi di San Martino*, who were to distribute it to the poor, "principally the poor of the Carnesecchi family, and then to others as they see fit."[80] These instances appear to support the larger trend noted by Cohn for Sienese testaments, which increasingly in the sixteenth century made some sort of public provision for the testator's illegitimate children and which again suggest that direct bequests were also part of the arsenal of strategies families used to assist children who fell off of the inheritance grid.[81] Whether testators were supporting their own legitimate or illegitimate children, the mechanism of depositing sums of money or of leaving real estate to support them either in convents or charitable institutions was both uniform and widespread.

Perhaps the most illustrious example of this sort of provision was Giorgio Vasari's arrangement for his illegitimate son. The codicil to Vasari's will left 500 scudi to Antonio Francesco, who was the son of Vasari's Moorish servant Isabella. The five hundred florins were deposited with the Innocenti and the interest was to be used for Antonio's maintenance until age eighteen. Once Antonio reached eighteen, he had until the age of thirty the option to use the money to buy property. If he died in the meantime, the five

---

[78] AOIF Ricordanze A (XII,7) Libro segreto de' ricordi del nostro spedale dall'anno 1528 all'anno 1630, fol. 7v, 24 January 1530.

[79] AOIF Ricordanze (XII, 11), fol. 23r, n.d. [July 1577].

[80] AOIF Ricordanze A (XII, 7), fol. 41r, 1 January 1570: "principalmente di casa Carnesecchi et subsequentamente a altri come a loro paresse, secondo l'ordine distintamente datone in detto testamento."

[81] Cohn, *Death and Property*, 133.

hundred scudi would belong to the Innocenti. Here Vasari also provided for an alternative in case he decided before his death that Antonio should return to live with his relatives. In that case, the five hundred scudi should be used for the expenses the hospital had incurred in raising and feeding him.[82] Here, then, is a clear case of institution and family as possible alternatives even within the same will, with one as a backup system for any anticipated failure of the other.

Testators who were wealthy also used charitable institutions as an intermediary both for conserving dotal assets for themselves and for charity to the poorer members of the lineage. When the archbishop of Florence Andrea Buondelmonte died in November 1542, his testament instituted the Innocenti as his universal heir on the condition that it provide dowries for three girls of the Buondelmonte family. In August 1542, the archbishop had left nearly nine thousand florins on deposit in a strongbox at the Innocenti's depository, and in October 1542, two thousand were designated for Lucrezia di Giovanbattista Buondelmonte and another three thousand for the dowries of Giovanbattista's other daughters (present and future).[83]

Another six thousand florins were designated as "alms" for the Innocenti, from which the Innocenti paid for the dowries of "three poor girls" from the *casata* of the Buondelmonte. In 1551, the Innocenti paid a thousand florins of Lucrezia's dowry out of this account when she married Benedetto Ughuccione, and in 1554, Manente, one of Giovanbattista's sons, elected the three Buondelmonte poor girls to receive the dowries, each of whom received 150 florins and at least one of whom used her payment as a conventual dowry.[84] In short, charitable institutions did not necessarily even house family members who were recipients of charity but in many cases simply acted to conserve and transfer wealth from richer to poorer members of the same lineage.[85]

Conclusion

This chapter has shown that the crisis that forced young men and women into institutional care beginning in the late fifteenth century was not gender

---

[82] AOIF Filza d'Archivio (LXII, 7) fol. 49r, 28 June 1574. Cf. Patricia Rubin, *Giorgio Vasari: Art and History*, 53n.

[83] AOIF Giornale K (XIII, 17), fol. 59r, 27 November 1542.

[84] Ibid., fol. 170r, 30 October 1551 and fol. 189v, 2 July 1554.

[85] Cf. Richard Trexler, "Charity and the Defense of Urban Elites in the Italian Communes," in *The Rich, the Well Born, and the Powerful,* ed. F. Jaher (Urbana: University of Illinois Press, 1973), 64–109, at 77–8.

ideology but lineage ideology. In this respect, this chapter's findings cast doubt on the myth of the efficacy of the extended family and lineage in protecting and caring for each of its component parts. Seen in this wider perspective, the views of Richard Goldthwaite that this age saw the birth of familial and economic individualism are no longer irreconcilable with F. W. Kent's observations on the importance of lineage solidarity. Certainly Goldthwaite's study, by focusing on the economic fortunes of Renaissance Florentine families, underemphasized the extended lineage ties that bound them together. Certainly Kent, by focusing on the social networks that bound Florentine families of high social standing, neglected some of the economic issues that often divided families within the same lineage. Furthermore, both historians, by defining the family in terms of the fortunes of its male actors in the public world, certainly missed the social and psychic toll that lineage solidarity took on members of the family who were juridically disadvantaged in the inheritance grid.

Indeed, the evidence presented here suggests that the psychic and social toll was not limited to the weaker members of these families of high social status. The acquisition of land and other resources, that very materialism deplored by Silvio Antoniano in the context of post-Tridentine Milan, was central to the definition and maintenance of that social status. As Kuehn has pointed out, if the demands of agnatic succession placed constraints on women, even more so did such demands place constraints on how men could draw up their testaments and all the more did male heads of household have to "dower, feed, and shelter women before and after marriage."[86]

Most of the families studied here, callous as they may have sounded in their treatment of some family members, nonetheless applied themselves diligently to finding solutions to their social and economic dilemmas. Such families used the acquisition of land not only for the maintenance of their most favored members but also, on a much smaller scale, combined the acquisition of land with the use of convents and charitable institutions to obviate the consequences of an increasingly severe inheritance system – a system, it must be added, that families pursued with such vigor precisely because, in their view, it preserved wealth, social status, and the interests of succeeding generations. As solicitous as these *padri di famiglia* were, however, the example of Ser Andrea Nacchianti, among many others, suggests that if family solidarity was the intended consequence of rigid inheritance strategies, the unintended consequences tore families apart to the extent that even granddaughters or sons of first marriages were burdens that prosperous

---

[86] Kuehn, "Person and Gender," 96.

notaries, never mind less wealthy heads of household, endured with little grace. The next two chapters treat the varied fortunes of those boys and girls who, for whatever reason, could not be endured within the household at all and who had to exchange the discipline of the *padre di famiglia* for the discipline of charitable institutions.

4

INNOCENCE AND DANGER: PEDAGOGY, DISCIPLINE, AND THE CULTURE OF MASCULINITY

T HIS CHAPTER TREATS THE LIVES OF THOSE BOYS WHOSE FAMILY AND inheritance systems failed to provide the sort of economic and social support that Ser Andrea Nacchianti, however grudgingly, provided for the boys and girls in his kinship network who fell outside the categories of the statutory inheritance grid. Although much recent scholarship has focused on the problems this created for women, only a handful of scholars has explored the social consequences of homelessness for boys. In particular, Ottavia Niccoli has juxtaposed the perceptions and realities of links between undisciplined boys and violent criminality, as well as noting their vulnerability to exploitation. For the fifteenth century, Michael Rocke has analyzed the social boundaries of cross-generational homoerotic bonds as a foundation of patronage and male sociability. Konrad Eisenbichler's more chronologically extended study of a youth confraternity across the entire early modern period has brought the techniques of confraternal discipline into much sharper focus. More recently, Ilaria Taddei has chronicled the lives and childhood careers of boys in various Florentine youth confraternities, and Nicholas Terpstra has done the same for boys in orphanages in Florence and Bologna.[1]

---

[1] Ottavia Niccoli, *Il seme della violenza: Putti, fanciulli, e mammoli nell'Italia tra cinque e seicento* (Bari: Laterza, 1995), xix, cites two cases from the Bolognese archives in which a nine-year-old and ten-year-old boy respectively were pulled from the bed of the local priest, who gave them soup and bread in exchange for their sexual favors. Cf. Giovanni Antonio Flaminio, *Dialogus de educatione liberorum ac institutione* (Bologna, G. de Benedetti, 1523), 16v, cited in Niccoli, 102. Flaminio warns boys that "near schools young hoodlums circle a young boy like vultures around cadavers, sitting next to him, shamelessly placing hands on his back and showing him their purses and making grand promises." For the connection between homoerotic bonds, male sociability, and patronage in fifteenth-century Florence, see Michael Rocke, *Forbidden Friendships*. For boys and youth confraternities, see Konrad Eisenbichler, *The Boys of the Archangel Raphael* (Toronto: University of Toronto Press, 1998) and Ilaria Taddei, *Fanciulli e Giovani: Crescere a Firenze nel Rinascimento*, Biblioteca Storica Toscana a cura della Deputazione di storia patria per la Toscana,

Primary sources themselves, however, make clear that in the perception of sixteenth-century Tuscans, at least, bands of roving boys and young men constituted both a difficult social problem and a major threat to an already tenuous social and political order. Yet their ritual violence, although prohibited frequently by edicts and decrees, was encouraged and even assisted by adults, especially when ritual violence involved playing with the cadavers of notorious criminals and outcasts and even eating the hearts of political enemies.[2] Indeed, the very innocence of children demonstrated that through their violence, the hand of God was at work.[3] When violent groups of children turned against each other, contemporaries saw this as a prophecy of war and mortality, much the same as flocks of bickering birds and fluttering butterflies prophesied "God's judgment among men."[4]

In the last two decades of the fifteenth century, bands of roving children turned their physical aggression against Jews and other moneylenders, largely under the influence of such preachers as Bernardino da Feltre. Although Bernardino himself counseled prayer as the only efficacious weapon against Jews, children went well beyond that, to such an extent that the Otto di Guardia of Florence issued an edict forbidding violence against Jews. When a functionary of the Otto actually went into the piazza to proclaim the edict, however, a youth hit him in the face with a cane and was promptly arrested.[5] Indeed, in the later fifteenth and early sixteenth centuries, preachers such as Bernardino da Feltre and Savonarola attracted virtual armies of pious youths who attempted to enforce social mores and to punish transgressors.

As Ottavia Niccoli has pointed out, the violent society of late medieval and early modern Italian cities "fully involved children in its conflicts and sexual tensions, and even encouraged the presence of children and their active role. . . . The well-educated child will certainly be a perfect man and Christian. But to achieve such a goal without a radical change of the family environment and of society would certainly seem unrealizable." Niccoli argues that this attitude led to a massive change in the relationship between families and children, namely, that humanist and religious social reformers increasingly sought to exclude parents from participation in the educational and moral aspects of their children's upbringing.[6] In a passage that looks

---

vol. 40 (Florence: Leo S. Olschki, 2001). On boys in Bolognese and Florentine orphanages, see Nicholas Terpstra, *Abandoned Children of the Italian Renaissance,* 149–86.

[2] Ottavia Niccoli, *Il seme di violenza*, 27–39.

[3] Ibid., 38–9.

[4] Ibid., 53.

[5] Ibid., 76–7

[6] Ibid., 102–3.

back to the guardians of Plato's Republic as well as forward to Rousseau's Enlightenment and the French Revolution, Giovanni Maria Memmo wrote:

> The child entrusted to the wet nurse should be taken outside the father's household equally far from the mother and the father, because the one and the other, overjoyed by the delight and sweetness that children provide at that tender age, prove more damaging than useful. In which case I praise highly the custom of some, who serve in such a way as not to admit children into the father's presence until they are well-brought-up and well behaved.[7]

Although Niccoli's observations ring true, and there is no doubt that humanist, Catholic, and Protestant moral reform sought to separate parents and children to apply the discipline of church and state with less interference, I question the assumption that children and parents were not already separated in the high Middle Ages. Indeed, to re-create the pedagogical circumstances of an idealized classical past, reforming pedagogues undoubtedly overstated the extent to which such practices were not already part of current practice. Injunctions concerning dignity, decorum, and body language were monastic as well as classical in origin, and cathedral and monastic schools extended their prescriptions to medieval children as well.[8] Moreover, as Niccoli herself points out, not all reformers (Sadoleto is the exception Niccoli cites) found the early modern home an environment hostile to a disciplined, Christian upbringing. Alessandro Piccolomini (1508–78), for example, emphasized the mother's role in making sure that the infant drank in the fear of God along with its mother's milk, and in fashioning the pure speech of the young child.[9]

Pedagogy and Discipline in Boys' Institutions

To what extent, then, did the fusion of pedagogy, confessionalization, and discipline affect the actual organization of care in boys' institutions? Vittorio Frajese's important work on the disciplinary regime proposed by Cardinal Antoniano shows even more clearly the intention to unite religious and literary topoi with the actual practice of conventual discipline in

---

[7] Giovanni Maria Memmo, *Dialogo del magn. caualiere M. Gio. Maria nel quale dopo alcune filosofiche dispute si forma un perfetto Principe, et una perfetta Republica, e parimente in Senatore, un Cittadino, un soldato et un Mercante* (Venice: Gabriel Giolotto di Ferrari, 1563), 22, cited in Niccoli, *Il seme di violenza*, 104.

[8] Dilwyn Knox, "Disciplina: The Monastic and Clerical Origin of European Civility," 123.

[9] On drinking in the fear of God with mother's milk, see Piccolomini, *De la institutione*, 22r. On fashioning the child's speech, see ibid., 24v.

sixteenth-century Rome.[10] At the Ospedale degli Innocenti in Florence, the primary focus of this section, it is clear that by the 1570s, if not well before, hospital officials had constructed a division of care allowing for the allegedly different capacities of males and females. There was virtually no limit to the number of skills boys could learn:

> Because the dangers to males are neither as frequent nor as overwhelming as for females, the rule and custom of this house has been to raise them and instruct them during their youth in all the skills they are capable of learning and which the hospital is capable of teaching.[11]

By the same token, the Innocenti in the case of boys had the luxury of retaining them forever in the service of the institution through old age until death. Those boys whose fate was to end up outside the institution could expect "a little care." Borghini noted that the hospital's trustees, for example, often intervened to make sure young apprentices got paid or would put a stop to their mistreatment. This was rarely necessary, Borghini wrote, and as a result, it was not difficult for the hospital to discharge boys, and therefore no danger existed that their numbers would increase extraordinarily. Expenses for wet nurses and foster parents were thus proportionately reduced for boys, who in most cases could be discharged at the age of fourteen or fifteen.[12]

Not only did the division of care by gender suggest that hospital discipline was monastic in origin, but, as Goldthwaite and Rearick have shown, the architecture of Tuscan hospitals even in the fourteenth century was consciously modeled on that of the cloister.[13] When Vincenzio Borghini first assumed the post of superintendent of the Florentine foundling hospital in 1552, he fell naturally, even ironically, into the use of the monastic metaphor. Complaining in a letter to Vasari, Borghini wrote:

> It arrived just as I got the news that, in order to purge my sins, of which there is more than one, our Father Superiors have made me prior of this

[10] Frajese, *Popolo fanciullo*, 95, citing Biblioteca Vallicelliana di Roma, cod. G.43, Regole et ordini che s'haveranno da osservare nella Santa Casa della S.ma Madonna del Rifugio nuovamente eretta dalla Santità di N.S. Clemente VIII, fol. 2v. Although Nicholas Terpstra, in *Abandoned Children of the Italian Renaissance*, 151–2, doubts that administrators of orphanages had the time or inclination to read the advice of moralists, their "instincts, experience, and connections" surely shaped and were shaped by the advice of "a celibate clergyman." The administrators of S. Maria del Rifugio, at least, would have had little choice, because Silvio Antoniano wrote the orphanage's statutes.

[11] Vincenzio Borghini, *Considerationi sopra l'allogare le donne delli Innocenti fuora del maritare o monacare*, ed. Gaetano Bruscoli (Florence: E. Ariani, 1904), 29. The original manuscript exists in two copies: AOIF Filze d'Archivio (LXII, 17) fol. 39r–46r, n.d., and fol. 107rff.

[12] Borghini, *Considerationi*, 29–30.

[13] R. Goldthwaite and W. R. Rearick "Michelozzo and the Ospedale di San Paolo in Florence," 269.

monastery, over which I am in the worst sort of anguish, seeing as I am deprived of that quiet, leisure, and ability to study, that I have always sought and desired.[14]

Just as early medieval monks prayed for the penance that their patrons did not have enough lifetimes to sustain, so did the inmates of hospitals, including children, pray for the souls of their benefactors, reminding God, as it were, and as only beneficiaries could, of the benefactors' earthly good works.[15]

However, prayer for benefactors comprised only one small, if symptomatic part of institutions' larger efforts to effect a transformation from disorder to discipline, not only administratively but also in the lives of boys under their care. Building on the humanist pedagogy that characterized their mission in the fifteenth century, hospital officials consciously directed their pedagogical efforts to the work of moral reform. At the Ospedale degli Innocenti in particular, if in the fifteenth century hospital officials undertook to make each of their male charges "a gentleman, or at any rate, a rich man," the model for reform in the sixteenth century was confessional and disciplinary – more along the lines of oratories, confraternities of Christian doctrine, and Jesuit programs of reform.

The pedagogy of the Innocenti is also evident from contracts between the hospital and the masters it hired for the hospital's classrooms. In June 1534, the Innocenti supervised 1,766 children, of whom 1,000 were at wet nurse and 550 were in house: 420 girls and 130 boys. At this point, the institution had a single master for the girls, and one for the boys; each master was paid fifteen ducats per year. In addition, a hosier and a governor were employed at half-salary.[16] Moreover, at this stage, the hospital gave priority to the hiring of grammar masters as well as masters who did not specialize in the teaching of a single subject. This was a skeletal staff at best for such a large group of children, and hospital officials must have been making similar observations, because they added several pedagogues to the roster in the summer and autumn months of 1534.

Although the full import of the involvement of the hospital's masters in its ritual life will become apparent later in the chapter, the contracts

---

[14] Archivio di Stato di Arezzo (ASA), Archivio Vasari, cod. 48, fol. 194r, 22 October 1552. Cf. Karl Frey, ed., *Der Litterarische Nachlass Giorgio Vasaris* (2 vols., Munich: G. Müller, 1923), 1: 337.

[15] For a particularly good example of a benefactor requesting the prayers of children for the sake of his soul, see AOIF Ricordanze A (XII, 7): Libro segreto di Ricordi del nostro spedale, fol. 7v, 24 January 1530.

[16] AOIF Filza d'Archivio (LXXII, 12) fol. 331r, 24 June 1534 lists a "Maestro de le figliuole" (fifteen ducats), a "maestro de la gramaticha" at the same salary, "il governatore della volta de' fanciuli" (eight ducats, four soldi), and a "maestro de' chalzolai" (ten ducats), whose rate of pay had not yet been firmly established.

between pedagogues and the hospital drawn up in the 1530s show just how closely tied devotion and pedagogy were in the decades before Trent. Most, if not all of the hospital's grammar masters were clerics and were expected to say mass.[17] In addition, they were responsible for the purchase of wax and candles.[18] For example, Vincenzio Borghini drew up a contract with Ser Virgilio di Giubileo Malossi from Monterchi, who agreed "to teach grammar, reading, and writing, and to do everything that is usually expected of good masters, and similarly to celebrate mass and to rehearse the chorus as the other [masters] do."[19] This connection between pedagogy and devotion, reinforced by musical training, occurred outside the Innocenti as well: in 1554, the clerical school run by the canons of San Lorenzo made provision for "a schoolmaster for the clerics to teach them grammar and *cantus firmus* according to the usual."[20] A contract of 1561, redolent of Tridentine pedagogy, stipulated that the two masters "must teach our boys to read, write, and whatever [else] is required to instruct them well, so they will be well-mannered."[21] An interest in close supervision informed other requirements for the position as well:

and always at school, at dinner, at supper, in the loggia or in the courtyard, or at psalms, or during masses, [at least] one of the masters must accompany the said boys, nor should any [of the boys] ever be left alone.[22]

Moreover, these two masters, Ser Bartolomeo di Giovanni da Galatea di Romagna, and Ser Raffaello di Giovanni da Scarperia, supervised the boys

---

[17] AOIF Giornale I (XIII, 16) fol. 19r, 2 October 1533.

[18] AOIF Ricordanze E (XII, 5) fol. 11v, 31 March 1531.

[19] AOIF Giornale L (XIII, 18) fol. 72r, 24 July 1560: "Ricordo questo dì 24 sopradetto come la Reverendo del nostro priore D. Vincenzo Borghini ha tolto per maestro de' nostri fanciulli il Reverendo Ser Virgilio di Giubileo Malossi da Monterchi per insegnare gramatica, leggere, et scrivere, et fare tutto quello è solito de' buoni maestri per F. xii l'anno, obrigato similmente à celebrare la messa, et exercitare il coro come gli altri et per osseruanza del tutto si è appie."

[20] Florence, Biblioteca Medicea Laurenziana, Archivio di San Lorenzo 2157, fol. 78r, 8 May 1554: "far provisione di un maestro di scuola per e cherici di nostra chiesa per insegnar' loro grammatica et canto fermo secondo il solito." San Lorenzo, however, paid its schoolmasters forty-eight scudi per year, more than three times what Innocenti masters received. It may well be that San Lorenzo was perceived as an especially difficult place to teach. In 1520, a maestro at San Lorenzo was sacked for negligence, and the scribe complained that "la nostra squola al tutto era guasta e corrotta" (ASL 1, fol. 38r, *anno* 1520, cited in *San Lorenzo: i documenti e i tesori nascosti*, ed. Marco Assirelli et al. [Venice: Marsilio, 1993], 59). In 1542, a decision of the capitolo affirmed that the church "is badly served by our scholars, who do not want to serve the mass" (ASL, 1, fol. 166v, *anno* 1542, cited in *San Lorenzo: i documenti*, ed. M. Assirelli et al., 59).

[21] AOIF, Giornale L (XIII,18), fol. 90r, 17 October 1561. Information on this contract and on the two masters from Galatea di Romagna and Scarperia is also found in Gavitt, "Charity and State-Building," 250–1.

[22] AOIF, Giornale L (XIII, 18), fol. 90r, 17 October 1561. Cf. Gavitt, "Charity and State-Building," 251.

who had been sent out to work by visiting them every week and making sure they had everything they needed. On feast days, masters made sure that the boys who normally left the hospital on workdays should stay together and not leave without permission. These masters also had to ensure that there were at least twelve choristers who were to be taught singing and the recitation of penitential psalms twice a day, "once when they get up in the morning and again at noon when the priests go to mass." The masters had to be available to sing the mass as well as Vespers and therefore were not to officiate outside the hospital without the knowledge and consent of the prior. These two masters were also responsible for burying the dead "in the evening after supper," and for ensuring that whenever boys had to leave the premises to attend to the needs of the women's cloister, that they should always go in twos, "so that one will fear the other."[23] In addition to these obviously time-consuming duties, at least one master, once a week, "or at most every fifteen days," had to visit boys who had been placed out of the hospital as apprentices.[24]

Reliable evidence for the hospital's pedagogy comes from a 1581 inventory of the books of Ser Agostino di Bartolomeo Tombi, who occupied a room at the Innocenti. This may well mean that he taught, although there is some evidence that the Innocenti would house guests for extended periods of time who had little to do with the daily life of the hospital. Nonetheless, his book collection contained an "esercitio della lingua latina," a Greek grammar, a collection of "examples and sayings from Holy Scripture," all of which strongly suggest at least that such books had been used for pedagogical purposes. Other staples of Renaissance curricula, including Cicero's letters, Horace, Lucan, Juvenal, Vergil, and Ovid, make up a considerable proportion of the list. Even though these books were appraised and sold at his death, the likelihood is substantial, on the basis of Ser Agostino's residence at the Innocenti and the overtly pedagogical content of the collection, that this collection was of some use to the Innocenti's children during his lifetime.

Complementing this collection of books, the inventory lists a painted green harpsichord, and a second harpsichord about to be painted that had "belonged to a nun in Santa Marta" and that was returned to her.[25] Since a large number of masters' contracts specified duties that involved teaching and

---

[23] AOIF, Giornale L (XIII, 18), fol. 90r, 17 October 1561. Gavitt, "Charity and State-Building," 251.

[24] AOIF, Giornale L (XIII, 18), fol. 90r, 17 October 1561: "[H]anno ancor' esser' obbligati una volta la settimana, o, al più ogni 15 giorni di andar a visitare e' fanciulli che fanno al'arte per Firenze a' tessitori, et altro, et vedere quel che ara esse occorre."

[25] AOIF, Filze d'Archivio (LXII, 7) fol. 537r–537v; 553r–557r, 13 October 1581: "Un arpicordo dipinto di fuori verde; un altro Arpicordo che sta a dipigner' dicono esser d'una monaca de' Doni

leading the Innocenti's choristers, the presence of these two harpsichords may also be evidence that Ser Agostino was one of the hospital's pedagogues.[26] If Ser Agostino's book list does reflect what the Innocenti was teaching in the late sixteenth century, it represents a combination of what Paul Gehl described as the "moralizing conservatism" of Florentine trecento grammar masters and the unmistakable infusion of humanist pedagogy, which used the letters of Cicero as stylistic models and the major Latin lyric poets: Vergil, Horace, and Ovid.[27]

From the state of the evidence, it is extremely difficult to gauge what proportion of the Innocenti's boys might expect to be taught a humanist curriculum. A document of 1586, for example, proposing the reform of the hospital and the dismissal of several employees, notes that there were only two regular masters and a master of music for the entire hospital and that only one of these was actually needed, so certainly in the post-Borghini years the commitment to a broadly available education was no longer there, and perhaps had never been meant for the majority of children. Just as the reform commission of 1582 had recommended dismissing the painters to whom Borghini had given shelter, the reform of 1586 suggests the richness of the hospital's musical life under Borghini when it recommended that "the one who plays the cornet above the organ: both the one and the other expenses are superfluous."[28] Clearly, reformers, whether consciously or not, were working toward greater emphasis on manual labor and attempting to reduce the scale on which the Innocenti operated as a sort of children's city, which however illustrious, was also expensive.

Discipline and the Vocational Curriculum

Officials at the Innocenti foundling hospital distinguished between those boys able to pursue more advanced scholarship and those destined for work in the trades. In addition to apprenticeships with *bottegai* off the institution's

in S. Martha. Resi i libri e arpicordo a Meo Monti adì 15 Octobre 81. [altro arpicordo] A meo che lo renda alla padrone d'esso."

[26] Cf., for example, AOIF Giornale L (XIII, 18), fol. 72r, 24 July 1560.

[27] Paul Gehl, *A Moral Art: Grammar, Society, and Culture in Trecento Florence* (Ithaca: Cornell University Press, 1993), 54. Robert Black, "The Curriculum of Italian Elementary and Grammar Schools," in *The Shapes of Knowledge from the Renaissance to the Enlightenment*, ed. Donald Kelley and Richard Popkin, vol. 124 of Archives Internationales d'Histoire des Idées (Dordrecht/Boston/London: Kluwer Academic, 1991), 137–64, at 147–54.

[28] AOIF Filza d'Archivio (LXII, 13) fol. 306r, 24 December 1586, contains a partial list of employees to be dismissed: "2. Uno maestro de' fanciulli delli dua che vi sono, perche risolvemo che uno di loro fussi abbastanza per hora 3. Il maestro della musica, et ancora 4. Quello che suona la cornetta in su li organi sendo l'uno et l'altro spesa superfrua."

premises, the Innocenti also pursued vocational instruction in a variety of manual work for both boys and girls. Although there was wide variation in the number of trades taught, during the sixteenth-century the Innocenti's chief "exports" were carpenters, masters of hosiery, tapestry weavers, and painters.[29] By the late 1570s, before the cost-cutting reforms of 1582 and 1586, the hospital had as pedagogues four hosiers, four gardeners, two wool workers, a butcher, a baker, a *granaiuolo* (in charge of the grain stores), two carters, a *rotaio* (in charge of keeping track of admissions), three painters, six musicians, and five clerics.[30]

Those hired to teach vocational subjects also doubled as in-house suppliers of the Innocenti's daily needs. Thus, in December 1562, the Innocenti hired Maestro Luca di Domenico d'Arezzo as a shoemaker, obligated to "cut whatever needs to be done in the said shop, to sew, and to teach those children we send to him," for a salary of twelve florins a year, a full set of tools, and a furnished room in the institution.[31] In December 1569, the Innocenti hired "at our expense for our carpenter and cooper" Agnolo di Ceseri from Florence, who must "work entirely for the benefit of our hospital, and teach those children sent to him, with the sort of kindliness and diligence as though they were his brothers."[32] Similarly in 1573, Bartolomeo di Marco da Bologna was hired as master of the hosiery shop "to do all the work there is to do, and to sew, and to teach all our boys who will be sent to him daily." In addition to thirteen florins per year Bartolomeo had all his room expenses paid and a pair of shoes "for his own use," an agreement also forged with the next calzolaio, Scipione di Antonio Alleotti da Faenza.[33]

---

[29] On hospital apprenticeships as part of Cosimo's larger economic program, see the section, "The Cultural Life of an Early Modern Charitable Institution" later in this chapter.

[30] AOIF Filze d'Archivio (LXII, 15) fol. 177r, n.d., lists *calzolai, ortolani, lanaiuoli, beccaio, fornaio, granaiuolo, vetturali, rotaio, pittori, musici,* and *cherici*.

[31] AOIF Giornale L (XIII, 18), fol. 103v, 1 December 1562: "Ricordo come la reverentia del nostro Priore D. Vincenzo Borghini hoggi questo dì primo di dicembre 1562 ha tolto per maestro della nostra calzoleria Maestro Luca di Domenico d'Arezzo con patti sia obligato a tagliare ciò che fa di bisogno a detta calzoleria et cucire, et insegnare a quei fanciulli che d'in mano in mano li saranno conseganti et usati ogni diligenzia attenente al suo offitio; et per salaro di detto saranno l'anno fl. 12 dodici d'oro di moneta da cominciarsi il dì sopradetto, et di più le scarpe suo per consumo, et le spese, et ha stare fermamente in casa, et albergo; et di tutto siamo convenuti con esso lui d'accordo questo dì sopradetto."

[32] AOIF Giornale M (XIII, 19) fol. 46r, 12 December 1569: "Ricordo come sino al primo di novembre prossimo passato noi togliemmo un casa alle spese per nostro legnaiulo et bottaio Agnolo di Ceseri di Firenze con patti si debba interamente exercitare per utile del nostro spedale, et insegnare à questi fanciulli che di mano in mano li saranno consegnati, con quella amorevolezza et diligentia proprio com el fussino suoi fratelli."

[33] Ibid., fol. 143r, 26 March 1573: "Ricordo com' insino adì 26 di marzo 1573 ni togliemmo per maestro [della] nostra calzoleria Bartolomeo da Bologna con obligo di tagliare con diligentia tutto

In at least a few cases, the Innocenti clearly intended its system of apprenticeships to train boys so that they could stay on and teach various trades to younger boys. Although most examples date from the 1570s, the practice is documented at least as early as 1535, when Antonio, "son of our hospital and a master of hosiery" was paid for ninety lire covering his work from 21 September 1532 to 1 November 1535 and hired at the rate of six lire per month.[34] Five of the Innocenti's boys were hired as of the beginning of April 1574 as a sacristan, carpenter, weaver, hosier, and gardener at salaries of about eight to ten florins per year – competitive with apprentices and journeymen although not with those of masters.[35] The master carpenter who was hired in 1576 "for our shop," for example, received a salary of twenty florins, for which he had to practice his trade "faithfully," keep track of all the hardware and arms, and, "like a good master and father, teach all the boys we will send him each day."[36]

An undated list drawn up most likely before 1580 listed the masters outside the hospital with whom the Innocenti had contracts, including a goldsmith, two "alla polvere" (presumably the gunpowder magazine), four tapestry masters, six musketeers, four armorers, four artillery specialists, six weavers, two sculptors, a painter, a lute manufacturer, a milliner, a glass maker, a fringe maker, and an *aggiudicatore*. The range is surprising; a considerable number of apprenticeships, it seems, were available in various military occupations, but it was also possible to find work in sculptors' and painters' workshops.[37]

The personal patronage of the grand dukes also meant that the foundling hospital's boys could be pressed into the military service of the state. In 1548, Cosimo de' Medici wrote to Francesco di Ser Iacopo to inquire whether about a dozen of the Innocenti's boys could be found to work as carpenters on the galleys.[38] On 3 April 1559, Borghini wrote to Bartolomeo Concini,

el lauoro che vi si farà, et di cucire, et insegnar' a' tutti nostri fanciulli che alla giornata vi si consegnareranno, et per suo salario oltre alle spese et camera gli promettiamo fl. 13 di moneta l'anno, et le scarpe per suo uso." Cf. fol. 147v, 5 June 1573.

[34] AOIF Giornale I (XIII, 16), fol. 58v, 10 September 1535.

[35] AOIF Giornale M (XIII, 19) fol. 177r, 14 April 1574.

[36] Ibid., fol. 252r, 28 May 1576: "Ricordo come questo dì decto noi habbiamo tolto per maestro di nostri legnaiuoli et botai Lorenzo di Cresci di Nicodemo con patti deba lavorare et esercitarsi in nostra bottega fedelmente e lavorare se non per nostro spedale secondo che di mano in mano gli serrà ordinato alla giornata et tenere conto di tutti e ferramenti et armi che gli saranno consegnati et con patto ancora debba insegnare a tutti quelli nostri fanciulli che alla giornata gli saranno consegnati come buono maestro et padre."

[37] AOIF Filze d'Archivio (LXXII, 15), fol. 117r, n.d., lists external masters as *orafo*, "*alla polvere*," *arazzieri, archibusieri, armaiuoli,* "*alle fiasche d'Archibusi*," "*alle artiglierie*," *tessitori di drappi d'oro, tessitori di rasi, scultori, pittore, liutaio, aggiudicatori, cappellaio, biccieraio,* and *frangiaio*.

[38] Elizabeth Pilliod, *Pontormo, Bronzino, Allori: A Genealogy of Florentine Art* (New Haven and London: Yale University Press, 2001), 78 and 248n, citing ASF Carte Strozziane ser. 1, Filza XXXIV, fol. 107r.

one of the secretaries of the grand duke of Florence, Cosimo I. Borghini, clearly conscious of his obligations and position in the matter, wrote back:

> In response, I say briefly to your lordship that it being my duty always to obey willingly the dictates of that most Illustrious Lord our patron, I gave the order to do it right away, and tomorrow, God willing, or at the latest, the day after tomorrow, I will send some of them – twelve or fourteen. As to the remaining eight or so, I have sent for them where I have them, who will be in order within eight days at the most. And as much as possible, they will be of the nature and qualities demanded by Your Majesty. I am writing a word, to be saved for when the boys actually arrive, to His most Illustrious and Excellent Lord [Cosimo], . . . that he take special care of the them, that as they are still tender boys, scarcely expert, and quite terrified, they need to be introduced with patience and discretion, at least to the point where they have had a little practice.[39]

If Borghini's misgivings were a gentle attempt to dissuade Cosimo from his intentions, the subtlety was certainly lost on his secretary and the *provveditore* of the galleys, Luca Martini. On 11 April, Martini could report confidently that "we got twelve boys from the superintendent of the Innocenti, whom I will keep here until the *commissario* of the galleys returns to Livorno. It seemed to me best that they not be badly supervised and controlled there."[40]

Nor were the fears of the boys themselves unfounded. Forced service in the galleys was one option in a range of punishments meted out to the more recalcitrant of the criminals in the grand duke's dominion. In the summer of 1558, for example, nine months before twelve of the Innocenti's boys would face the rigors of the sea, one of Cosimo's functionaries drew up a list of twenty-six criminals condemned to the galleys. Although most of these criminals were thieves who had been sentenced to two to three years on the galleys, at least one had been convicted of ambushing and then seriously

---

[39] ASF, Archivio Mediceo del Principato 478, fol. 37r, 3 April 1559: Letter from Vincenzo Borghini to Bartolomeo Concini: "In risposta dico brevemente a V.S. che sendo obligo mio sempre, obbedire et di buona volontà a' cenni dello Ill.mo S. mio padrone, subito ho dato l'ordine d'esseguir'. Et domani piacendo a Dio al più lungo l'altro, ne inviero una parte di 12 fino in 14: et pel resto ho mandato dove gli ho di fuori, che saranno a ordine fra viii dì al piu lungo. Et saranno il più che si potra di quella sorte e qualità, che per la vostra mi dice. Et perche V. S. desiderava intendere quello seguiva, quanto più presto: scrivo questa per questo effetto solo. Riserbandosi alla venuta de' detti putti a scrivere non molto a S. E. I. alla quale desidero sieno raccomondati d'una parola a quello che si hara auta, che essendo putti, teneri, poco esperti, et spauriti, hanno bisogno d'esser introdotti con patienza et discretione almanco finche venghino pigliando un poco di pratica."

[40] ASF Mediceo del Principato 478, fol. 153r, 11 April 1559, letter from Luca Martini to Cosimo I: "Dallo spedalingo delli Innocenti di Fiorenza si sono havuti 12 fanciulli, li quale gl'ho qui che non essendo il commissario delle galee à Livorno mi ha detto lo scrivano . . . che io li tenga qui fino al ritorno d'esso, e mi e parso bene acciòche non fussino la mal custoditi et governati."

wounding a gardener. Two friars in this group would have been able to provide little spiritual consolation: one had been convicted of counterfeiting by the court of the archbishop of Siena; the other, a Carmelite, had been condemned by the order's vicar general to serve a life sentence in the galleys that the offending friar might be "reduced to skin and bone."[41] Finally, Nicholas Terpstra has observed that the early governors of the Ospedale degli Abbandonati in Florence were also "eager to send malefactors to pull the oars on Florence's galleys."[42]

Despite the apparent diversity and variability of placements, beginning with Vincenzio Borghini's tenure as superintendent in 1552, hospital officials attempted to formalize apprenticeships and to concentrate them among cloth weavers. Especially beginning in the early 1560s, Borghini arranged a large number of apprenticeships with these *tessitori di drappi*. Indeed, of sixty-six cases of boys apprenticed from 1534 through 1564 (these are recorded in the hospital's *giornale*; there are likely to have been more cases), forty-one were apprenticed with *tessitori di drappi*. In these cases, the contracts are virtually invariable and much to the advantage of individual boys, who had guaranteed employment for five years while they learned the trade, at wage rates up to five times what boys who worked in other enterprises earned. These contracts, in a pattern that eventually became adopted in other types of contracts as well, specified a pay rate that grew year by year in proportion, presumably, to the apprentice's increasing level of skill and usefulness to the *bottega*. Thus, the first year of apprenticeship paid six florins (forty-two lire), the second year eight, the third year ten, the fourth year twelve, and the fifth year fourteen, for a total of fifty florins.[43] In general, the higher wages paid to apprentices learning to be *tessitori di drappi* also began to be reflected in other types of *botteghe* as well, perhaps suggesting that at least by the 1560s, the Innocenti was nearly in a position to price the labor of its skilled apprentices. Although in most cases, the age when boys were first apprenticed is not given, in the few examples in which the age is indicated, it seems clear that apprenticeships started between the ages of ten and fourteen and lasted until boys were in their late teens (Table 4.1).

Just as striking was the tendency for the Innocenti's boys (but not girls) to have nicknames – "cacabasso"(low shit), "billera" (bad joke), "gonzo" (gullible), "meschino" (miserable, in the economic sense), or "morossino" (miserable in the emotional sense), which from their insulting and even

---

[41] The list of criminals and their sentences is found in ASF, Mediceo del Principato 471, fol. 687r, and fol. 688r, 22 June 1558. The two friars are listed in ASF, Medici del Principato 472, fol. 447r, 24 July 1558.

[42] Nicholas Terpstra, *Abandoned Children of the Italian Renaissance*, 186.

[43] AOIF Giornale L (XIII, 18) fol. 62r, 18 November 1558.

TABLE 4.1. *Apprenticeships at the Ospedale degli Innocenti, 1534–64*

Apprenticeships	N	Average annual wage (in lire di soldi di piccoli)
Tessitore di panni lanni (weavers of wool)	7	8
Tessitore di drappi (weavers of drapes)	41	40
Arazieri (tapestry and rug makers)	8	38
Musini	2	40
Saie (serge makers)	6	22
Rimettetori di drappi (repair of heavy cloth)	1	40
Tessitore d'ermisini (weavers of light silk)	1	40

Source: AOIF Giornale I–L (filze 16–18) 1534–64.

occasionally scatological character can be assumed to have been conferred on them by each other and then used in the day-books as a way of distinguishing one from another. Sometimes nicknames were more benign, "San Gimignano" or "Vichio," denoting a place of origin rather than particularly unattractive characteristics.[44] Although apprenticeships were usually set for periods of four and five years, mobility between shops seems to have been possible, if not frequent. In such cases, the employer had to pay any salary still due to the hospital, provided that the prior was willing to have him back in the hospital and he had not simply fled.[45]

A comparison with similar sources for the mid-seventeenth century reveals the extent to which the placement patterns of the Innocenti's boys had changed. Where during the sixteenth century boys had been apprenticed for terms of five years and occasionally even longer, in the seventeenth century, boys were placed out only for a year or two at a time, not so much to learn a specific trade, as had been true earlier, but to gather experience in a number of trades. Indeed, a considerable proportion of boys moved among several occupations within a short time, suggesting perhaps that the object was not so much to train them to earn a livelihood as it was to implant the notion that they should avoid idleness.[46] In particular, boys were often described not as apprentices but as "fattori."

---

[44] Ibid., fol. 89v, 17 October 1561, for "gonzo"; ibid., fol. 99r, 21 July 1562 for "meschino," "San Gimignano," and "billera"; ibid., fol. 102r, 3 July 1559 for "cacabasso"; ibid., fol. 102v, 15 November 1562 for "Vichio"; and Giornale K (XIII, 17), fol. 144r, 7 October 1547 for "morossino." This practice was not limited to the Innocenti: in the seventeenth century, the boys at the hospital of Santa Caterina degli Abbandonati were distinguished by similar nicknames: ASF Bigallo, 1675, fasc. 52, 27 May 1642.

[45] AOIF Giornale L (XIII, 18), fol. 130v, 9 July 1564.

[46] AOIF Ricordanze (XII, 14) fol. 26v ff., 31 March 1636–53.

These changes were also an organizational necessity stemming from the severe contraction of the economy toward the end of the first quarter of the seventeenth century. Wages were a good deal lower – the wage for the 170 placements described from 1636 to 1653 ranged from twenty-four to thirty lire per year, only half to three-quarters of the amount apprentices to *tessitori di drappi* had been earning in the third quarter of the sixteenth century. Concomitant with the scenario that Carlo Corsini has drawn for the mid-seventeenth century, in which foundling hospitals relinquished responsibility for boys once they reached age ten, the arrangements for placement suggest much more of a workhouse mentality arising from the increasing difficulty of assimilating foundlings into the economic life of the city.[47] As would be true in the Napoleonic era in France, this made the boys of foundling hospitals ideal draftees, like their counterparts who went to the galleys in the sixteenth century. In April 1646, several boys were chosen by the grand duke's drum major to serve as drummers "in the war in the direction of Pisa and Livorno."[48]

Pedagogy and discipline at the Innocenti reflected larger changes taking place within Italian schools. In Arezzo, masters' contracts in the 1490s began stressing schoolmasters' duties to instruct children in moral values and in how to live an upright life.[49] When Jesuits first began their schools in Monreale (Sicily) in 1541, for example, they taught reading and writing first, then as children matured, they taught them the Latin classical humanist curriculum. By the time of the foundation of the Collegio Romano, however, Jesuits were demanding that children entering the Collegio should already know how to read and write and, preferably, should already have some Latin. Such changes were part of a larger program to orient Jesuit teaching to the children of the elite to educate for leadership and seem to have been part of a larger conscious effort by humanist pedagogues to separate, as Borghini did at the Innocenti, those boys who could most profit from advanced study from those who could most benefit from learning manual trades.

The increasing formalization of class divisions from the sixteenth into the seventeenth century is amply illustrated by the fate of the *scuole pie*. The first *scuola pia*, founded in the Roman quarter of Santa Maria in Trastevere by

---

[47] Carlo Corsini "'Era piovuto dal cielo e la terra l'aveva raccolto: il destino del trovatello,'" in *Enfance Abandonee et Société, XIVᵉ–XXᵉ siècle: actes du colloque international*, Collection de l'École Française de Rome 140 (Rome: l'École Française de Rome, 1991), 109.

[48] AOIF Ricordanze (XII, 14) fol. 60v, 27 April 1646: "Nota di nostri fanciulli andati alla guerra alla volta di Pisa e Livorno per tamburini d'ordine di serenissimo G. Duca dato al signor Sandri collaterale e scelti da Simone Landini tamburo maggiore."

[49] Robert Black, *Studio e scuola in Arezzo*, 126.

José Calasana and with the support of Cardinal Silvio Antoniano, among others, admitted exclusively those children who could produce certificates of poverty. Only reluctantly did *scuole pie* eventually admit the sons of the wealthy. By the seventeenth century, Tommaso Campanella felt constrained to defend the *scuole pie* from critics who complained that to teach poor children the Latin classics subverted the hierarchical order of society. By encouraging social mobility, these critics argued, *scuole pie* ran the risk of creating labor shortages among skilled artisans and tradesmen. Despite these obstacles, the Florentine *scuole pie* continued throughout the seventeenth century to provide both a classical and a scientific education to boys from the most humble backgrounds. Yet the same social prejudices that made the Scolopi (a religious order founded in 1597 devoted to the education of poor children) in Florence so outstanding may well have taken their toll on the pedagogical resources of charitable institutions themselves. The *scuole pie*, however, did appropriate the sixteenth-century penchant for moral and disciplinary reform, especially in the form of religious training, and in this respect, by the second half of the sixteenth-century such charitable institutions as the Innocenti had made regular devotional practices a central part of their disciplinary regime.[50]

The evolution of codes of expected behavior for boys is nowhere clearer than in the set of house rules published at the Ospedale degli Innocenti in October 1618. Issued by the prior Marco Settimanni as "rules for the hospital's boys given to masters," they prescribed a daily routine of devotion and ritual prayer identical to the activities of *scuole pie*. "All the apprentices who live in the hospital" rose at dawn to say the Ave Maria and attend mass in the chapel. Prefects (*lettai*) enforced periods of silence and called each group of boys in turn according to whether they were sent out each day as apprentices. Each was then given his morning ration of bread, after which the boys went in twos to the church of SS. Annunziata, where they prayed thanks to God "for their good fortune, for the hospital's benefactors, and especially the Grand Duke."[51] The tradition of praying for the grand duke had been part of the hospital's ritual life at least since 1539, when Cosimo and two of his customs officials donated "seventy-five black berets to be worn by our children, and [in return] we are obligated to have them

---

[50] On the history of the *scuole pie*, see Paul Grendler, *Schooling in Renaissance Italy: Literacy and Learning, 1300–1600* (Baltimore: Johns Hopkins University Press, 1989), 381–90.

[51] AOIF Filze d'archivio (LXXII, 25) fol. 741r, 1 October 1618: "et ivi preghino Dio che dia loro buona fortuna, et gli benfattori et massime per il Serenissima Gran Duca."

pray for his most Illustrious Lordship and his aforesaid customs officials."[52] This tradition of praying for benefactors reflects practices also carried out in seventeenth-century *scuole pie*, which "practiced perpetual prayer during the day: a priest and nine students knelt and prayed in the church for fifteen to thirty minutes until relieved by the next group."[53]

Those children who stayed in the Innocenti's school and who were therefore not sent out were to remain in bed and quiet until the prefect summoned them "at an early hour," at which point they were to "dress themselves as well as give their help to the little ones who do not know how to dress by themselves." Once dressed, the boys proceeded two by two to the chapel, where "with devotion they must say the seven penitential psalms and prayers, reading loudly and distinctly so that they can be well understood by the others who must give their responses from the choir."[54] After breakfast, the schoolmaster was already in the schoolroom when, as the boys came in, he assigned them to their places where they were to remain silently listening as reading lessons, grammar, and Latin (or other subjects) were taught. Once the morning lessons were over, the master led the boys in saying the Ave Maria and the Salve Regina and then took them to the courtyard where they waited until the sounding of the dinner bell. At the bell's first sound:

> everyone shall wash and say grace standing in silence, and shall eat with good table-manners. The masters must supervise the boys using fear, and for those who do not behave modestly the master shall mete out punishment, consisting either of having [the miscreant] kneel in the middle of the room, or replenish the water, or whatever punishment the master deems appropriate, saying to them that it is important to make an example out of one for those who misbehave anywhere.[55]

[52] AOIF Giornale I (XIII, 16) fol. 157r, 29 December 1539: "per li speciali signori anzi lo illustrissimo signore duca et sua maestri di dogana chi l'anno fatto donativo di settantacinque berettini neri a tutta piegha per servitio delli nostri orphanelli et siamo oblighati fare preghare per sua Illustrissima Signoria et sopradetti maestri."

[53] Grendler, *Schooling*, 383. Cf. A. K. Liebrich, "Piarist Education in the Seventeenth Century," *Studi secenteschi* 26 (1985): 225–77; 27 (1986): 57–88, at 73–4.

[54] AOIF Filze d'archivio (LXXII, 25) fol 741r, 1 October 1618: "Quelli che stanno a scuola non si levino da letto fino che dal lettaio non saranno chiamati, il qual li facci levare a buon'hora et faccili stare nel loro dormentorio sino non sieno tutti vestiti et dieno aiuto a quei piccolini che non sanno vestirsi da loro. Et tutti levati faccili andare a due a due al chiesino, et ivi con devotione dichino i sette salmi penitenziali et orationi legendo forte et distintamente acciò sieno bene intesi da gl'altri che devon' risponde a coro."

[55] Ibid., fol. 741v: "persino che sonera il campanella a desinare, a qual tocco tutti vadino si lavino, e faccia beneditione tutti in piedi et con silentio, e buone creanze mangino, et il maestro stii per il refettorio acciò s'alevino con timore, et quelli che non stanno con modestia gli dii castigo, o di

After lunch, the boys washed again and then went into the chapel by twos, praying for the dead and for the souls of the hospital's benefactors and former priors. Once again, the boys recited the seven psalms and were brought to the courtyard or loggia to wait until the master called them for writing lessons. They practiced writing all afternoon, while the master ensured that they write "with great care, that they be given models of good and accurate handwriting with which to practice, and that the boys apply themselves with diligence" to the tasks at hand, "because when they acquire virtue God will give them good fortune as well."[56]

At the sounding of the bell for Vespers, the masters were to give instruction, test the pupils on what they had learned, "and then have them repeat what they had learned in the morning." A repetition of the Salve Regina and Ave Maria, as well as a recitation of the Our Father, concluded the school day, at which point the boys were dismissed and sent "without commotion" into the courtyard, where they were to wait until the supper hour. At supper as well, in addition to the usual prayers and washing, the boys were to eat "with fear and in silence." Another procession into the church followed, succeeded by a procession onto the loggia before the final Ave Maria. After the final Ave Maria, the boys went up the stairs, pausing in the upper part of the chapel for a final devotion and then went to their rooms where they undressed and went to bed. The master had to make sure that the lamp stayed lit through the entire night and in general to behave toward the boys with "charity always before his eyes" as his major guide to supervision.[57]

On Sundays and feast days, the masters taught something resembling a catechism, insofar as the learning required both memorization and the recitation of question and answer. In addition, the boys were taught to sing lauds in honor of the Madonna, "ad alta voce." These devotions did not take up entire Sundays, however, and at some point the boys were dismissed and free to roam the premises provided they conducted themselves "with modesty." In good weather, masters were instructed to take the boys outside "to get a little fresh air, either outside the gate at the end of Borgo Pinti, or

---

farli inginochiare in mezzo, o di farli bene aqua o quelli che li parrà più a proposito, dicendoli di piùche è sempre bene che facci tener la norma a uno, che accusi quelli che fanno del male in ogni luogo."

[56] Ibid., fol. 741v: "li facci scrivere, et habbili buona cura, che habbia buoni esempi et acurate, et diligente all'imparare, perche quando haranno le virtù Dio li porgera anco buona fortuna."

[57] Ibid., fol. 741v–742r: "Sonato che sarà vespro d'inverno tutti sene vadino in scuola, il maestro gli dia la lettione, gli faccia l'esamine, et li faccia replicare le lettioni della mattina...e poi li licentii, i quali licentiati vadino senza strepito nella corte...si lavino le mani, faccia la beneditione della tavola, mangino con timore ed silentio....Et le cose che toccan a far alli lettai il maestro n'habbino cura si faccino, et habbin tutti la carità sempre avanta gli occhi."

at the Villa degli Alberi."[58] Boys who normally went as apprentices during the day were included in all of the hospital's devotional activities, referred to as "spiritual exercises."[59]

Those boys who seemed to excel at such devotions became part of the group known as "seminarians," *cherici di seminario*, who were to be well-trained and placed in the holy fear of God, "with all the virtues that they need to be taught in order that they can call themselves clergy." To these spiritual types were assigned the duties of acolytes—serving mass, and keeping the chalices and the chapel clean. A subgroup of these aspiring clergy consisted of choral scholars. This last group had a special obligation to stay cleaner and to live more upright lives than the other boys, and on this group especially the masters should concentrate their attention on inculcating virtue, "as if they were sons of a noble family." Among this select group, the prior should be notified whenever one of them was found to be "especially clever at arithmetic, mathematics, or other skills." To this category of student the prior and the masters were to "do everything" to make sure that such pupils learned and became skillful.[60] It may well be that from this latter category of boys, hospital officials chose representatives to attend the funeral rites of deceased officials from the city's other charities. In 1703, for example, Claudio Ferrari, "maestro di nostri fanciulli," participated in the funeral of the defunct prior of San Paolo, along with four of the hospitals children. In 1704, Maestro Ferrari and six of the Innocenti's boys participated in the funeral rites of the prior of San Matteo, with Maestro Ferrari as the celebrant of the Mass and the boys each carrying a processional candle.[61]

The 1618 set of rules took great care to regulate as much behavior as its compilers could imagine. Scattered throughout all the admonitions to good behavior were references to comportment, modesty, and tranquillity.

---

[58] Ibid., fol. 743v: "Il maestro quando è bel tempo menerà fuori li fanciulli a pigliar un po d'aria, come sarebbe fuor della Porta a Pinti, a gl'Alberi o altrove, facendo che sopratutto vadino con modestia."

[59] Ibid., fol. 742r–742v: "E perche il giorno delle feste non si va a bottega, faccia il maestro che tutti tanto li scolari, quando li bottegai vadino a far tutti gl'esercitii spirituali come s'è detto di sopra." For Borghini and the Villa degli Alberi, see B. Varchi, "L'Ercolano, ovvero: agli Alberi," in *Opere di Benedetto Varchi* (Trieste: Lloyd Austriaco, 1858) 2: 11, 23, and 33.

[60] AOIF Filze d'archivio (LXXII, 25) fol. 742v, 1 October 1618: "prima in avezzarli bene e col santo timor di Dio, et con tutte le virtù, che possino imparare, queli si chiamino li Cherici … et si tirino in somma inanzi con tutte le virtù, come se fossero figli di famiglia nobile. Et perche tra di loro ci potrebbe esser qualche d'uno che inclinassi all'Abaco, alle matematiche, o altre virtù, il maestro osservi et n'avertisca il priore, che non guarderà a cosa alcuna farli imparare, et divenghino virtuosi."

[61] AOIF Ricordanze (XII, 17) fol. 38r, 7 May 1703. For San Matteo, see ibid., fol 38v, 19 August 1704.

Boys could wander freely through the hospital's premises but rules cautioned them not to associate with seedy-looking characters (*pestine*), "especially not to loiter near the *baroni* who come to sun themselves along the entire length of the loggia." The rules also forbade boys to indulge in "horseplay, blaspheming, or to use indecent language," and the masters were responsible for making sure that the children swept the floors of the hospital and kept the premises clean. Boys were specifically excluded from the "food cellars, the vaults, and the garden, and on feast days they should be ready to hear Vespers, and should neither make a commotion nor bring into the chapel things to eat, or deface the church."[62] The penalties for lack of modesty were, in theory at least, severe. Boys who failed to heed the admonition that at night they were to stay in their beds and not move could be "sent outside the hospital."[63]

The goal of such discipline was that the master should raise his pupils "with the fear of God," so that they could inspire the skills, virtues, and good manners that would make them men. Hospital officials saw such pedagogy as developmental, as a process focused on "helping them and making them progress."[64] In this respect, devotion, ritual, and class work each played an equal role in the larger enterprise of discipline and the control of impulse. The inculcation of discipline, manners, and *civiltà* served not only to increase the chances of success for select pupils but also to assist the hospital in presenting its charges publicly to the outside world. Daily, masters checked for torn clothes, sending the younger children back with an older child to help them and to make certain that shoes were "tied, buckled, and stayed clean."[65] The rules, at least, demonstrated tremendous concern for cleanliness and order. In particular, masters were instructed when the grand duke, archduke, or their consorts arranged a visit to the Innocenti that the children should line up along the front of the loggia, and as the carriage drew up alongside, "to

---

[62] AOIF Filze d'archivio (LXXII, 25) fol. 743r, 1 October 1618: "Non prattichino con altra specie di pestine, et in particolare non stieno mai a canto a quei baroni che voglian venire al sole tutta la loggia, e non vadino fuora senza licentia.... Non giuochino, non bestemino, et non dichino parole indecenti si tenga conto che dee spazzare, et tener pulita la casa, et il maestro habbi cura lo faccino. Non vadino per le stalle, per le cantine, per le volte, et per l'orto. Sieno pronti ad udir il vespro, li giorni festivi, et non faccino strepito, ne portino cosa nè di mangiare, nè di imbruttare la chiesa."

[63] Ibid.: "Stiino nelli lor letti quando sono a dormire, et non si muovino, perche se saranno veduti far altrimenti, saranno mandati fuor di casa."

[64] Ibid.: "Et in effetto il maestro gli alievi con il timor di Dio, con le virtù, et con quelle buone creanze, che li possono far di venir' huomini, acciò nio ancora potteamo pigliare l'animo d'aiutarli et tirarli innanzi."

[65] Ibid.: "tenga uno che habbi la cura di far tener allaciare bene le raspe, e calze, et star puliti al possibile."

do them reverence by bowing their heads," and when they left the nearby Church of the Annunziata to do the same.[66]

Two rather poignant letters written to the prior of the Ospedale degli Abbandonati in 1639 by a father who had temporarily abandoned two sons, one to the Innocenti and one to the Abbandonati, reinforce the connection between devotion and discipline as perceived by those who availed themselves of the services of charitable institutions. The father, Bernardo Chimentelli, had heard by way of his own brother Don Vigilio that Giuliano, the son at the Abbandonati had been misbehaving and was about to be expelled. He wrote from Rome to the prior, Ulisse Nucci:

> I come with this letter to greet you wishing you happy holidays, and I also beg you to have compassion and patience concerning the liveliness of Giuliano my son. My brother Don Vigilio has written to me that he [Giuliano] is not working out well and is not learning, I don't know where that comes from – only that when I was overtaken by the wrath of my relatives; I had to abandon my sons. He was never an idiot as I understand he is now, even if he was always full of fun, shy and a quick learner. They tell me that he has come into the disfavor of your Lordship and that you do not want to keep him any longer. . . . I had hoped to have him close by me in Rome, but since Carnival I have been afflicted with liver disease, and I suffer such pain from urine that I cannot leave my bed and with fever and almost every other ailment that I do not have the words to express. . . . I pray that you say a *salve* to the Most Holy Annunciation that we might pray to God most high for very a miracle and to San Filippo Neri who does very great miracles for our children.[67]

Bernardo wrote a second letter the same day to his son Giuliano at the Abbandonati in which he made even clearer the connection between devotion and discipline:

> My honorable son:

> Don Vigilio my brother has written to me that you are not behaving as a good son, and that you are not learning any skill, and that you spend the entire day scandalizing Sir Ulisse to whom I entrusted you. You are to behave well, to pray God for him, and not spend the whole day as you have done on the school grounds, making a ruckus with the other children instead of keeping your books in hand and taking up pen to learn how

---

[66] Ibid., fol. 742v–743r: "et quando le loro carozze sono di rimpetto li faccino reverenza col capo."

[67] ASF Bigallo 1675, fascicolo 7, 4 June 1639, unfoliated: Bernardo Chimentelli in Rome to Ulisse Nucci at the Spedale degli Abbandonati in Florence, cited in Maria Fubini-Leuzzi, *Condurre a onore: famiglia, matrimonio, e assistenza dotale a Firenze in età moderna* (Florence: Leo S. Olschki, 1999), Appendix III, 256–7.

to write. Always remember and recognize that you are poor, and you will have no income except for your skills, what you are and what you must learn. In future do not behave as I have heard you have, that you were not learning and not being good, but instead show good will and obedience to your elders. Remember to pray God and the Most Holy Annunciation for me, that this little infirmity that has afflicted me will be taken away, and pray for your mother, too, who begs you to be good and to learn. And if my father or brothers ask or want that you become a priest, you tell them that you do not want to be one on any account, as you have always told me, and that if you do, you will always be cursed. Commend me to everyone and obey everyone. You will go to Signora Caterina, wife of Carlo Massini who, as you know, stays at the Innocenti. You will treat them reverently, kissing their hands on our behalf. You will tell them that you commend your brother to them and to the Prior of the Innocenti, because God knows how he is treated and how he is doing. You will pray God for your grandfather and your uncles that for the love they bear toward God they will rescue your brother Giovanbattista degli Innocenti. Pray to the most Holy Annunciation for him, and for those who are taking care of him, and make sure that you say every day that prayer I taught you that day in the Office, that goes "O dulcissime Iesu Christe verus deus" and teach it to Signore Ulisse, and say it every day. I'm sending the oath that says that I married your mother (since you were born illegitimate I made you legitimate). Keep that proof next to you and keep it in mind for when you might need it . . . Even to God I beg you to be good and to learn, and to pray God for us as we do for you. Write me a letter. Your most loving father, from Rome, 4 June 1639. P.S. Your mother is ill but getting better.[68]

Thus, the exhortations and frequent prayers provided in the rules of 1618 were not so much a retreat for the soul as they were the extension of the patronage of benefactors and relatives to incorporate the Virgin Mary and the entire celestial court. If in this case the father hoped the sojourns of his two boys in charitable institutions would be brief, what is striking is the inability or unwillingness of the extended family network to provide concrete assistance, although clearly they formed part of the more general network of benefactors and intimates who expected the beneficiaries of their charity to pray for them. The father died six months later, as poignantly recorded in a letter from Giovan Battista degli Innocenti (now at home and

---

[68] ASF Bigallo 1675, fascicolo 7, 4 June 1639, unfoliated: Bernardo Chimentelli in Rome to Giuliano Chimentello at the Spedale degli Abbandonati in Florence, also cited in Maria Fubini-Leuzzi, *Condurre a onore*, 257–8.

calling himself Giovanbattista Chimentelli) to Ulisse Nucci, who in early
December "passed away in much agony."[69]

Two Alumni Careers: Giovanbattista (Fra Iacopo) Nacchianti (1502–69) and Costantino Antinori (1530–78)

In one of his memoranda to Grand Duke Francesco I, the Innocenti's superintendent, Vincenzio Borghini, wrote:

> Whether foundlings come here because of poverty or scandal, or because
> of the death of relatives, or to hide secret births, or whatever reason there
> might be, we treat them as follows: as soon as we receive these creatures
> they are given to wet nurses and then weaned. Then they are welcomed
> back into the hospital, and we teach the boys, according to their ability,
> various skills. And there is a school and master for anyone who is skilled
> at reading and writing. If anyone is discovered who is worth it, he is made
> to study, and good pupils come of it, even prelates.[70]

One such prelate, a pupil of the Innocenti before Borghini's time, was
Giovanbattista Nacchianti, born legitimately in 1502 to the Innocenti's
notary Ser Andrea di Cristoforo Nacchianti and who left his portion to
the Innocenti in 1517.[71] Giovanbattista, according to Vincenzio Borghini,
"who wrote so much and in a very learned way, was a pupil in this house,
and was the little Innocenti bishop."[72] When Andrea Nacchianti died in
March 1510, Giovanbattista was seven years old, and on 12 May, Maestro
Francesco Petrucci, the Innocenti's superintendent, along with Antonio di
Lodovico Sassolini, a Franciscan at Santa Croce, became one of the guardians
appointed to oversee the estate.[73]

---

[69] ASF Bigallo 1675, fasc. 7: Giovan Battista Chimentelli in Florence to Ulisse Nucci in Florence,
10 December 1639, cited in Fubini Leuzzi, *Condurre a onore*, 258: "Devo dar' parte a V. S. con
amare lacrime approssimarsi la perdita di mio padre dalle 5 ore in qua della notte passata sta
agonizzando."

[70] AOIF, Suppliche e sovrani rescritti (VI, 1), fol. 138r, n.d.: "o, per povertà, o per disgratia di morte
de' parenti, o, per celare i parti furtivi o, per qualunque altra cagione si sia: si governa in questo
modo: Che ricevute le dette creature si danno à balia et divuezzi che sono: si ricevono in casa, et
si allievano, insegnando à masti secondo a loro dispositione della capacità loro, diverse arti: et ci
è scuola et maestro per chi è atto à leggere, et scrivere, et se si scuopre alcuno spirito ch'e vaglia;
si fanno studiare, et ne sono usciti de' buoni allievi et prelati sino a' vescovi."

[71] AOIF Estranei (CXVLIV, 633) fol. 128r, 15 October 1502. His wet nurse was Mona Piera da
Prato: ibid., fol. 128v, 29 October 1502. Giovanbattista was taken care of by Mona Piera da Prato
until at least 3 October 1507, just before his fifth birthday (ibid., fol. 135r).

[72] See below, n. 147.

[73] For a discussion of Ser Andrea Nacchianti's will, cf. supra, Chapter 3.

It is most likely that at Andrea's death in 1510, Giovanbattista actually began to live at the foundling hospital, for his donation, drawn up on 22 February 1517, mentions his earnest concern, confided in secret to a Dominican friar at San Domenico di Fiesole, to satisfy the debts he had incurred while he "stayed at the Innocenti." These debts were for his feeding, loans, and other expenses borne by the hospital and by Petrucci, its prior, as well as Petrucci's expenses for his guardianship. The two thousand florins he left to the Innocenti when he joined the Dominicans at San Marco suggests that he still had some controlling share in the wealth of the Nacchianti family, a suggestion confirmed, in fact, by the 229 florins his father deposited for him in the Innocenti in 1510. In addition to the deposit to the Innocenti, his father also left on deposit a sum of money at the hospital of Santa Maria Nuova as security.[74]

Giovanbattista's decision to join the Dominicans was almost certainly a result of Francesco Petrucci's guardianship. Petrucci was one of two of the Innocenti's superintendents to be actively involved in the Savonarolan movement during the first quarter of the sixteenth century (indeed, members of the silk guild, the Innocenti's official patron, figured prominently in the continued flourishing of Savonarolan ideas and organizations). In 1503, Petrucci had also successfully negotiated an agreement between the youth confraternity of San Zanobi and the Dominicans of San Marco to give San Zanobi's members more meeting space. Another *piagnone* silk guildsman, Ser Lorenzo Violi, whose family ran a flourishing firm of dyers that had branches as far flung as Bruges and Alexandria, notarized the agreement, and the guarantors were two more prominent silk guildsmen, Francesco del Pugliese, the son of Piero di Cosimo's patron, and Niccolò del Nero. An

---

[74] For Borghini's notice, which occurs in the first draft of his *Consideratione sopra l'allogare le donne delli innocenti fuora di maritare o monacare*, see AOIF Filza d'Archivio, 17, fol. 39r: "et il vescovo di Chioggia Nacchianti, che ha scritto tanto et si dottamente, fu allevato in questa Casa et fu il vescovo nocentino." For the amount left by his father in trust, see AOIF Ricordanze (XII, 6) fol. 4r, 10 March 1509. In 1510, we know that he was living with his mother in the parish of San Simone. By 1 July 1511, however, the house was rented "di nuovo" [again] to two widows, who were to pay the eight-year-old Giovanbattista fourteen florins every six months in rent. On 1 August, moreover, Ser Andrea's executor bought a farm in San Casciano using money that had been deposited by Ser Iacopo (AOIF CXLIV 634, fol. 212r and 212v, 1 July and 1 August 1511). Furthermore, Messer Francesco Petrucci and Giovanbattista's mother, Mona Dianora, were his guardians: AOIF Estranei Debitori, Creditori, e Richordi (CXLIV, 634), fol. 208v, 12 May 1510. See ASF Notarile antecosiminiano 16279, Antonio Parenti 1509–11, fol. 72r–74v, 86r-v, for details of the appointment. For the statement in his will that he "spent time" at the Innocenti and owed the hospital and its prior for his care, see ASF Diplomatico Spedale degli Innocenti, 22 February 1517.

astonishing proportion (94 percent) of members of San Zanobi who were already destined for the religious life between 1501 and 1530 were persuaded to join the Dominicans at San Marco. Although Giovanbattista Nacchianti, regrettably, is not listed among the members of that confraternity, nor, for that matter, were the Nacchianti numbered among the *piagnoni*, circumstantial evidence virtually forces the conclusion that Petrucci's guardianship moved Giovanbattista in the direction of a career with the friars at San Marco.[75] Certainly he would have inherited from them the reforming zeal that more than once in his later life would be a source of political tribulation.

When Giovanbattista joined the Dominicans, he took the name Iacobus. After nine years at San Marco in Florence, he was sent to Bologna to study theology in 1528, where he came under the supervision of Michele Ghislieri, the future Pope Pius V. In 1534, he taught at the Dominican monastery in Perugia, and on his thirty-fourth birthday in 1536, he became prior of the monastery in Pisa, where the local chronicler described him as a "son of San Marco, a very learned man of angelic customs."[76] In 1537 he became prior of the monastery in Lucca. In 1538 he returned to Perugia, where he taught philosophy and theology until 1541. In that year he taught philosophy at the Minerva, the church in Rome where the feast of Saint Thomas Aquinas was celebrated annually with a mass and an oration, and where the Carafa had

---

[75] On the Innocenti's priors (Petrucci and Buonafè) as Savonarolans, see Lorenzo Polizzotto, *The Elect Nation*, 35. On Petrucci negotiating the agreement for more space for the youth confraternity of San Zanobi, see idem, 193. On San Marco's remarkable success in controlling this confraternity and recruiting its young members to the Dominican order, see Polizzotto, 194–5. Ser Lorenzo Violi, whom Polizzotto describes as the "piagnone" notary, belonged to the family of prominent and successful silk merchants. The family business had commercial contacts as far-flung as London, Bruges, and Alexandria. The painter Cosimo Rosselli, the recipient of a commission from Ser Andrea Nacchianti to paint his chapel, was connected to the confraternity of San Zanobi. On the commission, see Dario Covi, "A Documented Altarpiece by Cosimo Rosselli," *The Art Bulletin* 53.2 (1971): 236–8, and on Cosimo Rosselli's connection to San Zanobi, see Eisenbichler, *The Boys of the Archangel Rafael*, 258–9. Francesco del Pugliese, another prominent "piagnone," also was part of a family prominent in the silk guild. Another del Pugliese (Raffaello) commissioned Piero di Cosimo's altarpiece (now in St. Louis) of the Virgin with Saint Nicholas, possibly a reference to the Monte delle doti or the newly formed Monte di Pietà, whereas another glorious Piero di Cosimo painting of Madonna, child and saints (including Saint Catherine of Alexandria) was painted for the Spedale degli Innocenti. For the connection between Piero del Pugliese and the Savonarolan movement, see Laura Cavazzini, "Dipinti e sculture nelle chiese dell'Ospedale," in *Gli Innocenti e Firenze nei secoli: Un ospedale, un archivio, una città*, ed. Lucia Sandri (Florence: Società per Edizioni Scelte, 1996), 113–50, at 119, 122. Francesco del Pugliese's close ties with the Savonarolans are much more amply documented. See Polizzotto, *Elect Nation*, 234n.

[76] Pietro Mozzato, *Jacopo Nacchianti: un vescovo riformatore (Chioggia 1544–1569)* (Chioggia: Edizioni Nuova Scintilla, 1993), 10–12. I thank Dr. Susan Schulze for finding and making available a wealth of primary and secondary source material on Nacchianti.

an important chapel.[77] According to an entry of January 1546 in the diary of the secretary and chronicler of the Council of Trent, Angelo Massarelli:

> That man [Nacchianti] is a Dominican friar, who, after he was kicked out of his order, his Holiness rescued him out of compassion and gave him 15 *scudi* a month for his entertainment, and placed him in the middle of debates while he was eating – he was in such favor with the Pope, that he made him confessor to his son, the Duke of Castro.[78]

Nacchianti's erudition and bearing during these debates so impressed Pope Paul III that in 1544, he appointed him bishop of Chioggia, a small fishing village just south of Venice.[79]

Nacchianti attended all three sessions of the Council of Trent, arriving at the first session in May 1545.[80] Although Nacchianti drew a stipend from the papal legates and stayed as the cardinal of Trent's houseguest, the bishop of Chioggia felt under no subsequent obligation to support the papal party's agenda.[81] Drawing the wrath of the Council's secretary, who accused him of gross ingratitude, Nacchianti opposed virtually every plank of the papal platform. He sided with those, including the cardinal of Trent, who wished to discuss abuses first and dogma second. He got into a dispute over the canonicity of the Scriptures approved at the Council of Ferrara-Florence in 1439, a dispute that was clearly a prelude to his more radical views

---

[77] John W. O'Malley, "Some Renaissance Panegyrics of Aquinas," Renaissance Quarterly, 27.2 (1974): 174–92. On this chapel, see Gail L. Geiger *Filippino Lippi's Carafa Chapel: Renaissance Art in Rome*, Sixteenth-Century Essays and Studies, vol. 5 (Kirksville: Sixteenth Century Journal Publishers, 1986).

[78] *Concilium Tridentinum: Diarorum, Actorum, Epistularum, Tractatuum nova collectio*, ed. Societas Goerresianae (Fribourg: Herder, 1901) 1: 382.19, diary of Angelo Massarelli, 22 January 1546. See also Gottfried Buschbell, *Reformation und Inquisition in Italien um die Mitte des 16 Jahrunderts Quellen und forschungen aus dem gebeite der geschichte* (Paderborn, F. Schöning, 1910), 155, cited in Colomban Fischer, "Jacques Nacchianti, O. P., évêque du Chioggia (Chiozza) + 1569 et sa théologie de la Primautè absolue du Christ," *La France Franciscaine* 20 (1937): 97–174, at 100. There is no evidence in these or any other sources concerning why Nacchianti might have been expelled from the Dominicans. Serafino Razzi's brief biography makes no mention of it; perhaps Pope Paul III's "rescue" included Nacchianti's reinstatement. See Serafino Razzi, *Istoria de gli uomini illustri così nelle prelature Come nelle Dottrine, del Sacro ordine degli Predicatori. Scritta da F. Serafino Razzi dell'istesso ordine, e Dottore Theologo, della Prouincia Romana* (Lucca: per il Busdrago, 1596), 116–17.

[79] *Concilium Tridentinum*, 1: 382.26–383.3, diary of Angelo Massarelli, 22 January 1546. On Chioggia as a plum benefice for diligent inquisitors, see Pullan, *The Jews and the Inquisition of Venice* (London: I.B. Tauris, 1983), 32. See Biblioteca Apostolica Vaticana (BAV), Barb. Lat. 2879, fol. 272v, 30 January 1543: Atti Concistoriali for Nacchianti's elevation to the see of Chioggia.

[80] *Concilium Tridentinum* 1: 184.19, diary of Angelo Massarelli, 6 May 1545.

[81] *Concilium Tridentinum* 1: 383.3–11, diary of Angelo Massarelli, 22 January 1546.

that the authority of Scripture should supersede ecclesiastical tradition.[82] The account by Cardinal Girolamo Seripando, archbishop of Salerno, of the Council of Trent also records on 5 April 1546 "great tumult against the Chioggian bishop, when he called ungodly those who put the apostolic authority of the Church on the same level as the books of Holy Scripture."[83] Nacchianti left Trent a few days later and never returned to the first session.

Nacchianti's views that Scripture constituted a higher authority than apostolic or ecclesiastical tradition, as well as other signs of sympathy with Lutheran ideas, also brought attempts by the Venetian Signoria to have him transferred from the see of Chioggia, and a trial for heresy.[84] The first documented attempts to have Nacchianti transferred away from Chioggia came in August 1546. His lack of secure doctrine made the Venetian Signoria nervous about having him so close to such a large city of influence as Venice, and they wished to substitute for him Tommaso Stella, the bishop of Salpe, whose anti-Lutheran preaching was well known and whose views were much safer. Even as late as December 1547, Nacchianti's transfer from Chioggia was still the subject of correspondence, but his tenacity ensured that the Venetian Signoria's hopes of having a fiery anti-Lutheran preacher in Chioggia would not be realized.[85]

Massarelli's investigation of Nacchianti resulted from an accusation by the Chioggian schoolmaster Giuliano Ercolano that at some point during Lent 1548, Nacchianti had heard a pro-Lutheran sermon by Fra Girolamo da Siena and had come up to him afterward full of praise, saying, "you preached a beautiful sermon this morning." Massarelli journeyed to Venice and Chioggia at the end of 1548 and beginning of 1549 to interview witnesses. As a result of these investigations, Nacchianti and his supporters charged that Massarelli had conducted the investigation improperly. Nacchianti's party appealed to Marcello Cervini to review Massarelli's actions. Cervini found

---

[82] On 8 August 1545 at a banquet and again in front of the full assembly in April 1546, he argued that Scripture should be considered more important than ecclesiastical tradition. Cf. the letter of Giacomo Giacomelli to Cosimo Giacomelli, in *Concilium Tridentinum*, 10:173.37–46, 13 August 1545, cited in Massimo Firpo and Dario Marcatto, *Il processo inquisitoriale del cardinal Giovanni Morone* (Rome: Istituto storico italiano per l'età moderna e contemporenea, 1981–9), 1: 270.

[83] *Concilium Tridentinum* 2: 433.5–6, Hieronymi Seripandi, *Commentarii de vita sua*, 5 Aprilis 1546.

[84] Luigi Carcereri, "Fra Giacomo Nacchianti vescovo di Chioggia e fra Girolamo da Siena inquisiti per eresia," *Nuovo Archivio Veneto*, 21 (1911): 468–89, at 469–70. Cf. Hubert Jedin, *A History of the Council of Trent*, trans. E. Graf 1961 (2 vols., London: Thomas Nelson & Sons, 1957–61) 2: 64, and Buschbell, 155–73.

[85] Carcereri, "Fra Giacomo Nacchianti," 471–2, citing Carte Farnesiane di Parma for 26 May 1547 and ASF Manoscritti, Carte Cerviniane 42, n. 169 for 10 December 1547.

Massarelli blameless and Nacchianti's charges groundless.[86] Nacchianti eventually escaped persecution by recanting so persuasively that he reassumed his seat at the second and third sessions of Trent.

In an explicit comparison between the case of Pier Paolo Vergerio's condemnation and Nacchianti's exoneration, Silvana Seidel-Menchi notes that despite the example Nacchianti set during the conciliar debates, in his own diocese he kept his more radical views private, allowing the faithful to continue their attachment to rites and ceremonies that Nacchianti himself considered superstitious. Thus a review of the Chioggian clergy undertaken by Annibal Grisonio in 1549 elicited some surprising testimony from the cathedral's canons:

> Several times walking along with him in church, and seeing some women kneeling before images, the bishop inquired of the other canons who were with him, "what's that woman doing?" And when we told him that she was doing her devotions, he smiled condescendingly. And when we asked him, "why are you laughing, monsignor," he kept on smiling and alternated between not answering, and saying, "they are simple people."[87]

Although the cathedral's canons had also heard him laughing to himself about the sale of indulgences, Nacchianti apparently did nothing to prohibit them. Similarly, when processions of flagellants came to Chioggia, Nacchianti made something of a game of them, and when he tried to abolish the annual January 2 procession led by "two canons of the cathedral, two children, a crib, and an infant," the canons and the faithful defended the procession as being of "longstanding custom and great utility." Nacchianti abandoned his efforts to put an end to this ritual as well. Admittedly, Nacchianti's split between word and deed did not fool the local schoolmaster, who turned him in to the authorities of the Inquisition. When he did take the pulpit, he apparently succeeded in keeping his discourses sufficiently abstruse to conceal his Lutheran sympathies. As one local fisherman testified, "His

---

[86] The account of William Hudon, *Marcello Cervini and Ecclesiastical Government* (De Kalb: Northern Illinois University Press, 1990), 122, which puts Nacchianti under arrest in a Bolognese monastery, appears to be a conflation of his fate and the fate of the preacher whose sermon Nacchianti praised. Fra Girolamo of Siena, not Nacchianti, was arrested in February 1549 and escaped from custody two months later, on 3 April. See Massarelli's diary in *Concilium Tridentinum* 1: 825.5.

[87] Silvana Seidel-Menchi, *Erasmo in Italia 1520–1580* (Turin: Bollati Boringheri, 1987), 373n, citing Archivio di Stato di Venezia (hereinafter ASV), busta 8, fascicolo 11 (now renumbered as fascicolo 3): *Inquisitione fatta per il reverendo messer Annibal Grisonio sopra la vita e costumi delli canonici et preti di Chioggia con il reverendo maestro Adriano Veneto dell'anno 1549*, fol. 2v. This inquisition file has now been transcribed in full by Mozzato, 113–94.

preaching displeased me not because he said bad things, but because it couldn't be understood."[88]

At the third session of the Council of Trent, Nacchianti spoke up on 15 December 1562 concerning the issue of episcopal residence, about which he had written a treatise in 1554 dedicated to Marcello Cervini. Following the suggestion of a French bishop that episcopal residence had been established "by divine law," Nacchianti argued that the wording should be changed to "canon or ecclesiastical law." His careful and attentive administration of the diocese of Chioggia was considered a model for implementation of the Tridentine decrees.[89]

The view of at least one neo-Savonarolan, Serafino Razzi, in his catalog of Dominican prelates published in 1596, suggests that Florentine Dominicans revered Nacchianti's memory:

Iacopo Nacchianti, a Florentine, who made his profession of faith at the monastery of San Marco in Florence, [was] a father of singular intelligence, and very learned (such that at the Council of Trent he was believed to be the most knowledgeable bishop there). When he was a reader at the Minerva in Rome, he attended disputations at the papal table in the company of the most learned men who were in Rome at that time. In that way, he earned the favor and kindness of Paul III, who pronounced and created him bishop of Chioggia. He wrote some excellent works, of which I will say more below. He was always beloved by his mentors, and when he came to visit San Marco, while I will still a novice, he was lovingly received by everyone, and sang us an episcopal mass. Father Nacchianti was tall,

---

[88] Seidel-Menchi, *Erasmo*, 69, citing ASV busta 8 fascicolo 3, fol. 25v. Cf. Dino De'Antoni "A proposito di Erasmo e Nacchianti," in *Chioggia: Rivista di studi e ricerche* 3.4 (1990): 176–9.

[89] *New Catholic Encyclopedia*, vol. 10, s.v. "Nacchianti." Nacchianti's printed works, all published at Venice after his encounters with the Inquisition, can surely be seen as an effort to reestablish his credibility with Rome, and especially with his patron, Marcello Cervini. See bibliography for a full list. Indeed, the late-seventeenth-century ecclesiastical historian Richard Simon's compilation of commentators and commentaries on the New Testament dismissed Nacchianti's contributions as so polemical and anti-Protestant that his work could not be considered commentary. The Chioggian bishop's collected works are in *Iacobi Nacchianti Clugiensis episcopi operum tomus primus* (Venice, 1567, 1569; Lyon, 1657), the first edition of which Vincenzio Borghini himself owned a copy.

For Nacchianti's treatise on episcopal residence, including a dedicatory letter to Cardinal Marcello Cervini, see Biblioteca Apostolica Vaticana, Codices Ottoboniani Latini 465, fol. 215r–236r. For an abridged transcript of Nacchianti's interventions at the Council of Trent, see D'Addario, *Aspetti della controriforma a Firenze*, 371. On Nacchianti and Cervini, see William V. Hudon, *Marcello Cervini*, 56, 62, 122–3. The trial is described in Massimo Firpo and Dario Marcatto, *Il processo inquisitoriale del cardinal Giovanni Morone* 1:269–71 and in Benedetto da Mantova, *Il beneficio di Cristo*, ed. S. Caponetto (De Kalb: Northern Illinois University Press, 1972), 441–3, 493–4. On Borghini's ownership of Nacchianti's opera, see Matteini, "La biblioteca erudita," 635.

with a dry complexion, and with his long beard and bishop's raiment, had a handsome and commanding appearance. He built on the monastery of Chioggia a funerary chapel, in which, dying at an advanced age on 24 April 1569, he was buried in front of the altar, under a white marble slab, with the following epitaph: Iacopo Nacchianti, order of preachers, bishop of Chioggia.[90]

There is also a contemporary portrait of Nacchianti in Vasari's corridor, which links the Uffizi to the Palazzo Pitti in Florence.

Although Nacchianti had been an *allevato*[91] before Borghini's time, another example of the Innocenti's solicitude, Costantino Antinori, had been abandoned at the Innocenti during the 1530s. In 1550, he obtained from Niccolò Durante di Montaiuolo, the vicar of the archbishop of Florence, a "dispensa di legittimatione" that would allow him to join any of the four minor orders. This legal instrument noted that Antinori was still "a youth, and one of those destitute and abandoned boys who from his infancy was left at the hospital of Santa Maria degli Innocenti and who for several years was laudably educated there."[92] He was twenty-two years old when Borghini became prior in 1552, and shortly after that date, Borghini appointed him as assistant prior. In 1555, as a sacristan at the Innocenti, Antinori provided a proxy signature for Benedetto di Giovanni da Vernia, who was about to take on an Innocenti foundling as an apprentice, because Benedetto "did not know how to write."[93] In 1558, Antinori witnessed the last will and testament of Raffaello Borghini.[94] In early 1564, Antinori was elected as rector of the Oratory of San Martino all'Alba.[95]

---

[90] Serafino Razzi, *Istoria*, 116–17.

[91] I use the term *allevato* to describe children who were educated at the Innocenti, whether or not they had been brought there as infants, which is sometimes difficult to determine. In the case of Nacchianti, there is secure documentation fixing his arrival at the hospital at age seven in 1509. Franceso Morandini da Poppi did not arrive at the Innocenti until he was at least nineteen. Giovanbattista Naldini arrived very shortly after his birth on 3 May 1535. On this revised birth date, see Elizabeth Pilliod, *Pontormo, Bronzino, Allori*, 77. Documents relating to Costantino Antinori describe him as "abandoned in the hospital of the Innocenti since infancy."

[92] AOIF, Filza d'Archivio (LXII, 3) fol. 467r, 5 December 1550: "discretus iuvenis Constantinus unum de pueris ab eius infantia destitutis et expositis in hospitale Sancte Marie Innocentium de Florentie et ibi per plures annos laudabiliter educatus."

[93] AOIF Giornale L (XIII, 18) fol. 13v, 27 July 1555: "Et io Ser Constantino sopradetto fui presente quanto di sopra si contiene, et in fede del vero a preghiera del detto Benedetto perche disse non sape scrivere ho fatto questi versi di mia propria mano hoggi questo dì sopradetto in Firenze."

[94] AOIF, Filze d'Archivio (LXII, 19) fol. 263r, 26 August 1558. Raffaello Borghini was the brother of Vincenzio, the prior, but not the Raffaello Borghini who in 1580 published *Il riposo*, a work containing biographies of artists.

[95] On Antinori's election as rector of San Martino all'Alba, see AOIF, Filza d'Archivio (LXII, 3), fol. 469r, 18 January 1563.

His career did not proceed as smoothly as these events might make it appear: shortly after his election as rector of San Martino all'Alba, Antinori was under investigation for the homicide of Betto di Giano from San Donato in Poggio, who was a servant of "the sons and heirs" of Alfonso de' Pazzi. On 3 May 1564, Costantino and Betto were playing pall-mall at the Villa degli Alberi, the Innocenti's country property just outside the Porta San Gallo.[96] Costantino, according to the indictment, hit the ball, which bounced off Betto di Giano's head and wounded him so gravely that within a few days, he had died from his injuries. The archiepiscopal court summoned witnesses, including Antinori himself, who were all in accord that Costantino had shouted "guarda, guarda!" as a warning, but to no avail.

The court ruled that the killing had been accidental and "counter to the intention of the priest Costantino, alumnus of the said hospital"; nonetheless, for his frivolity, the court condemned him to say every Friday for a year the seven penitential psalms and to celebrate at least once a Saint Gregory Mass for the benefit of Betto's soul. Costantino was also confined to the city of Florence for a year under pain of excommunication and a fine of fifty scudi if he were discovered to have left the city.[97] His conscience apparently tormented by this wrong he had committed, Costantino presented himself before the archiepiscopal court on 12 September 1564 and offered to serve jail time. The archiepiscopal court sentenced him to jail, ordering him to appear three days later, at which point his jail sentence was suspended, and notwithstanding the rules promulgated at the Council of Trent, Antinori was neither excommunicated nor barred from administering the sacraments. These proceedings were clearly a preliminary step leading to his appointment on 14 November 1564 as rector of the parish of San Quirico a Legnaia.[98]

In a 1569 letter, the superintendent of the hospital of San Paolo, identified by Carol Bresnahan as Antinori, wrote to Cosimo just as San Paolo was about to undergo a new set of reforms designed and implemented by Vincenzio

---

[96] Pall-mall was an extremely popular game in sixteenth- and seventeenth-century Italy and France and was the immediate ancestor of cricket, golf, and croquet. Its earlier version usually involved hitting a large wooden ball with a mallet and seeing either how far it could go or how close it could come to a specific target. Pall-mall brought a similar, if less severe misfortune on the young Jean-Jacques Rousseau: "I was playing pall-mall at Plain-Palais with one of my comrades named Pleince. We quarreled about the game, fought with each other, and during the fight he hit my bare head with such a well-placed mallet blow that with a stronger hand he would have knocked my brains out." Rousseau, *Reveries of a Solitary Walker*, trans. Charles E. Butterworth (Indianapolis: Hackett Publishing, 1992), 56.

[97] ASF Diplomatico, Spedale degli Innocenti, 16 June 1564.

[98] ASF Inventarii, spoglio del fondo Diplomatico ≪Spedale degli Innocenti≫, 246–47; ASF Diplomatico, Spedale degli Innocenti, 16 June and 12 September 1564.

Borghini himself.[99] Sometime thereafter in an undated *supplica*, Borghini wrote to the grand duke:

> I have in the service of this hospital a certain Costantino Antinori, illegitimate son of Alessandro Antinori, raised here and trained by me with special care, and today forty-two years old. In addition to being virtuous and of the best moral character, he is the most faithful and the greatest help that I have in the affairs of this hospital, and almost the entire administration of the hospital. Over his account books he works with such love, faith, and to both my satisfaction and that of the entire family and of the matters themselves, that I am forced not only to love him but also to think about how I can help and favor him in any way I can.[100]

This favor assumed the specific form of nominating Costantino for the post of "supernumerary" canon of the Florentine church of San Lorenzo. As Borghini wrote, Antinori was of sufficiently good character to be worthy of such a post, adding that he "would not be useless in that place." Further evidence of Borghini's confidence in Antinori comes from the latter's role in transferring 40,000 scudi from the Innocenti's depository to Francesco de' Medici in October and November 1570.[101] In August 1572 the canons of San Lorenzo, at the direct urging of Grand Duke Cosimo, unanimously recommended to Archbishop Antonio Altoviti that Antinori

---

[99] Carol Bresnahan Menning, "Loans and Favors," 507, n71, and *Charity and State*, 186. I have been unable to confirm independently that Antinori was superintendent of S. Paolo, and the superintendent of San Paolo in 1569 was Ilario Zanpalochi. The superintendent's letter is in ASF, Monte di Pietà 266, 14 February 1568. It was apparently not unusual for former inmates to take a post as administrator of a charitable institution, for in 1569, the superintendent of the hospital of San Matteo was accused of misappropriating funds given him by the Arte del Cambio. He wrote to the grand duke, mentioning that he felt extreme affection for the institution where he had spent his childhood. See AOIF Suppliche e sovrani rescritti (VI, 1) fol. 412r, 20 September 1571. This affection was reciprocated when Borghini and Don Isidoro di Monteacuto, fellow Benedictine and superintendent of Santa Maria Nuova, attempted to mediate the dispute between the Arte del Cambio and the superintendent of San Matteo, ultimately concluding that the imputation of wrongdoing was false and motivated by passions and interests and that the superintendent of San Matteo should be cleared (AOIF Suppliche e sovrani rescritti (VI, 1) fol. 409r and fol. 414r, 30 October 1571). The correspondence among the superintendents of San Matteo, Santa Maria Nuova, and the grand duke is in AOIF Suppliche e sovrani rescritti (VI, I) fol. 409r–427r, with dates ranging from 1544 to 1571.

[100] AOIF, Suppliche e sovrani rescritti (VI, 2), fol. 104r, [n.d., but on fol. 103r Borghini writes that he sent the letter "at the end of March 1572"]; Gavitt, "Charity and State Building," 250. Costantino's natural father was Alessandro Antinori (1481–1557), s.v. "Antinori, Alessandro," *Dizionario biografico degli Italiani*. Alessandro had been in exile as a merchant in Lyons when in 1532 he returned to Florence under the protection of Alessandro de' Medici. He subsequently served on the Council of 48.

[101] Maria Fubini-Leuzzi, "Le ricevute di Francesco de' Medici," 363–4.

be appointed, followed by appointment as a regular canon in October.[102] Borghini's connections with the canons of San Lorenzo were extensive, if not always unruffled, and such connections undoubtedly account for the ready acceptance of his nomination of Antinori as supernumerary canon.[103]

Antinori, after becoming a permanent canon in 1573, continued to serve as assistant superintendent of the Innocenti, even assuming the superintendency when Borghini was absent or ill, and acting as the hospital's attorney. He also deposited 270 florins with the Innocenti from which he drew annual payments of 24 florins per year.[104] In the life of the San Lorenzo chapter itself, in early 1574, he was part of a delegation of three canons sent to "Illustrissima et eccelentissima Signora Doga Isabella Medici Orsina" to divine Cosimo's choice to replace the late Ser Filippo Franchini as chancellor. At the end of December 1575, Antinori was awarded a doctorate in Theology from the Ginnasio of the Apostolic Chancery of Pisa.[105]

Although Antinori's diploma from the Ginnasio of Pisa makes no explicit mention of his long association with the Innocenti, his degree was conferred on 28 December, the feast day of the Holy Innocents. The diploma, approximately 100 centimeters wide and 100 centimeters long, depicts in blue, green, and gold leaf various mythical and bare-breasted feminine creatures with cornucopia and holding flaming torches, as well as other delightful grotesques holding ornamental curtains in their mouths. At the end of the document, the notary's seal is held up by two *putti*, each standing on a small blue and white cloud. The text itself identifies his mentors as well as celebrating his skill in disputation, which was held on the topic of the fourth distinction, second book, and third distinction, fourth book, of Peter Lombard's *Sentences*. In addition to celebrating the actual conferral of the degree, the diploma also mentions that he has been examined on matters of faith and contains Antinori's own subscription of belief not only to the Nicene Creed but also to all the doctrines, individually identified, and promulgated and clarified by the Council of Trent. On 18 June 1578, he was

---

[102] AOIF Filza d'Archivio (XLII, 3) fol. 471r-v, 6 August 1572.

[103] Eric Cochrane, *Florence in the Forgotten Centuries, 1527–1800* (Chicago/London: University of Chicago Press, 1973), 61.

[104] For the document in which Luca, "son of the Innocenti," made Costantino Antinori his procurator, see AOIF Filze d'Archivio (LXII, 6) fol. 211r: 11 March 1568. AOIF Giornale M (XIII. 19) fol. 126v, 25 September 1572, describes Antinori as "canonico di Sancto Lorenzo et procurator' di detto spedale et spedalingho in nome di detto spedalingo." For Antinori as *spedalingho* during Borghini's illness, see AOIF Filze d'Archivio (LXII, 5) fol. 300r, 13 September 1575. For Antinori's deposit, see AOIF Ricordanze A (XII,7), fol. 42 r, 1 February 1572.

[105] ASL 2325, fol. 79v, 11 March 1573.

invested, following a papal decree of 1 June, as a Canon of the Duomo of Florence.[106]

Although the careers of these two boys are not representative of the experience of the majority of children at the Innocenti, they suggest that by the middle of the sixteenth century, the Innocenti had come to play a central role in the social, economic, ecclesiastical, and intellectual life of early modern Florence. Moreover, the experience of Nacchianti challenges the notion that family and inheritance strategies exclusively put females at a disadvantage. At the same time, Costantino Antinori's personal history at the Innocenti demonstrates that charitable institutions figured into the family strategies of both mercantile and patrician families. These two personal experiences also suggest that for a small group of elite boys, the patrons of the Innocenti were willing to invest considerable time and energy into a first-rate education to prepare boys for ecclesiastical careers. Just as important, however, was the role that charitable institutions came to play in the city's cultural life, a role that not only tied them to the splendor of Medici rule but also, in the case of tapestry manufacture, to the conspicuous consumption that consciously accentuated the definition of a Florentine aristocratic class.

The Cultural Life of an Early Modern Charitable Institution

The place of music and the visual arts in the hospital's curriculum, and, indeed, in the practices of convents and confraternities, had a specific disci-plinary purpose. The masters who supervised the disciplinary lives of boys most closely also taught them to sing masses and to perform other liturgical rites. Especially from the second half of the sixteenth century forward, the Innocenti's account books record purchases of "notebooks of lined paper for writing musical passages."[107] In addition to the harpsichords that Ser Agostino Tombi had brought to the Innocenti, the hospital's organ was also the site of lessons taught to the Innocenti's boys by Fra Mauro of the Servite order.[108] Moreover, the Innocenti's account books record payments by tech-nicians whose job it was to "adjust and tune" the hospital's instruments,

---

[106] ASF Diplomatico Spedale degli Innocenti (pergamene lunga), 28 December 1575, is Antinori's diploma in theology. For his appointment and investiture as canon of the Duomo, see ASF Diplomatico Spedale degli Innocenti 1 June and 18 June 1578.

[107] 1 AOIF Quaderno del Camarlingo (CXXVI, 46), fol. 223r, and AOIF Quaderno del Camarlingo (CXXVI, 35), cited by Lucia Sandri, "L'assistenza nei primi due secoli di attività" in Lucia Sandri, ed., *Gli Innocenti e Firenze nei secoli*, 73. I am heavily indebted to Lucia Sandri's article for this section on the Innocenti's musical pedagogy.

[108] Ibid., 72.

which included a cornet, a trombone, and a monochord, an instrument with one flexible string that could be used like the modern tuning fork but also used in antiquity to demonstrate acoustical properties.[109]

The neighboring Annunziata Servites appear to have specialized in such musical training, judging by the hiring of the Servite Fra Maurizio, who gave private music lessons to Luigi Strozzi, one of the Innocenti's pupils.[110] In 1585, the prior Fra Niccolò Mazzi made a token payment to one of the Innocenti's foundlings to "sing accompanied by the organ."[111] The preparation of the Innocenti's boy foundlings for a vocal career even extended to castration: in 1572 and 1573, the hospital summoned Maestro Sisto Sisti and his son Niccolò "to castrate big Antonio" and "Lattanzio from San Gimignano," respectively.[112] Such a heavy investment in masters, instruments, and even surgeons strongly suggests that public musical performances enhanced the hospital's participation in the cultural life of the Medici court. Perhaps more important, castration marked a way for otherwise impoverished boys to earn a living, especially from the early seventeenth century onward, when demand for castrati in operatic performance and ecclesiastical liturgy was high and employment in the cloth industry became more limited. Nonetheless, castrati were not a numerically significant phenomenon even in Italy, where their numbers in the seventeenth century never exceeded more than a few hundred boys across the entire Italian peninsula.[113]

Cultural involvement with the Medici court is far more demonstrable with regard to the visual arts.[114] The appointment of Vincenzio Borghini as prior in 1552 deliberately reinforced this link, because Borghini and Vasari were collaborators in such projects as the second edition of Vasari's *Lives of the Artists* and the ceiling of the Salone dei Cinquecento. Perhaps at Vasari's suggestion, shortly after Cosimo had entrusted him with directing the tapestry shops begun by Jan Rost and Nicholas Karcher, Cosimo introduced

[109] Ibid., 73.

[110] Ibid.

[111] Ibid.

[112] Ibid.

[113] See John Rosselli, *Singers of Italian Opera: The History of a Profession* (Cambridge: Cambridge University Press, 1995), 38–9, for the example of Domenico Melani from Pistoia, who had three of his sons castrated so they could pursue musical careers, as well as the petitions of Roman boys asking musicians, surgeons, and even patrons to castrate them or to provide financial assistance for the surgery so that they could lift themselves out of poverty. For highly tentative estimates of how many castrati were in Italy at any one time, see ibid., 40–1.

[114] This final section reproduces a portion of my earlier article, "An Experimental Culture: The Art of the Economy and the Economy of Art under Cosimo I and Francesco I," in *The Cultural Politics of Duke Cosimo de' Medici*, ed. Konrad Eisenbichler (Aldershot: Ashgate, 2001), 205–22.

a tapestry workshop into the Innocenti itself.[115] Even Rost's contract of 1549 specified that he was to teach tapestry manufacture to

> boys and youth, so that the arts of tapestry weaving, and the secrets of dyes ... can be learned, acquired, and established in the city of Florence, and in such a way that without the support or training of any foreigner whatsoever, the said skill and dyeing can be accomplished and practiced in the city of Florence.[116]

Certainly there is no doubt that by 1565, two years after the foundation of the Accademia del Disegno, Borghini was teaching drawing to some of the Innocenti's foundlings. In a letter to Vasari, Borghini wrote:

> I am giving the children practice in exercising their caprice a little, so that when they draw an outside figure they have free reign to put in little embellishments. I have them do little partitions, frames, columns, pilasters, and so on. I have them do such drawings in abundance, as might decorate a nice book.[117]

Vasari, in turn, in the *Lives of the Artists*, identified at least two of Borghini's protégés as Battista Naldini (1535–91) and Francesco Morandini da Poppi.[118]

Battista Naldini had been an *allevato* of the Innocenti and, before Borghini's tenure began in 1552, had been placed as an apprentice with Jacopo Pontormo. According to Vasari, Pontormo "in his last years adopted Battista Naldini, a youth of good intelligence, who took as much care of Jacopo as the latter would permit. Under Jacopo, he made considerable progress in design, and excited the highest expectations." Vasari also lists Borghini as one of the close friends with whom Pontormo "relaxed over a meal" and also noted that above all, Pontormo loved Bronzino, "who loved him equally in return

---

[115] Cf. Gavitt, "An Experimental Culture," 207; Laura Cavazzini, "Dipinti e sculture," 127.

[116] Gavitt, "An Experimental Culture," 207, citing C. Adelson, "Cosimo I and the Foundation of Tapestry Production in Florence," 910.

[117] Karl Frey, *Nachlass*, 2:24, cited by Cavazzini, "Dipinti e sculture," 127.

[118] Giorgio Vasari, *Le vite de' piu eccellenti pittori, scultori, e architettori* (Florence: Tipografia Giunta, 1568), 6: 240. On Naldini's birth date, 3 May 1535 (not 1537) and on his association with the Innocenti, see Pilliod, *Pontormo, Bronzino, Allori*, 78–9. Pilliod's speculation that Vincenzio Borghini may have put forward the ten-year-old Naldini for adoption by Pontormo is not supported by the chronology, because Naldini would have been ten years old in 1545, seven years before Borghini became the Innocenti's superintendent. It is likely that the hospital's superintendent at that time, Luca Alamanni, recognized Naldini's talent. His apprenticeship to Pontormo, including his residence in Pontormo's house and the fictive father-son relationship that fell short of legal adoption all follow a pattern quite common for Innocenti boys who survived infancy and early childhood. See Thomas Kuehn, *Illegitimacy in Renaissance Florence* (Ann Arbor: University of Michigan Press, 2002), 168.

in gratitude and acknowledgment of the benefits received from him."[119] In 1554, the nineteen-year-old Naldini was engaged to teach drawing to the Innocenti's children, and in 1555, he was paid to paint candles.[120] In 1560, Borghini sent him to Rome and eventually placed him with Vasari. In particular, Borghini requested Vasari to plan Naldini's program of study: "Thus, please write a few lines for him, telling him all the best things about his vocation that are in Rome, so that once he has been there a few months, he can profit from them and produce good things."[121]

By 1565, Naldini was already working with Vasari both on the Salone dei Cinquecento in the Palazzo Vecchio, as well as contributing two panels to Francesco's *studiolo*. In 1569, 1578, 1579, and 1585, Naldini held the office of consul in the Accademia del Disegno, which Cosimo had founded and officially inaugurated in 1563. In a somewhat less spectacular manner than Bishop Nacchianti, Naldini's work also roused the suspicion of post-Tridentine censorship, when in completing Maso di San Friano's altarpiece of the Ascension at Santa Maria del Carmine he included Saints Helena and Agnes, as well as portraying the Virgin Mary as still young. Raffaello Borghini noted that blame should be attached not to Naldini but to the patron, a view now supported by the publication of the donor's testament and codicil.[122] Art historians unsympathetic to late mannerism in general have not been kind to Naldini's work, but apart from recent rehabilitation of his artistic reputation, his skill in *disegno* has been almost universally admired and recognized since Raffaello Borghini's positive assessment in 1584 of Naldini's "facile, e bella maniera, e vago modo di colore."[123]

---

[119] Vasari, *Vite* 5: 333–4; English translation by George Bull as *Lives of the Artists* (New York/London: Penguin, 1987), 2: 272.

[120] Elizabeth Pilliod, *Pontormo, Bronzino, Allori*, 216, citing AOIF, Entrata e Uscita AA (CXXII, 104), fol. 76v, 28 August 1554.

[121] Frey, *Nachlass*, 1:582. For an illustrated catalog of the sketches Naldini produced in Rome, see Christle Thiem, *Das römische Reiseskizzenbuch des Florentiners Giovanni Battista Naldini 1560/61* (Munich/Berlin: Deutscher Kunstverlag, 2002). Apart from the detailed views of mid-sixteenth-century Rome these sketches provide, several of them are studies of contemporary works of art. Naldini was specifically commissioned, for example, to "translate" one of Vasari's drawings of Judith and Holofernes into a painting – see Alessandro Cecchi, "Borghini, Vasari, Naldini e la 'Giuditta' del 1564," *Paragone* 28 (1977): 100–7, and Naldini's *modello* for the Vasari is in the Musée de Beaux-arts in Lille.

[122] Catherine Clover, "Documentation on Naldini's Ascension for S. Maria del Carmine in Florence," *The Burlington Magazine*, 141 (1999): 615–17, citing Raffaello Borghini, *Il Riposo* (Florence: G. Marescotti, 1584), 114–15.

[123] Raffaello Borghini, *Il riposo*, 619. Naldini's participation in the Salone del Cinquecento is mentioned in Vasari, *Vite*, 5: 567. On Borghini's tutelage of Battista Naldini, see Zygmunt Wazbinski, "Giorgio Vasari e Vincenzo Borghini come maestri accademici: il caso di G. B. Naldini" in *Giorgio Vasari: tra decorazione ambientale e storiografia artistica, Convegno di studi (Arezzo, 8–10*

In 1566, Borghini commissioned Naldini to paint a Deposition depicting Saints Jerome and Catherine, which was unfortunately lost in an attempt to detach it in 1659. The sketch for it, however, Borghini admired so much that he hung it above the door of his own quarters at the Innocenti, and it can now be seen in the hospital's museum. Naldini is also one of Vasari's four assistants who can be seen peering down from the north wall of the Salone dei Cinquecento. Likewise, Borghini commissioned Francesco Morandini da Poppi, another protégé, to execute an altarpiece depicting the Nativity, which eventually found its way to the abbey of San Salvatore a Spugna, near Colle Val d'Elsa. Borghini also pressed Francesco Morandini da Poppi into service collecting inscriptions for his research on the early history of Florence.

Although Francesco Morandini da Poppi lived with Borghini at the Innocenti, it is unlikely that he was an *allevato*, because his presence in Florence cannot be documented before he was nineteen years old. According to Raffaello Borghini's *Il riposo*, Morandini's father sent him to learn grammar with an eye to having him become a notary. After the younger Morandini copied a series of prints, his uncle, a friend of Giorgio Vasari's brother Piero, introduced him to the Aretine painter, who in turn recommended that Francesco Morandini come to Florence to study under Borghini's protection. According to Raffaello Borghini, the Innocenti's prior "received [Morandini] very courteously, and gave him every comfort so he could dedicate himself to the study of drawing." In executing the San Salvatore altarpiece, Morandini availed himself of the services of a young *allevato*, Ulivo Ulivieri, to whom Borghini himself had taught drawing.[124] Finally, Francesco Morandini da Poppi, in his last will and testament of 3 April 1597, continued the tradition of encouraging the hospital's foundlings in their artistic aspirations by leaving to Curtio degl'Innocenti, "who at present works in the said testator's workshop, the use and enjoyment" of one of his apartments in his house in via S. Gallo, as well as leaving his artists' supplies for Curtio to purchase at a steep discount.[125]

ottobre 1981), ed. G. C. Garfagnani (Florence: Leo S. Olschki, 1995), 285–9. One of Naldini's panels in Francesco's studiolo has drawn attention in Harvey Hamburgh, "Naldini's *Allegory of Dreams* in the Studiolo of Francesco de' Medici," *Sixteenth Century Journal* 27.3 (1996): 679–704. On Cosimo, discipline, and the Accademia del Disegno, see Karen-edis Barzman, *The Florentine Academy and the Early Modern State.*

[124] Raffaello Borghini, *Il riposo*, 640. Cf. Cavazzini, "Dipinti e sculture," 127–30. On Francesco Morandini da Poppi's early education, see Alessandra Giovanetti, *Francesco Morandini detto il Poppi* (Florence: EDIFIR, 1995), 17–22.

[125] AOIF Filze d'Archivio, 23, fol. 24r–24v, 3 April 1597.

Close ties among the Accademia del Disegno, Borghini (its first director), and the Innocenti's foundlings established the foundling hospital as a major center of the city's artistic life. The founding statutes of the Accademia del Disegno, which held its first exhibition at the foundling hospital, show Borghini's intentions that drawing, painting, and sculpture should in some cases provide a material remedy for poverty. The statutes set up a special fund, subsidized by sales of donated property:

> for the benefit and help of poor boys who are practicing said art, as well those desirous of practicing it but who are prevented by their poverty from doing so. Every week the Academy must distribute to those boys who have been approved, a sum to be decided . . . starting from when they are eleven years old until they have reached the age of fifteen.[126]

One of the Innocenti's foundlings, who described himself as "Ventura di Vincenzio Ulivieri, painter, tapestry maker, rug-maker, and pupil of the house of the Innocenti," directed a tapestry and rug workshop at the hospital. In his account book, he promised to "keep accounts of all materials and of all stamen, wool, and goats' hair used in house, as well as every other thing that comes into our hands that is so derelict it can [only] be used for said products."[127] This tapestry workshop maintained a very close relationship to Grand Duke Francesco and his consort, Bianca Cappello, weaving rugs and tapestries specifically on commission for them, and, on one occasion, producing a piece made from dog hair as a joke to see whether Francesco could tell the difference from the normal product. Although the Accademia del Disegno sought through tapestry manufacture to alleviate the poverty of boys, Ulivieri also supervised a staff of girls. The social milieu of the Innocenti's girls, as well as those housed in various Florentine conservatories, is the subject of the following chapter.

---

[126] Bibiloteca Nazionale Centrale di Firenze (BNCF) cod. Magliabechiana, II, I, 399, cap. VII, cited in Wazbinski "Giorgio Vasari e Vincenzo Borghini," 297.

[127] Gavitt, "An Experimental Culture," 212, and Biblioteca Moreniana, Florence (BMF), Fondo Bigazzi 168, fol. 1 right, 15 May 1581.

5

FROM *PUTTE* TO *PUTTANE*: FEMALE FOUNDLINGS AND CHARITABLE INSTITUTIONS IN FLORENCE

Introduction: Honor and Savonarolan Reform

WELL AFTER THE DEATH OF SAVONAROLA, LORENZO POLIZZOTTO HAS shown, Savonarolan piety continued to influence lay devotion and lay religious organization until Grand Duke Cosimo's "dissolution" of the monastery at San Marco in 1545. Savonarolan reformers knit together a system of charitable institutions that by 1530 already suggested that care of vulnerable females – young girls, adolescent girls, and widows, especially – was to be the major focus of charitable concern. Even as early as the 1490s, Savonarola and his followers had put before the government of Florence a proposal for the reform of women.[1] This chapter examines the proliferation of charitable institutions for girls and women and the origins of this concern in terms of family strategy, inheritance practice, and "preventive" approaches to the problems of prostitution. In addition to abundant evidence from the Ospedale degli Innocenti, this chapter also examines the statutes, admission records, and disposition records of the girls' homes of Santa Maria e San Niccolò del Ceppo, the Pietà, Santa Caterina della Ruota, and the widow's asylum of Orbatello as a means to understand sixteenth-century Florentine perceptions of marginalization as well as the material realities of a group of women who, although marginalized, represented a problematic that drove straight to the heart of the central values and gender constructs of premodern Mediterranean systems of honor and shame.[2]

---

[1] F. W. Kent, "A Proposal by Savonarola for the Self-Reform of Florentine Women (March 1496)," *Memorie Domenicane,* nuova serie 14 (1983): 334–41.

[2] An abbreviated version of this chapter has been published as "From *putte* to *puttane*: Female Foundlings and Charitable Institutions in Northern Italy, 1530–1630," in *At the Margins: Minority Groups in Premodern Italy,* ed. Stephen J. Milner (Minneapolis: University of Minnesota Press, 2005), 111–29. For a comparison between these institutions and similar initiatives in Bologna, see Nicholas Terpstra, *Abandoned Children of the Italian Renaissance,* especially 103–48. On the

Just as during the republican period Florentine humanists linked civic wealth, moral reform, and Christian charity to the collective salvation of the *civitas*, so did Savonarolan piety, as Donald Weinstein has shown, place the practice of charity at the forefront of the Christian *renovatio* that would render Florence worthy of salvation. Savonarola's "new Jerusalem" would be one in which every citizen sacrificed his own interests to those of Christian community. The Savonarolan regime acted quickly to associate itself with the city's major charitable institutions, placing the foundlings of the Innocenti, in particular, at the center of ritual devotion. Savonarolan-inspired processions of children dressed in white moving their elders to tears on Palm Sunday, as well as substituting for their usual carnival pranks the distribution of alms to the poor, firmly fixed the association between radical Christian reform and charity.[3] The anti-Jewish flavor of many of these processions also found an echo in the Savonarolan intervention that led to the official foundation of the Florentine Monte di Pietà as a replacement for Jewish money lending in 1495.[4]

Less publicly visible, but no less important, were the links that Savonarolan reformers already had to the Innocenti. Although Polizzotto describes both the Innocenti and Santa Maria Nuova as too complex to fall completely under Savonarolan control, I would argue that he underestimates the hold that the prophet's followers had on the foundling hospital. Indeed, a comparison of the families who occupied the consulate of Florence's prosperous silk guild, the Innocenti's patrons and putative founders, with Polizzotto's list of families involved with the *piagnoni* (sympathizers with Savonarola), shows a truly remarkable correspondence.[5] The del Pugliese family, for example,

relationship of Savonarolan reform to the conservatory of Santa Maria e San Niccolò del Ceppo, see Rosalia Manno Tolu, "Echi Savonaroliani nella Compagnia e nel conservatorio del Ceppo nei secoli XVII–XVIII," in *Savonarola e la politica*, ed. G. C. Garfagnini (Florence: Edizioni del Galluzzo, 1997), 209–24.

[3] On Savonarolan reform, see Donald Weinstein, *Savonarola and Florence: Prophecy and Patriotism in the Renaissance* (Princeton: Princeton University Press, 1970), and Polizzotto, *Elect Nation*. On processions of children, see Luca Landucci, *Diario fiorentino dal 1450 al 1516, continuato da un Anonimo fino al 1542* (Florence: G. C. Sansoni, 1883), 53; Richard Trexler, "Adolescence and Salvation in the Renaissance," in *The Pursuit of Holiness in Late Medieval and Renaissance Religion*, ed. C. Trinkaus and H. Oberman (E. J. Brill: Leiden, 1974), 200–64, at 261–3; Philip Gavitt, *Charity and Children*, 296–7; Domenico di Agresti, *Sviluppi della riforma monastica Savonaroliana* (Florence: Leo S. Olschki, 1980), 7.

[4] On the foundation of the Florentine Monte di Pietà, see Menning, *Charity and State in Late Renaissance Italy*, 37–63.

[5] Of the surnames listed for the Silk Guild's consulate in 1474 and 1475 (the latest year for which I have an available list) the families represented are Antinori, Banchi, Rustichi, della Casa, da Verrazzano, Bartolini, Bartoli, Berardi, Carnesecchi, Bonsi, Aldobrandini, Ginori, Pandolfini, Falconieri, Berlinghieri, del Giocondo, Canigiani, Lippi, Lotti, Cambini, del Nero, del Scarlatto, Vespucci, Mori, and Deti. Only seven surnames among the twenty-five guild consuls – the Antinori, Banchi, Rustichi, Berardi, Falconieri, del Scarlatto, and Deti – are missing from Polizzotto's

prominent Savonarolan sympathizers, were also generous patrons of the hospital's church.

Piero del Francesco Pugliese, in particular, commissioned Piero di Cosimo's painting of the *Madonna con Bambino e santi,* which has formed part of the Innocenti's artistic patrimony since 1493 and which is now visible in the hospital's museum gallery. Another Piero di Cosimo tempera and oil glazed panel, a *sacra conversazione* with the Madonna and Saints John the Baptist, Peter, Dominic, and Nicholas (holding the traditional three balls that symbolize his association with dowries) hangs in the St. Louis Art Museum and bears the del Pugliese family coat of arms. Even the relationship among this seemingly odd assortment of saints ties together Florence's patron saint, the founder of the Dominican order, and Saint Nicholas's protection of girls, in which Saint Peter stands not merely as the foundation of the church but also as holder of the keys to communal salvation. Saints Nicholas and Dominic kneel in adoration before the Madonna and Child, and Saints John the Baptist and Peter place sponsoring hands on the shoulders of Dominic and Nicholas, respectively. As further reinforcement of the Dominican connection to this devotional piece, its predella illustrates scenes from the history of the Dominican order.[6]

Putte to *Puttane* at the Innocenti: Discipline and Its Discontents

At some point in the first three decades of the sixteenth century, the hospital's scribes stopped using the terms *fanciulla* (singular) and *fanciulle* (plural) and began to refer to the hospital's boys as *putti* and the hospital's girls as *putte.* If it is perhaps too crude an analysis to attribute this early shift to increases in infant mortality, the terms nonetheless suggest not only the innocence associated with *putti* in Italian painting but also the otherworldly fate that awaited most infants admitted to the Innocenti during the sixteenth century. Although this usage continued throughout the sixteenth century, by the last quarter of the sixteenth century the Ospedale degli Innocenti called up images of prostitutes (*puttane*) as readily as images of more ethereal beings. Francesco Settimanni's eighteenth-century compilation of cinquecento chronicles, for example, charges that the Innocenti became so overcrowded and mismanaged during the last years of Borghini's tenure

list of families who numbered Savonarolan sympathizers among their kin. Moreover, a number of prominent silk guild families, including the del Benino, Parenti, and del Pugliese, were prominent among the *piagnoni*. For a list of the silk guild's consuls and the *operai* of the hospital of the Innocenti, see ASF, Arte della Seta, 246, *passim*.

[6] Laura Cavazzini, "Dipinti e sculture nelle chiese dell'Ospedale," 119–20, and *The Saint Louis Art Museum Handbook of the Collections* (St. Louis: The Museum, 1991), 84.

(1579–80) that hospital officials released hundreds of adolescent girls into the streets of Florence, "where out of necessity they became prostitutes." Although Settimanni's history is exaggerated, it is not without truth, because the Orbatello, the institution to which the hospital's older women were discharged, aroused suspicions among those who saw young silk guildsmen frequenting it in 1585.[7]

Pietro Aretino's tripartite division of feminine careers into wives, nuns, and prostitutes was hardly unique either to Tuscany or to pornography: even Silvio Antoniano's 1595 statutes for a shelter for poor girls and widows correspondingly classified the inmates into "zitelle, vedove, convertite."[8] In mid-sixteenth-century Florence as well, a treatise written by the Innocenti's superintendent, Vincenzio Borghini (whose tenure lasted from 1552 until his death in 1580), *Consideratroni sopra l'allogare le donne delli Innocenti, fuori dal maritare o monacare*, took as its major assumption that without some sort of opportune remedy, the only alternative to marriage or becoming a nun was prostitution. Borghini's proposal that the Innocenti should reintroduce household service did not so much expand girls' occupational options as it provided a means for girls to finance meager dowries through the wages of their own work rather than from the hospital's coffers. Moreover, the increasing toll that the overwhelming presence of girls took on the resources of the Innocenti could be somewhat mitigated by sending them out to live as household servants. This was an option unavailable to girls between the end of the fifteenth century and Borghini's tenure. At comparable institutions for girls, such as that of the Santissima Annunziata della Minerva at Rome, founded by Torquemada in 1466, girls who had merely had a history of domestic service were already barred from entering.[9]

By the middle of the sixteenth century, girls at Florence's Ospedale degli Innocenti had become the major preoccupation and care of hospital officials, because their sex was "more fragile and disposed to many more and greater dangers."[10] These girls has been abandoned precisely because they had no one to take care of them, and left alone they might easily *capitar male,* or end up badly (Borghini's euphemism for prostitution).

The hospital thus had to take care of them until death (or at least until they found a safe haven) because to be without family or without the protection of the convent meant they were left to the winds of chance, without

[7] Francesco Settimanni, "Memorie Fiorentine," ASF Manoscritti 129, 212v. For the 1585 charges, see ASF, Parte Guelfa Nero, fol. 75r, 17 January 1584 [s.f.], cited in Richard Trexler, "A Widows' Asylum," 149n.

[8] Vittorio Frajese, *Il popolo fanciullo,* 94.

[9] Ibid., 93–4.

[10] Vincenzio Borghini, *Consideratroni,* 29.

special boundaries or rules; in fewer words, in a state of disorder.[11] As the job requirements for their governesses (*priore*) indicated, the supervision of girls required "charity, vigilance, and discretion."[12] Girls were certainly capable of profiting from instruction, according to the hospital's priors, and as was true for boys, pedagogy was to "lead them to their desired goal and to the perfection of other virtues."[13] Indeed, the Innocenti did teach a limited number of girls to read, especially those whose occupations within the hospital, such as those of physician and superintendent of wet nurses, made reading a valuable skill. Thus, women without familial or institutional ties were, by definition and regardless of their individual character traits, naturally in a state of disorder, which only paternal or ecclesiastical authority could properly confine.

Two models governed the organization of care in institutions for girls: the family and the cloister. An overwhelming proportion of such care was religious and disciplinary in nature, specifically focused on devotional practices. At the same time, however, reclusion was gender-specific only to the extent that traditionally men properly inhabited the public world and women the private world. Reclusion was the solution to disorder of all sorts, even if women were more likely to require reclusion than men. For both genders, the monastic, conventual model of the Benedictine or the Basilian rule governed the demands of discipline.[14]

The power of the monastic or conventual model also moved charitable institutions to copy the hierarchy, with its prior, lay brothers and sisters, and even patients bound to the hospital's prevailing *regola*. Another application of monastic discipline to female foundlings was the discipline of work and in particular work suited to the demands of female honor. The notion that sewing and other occupations having to do with cloth was a proper occupation for young women was explicitly stated in treatises that outlined their upbringing and education.

As early as the 1530s, and possibly earlier, girls at the hospital of the Innocenti were engaged in weaving, and the Innocenti clearly kept track of what the girls were earning. For example, in April 1533, the Innocenti received

---

[11] Borghini, *Considerationi*, 30.

[12] AOIF Nota di ufizi e arti di donne di casa (XLVI, 1) fol. 1v, *anno* 1581: "Che, la priora e vicepriora e l'offitio delle quali debbe esser' sopra la cura e governo di tutte l'altre donne grandi e pichole di decto spedale le quali come principale capi e governatrice debbe esser' piena di carità e di vigilanza et di discretione."

[13] Ibid., "acciò possa conducere al desiato fine e alla perfectione dell'altre virtù."

[14] Indeed, where Norbert Elias argued that discipline originated in the princely courts of early modern Europe, Dilwyn Knox, by contrast, has shown the importance of the monastic model as the source of *disciplina* and *civiltà*. See Dilwyn Knox, "Disciplina: The Monastic and Clerical Origin of European Civility," 123.

a payment of thirty-five lire from the silk company of Giovanni Borgherini "for the account of the earnings of our women."[15] Similarly, in August 1534, the hospital's *ricordanze* noted two payments amounting to a total of seventy lire for "the gains of our weaver."[16] By the mid 1540s, this work had reached sufficient proportions that hospital officials decided to enlarge the hospital's physical structure, both to keep a separate place for the wet nurses and so that the hospital's girls would have more space for their activities connected to weaving.[17]

In 1581, Borghini's successor at the Innocenti, Fra Niccolò Mazzi, pulled together a summary of "the duties and occupations of the women" of the Innocenti.[18] Noting that "there is no doubt to any who consider the matter that there is no work of greater piety and charity, or more pleasing to God or closer to the heart of the Republic, nor more necessary to this city, than this House of the Innocenti," Mazzi devoted the remainder of his summary to the successful efforts of the institution in placing out girls for household service, convents, and marriage.[19] Nonetheless, despite Borghini's efforts to reduce the number of women in the hospital (somewhat successful, because the hospital's census of women had declined from 980 to just under 700), they still, in Mazzi's view, represented too great a drain on the hospital's resources. He resolved, therefore, to "reorder" their supervision and care, and "to address [the problem] of how to instruct and encourage them in all those crafts and feminine manual work that can possibly be introduced."[20] Mazzi explicitly set out the financial rationale behind the scheme: "so that with their effort and skill, these women can contribute to their own upkeep." At the same time, the work will "make them industrious so they can have better results when they wish to be placed."[21] Left unspoken was that this, too, would contribute to easing the hospital's financial burden.

---

[15] AOIF Ricordanze E (XII, 5) fol. 62v, 5 April 1533: "Da Giovanni Borgherini e chompagni setaioli y. trenta cinque per li per conto de' guadagni di nostre donne rechò Michele d'Alexo contanti l. 35."

[16] Ibid., fol. 112v, 22 August 1534: "Guadagni di nostre tessitore deono hauti adì 22 d'agosto y. sexanta sei piccioli portò contanti messer Luca nostro priore–y.66. E addì xxiii detto y. quattro piccioli portò contanti messi a entrata D @11 sotto dì xxii d'agosto 1534–y.70."

[17] AOIF Giornale K (XIII,17), fol. 93v, n.d., but most likely in January 1545.

[18] AOIF, Nota di Uffizi e arte di donne di casa (XLVI, 1), anno 1581.

[19] Ibid., loose fol.: "El non à dubio a chi ben considera che l'opera di questa casa dell'Innocenti non sia delle maggiori e di pietà e carità acepta a Dio e grata e a cuore a lor A. A. e a tutta la Republica necessaria che nessuna altra di questa città."

[20] Ibid., fol. 1r–1v: "ha pensato di riordinar' la cura e gouerno di dette creature e maxime delle donne che di presente ascendono al numero di 700 e sempre crescono con indirizzarle à farle instruir' e exercitar' in tutte quelle arti e opere manuali femminili che possibil' sia introdursi."

[21] Ibid., fol. 1v: "acciò che con le fatiche e virtù loro possino in parte aiutare l'hospedale alla stessa lor' alimentatione. Et di poi fatte industriose possino anchora trovar' miglior partiti quando allogar' si volessino."

The reformers who attempted to patch together the hospital's finances after Borghini's financial catastrophe had in fact recommended that tapestry and other forms of cloth production should cease, and although this was the single recommendation that Francesco I had vetoed, there is in this sudden rush to account for production and profits more than a hint that these activities still had to prove their usefulness – in short, they had to turn a profit. Such accounts were used not only to justify this form of workfare but also as encouragement to the girls to understand the importance and value of their work. To this end the weekly posting of earnings was made for each worker so that she could be rewarded and recognized for her efforts.[22] Moreover, a certain portion of each worker's weekly earnings was posted to her account to be spent on her clothing and other "comforts," with the most industrious worker to receive a bonus.[23] This was only one step shy of what Sandra Cavallo documented for the Casa del Soccorso in Turin beginning in 1682, where high productivity and earnings "were also an essential requisite in order to obtain a dowry."[24] Even women who worked outside the hospital had to remit a portion of their earnings to it, and after the reforms of 1581, those who became victims of unemployment could not return to the Innocenti but had to go the hospice of Orbatello instead.[25] In 1591, a certain Pulidoro Ferrarese petitioned the Innocenti to allow him to take girls as apprentices in his packaging operation, but officials denied his petition because he insisted on paying the girls directly instead of allocating some of their salaries to the hospital's treasury.[26]

The tapestry workshop at the Innocenti, even though directed by a former male foundling, also functioned to keep the hospital's girls and women gainfully employed, as is clear from the petition that Fra Niccolò Mazzi and Ulivo Ulivieri submitted to Grand Duke Francesco requesting his formal approval of the workshop:

> Fra Niccolò da Cortona prior of the Innocenti hospital and Ulivieri alumnus of said hospital, and painter and tapestry-maker, humble servants of your Serene Highness, explain to him with all humility that they have brought to fruition and placed into operation the process of using goat hair to make rugs, and, through Ulivieri's work, after much difficulty, have

---

[22] Ibid.

[23] Ibid., fol. 12r.

[24] Sandra Cavallo, *Charity and Power in Early Modern Italy*, 113, although the supporting archival reference mentions only that a confraternity of women gave out medals for especially noteworthy productivity.

[25] AOIF Deliberazioni e Partiti degli Operai (VIII, 3) fol. 3v, 29 November 1581.

[26] AOIF Filza d'archivio (LXII, 15), fol. 409r, 9 March 1592.

brought to perfection the ability to do not only rugs, but also tablecloths, tapestries, large combed woolens, and garlands similar to ones from Calabria. Given that this activity is to the benefit not only of the hospital . . . but also of the women of the hospital . . . the petitioners on their knees beg Your Highness to deign to concede them the favor and patent to the said hospital and to Ulivieri for twenty years.[27]

As the committee of nine appointed to reorder the hospital's finances contemplated various solutions to its overcrowding, including shipping off a proportion of the older women to the widows' hospice of Orbatello, a small contingent of three women refused to go along with the commission's plans and were consequently jailed until they relented. The commission nonetheless went ahead to apportion various tasks among the hospital's remaining female population, with the object in each case to reduce the financial burden they represented. Thus, one contingent would be sent out as servants; another contingent sewed and wove wool and silk "and other duties throughout the hospital, so that all would be earning money for the hospital."[28] Finally, "one part shall serve in the craft of rug-making and within four months shall have taught the skills involved in it to all the [resident] women of the hospital."[29] Hospital officials destined another group of girls to work Perpignan cloths "which have not yet been introduced."

Not all of women's work, however, was dedicated to the *bottega*. The hospital's female staff included four sacristans:

whose duties are to take care of the vestments and decorations of the church, to rouse all the girls to hear mass and to the devotion and fear of God, as well as to make sure that the girls pray for the remission of sins for all the benefactors as well as for the salvation of the city and its state.[30]

The hospital also employed four female pharmacists and three female physicians (plus another two in training), who had to "order and keep track of the spices and medicine and to minister according to their craft."[31] At least some of these female physicians, moreover, were not hired from outside

[27] Philip Gavitt, "An Experimental Culture," 212, citing AOIF Filze d'Archivio (LXII, 31) fol. 36r, 6 March 1582.

[28] AOIF Filze d'Archivio (LXII, 17), fol. 397r, n.d.

[29] Ibid.: "Una parte servirà al Arte de' Tappeti alle quale si acommodano molto bene e fra 4 mesi al più lungo si ridurrà tutta l'arte fra le donne."

[30] AOIF Note di ufizi e arti di donne di casa (XLVI, 1) fol. 2v, anno 1581: "L'offitio de' quali si e di tener cura de' panni e paramenti della chiesa e chiamar' e indur' le fanciulle e tutta l'altre alle messe e offitie alla devotione e timor del Dio e preghar' per la remission' de' peccati per tutti i benefactori e salvationi della città e stato."

[31] Ibid., fol. 2v: "l'offitio delle quali si è ordinar' e tener' conto della spetiera e medicina e medicare secondo l'arte loro."

but rather were foundlings themselves, as is clear from a list of fourteen girls who were learning to read, two of whom were Lisabetta, *medica*, and Pasquina, *medica*. One of the other female physicians was a Mona Lorenza from Bologna, raising the possibility that she had been trained there. The office of physician was conceived differently from that of the six nurses, whose function was "to administer medication and to supervise the sick with charity and diligence."[32]

In addition to this phalanx of pharmacists, doctors, and nurses to treat the sick, women also participated in the administration of the women's convent and supervised some of the boys. Four *rottaie* could be pressed into service at the wheel where infants were admitted, as well as three porters to guard the door. Those women who addressed themselves directly to the care of children either supervised them or their clothes, including two women who were assigned to taking care of the hosiery. In addition, seven women were assigned to the storeroom and kitchen. In at least one instance, this made them somewhat vulnerable to exploitation, as in 1575, when a baker and a bricklayer gave three of these kitchen workers lemons, cheese, and fruit in return for being allowed to pilfer as much of the hospital's flour as they could carry away.[33] Altogether, the statistical profile accounted for 586 women within the hospital in 1581, about 80 percent of whom were involved in the production of the hospital's *bottega*.

Some girls who were especially apt would be kept aside to do the errands and administration for the institution, and some could even be slated for training so they could take up administrative and direct-care posts at the Innocenti and at other charitable institutions in Florence. Such was the case in 1551, when Prior Luca Alamanni installed Mona Dorothea, "raised in our hospital." She was fifty-four years old at the time of her appointment and had previously worked "for several years" as kitchen staff.[34] Her predecessor, the "legitimate and natural" daughter of Landozzo degli Albizzi, had also been fed and raised in the Innocenti and had gone on in 1511 to serve as prioress "forty years, five months, and nine days with the highest degree of prudence, care and rectitude."[35]

Mona Gostanza appears to have been especially beloved by "all her daughters" as well the prior, who "out of respect for her nobility and outstanding

---

[32] Ibid.: "l'offitio delle quali se a di dar' la medicina e governar' l'infermi con carità e diligentia."

[33] AOIF Deliberazioni e Partiti degli Operai (VIII, 1) fol. 13v, 3 August 1575.

[34] AOIF Giornale K (XIII, 17) fol. 173r, 30 December 1551: "elexie et consitui Priora mona Dorothea allevata del decto spedale d'anni 54 in circha et stata più anni dispensiere della cucina."

[35] AOIF Giornale K (XIII, 17) fol. 171v, 28 December 1551: "Mona Gostanza suta nostra priora quale fu figliuola legitima et naturale di Landozo delli Albizi benchè nutrita et allevata del nostro spedale poi che per anni quaranta mesi conque dì nove con ottima prudentia sollecita et rectitudine hebbe administrato l'offitio della priora nel decto spedale."

TABLE 5.1. *Occupations or other status of women in the Innocenti, 1581*

Production workers	484
Administrators	57
Direct care of children	20
Students	14
Ill	11
TOTAL	586

Source: AOIF Nota di ufizi e arti di donne di casa (XLVI, 1) fol. 10r, anno 1581.

merit" had a Saint Gregory mass celebrated in her honor. The prior invited the friars of San Marco, San Francesco, the Servi, and San Gallo to be in attendance, as well as the congregation of the priests of the Visitation. The rector of the local parish of San Michele Visdomini presided over the interment. Even though the solemnity and magnificence of the funeral rites for prioresses was traditional, Prior Alamanni went even further in this case and buried Mona Gostanza in accordance with her express wish to be buried next to the body of her predecessor. This was no mean feat, it turned out, because officials had trouble remembering the exact location of her burial site. Moreover, the space next to Mona Agatha was already occupied by the Innocenti's first prior and treasurer, Lapo di Piero Pacini, whose tomb had to be cleaned out and his bones somewhat unceremoniously removed and reburied under the hospital's loggia to accommodate Mona Gostanza's body.[36]

Although Borghini's view of the hospital's women as fragile creatures with little judgment certainly runs counter to claims that Tridentine reforms bolstered the status of women in the late sixteenth century, his unrelenting obsession with monastic isolation and protection did not comprise the entirety of his attitudes toward women.[37] His funeral praise for Mona Maria, the woman who had governed as *priora* for nineteen years and *sottopriora* of the hospital's girls for the previous twenty, and who had been a foundling herself, noted that she had served "very affectionately and to the great contentment not only of our reverend prior Don Vincenzio Borghini but also of the entire hospital, the men's side as much as the women's."[38] Her death was

---

[36] Ibid., fol. 172r.

[37] S. K. Cohn, "Donne e controriforma a Siena: autorità e proprietà nella famiglia," *Studi Storici* 29.1 (1989): 203–24. The remainder of this subsection is taken from my article "Charity and State Building," 256–9.

[38] AOIF, Giornale M (XIII, 19), fol. 197r, 3 November 1574, cited in Gavitt, "Charity and State Building," 257. For the job description of the *priora*, see supra, n. 13.

greeted with "great sorrow, not only by our reverend prior, and the entire hospital, who wept openly as is done for a great loss, but also the entire city, by the grace of her good character, which in truth was loving, kind, ready to serve her neighbor, and endowed with every good quality."[39]

If the ritual ostentation of funeral rites bespoke both social standing and respect, as Lauro Martines has suggested for fifteenth-century humanists, the funerals accorded the prioresses of the Innocenti suggest that Borghini's praise was more than formulaic.[40] Mona Maria's funeral included thirty masses for the dead, in which "all the women, as well as the boys and the girls, prayed to God for her soul."[41] Although the hospital's chapel decorations were not as elaborate as the funeral preparations for Michelangelo, Mona Maria's mourners nonetheless would have seen that "the chapel was organized with stringers full of church candles inside up to the chapels of San Piero and Santa Caterina, and in the midst of the church one of the arches was full of candles, and all the altars were adorned in brown with candlesticks full of wax."[42] The iron gate to the women's cloister was also highly decorated and draped, and Mona Maria's body was placed on a "brown table with four very beautiful brass candlesticks resting in four candle holders."[43] As her corpse was being prepared for the procession, clerics "both from the hospital and other priests sang psalms and offices for the dead in the *loggetta*."[44]

Nor were the funeral rites for Mona Maria in any sense private. After the thirty masses for the dead had been sung, friars and priests from San Marco, Santa Croce, Santissima Annunziata, and San Michele Visdomini congregated in the Piazza de' Servi before beginning a procession that took them south down the Via de' Servi to the church of San Michele Visdomini, then west to the Medici palace, then north to San Marco, and finally east again to the church of Santissima Annunziata and back to the Innocenti. At the Innocenti, the hospital's children "dressed in brown and wearing their civilian berets, and accompanied by their tutor," knelt while her body was lowered into the grave inside the hospital's chapel.[45]

[39] Ibid.

[40] On the relationship between funerals and social standing in the fifteenth century, see Lauro Martines, *The Social World of the Florentine Humanists, 1390–1460* (Princeton: Princeton University Press, 1963), 243–5 and Sharon Strocchia, *Death and Ritual in Renaissance Florence* (Baltimore/London: Johns Hopkins University Press, 1992), 149–235.

[41] AOIF, Giornale M (XIII, 19), fol. 197r, 3 November 1574, cited in Gavitt, "Charity and State Building," 257.

[42] Ibid.

[43] Ibid.

[44] Ibid.

[45] Ibid., fol. 198r, cited in Gavitt, "Charity and State Building," 257–8.

The installation of Mona Maria's replacement, Mona Fiammetta, who at age fifty had been in the hospital her entire life and who had served in the hospital's dispensary for ten years, occasioned both ceremonial and ritual emotion that was no less elaborate. Borghini wrote extensively of the consultations he had undertaken, "because of the importance of the office of prioress," with the entire governing body of the Innocenti's patrons, the Arte della Seta. On the day of the installation, Borghini himself celebrated a mass of the Holy Spirit, in which both the "little girls and the women" prayed for God's continued favor. Then, "going with two priests into their [the women's] church where 500 of the older girls had gathered, he gave a very beautiful sermon exhorting them to live in fear of God, and to render obedience to the new prioress, and he [in turn] promised to be a good father to them."[46]

Borghini's feminine audience was so moved to tears that "everyone continued to cry for quite a long time."[47] Borghini, according to his own account, leaving the girls to say their prayers, gathered the old women and the hospital's officials, and in the presence of the new prioress, repeated a similar peroration.[48] Indeed, Borghini's florid descriptions of his own elaborate preparations and his moving eloquence combined a descriptive formula developed during the sixteenth century with an agenda that emphasized his ceremonial importance.[49] Yet Borghini's seemingly self-serving descriptions of his own eloquent and moving sermons provided both a literary model and a ceremonial order that housed and circumscribed feminine behavior in general and feminine mourning in particular.

Quasi-Conventual Institutions for Poor Girls: S. Maria e San Niccolò del Ceppo (1551), the Fanciulle della Pietà (1554), Santa Caterina (1590), and the Widows' Asylum of the Orbatello (1372)

The Conservatory of Santa Maria e San Niccolò del Ceppo

At Florence, the founding statutes of the convent of Santa Maria e San Niccolò del Ceppo make abundantly clear that avoidance of prostitution

---

[46] Ibid., cited in Gavitt, "Charity and State Building," 258–9.

[47] Ibid., cited in Gavitt, "Charity and State Building," 259.

[48] Ibid., fol. 198v; Gavitt, "Charity and State Building," 259.

[49] The descriptive formula, for example, was much the same as for the death of the prior. See AOIF, Giornale K (XIII, 17), fol. 173r, 30 December 1551 for a description of Luca Alamanni's funeral rites, which are substantially similar to Mona Maria's, although the prior's procession covered more distance and had a greater number of participants.

was the principal motive for the foundation of this congregation.[50] In 1551, "the bounty of God inspired some citizens of this city of Florence to make some provision for the many abandoned girls who because of these calamitous times were forced to wander begging throughout the city, in manifest danger of *capitar male*."[51] The citizens who took part in this pious enterprise were a diverse group socially. Initially founded in 1541 by Leonarda Barducci Ginori, Cosimo closed it in 1551, but the confraternity known as the Compagnia di S. Maria Vergine, itself a new foundation, took over its administration that same year.[52] In addition to such venerable Florentine family names as the Frescobaldi, the Velluti, the Pandolfini, and the Portinari, this confraternity of eighteen founders (all men) included a dealer in secondhand goods, a priest, and several less well-known surnames, including a certain Antonio da Milano. The membership of the men's congregation responsible for this abandoned girls' convent grew incrementally, not for lack of interest but because the numbers were deliberately kept restricted. In 1564, it took over the conservatory of San Niccolò, founded by the Otto di Guardia e Balìa eight years earlier. Although administered together, they took in separate groups of girls.[53]

On 1 March 1552, Cosimo I bestowed his formal approval on the enterprise, and the initial group of eighteen founders collected eighteen girls who were ten years of age or older. The founders housed the girls in a group of rental apartments "converted to convent use with sufficient *clausura* [cloistering]" above and next to the church of San Felice in Piazza in the Oltrarno, appointing as their governess for bodily needs "a mature woman of good

---

[50] For accounts of the daily lives of the girls of this conservatory, see Rosalia Manno Tolu. "Ricordanze delle abbandonate fiorentine di Santa Maria e San Niccolo del Ceppo nei secoli XVII–XVIII," in *Studi in onore diArnaldo d'Addario*, ed. L. Borgia (Lecce: Conte Editore, 1995) 3: 1007–1024.

[51] Nicholas Terpstra's assertion in *Abandoned Children of the Italian Renaissance*, 77, that "significantly, none of the Florentine conservatories mentioned the threat of prostitution in their statutes," although perhaps literally true, does not mean that compilers of such statutes did not have anxieties regarding the issue, because "manifesto pericolo di capitare male" must surely refer at least in part to the prospect of prostitution. ASF Monastero di S. Maria e S. Niccolò del Ceppo, Capitoli MS ibis, fol. ir: "la bontà di Dio ispirato alcuni cittadini di questa città di Firenze in questa presente narratione i nominati a desiderare et colere provedere, che molte fanciulle abbandonate che per i tempi calamitosi erano necessitate andare accatando per la città, con manifesto pericolo di capitare male."

[52] For providing information on this foundation as well as the other Florentine foundations for girls discussed here, I thank Nicholas Terpstra for generously sending me in advance a draft of his book chapter, "In loco parentis: Confraternities and Abandoned Children in Florence and Bologna," in *The Politics of Ritual Kinship: Confraternities and Social Order in Early Modern Italy*, ed. Nicholas Terpstra (Cambridge: Cambridge University Press, 1999), 114–31.

[53] Ibid.

habits and exalted prudence" and for their spiritual needs "a religious man of good habits and fearful of God, so that with exhortations, confessions, and the sacraments he shall lead them to walk in the path of God."[54]

Highly restrictive admissions policies reinforced the congregation's disciplinary agenda, which expressly excluded girls in danger of being either morally or medically diseased.[55] According to the statutes, girls had to be "no less than ten years old and should be truly abandoned and without any support whatsoever, i.e., without father, mother, brothers, or paternal uncles older than twenty-eight."[56] Indeed, the statutes excluded any girl who had received shelter or support within the previous four months, unless it was from someone who also went out begging or otherwise posed a danger to the morality of the girl in question.[57] Even in these cases, the members of the congregation were advised to keep their eyes open for any signs of lapsed behavior. In such cases, the congregation "shall not accept her but rather she shall be dismissed immediately."[58] So insistent was the congregation to make sure it recruited girls who were salvageable, the statutes expressly stated that the inmates should "preferably be called repentant rather than abandoned."[59]

As was true with institutions for repentant prostitutes, repentance, an upright life, and good physical health were the preconditions, not the anticipated outcomes of internment, for fear that "our place might become infected." Moreover, before anyone could propose a girl for admission, the girl had to be brought before the prioress and a nurse, who inspected her for signs of incurable or contagious illness, and dismissed her immediately if she

---

[54] ASF Monastero di S. Maria e San Niccolò del Ceppo, MS. 1 bis, fol. 1r, 1 March 1551: "la quale chiesa et casa ridussono a uso di monasterio con sufficiente clausure ponendo al loro governo corporale una donna matura di buon costumi et di exalta prudentia, et quanto allo spirituale un religioso di buon costumi et timorato di Dio; accio con l'exortationi, confessioni, et sagramenti le andassi incaminando nella via di Dio."

[55] Terpstra notes that by the sixteenth century in both Bologna and Florence, conservatories for boys or girls developed along distinctly and deliberately different lines from the larger, crowded hospitals, hoping by restricting the definition of admissible "family" to provide better and more manageable surroundings for children. I am less inclined to agree with Terpstra that large institutions did not employ the metaphor of family as frequently as smaller ones.

[56] ASF, Monastero di S. Maria e San Niccolò del Ceppo, MS. 1 bis, fol. 11v: "Ordiniamo che non se ne possino accettare che non habbino meno di anni dieci finiti et sieno veramente abandonate et senza appoggio alcuno cioè senza padre et madre senza fratelli o zii paterni maggiore di anni vent'otto."

[57] Ibid.

[58] Ibid., "Et quando il sospetto fussi tanto grande e durato tanto tempo che la fanciulla o fanciulle habino potuto vedere et sentire parole et fatti disonesti per i quali vien machiata, la mente in tal caso non si accetino ma si licenzino subito."

[59] Ibid. "havendo con lungha sperienza conosciuto et provato gli panni che per questo verso vengho fatti alla nostra opera che più presto si potrieno chiamare fanciulle rincresciute che abbandonate."

found any.[60] Once a girl was proposed for admission, she still had to endure an eight-day wait while hospital officials interrogated her and conducted an investigation into her past, including where she had lived, who her mother and father were, and who had previously taken care of her. These measures were necessary, argued the compilers of the statutes, so that families could not defraud the hospice by using it to avoid having to fulfill their responsibilities of family support.[61] Despite the diligence of such investigations, a number of girls slipped through and were only returned to their parents, brothers, or even husbands, after having lived at the Ceppo for several years. Four of the five brothers responsible for deciding whether to admit a particular girl had to agree before she could actually be admitted. If any of the brothers were absent, the vote would go to the entire membership.

If admission required a sound mind and sound body, considerations of honor also applied when it came time to send these girls back out into the world. Congregation members were to take "diligent care" in housing girls, either "placing them out as servants, getting them married or into a convent, according to what it is possible to arrange for each one."[62] In particular, when the congregation placed out girls as servants, the brothers had to take special care that prospective employers were "fearful of God and of good reputation, so that they will bring up the girls religiously with good habits and as if they were their very own daughters." For this purpose, the confraternity established a two-month trial period before committing itself to a long-term contract.[63]

The statutes also established *clausura*, because "just as through the door of the heart when it is not well-guarded, thieves come in who rob souls of their spiritual treasure, so it is with doors of our hospice, which, if neglected, could cause disorder and dishonor to God." For this reason only the provost, the provveditore, or the company as a whole could allow visitors in, and only the same officials could give consent to girls who wished to leave.[64]

---

[60] Ibid., fol. 12r: "Nemeno si accettino quelle che fussino state per serve per guardiane di bestie o fussero andate accattando ma sieno fare et di corpo et di mente acio che ne per l'una ne per l'altra ... venissi infettato il luogho nostro."

[61] Ibid., fol. 12v–13r.

[62] Ibid., fol. 13v: "Sieno li detti cinque cioe proposto et consigli et oblighati havere l'ochio apore diligente cura quando si porgerà l'occasione d'allogare le fanciulle o porle con altri per serve o maritarle o monacharle secondo la possibilità se alcuna havesi da per se da potergli dare esito."

[63] Ibid., fol 13v–14r: "cerchino di acchomodarle con persone timorate di Dio et di buona fama accio sieno religiosamente ne' buoni costumi in quel modo come se fussino loro figliuole."

[64] Ibid., fol. 14r: "Et perche si come per la porta del cuore quando è benguardata, bene spesso v'entrono e ladri che rubono il tesoro spirituale del'anime cosi nel'essere trascurati intorno alla

As was true with the Innocenti's tapestry workshops, the Ceppo's officials kept track of the work that the girls did. For this purpose, the prioress, in addition to being "adorned with virtue, a good example to all, and of mature age, prudence, and discretion," had to know how to write so that she could "keep diligent account of what work the girls had done, showing the two visitors every Sunday and making sure that each girl worked not for herself but for the common good."[65] Again, economic and social discipline mixed, just as they did in the Innocenti's workshops, so that each girl had to "render every honor, reverence, and obedience" to her instructors, and the prioress had to "instruct, train, correct, and punish" those who strayed. In addition, one girl had to be trained to keep the account books that recorded all the prioress's income and expenditures.[66] Finally, the prioress's contract stipulated that she see to it that bedsheets were changed "frequently" and that if any provisions were lacking, she should tell the two visitors so that supplies could be replenished. Every evening, the prioress had to ensure personally that every girl was asleep and that once the Ave Maria had sounded, all the doors be locked "so that everything shall be to the praise of God and the peace and good government of this place."[67]

The Ceppo successfully placed out 275 girls altogether between 1558 and 1621. Almost all of them, even if at some point they became victims of urban poverty, had come initially to Florence from the countryside. Of a sample of 113 covering the years 1558 to 1580, only 20 at the most (assuming all the unspecified ones were Florentine in origin) were from Florence – 87 were from the Tuscan *dominio*, and the remainder were from Bologna, Genoa,

---

porta che conduce alle nostre fanciulle potrebbe accadere disordine et cosa che fussi disonore di Dio pero vogliamo che la cosa non possa entrare alcuno senza licentia del padre proposto etcetto il provveditore e la compagnia loro chi piacerà a essi."

[65] Ibid., fol. 14v: "bisognando una compagnia la quale sia ornata di virtù et exemprale [sic] a tutte di matura età di prudentia et discretione et governo sappia scrivere et si chiami priora tengha diligente conto di quello lavorano le fanciulle dandone ogni domenica conto a' due visitatori et habbia l'ochi che nessuna lavori per se propria ma per il comune." That such work involved more than the duties associated with maintaining the girls' quarters is clear from a reference in the same page to the account books the prioress had to keep of the silks that came into the institution to be worked on and that were sent back out to the shops. This suggests that although Terpstra's distinctions of scale between large foundling hospitals and small conservatories still apply, the small conservatories were also workhouses and that child labor prevailed as the disciplinary regimen in both settings.

[66] Ibid., fol. 14v–15r: "intendiamo che sia reso ogni honore reverentia et obedientia accio meglio possa l'instruire, ammaestrare, corregiere et gastighare chi errassi."

[67] Ibid., "Vegha frequentemente le letta accio stieno pulite et stesse et le faccia mutare di lenzuola quando sarà di bisogno . . . et ogni sera sonata l'avemaria sieno serrate le porte a chiave accio tutto sia allaude di dio et pace et reggimento di detto luogho."

Venice, Ancona, or Milan. Because the Ceppo only began keeping reliable statistics in 1570, and even then the reliability of estimates of age is suspect, it is only possible to know for a little over half the sample their age on admission. Of the sixty girls whose ages we know, fully eighteen had been admitted in violation of the statutes. Another thirty-one girls were at the age especially vulnerable to violations of honor (ages 10 to 16), and therefore also at the age where families concerned about the expenses of dowry might have been sorely tempted to abandon them to the streets.[68] Certainly, the number of girls admitted beyond the age of sixteen drops off sharply. Among the younger girls was a three-year-old whose mother "stayed with" the grand duke's secretary, Bartolomeo Concini, and who was returned to her mother shortly afterward.[69]

The Ceppo kept track of girls long after they married, went into household service, or went into convents. Lisabetta, for example, the nineteen-year-old daughter of Bernardo, a weaver from Radda in Chianti, when she was admitted in 1556 at age forty was found to have two or three brothers in Florence and was married to a worker in Borgo S. Niccolò. Antonio Manovelli from Piantravignia near Castelfranco di Sopra had two daughters who were accepted for admission: Lucretia, admitted in January 1558 as an eighteen year old, and Humana, admitted in 1559 at age twelve. Lucretia became prioress and died in 1603, leaving only Humana still in the care of the institution.

The Ceppo sent out its youngest girls as servants for terms of five to ten years and succeeded in placing virtually all its girls out for household service. At the very least, those employers who took on servants from the Ceppo had to provide clothes, shoes, and a basic wage averaging about ten lire per year. A few employers willingly committed themselves to arranging marriages and supplying a small dowry or eventually sending the girls to a convent. Of forty-three girls whose eventual fates after employment or service we know, ten married, sixteen returned home to a relative, one returned home to her husband, four took off from their employers without warning, and eight died.

---

[68] I have drawn all statistics and samples from ASF Monastero di S. Maria e S. Niccolò del Ceppo, MS. 59: Fanciulle accettate e di poi acconciate con altri, 1558–61, fol. 1r–17r, 105v–120v. The Ceppo's statistics are typical of Florentine conservatories in general: in Bologna age at admission, more often fixed by statute at ten years old, was much higher on average. Cf. Terpstra, *Abandoned Children*, 79, table 3.3.

[69] Ibid., fol. 113r: "Margherita Piccina da Terranuova senza padre ha madre che sta col secretario Concino mandòlla del monsignore Vicario. Venne l'anno 1565 d'anni alhora 3. Resesi a sua madre."

The Conservatorio delle Fanciulle della Pietà

This conservatory, located originally in Borgo Ognissanti, and after 1568 on the via della Mandorla behind the Church of Santissima Annunziata, also owed its foundation to a noblewoman, Margherita di Bonromei, and its survival to the influential Dominican reformer, Alessandro Capocchi, who in 1557 provided the spiritual leadership and organizational expertise of this new foundation. According to a marginal note in the conservatory's 1570 statutes, the Dominican influence persisted at least until 1728, at which time its workers wore the Dominican habit and were under the jurisdiction of the friars of San Marco. The Conservatorio della Pietà, unlike Santa Maria e San Niccolò del Ceppo, was a charity administered by a board of noble women, one of whom was to be named the "mother prioress," and the compiler of the 1570 edition of the statutes made this arrangement a prominent part of the Pietà's constitutions.[70]

These constitutions are valuable both for their prescriptive tone and their descriptions of how the compilers envisioned the ideal disciplined life for preadolescent and adolescent girls. Extremely detailed and consisting of twenty-six separate chapters regulating the daily life of the conservatory, the constitutions set the general religious and reformed tone by quoting the Old Testament to the effect that the girls were in all of their activities to "decline from sin and to do good." In particular, the constitutions were to encourage girls "to seek first the honor of God, then our own salvation, and then the peace and unity of our congregation," and to demonstrate it in their words. "These two parts [shunning evil and doing good] are each necessary to the other, because having only one but not the other one cannot proceed to the reward of eternal life. If one does good works but does not shun evil, or if one renounces evil but does not do good works, one will not be called to eternal salvation."[71]

What is striking about the constitutions of the Pietà is that a considerable amount of work was to be undertaken by the girls themselves – following, once again, a stricter conventual model of organization and internal

---

[70] Biblioteca Moreniana, Florence, Fondo Bigazzi 61, fol. 5v, 25 March 1570: "vogliamo che la nostra congregatione sia sempre governata da una congregatione di citadine le quale una si chiama la madre priore con le altre priore in suo aiuto."

[71] Ibid., fol. 4r–4v: "ci dieno gratia di fare tutte quelle chose che ci sia prima l'onore di Dio et di poi la salute delle anime nostre et pace et unione di nostra congregatione . . . dicendo declina a malo et fac bonum incuire pare et persequere eam vol dire partiti dal male et fa bene cerca la pace et seguitala nelle quali parole manifestamente ci dimostra essere dua parte necesarie perche avendo l'una senza l'altra non si puo pervenire a quel dolie premio di vita eterna imperoche facendo bene et non lassando al male et lassando el male et non facendo bene non si chiama via di salute."

discipline. Although two women served the girls, and the prioress and her assistant managed the daily life of the institution, the girls themselves carried out the duties, as necessary, of porter, housemistress, reader, a mistress for the novices, a tailor, someone to be in charge of the refectory, a doctor, a nurse, mistress of silk weaving, a loom threader, and a hosier.[72] The Pietà enforced internal discipline with strict rules concerning confession and communication. Girls had to confess at least once a month, and those who intended to become nuns more often than that – every Sunday, Wednesday, and Friday, as well as every feast day. Those who did not feel ready or worthy of receiving communion had to ask the father confessor's permission to miss it and had to stay in church with head uncovered.

Rules of decorum persisted beyond the mass itself and made themselves known through the language of the body as well. The rule of silence applied not only in church and other places of prayer but also to common areas, dormitories, and stairs, as well the common room. When summoned, girls were enjoined to answer "with humility" by saying "God be praised." When going outside "in formation," girls had to have their "eyes low and their hearts pure" without talking to one another. When they stood in line for confession, only four at a time could be in the church, and they were to speak of matters of confession only to the father confessor, and during the confession, they could not name other girls. In addition to private confessions, once a week, the prioress held a hearing at which girls confessed their defects and she then meted out "reproofs and punishments with love and charity." She also mediated disputes by sending the offending parties to church to be reconciled "in the presence of the holy sacrament."[73] At mass and on other occasions when everyone met in common, girls could not rise to leave without seeking permission from the *madre priora*, and when they sat together waiting for their work assignments, they were to sit distant from one another "so that they are not touching."[74]

Although the rules attempted to reduce public humiliation and ridicule by providing that when a girl did public penance, other girls were not to make

[72] Ibid., fol. 6r.

[73] Ibid., fol. 11v–12v: "et di piu che ogni venerdi o altro g[i]orno si facci la audientia di difecti dalla madre priore ordinata secondo li bisogni et quelli difecti riprendeli et gastigarli con amor' et carita et che ogni mese una volta si venga alla audientia delle ofitiale et quelle riprendere con carità et amore et di più ogni mese che si debba far la cercha per tutta la chiesa cerchando se nessuna tenessi cosa partiale et simil chose a quelle torle e decta cercha la debbi fare quelle persone che dalle madre priore sarà ordinato et di più quando una fanciulla avesi odio o ranchore con un altra vogliamo et ordiniamo che la sera le vadino in chiesa dinnanzi al santissimo sagramento a riconciliarsi."

[74] Ibid., fol. 7r–8v: "quando le fanciulle sono congregate in comune si alla messa come in sala o alla oratione che nesuna non sia ardita di levarsi di quivi se prima non domanda licentia alla madre o maestra secondo li lavori et di più star distante l'una dalla l'altra tanto che non si toccare."

fun of her, they also restricted girls from visiting their sick colleagues without permission from the prioress, and when it came time to wash hair and feet, girls should not do this for one another but leave it to those whose turn of duty it was. Undertones of repressed sexuality also dictated that clothes should be not only well sewn, but done so with simplicity and "reaching up as far as the neck so as not to show those things which ought to remain covered." Indeed, girls could not even speak about husbands or matrimonial ambitions to each other. Rather, "if some girl no longer wishes to serve our Lord Jesus in a perfect state of virginity," she must go to the prioress and place herself under her obedience. Even when working in the bakery, an older girl always had to be there with a younger one and had to take care not to wander alone through the parts of the complex where they could be seen from the street "so as not to give occasion for disgrace." Indeed, in making sure that the gates "in front and in back" were locked, the statutes exhorted girls to make explicit comparisons between the physical gates and "the gates of their bodies, so that our enemy does not enter them."[75]

Virtually every aspect of *clausura* that applied to cloistered nuns applied in the Pietà as well. The conservatory allowed in no men save the father confessor, except for construction workers when building was in progress or repairs were to be made. Even then, the mother prioress and at least one other woman accompanied them. The grate where one could make at least spoken contact with the outside world was also where beggars had to wait for alms and others who had business with the prioress could stay. Under no circumstances could girls linger at the grate longer than was necessary to transact business such as receiving raw materials for the workshops. In particular, girls "could not chat at the grate the entire day but instead must send every visitor on his way."[76] Men were not the only potential danger. Even alumnae who had chosen to marry and who came back to visit the prioress had to wait at the grate until the prioress's servants were authorized to allow her to enter the complex. Abuses of *clausura* and issues of patronage that plagued the convent of Santa Croce Val d'Arno (see Chapter 6) at precisely this time also find their way into the statutes of the Pietà. No woman from outside the Pietà could sleep there, and girls could not have their relatives visit except by permission of the prioress herself, because "it is

---

[75] Ibid., fol. 8v–9r: "li panni sieno cuciti et facti con simplicita et stare al collo amontate non mostrando quelle chose che si possano tener coperte et di più el lunedì et mercoledì non si mangiar carne senon per queste che anno causa legitima et di piu che in nostra congregatione non sia nesuna ardita di ragionar' di marito o cose di matrimonio ma quando qualche fanciulla non volessi servire a yesu nello stato perfecto cioè in virginita vadia adirlo alla madre priore o madre di casa et aspectar la obedientia di esse madre."

[76] Ibid., fol. 10v–11r: "et non istare tutto el dì a cicalare ma spedire ogni persona subito."

quite sufficient that we will see each other in Paradise if we're good." Girls could not sleep together, with the exception of the smallest ones, and not even then could the prioress mix the ill with the healthy.[77]

In addition to the armor of internal discipline and statute to ward off occasions of sin, rituals of prayer and devotion also structured the day to keep girls occupied when they were not eating, sleeping, or working. After specifying that all property was held in common and that no girls except the ones assigned to specific jobs should possess keys, the statutes forbade singing "worldly things such as love songs or the like" and proposed the substitution of "laude, hymns, and psalms" instead. The organization of the day was itself structured, just as was true in the more normal monastic setting, around devotions.[78]

At dawn, when the Ave Maria sounded, the mistress appointed for this task woke up the girls by saying the Ave Maria or the Pater noster. The girls then congregated in the prayer niche "praising God and saying 'blessed be the name of the Lord now and forever.'" The girls then repeated the Ave Maria and the Pater noster, then the Creed, "thanking our sweet Spouse for all the benefits received from His Majesty." After making the sign of the cross and repeating several more Ave Marias and Pater nosters, the girls prayed for mercy on their sins, taking as their model for grace and forgiveness the forgiveness Christ had shown "to the thief on the cross and to Mary Magdalene."[79]

The prayers themselves had an unmistakable church militant, Counter-Reformation flavor. Girls prayed "for the status of our holy mother church, that it successfully convert all sinners and infidels and preserve good people in her holy grace." Girls also prayed for "the temporal State and for all those who rule and govern the Florentine state, that they may govern our Florentine city in peace, in charity, and in evangelical faith."[80] Just as advice books on the family saw it as a microcosm of the state, so did the compilers of the statutes envision the broad scope of divine justice exemplified in

---

[77] Ibid., fol. 11v–13v: "basta bene che tutti ci rivedremo in paradiso se noi saremmo buoni."

[78] Ibid., fol. 14r–14v: "et di più non cantare cose mondane come canzone o simili ma cantare laude hinni et salmi."

[79] Ibid., fol. 15v–16r: "subito levate et congregate nel cluocho della oratione laudando idio dicendo sit nomen domini benedictam: ex [h]oc nu[n]c et usque in seculum et seguitando . . . rigratiando el nostro dolce sposo . . . pregando che chi abbia pietà de' nostri peccati et ci dia gratia di far' la sua sancta voluntà et di essere buone si chome delle questa gratia al ladrone in croce et a Maria Magdalena."

[80] Ibid., fol. 16r–16v: "et più uno pater nostro et avemaria pregando per lo sstato della santa madre chiesa con pregare che converta tutti li peccatori et infideli et conservi li buoni nella sua sancta gratia et ancora per lo stato tenporale et per tutti quelli che anno a reggere et governare lo stato fiorentino acio che governino la nostra città fiorentina in pace et in carità et fede evangelica."

the good governance of the state, which in turn was reflected in the good governance of the institution:

> And moreover we should pray God for our spiritual father so that he will govern our souls so that we may reach and enjoy the desired paradise, as well as for the prioress and the housemistress and staff, so that they all must always do those things that redound to the praise of God and the peace of our house. We should also say an Ave Maria and Pater noster for the girls of our House, both living and dead, for all those troubled and afflicted, that God may give patience to them and to those who rule and govern.[81]

Thus, the community of the Pietà embraced the living and the dead and, in particularly vivid imagery, solicited prayers "for the dead who are waiting in holy purgatory with their hands and feet bound in . . . atrocious suffering." These prayers took the form of reciting the psalm De profundis and the prayer Deus veni et largitor. These and further prayers to the saints and angels were merely preliminary to the formal mass, which all girls had to attend and "stay at the mass with devotion, silence, and meditating on the mystery of Jesus Christ's holy passion."[82]

Once the girls reached the posts where they worked, their supervisors entered upon another round of common prayer by saying the Pater Noster and the Deus adiutorium meum intende every half hour. At the end of the workday, the housemistress led the girls in another round of prayer "thanking God for all the benefits received on that holy day and then reciting the Litany of Saints." At bedtime, the fervent cycle of prayers continued, and in addition the girls prayed together "for the [re]union of all Christianity." The prioress then gave the sign of peace, which two appointed girls then passed on, hierarchically through the older girls and then the younger ones. The prioress then exhorted the girls to give their last thoughts before going to sleep to the "poor dead."[83]

[81] Ibid., fol. 16v: "et più pregare idio per el nostro padre spirituale che governi l'anime nostre acìo che le possino arivare et godere el desiderato paradiso così per la madre priore et madre di casa et hofitiale che tutti abbino a fare senpre tutte quelle cose che ritornino a laude di dio et pace di nostra casa con dire uno pater nostro et ave maria anchora per tutte le fanciulle di nostra casa si vive come morte per tutti li afflitti et tribolati che idio li dia patientia a loro et a chi li a reggere et governar."

[82] Ibid., fol. 16v–17r: "con dire uno pater nostro et una ave maria per li morti che stanno aspectando con le mani et piedi legati in quelle atrocissime pene del santo purgatorio . . . et ultimamente uno pater nostro et ave maria a riverentia della passione di iesu dolce sposo nostro."

[83] Ibid., fol. 18r–18v; fol. 20: "rigratiando idio di tutti li benefitii ricevuti in quel santo gorno et di più dire le letanie di tutti li santi: . . . dichisi uno paternostro et ave maria a honor dello santo spirito pregando per la unione di tutta la cristianità. . . . et finita la madre dicha consideriamo alli poveri morti et pregisi per loro con dire el salmo miserere mei deus."

Certain liturgical rituals also repeated themselves at set times of the year. The Fanciulle della Pietà prescribed the *quarantore*, or forty-hours devotion, at least three times a year (the feast of the Holy Spirit, the feast of the angels on September 7, and Christmas), and ideally also on the Monday and Tuesday of Carnival and Good Friday as well.[84] The forty-hours devotion for Carnival is especially significant because it corresponded with other initiatives taken after the Council of Trent to keep children's focus away from pre-Lenten festivities and to substitute for Carnival religious devotion and meditation. Even as early as the Savonarolan period, the pre-Lenten season, Palm Sunday, and Good Friday had been occasions for ritual processions of children dressed in white to go around the city; the *quarantore* devotion maintained the calendar but shifted the focus to a much more structured disciplinary piety.[85]

Indeed, most of the daily devotional practices that were not part of an official *quarantore* celebration still reflected both the letter and spirit of that devotion. Prayers for the reunion of Christians and the conversion of sinners and infidels were an important part of both, as was the exposition of the *santissima sagramento*. In the formal *quarantore*, which had its origins in Catholic reform devotion in the late 1520s or early 1530s and which was formally approved in 1539 by Pope Paul III, continuous prayer occurred in shifts for approximately forty hours, and the church doors were closed and women excluded, although no mention of the exclusion of girls was mentioned in the statutes. Because only one priest was available for this devotion, it seems likely that for whatever reason, the exclusion of women did not apply, at least in 1570, to this devotion at the Pietà. Like the entire cycle of prayer at the Pietà, the *quarantore* prayers were meant to be not only continuous but fervent supplication, to be used especially in times of common calamity or peril.[86]

In addition to surviving statutes, the Conservatory of the Pietà provides the most comprehensive demographic information of all of the girls' asylums in Florence. The Pietà accepted 917 girls between 1559 and 1623. During its first day of operation in January 1555, it accepted fifty-two girls, with

---

[84] Ibid., fol. 20r–21r.

[85] On Savonarolan processions, see Gavitt, *Charity and Children in Renaissance Florence*, 296–7, citing Luca Landucci, *Diario fiorentino dal 1450 al 1516*, 124–5.

[86] Indeed, Paul III's apostolic letter approving the devotion specifically linked the *quarantore* to the appeasement of God and the defeat of the Turks. This apostolic letter is quoted and translated in the 1909 edition of the Catholic Encyclopedia s.v. "Forty Hours' Devotion." On the *quarant'ore* devotion and baroque theater, see Mark Weil, "The Devotion of the Forty Hours and Roman Baroque Illusions," *Journal of the Warburg and Courtauld Institutes* 37 (1974): 218–48.

an average age of twelve and who ranged in age from five to twenty. This pattern remained remarkably consistent over the course of the sixteenth and seventeenth centuries, suggesting in this case as well that the precipitating factor for admission was parental concern over the approach of marriage. Such a suggestion takes on a firmer shape in light of Lucia Sandri's finding that girls of the Pietà (and the Ceppo) were among depositors to the Innocenti's deposit bank who were accumulating savings there for their dowries.[87] Approximately 20 percent of the girls came from Florence; most of the remaining 80 percent came from the surrounding countryside, especially the Casentino and the Mugello. By and large, the girls of the Pietà did not come from wealthy or even middling families but from families of artisans: tailors, dyers, carpenters, weavers, fishermen, grocers, bakers, weavers, and furriers.

Clearly the hopes of these families were that girls under the auspices of such institutions as the Pietà could either earn enough from being sent out as domestic servants to contribute to their own dowries, or in some cases, ease the family's economic burden for only a year or two. Some 49 girls among the first 359 admissions returned to their parents by prior arrangement, and two girls fled the institution, one while she was ill at the hospital of Santa Maria Nuova and the other – who found her way home – from the Pietà itself. One would expect, after all, that if feminine honor were the fathers' overriding concern, a large percentage of the Pietà's inmates would marry directly from the institution or become nuns. Instead, of 359 girls admitted between 1555 and 1560, only 22, or 6 percent, married, and only two girls took conventual vows. Indeed, one of the girls who took vows did not even do so under pressure from the institution but because the woman who had taken her on as a servant also decided to profess her vows.[88] Although it is tempting to argue that the quasi-monastic regimen of the Pietà discouraged most girls from the real thing, it is probably more realistic to speculate that the servant positions for which most of them were qualified were neither particularly desirable nor in great supply in the cloister. When, for example, Lucrezia from Montemignaio entered the convent of Santa Maria degli Angeli in working-class district of Borgo San Frediano, she did so as a servant rather than as a novice.

[87] Lucia Sandri, "L'attività di banco di deposito," 155–62. I thank Dr. Sandri for sending me an advance draft of this article.

[88] ASF, Corporazioni Religiose Soppresse dal Governo Francese, 112, Società dello Spedale di Pietà, 78: Libro Segreto A, fol. 57 right, n.d. The girl in question had been admitted at age ten to the Pietà on 11 November 1556–the date of her departure to the convent would no doubt have been sometime in the early 1560s.

Outside the cloister, however, positions for servants were much more plentiful, and fifty-two (14.4 percent) of the girls admitted in the first five years became servants in private households in Florence. In some cases, the length of service was left unspecified; in others it was specified in a contract. A certain Domenica, originally from San Gimignano, entered the domestic service of Domenico Dardano in 1557 when she was thirteen years old for a stipulated period of nine years, although she left after only a few months and went into the service of a weaver for a four-year contract instead. Placements could be somewhat modest, but a more fortunate girl might well end up as a servant to one of the duke's servants, as happened to a girl from Montelupo who worked for Girolamo Francioso "che sta con Sua Eccellenza."[89]

Another 67 girls of that first five-year cohort of 359 girls (or 18.7 percent) stayed resident in the hospital without ever being successfully placed out at all. Among these were Mona Brigida and Mona Caterina, who rose through the ranks, like many comparable women at the Innocenti and the Orbatello, to become prioress. Mona Caterina, in particular, who died in 1613, had supervised the weaving workshops at the Pietà before being elevated to the position of prioress. Those who were resident in the hospital would have benefited from the instruction provided by female weavers hired from outside to come in and teach, in return only for shelter, board, and clothes.[90]

Unfortunately, by far the most common fate for girls admitted to the Pietà was premature death. Of the 359 girls who arrived between 1555 and 1560, 46.5 percent died before their twenty-first birthday, and among the earliest arrivals, adolescent mortality reached levels of 60 percent. Given that these deaths occurred among a population that was biologically less vulnerable than most other sectors of the population, these figures are appalling. Certainly the first years of operation were years of both serious epidemic disease and outright starvation, but the pattern of abnormally high mortality persisted well into the 1560s, suggesting that however well intentioned the motives of founders and the patronage of grand dukes, these institutions were not receiving enough support to make them viable. Indeed, the Pietà did not even house girls who were ill but sent them to Florence's general hospital, Santa Maria Nuova, if beds were available there.

Lucia Sandri has revealed, on the basis of her study of the banking deposits at the Innocenti made by the girls of the Pietà, an even more sinister side to these mortality figures: the extremely heavy workloads undertaken by the girls of the Pietà in making brocades and other silk products for the grand ducal court. In an undated petition to the grand duke (answered by Cosimo's

---

[89] Ibid., fol. 26 right, 7 October 1556.
[90] Ibid., fol. 30 right, n.d.

secretary, Bartolomeo Concini, who served for at least three decades), the girls of the Pietà complained that their work was so tiring that they fell irremediably ill of catarrh, so that one of their teachers had died of it in the previous month, and although two girls were beginning to know how to do the work extremely well, one fell ill and the other was going blind. Of the ten women who taught and supervised the girls, only two were left, because "due to the worsening of the weather the healthy were falling ill quickly." The petition asked the grand duke to provide a more stable subsidy to the silk guild, and Concini wrote back saying that the guild should tell him what it required. In short, such institutions could not be havens from the economic, medical, and social problems that ravaged sixteenth-century Italy. If the institution was founded to prevent girls from wandering the streets and selling their bodies for food money, the Pietà successfully preserved their usefulness to the city's economy, but not their lives. Nicholas Terpstra's research, moreover, raises the possibility that the girls of the Pietà were victims of severe sexual exploitation by their benefactors during the period of time they lived on Borgo Ognissanti, and that both the move to via della Mandorla and the extremely detailed and severe statutes of 1570 were a direct response to these events.[91]

Santa Caterina della Ruota[92]

Founded in 1590 during the great famine, the hospice of Santa Caterina was patterned after the Ceppo and the Pietà and sounded many of the same post-Tridentine themes: an intense daily cycle of devotion and prayer, the daily discipline of work and earning one's own bed and board, strict *clausura*, extremely restrictive admissions policies, and a concern that hunger and desperation not drive small girls into a life of prostitution:

> In the reign of Don Fernando de' Medici Duke of Tuscany there was a great famine in which many poor girls gave themselves over to an evil

---

[91] Lucia Sandri, "L'attività di banco di deposito," 166. The petition to the grand duke can be found in AOIF Filze d'Archivio (LXII 61) fol. 323r, 12 May (no year): "tanto che ce gran perormento di tempo, è come sano presto si infermano." Nicholas Terpstra surmises, in my view correctly, that this list of symptoms (catarrh and blindness) indicates the high mortality at the Pietà was most likely due to syphilis. See Terpstra, *Abandoned Children*, 265–6. For greater detail concerning the lives of the girls of this conservatory, see idem, *Lost Girls: Sex and Death in Renaissance Florence* (Baltimore: Johns Hopkins University Press, 2010), which ties together in compelling detail this conservatory's high mortality rate, low external placement, the symptoms of syphilis, the use of abortifacients, and the relationship between the girls' low socioeconomic status and their exploitation.

[92] Much of what follows on Santa Caterina can also be found in John Henderson, "Charity and Welfare," 70–1.

life because of hunger. Wishing to obviate such evils and sins, several gentlemen, fearful of God and with the favor of His Most Serene Grand Duke dedicated themselves to shelter many poor girls who were wandering in the streets, so that they should not fall prey to evil.[93]

The original intention of the founders was to keep open the shelter only for three years in hope that once the famine ceased, so would the need for shelter. Instead, because within three years not all of the girls found placements elsewhere, the founders and the grand duke established for these girls a hospice in Via San Gallo, "all this for the honor and glory of God and to preserve these little girls from the Devil's hands."[94]

The founding statutes fixed the population of Santa Caterina at eighty girls, so that an entrant could only be accepted if a current inmate "dies, marries, or becomes a nun." Policies for admission were not merely strict but explicit concerning the categories of girls they excluded: "blind, deaf, mute, hunchbacks and cripples," although the statutes specified that the reasoning behind this exclusion was that such categories of girls were hardly vulnerable to the dangers of prostitution in the first place. The founders also excluded "daughters of bad women, or their nieces, or of persons of bad reputation, whom we do not want more than ever, nor should they even be allowed for a moment inside the place."[95]

As was true at the Ceppo and the Pietà, the hospice of Santa Caterina observed strict *clausura*. Because the hospice had no garden, girls were allowed to walk outdoors once a week "to get a little air" in well-supervised groups of six or eight girls. Relatives who wished to visit could only do so once a week and had to seek prior permission from the *madre priora*. Even then conversations had to take place in a voice loud enough for the appointed listener (*ascoltatrice*) to hear. Speaking in too low a voice was

---

[93] ASF, Monastero di S. Caterina 7: Capitoli et Ordinationi delle Fanciulle Abbandonate di Santa Caterina Martire della città di Firenze (1590), fol. 2v–3r: "Regnando Don Fernando de' Medici Gran Duca di Toscana fu per tutta Italia una grandissima carestia onde molte povere fanciulle per la fame si davano a mal'vivere. Volendo à tanti mali et peccati oviare, molti gentil'huomini timorati di Dio con il favore della Serenissima Gran Duca si dettero à raccorre molte povere fanciulle, che andavano per le strade, acciò non capitassero male, con animo in termine di tre anni di accomodarle." This codex has two versions of the statutes: an incomplete earlier version with numbered folios, which I cite with folio numbers, and a complete later version with unnumbered folios, which I cite by section (Distinzione) number and Chapter number.

[94] Ibid.: "et questo tutto per honore, et gloria di Dio et conservare tante fanciulle dalle mani del demonio."

[95] Ibid., fol. 4r–5v: "ordiniamo, che il numero delle fanciulle non eccedino il numero di ottanta à tale che se non ne muore, ò mariti, ò si monachi . . . che non sieno cieca, sorda, muta, gobba, stroppiata, et questo perche simille non sono così periculose à capitar male; non figlie di donne cattive, o nipote di tale, o di persone infame, le quali tutte non vogliamo che mai, ne per veruna sorte d'occasione siano intromesse dentro al luogo."

sufficient grounds for restricting visits from relatives for six months. Carpenters, builders, and repairmen had to get the prioress's permission to enter "to maintain a greater reputation for the place, to take away any opportunity for murmuring, which must never happen."[96]

All the girls, young and old, were required absolutely to confess once a month, but the older girls were to encourage the younger "by word and by example" to confess and to take communion often "by which we mean at the most twice a week."[97] Prayer was virtually constant when the girls were not actually working, and even more than was the case for the Ceppo and the Pietà, the girls of Santa Caterina prayed two or three separate times a day for their benefactors, both dead and living. "Every day the third part of the most holy Rosary will be said for the dead benefactors of the place. Every Wednesday an entire Office of the Dead for Our Lord, as well as one full Rosary for each girl who has died."[98]

Although the discipline of work was clearly an important part of the daily regime, at Santa Caterina the earnings of girls had no apparent link to their dowries, which were uniformly a hundred lire for girls who married and three hundred for those who wished to enter the religious life. Instead, "because this is a poor place, and alms are scarce, the Signor Provost will use every diligence that there shall never be lacking work for the girls to do, such as silk and gold work, and finally . . . that money from the shops except in cases of extreme necessity shall not be touched, but saved to buy grain."[99] Although the statutes of other institutions do not mention begging, it is clear that the girls of all these hospices were expected to support their institutions through rigidly supervised begging in churches. One of the instructions for the mistress of the novices, for example, was that the girls

> may not leave church by themselves to go anywhere else, and when they do go out begging, never to go without a companion. They must always stay in groups, not stopping to talk with relatives, or with the girls of the

[96] Ibid., Dist. II., Capitoli 7–8: "Considerando l'angusta del luogo, et che non ha un poco di orto, da pigliare un poco d'aria et di camminare una volta la settimana. . . . in verun' tempo ò hora mai entrerrà dentro il luogo un'operaio solo, ma chimando la nostra priora. . . . Et questo per mantenere il luogo con la maggiore reputatione, che sia possibile et levare l'occasione alla mormoratione, che mai potesse occorrere."

[97] Ibid., Capitolo 10: "et le grandi esorteranno le piccine con parole et buon esempli à confessarli, et communicarsi spesso, il che intendiamo che sia al più due volte la settimana."

[98] Ibid., Capitoli 2–3: "Ogni giorno si dirà la terza parte del Santissimo Rosario per i Morti Benefattori del luogo. Ogni Mercoledi tutto l'officio de' Morti per il Signor: così per ogni fanciulla che muora una volta tutto il Santissimo Rosario."

[99] Ibid., fol. 6r: "Per essere il luogo povero, et le limosine scarse il Signor proposto userà ogni diligenza, che non manchi mai loro da lauorar come seta, oro, et finalmente, che non si habbino da stare, et i denari delle botteghe senza estrema necessità, et senza l'ordine del proposto, non si tocheranno."

Pietà, of San Niccolò, or to the nuns who beg, or to abandoned boys. [They must] not stay outside of church, nor sleep, nor eat things that are given them, but bring them directly back to the hospice. If someone says to them, come into my house and I will give you alms, they are not to go in, they are not to bring news, or deliver messages.[100]

Yet maternal solicitude was not entirely absent: the mistress of these novitiates also had to make sure that the novices' faces were clean, to treat them as "special daughters of God," and even "to teach reading to those pupils who were apt."[101] The mistress of the novices was in theory the most important figure in shaping the discipline that these young girls would undergo to preserve their prospects for an honorable marriage or for entry into the religious life.

The Orbatello "Widows' Asylum"

Founded in 1377 by a member of the Alberti family, and ostensibly the beneficiary of the patronage of the Parte Guelfa, the so-called Widows' Asylum of Santa Maria in Orbatello is the only foundation solely for Florentine women that had its origins before the Savonarolan reform movement. It addressed the issues involved in gender and inheritance both innovatively and directly: when a male head of household died (or in some cases had merely abandoned his family), not only his widow but also her children could be admitted into the Orbatello's apartments, eventually to be supervised by elderly women who had become the matrons of the institution. As Richard Trexler has shown, even the architecture of the Orbatello attempted to preserve what was left of the integrity of the household unit. During the fifteenth and sixteenth centuries, Orbatello was thus not merely a widow's asylum but also a shelter for *malmaritate*. In this respect, it seems to have anticipated the kind of institution that would become much more numerous during the sixteenth century.[102]

---

[100] Ibid., Dist. III. Cap. 5: "non si partir di chiesa per andare in luogo veruno, non andare una senza l'altra, ma sempre stare accanto a la compagnia, non favellar con parente, o con le fanciulle della Pietà, di San Niccolò, ò à monache che accattano, ò à fanciulli abbandonati, non stare fuori di chiesa, non dormire, non mangiare le cose, che li sono date, ma portarle a casa, ma attendere a accattare, e se nessuno gli dicessi vieni a casa mia che ti darò la lmosina, non v'andare, non arrechar novelle, non portar imbasciate."

[101] Ibid.: "deve vedere che stiano pulite . . . et governarle in tutti i lor bisogni, et trattarle come particolare figliuole di Dio. . . . Deve insegnar' loro leggere à quelle che sono atte."

[102] Richard Trexler, "Widows' Asylum," 120–6. Admittedly, the Orbatello did not do much to solve gender and inheritance issues among the merchant elite, among whom in some respects they were the most pressing.

As Trexler documents, the Orbatello, like the girls' institutions we have been considering, drew the vast majority of its population from the Florentine countryside. As did the other institutions for girls, the Orbatello also provided a modest dowry, which these girls used almost exclusively for marriage rather than as an entry to conventual life. Although Trexler finds it surprising that during the sixteenth century the Parte Guelfa gave control over the Orbatello almost entirely to its resident matrons, such a pattern is entirely consistent with the monastic model of self-government that obtained in other girls' institutions as well. Only with the sudden influx of girls from the Innocenti did the stabilization achieved in midcentury become compromised and the overwhelming collision of family structures, gender roles, and demographic realities make the *putte* of the Innocenti vulnerable to becoming the *puttane* of the Orbatello.[103]

However, counter to the accusations of Settimanni's sources that the Innocenti's prior had relegated his excess girls to a life of walking the streets, the Innocenti sent thirty-six-year-old women, not young girls, and had sent them to Orbatello, not into the streets. Moreover, the Innocenti had four months from a woman's thirty-sixth birthday to find another place for her before sending her away with her clothes and thirty florins, and grand ducal officials, as part of the larger reforms to reconstitute the Innocenti after its 1579 bankruptcy, designated the Orbatello for all those women who could not look forward to the *honesto ricapito* of conventual or household service, "so that they can live the rest of their lives much more honestly than in some other place."[104] Nonetheless, the demand for space at the Orbatello certainly did outpace supply. By 1582, the officials of the Innocenti suggested to the Parte Guelfa that Francesco consider building an entirely new and separate convent for these women.[105]

By 1606, it was clear that the Orbatello was hardly the sheltered environment for which Innocenti officials had hoped, and criticism came from two directions, the Innocenti itself and Orbatello's inmates. The Innocenti's prior, Ruberto Antinori (who had been an Innocenti foundling himself), lodged two complaints with the grand duke against the Orbatello's chaplain, Don Alessandro Staccini, or as the women of the Orbatello scornfully referred to him, Stacciuolo. Antinori complained that Staccini failed to inform him when an Orbatello inmate died and failed to keep an accurate census. Both

---

[103] Trexler, "Widows' Asylum," 141.

[104] AOIF, Filze d'Archivio (LXII, 22), fol. 450r, 25 October 1580; "et in tal modo molte delle dette fanciulle et donne così licentiate potranno ricarsi in detto luogo à vivere il resto della lor vita molto più honestamente che in altro luogo."

[105] Ibid., fol. 602r, 23 August 1582.

these failures, Antinori charged, were deliberate attempts to stanch the flow of Innocenti women to Orbatello in direct violation of the grand duke's earlier directives. The grand duke remedied these problems easily enough by having the captains of the Parte Guelfa order Staccini to improve his record keeping.[106]

More serious, however, were the charges leveled by the inmates themselves, who in a letter to the grand duke accused Prior Staccini of exploiting their labor as well as confiscating such meager property as they might possess and keeping it after they had died:

> The poor Innocenti women living in Orbatello, most humble servants of Your Highness, explain to him with all due respect that for the past fourteen years or so they have been under the care of Don Alessandro Staccini, chaplain in the said place. These poor women have been very badly mistreated both physically and spiritually. Worse, he has always attempted to cheat them, and has cheated them, and robbed them of the effort of their labors which they need to survive and by which they are fed, having no other support in this world than the sweat of their brow, sewing day and night. Even very young girls are at risk of some accident. Those who have not already broken their necks cannot at their death expect to have more than four pennies at their disposal for a decent funeral mass.[107]

The petitioners provided extremely specific evidence, naming some seventeen women who had been victimized and enumerating how much the priest had taken from them. As if taking the very clothes off their backs were not sufficient, Staccini beat them publicly with sticks, and when these poor women died, they died "like animals, not even fed and nourished by those sacraments necessary for all good Christians, and without which their souls cannot even be recommended to heaven." The petitioners begged "by the bowels of Christ Jesus" that the grand duke remedy the problem by

---

[106] Ibid., fol. 450r–451r, after 22 March 1605.

[107] AOIF Filze d'Archivio (LXII, 25), fol. 764r, 21 April 1606: "Le povere donne nocentine habitante in Orbatello, humilissime servitrici di V. A. S. con ogni debita reverentia li espongano, come quattordici anni in circa sono state sotto il governo et custodia di Don Alessandro Staccini, cappellano in detto luogo dove che le poverelle sono state dal detto capellano, molto male bistrattate si del corpo loro come del' anime, oltre, che sempre ha cercato d'usurpalle, si come ha sempre usurpate, et tolto 'l loro la fatica delle loro braccia, della quale li convenivano vivere, et con quella nutrirsi, non havendo altro sussidio in questo mondo, che la fatica delle braccia loro, che giorno e notte stanno del continuo à incannare. Dando occasione ancora e di molte giovane di detto luogo, di farle capitare male, che da lui non è restato, che non hanno rotto il collo, si ancora, che alla morte loro, le poverelle non possono pur disporre il quattro cratie per far' fare un' poco di bene per l'anime loro non essere signore di far dire pur una messa."

removing Don Staccini and placing the girls back under Antinori's care at the Innocenti.[108]

Repentant Prostitutes and Recalcitrant Wives

All of the aforementioned institutions, however, attempted to provide some sort of middle ground between the lifetime commitment of the cloister and the dangers of the streets. Like convents, these institutions cultivated monastic discipline for personal salvation but, because of their necessary interactions with the wider world, also for reasons of public order. The girls' asylums I have been considering thus far offered rigorous preparation for the conventual life but also attempted to leave open a range, albeit a limited one, of other options for those girls either unsuited or unreceptive to a lifetime commitment. Institutions for repentant prostitutes and recalcitrant wives alike interacted most directly with those forces that attempted to enforce the norms of lineage, order, and decorum, and as a result, offered even more flexible programs, so that women could "cycle" in and out of such institutions much more easily.

Unlike the girls' refuges, however, convents, confraternities, and lay foundations for repentant prostitutes had a longer history that dated to the end of the twelfth century. In Florence, the convent of Santa Elisabetta ministered to converted prostitutes starting in the early fourteenth century. Such efforts received new impetus from late-fourteenth-century concerns arising from deliberate attempts to encourage repopulation, marriage, family life, and lineage solidarity. Such concern was formally institutionalized in 1403 by the creation of the officials of the Onestà, whose charge was to reduce the incidence of sodomy, which it proposed to do at least initially by promoting brothels as an alternative. Although the regulation of sodomy eventually came under the purview of the Ufficiali della Notte (officials of the night), the Onestà continued to regulate prostitution rather than make serious attempts to eliminate it. Only with the spread of syphilis in the early sixteenth century, as well as more generalized concern about young women's vulnerability to exploitation, did government agencies work more closely with the asylums for the *convertite*, not surprisingly at the same time that other public initiatives for the protection and shelter of older children were

---

[108] Ibid.: "moiano come bestie, che da detto prete non vengano à essere pasciute, et nutrite di quei santissimi sacramenti si come si conviene a' buon' cristiani, senza pur ricevere le raccomandazione de' anima à tale, che le poverelle ricorrono genuflesse à benigni piedi di V. A. S. suplicandola per le viscere di Jesu Cristo, che ci gli ripare, à un tanto disordine, con rimuovere detto D. Alessandro."

taking place. Where prostitution still actively flourished, authorities passed a series of measures taxing both income and inheritances of prostitutes to generate income for the institutions dedicated to their conversion.[109]

Indeed, the institutional profiles of Florentine asylums for repentant prostitutes resemble most closely the profiles of the Ceppo and the Pietà. Although the average age of ex-prostitutes who entered the ranks of the *convertite*, according to Sherrill Cohen's sample, was twenty-four, quite a bit older than the wayward girls who entered the Pietà early in their adolescence, the majority of ex-prostitutes came from vastly similar social backgrounds: fathers who were artisans, laborers, and craftsmen. The *convertite* houses sheltered many nonprostitutes as well, but in stark contrast to the girls' institutions described earlier, both institutions for *convertite* and *malmaritate* refused to accept young girls who were still virgins, for fear that proximity even to repentant prostitutes and other nonvirgins would lead the girls morally astray. Institutions for *convertite* and *malmaritate* also included girls who had lost their virginity through rape. Less clear was the status of daughters of prostitutes and children who were victims of rape, and in 1553, the grand duchy attempted to prohibit the acceptance of any women except converted prostitutes. Combined with severity applied by the new institutions for young girls that prohibited girls who had lost their virginity or whose mothers were prostitutes, the legislation created a serious hole in the social safety net. Consequently, the *convertite* houses were often besieged with requests to circumvent the rules.[110]

Institutions for *convertite* and *malmaritate* also differed from institutions intended for younger girls with respect to marriage. Among those demanding the services of the *convertite* were young widows and married women whose husbands were away, and married women whose marriages had become intolerably dysfunctional. Even convents had performed this service, as Vincenzio Borghini acknowledged in a report to Grand Duke Francesco's secretary:

> We also need to consider a point that experience proves every day: that young widows stay in convents who have no other convenient place to withdraw. It has been licit up to this point to keep them in reserve in a convent until a decision can be made about them. Similarly, sometimes either through the husband's absence, or some other reasonable motive, the same hospitality is given to married women. In these two cases, such [hospitality] removes from the many and significant scandals that would

---

[109] On the regulation of prostitution, see Sherrill Cohen, *The Evolution of Women's Asylums*, 42–53. On the control of sodomy, see Michael Rocke, *Forbidden Friendships*, 26–32.
[110] Cohen, 63–7.

otherwise follow, and causes infinite good, so that everything finally results in honor to God, and with great quiet and satisfaction to all.[111]

As both convents and institutions for the *convertite* tightened their regulations in response to the directives of the Council of Trent, married women became another population excluded from these traditional institutions. In 1579, a confraternity founded the Casa delle Malmaritate precisely to meet the needs of women who did not eventually wish to take monastic vows or to observe strict *clausura*. Nonetheless, by the early seventeenth century, the Casa delle Malmaritate, although still a more flexible kind of institution than the convent or the *convertite* asylum, only allowed its inmates to leave by a special vote of the confraternity, without which those who attempted to leave were subject to imprisonment.[112]

As significant as the differences among all these institutions were, however, they were united by important similarities. They all, either by restrictive admissions policies or other means, attempted to ensure that commitment to the goals of the institution had to be made before entrance. All imposed similar forms of monastic discipline: adherence to the common life, public penance, frequent prayer for their own souls and those of their benefactors, and an economic regimen based on the principle that women must support their stay in the institution through productive work. Prospective nuns had to bring at least a modest dowry to enter the convent, and in the refuges for laywomen and girls, such activities as weaving, sewing, and serving both supported the institution and, in most cases, helped girls who were not destined to the religious life to become economically self-sufficient, although hardly autonomous.

Even such institutions as the Casa delle Malmaritate, much more geared than similar institutions to reinserting its charges into the outside world, taught its girls skills that would be useful for women in the domestic economy. Moreover, it did so, as was the case with the Innocenti and other refuges, specifically with an incentive system that allowed girls to acquire a higher occupational status within the convent.[113] Laura McGough has

---

[111] BNCF Magliabechiana, Cl. VIII, 1393, fol. 106r, n.d.: "Sarebbe ancora da considerare un capo che tutto il giorno mostra l'esperientia, che rimanendo tal volta alcune vedove di poca età et che non hanno dove ritirarsi convenientemente à quel grado. È stato lecito fin qui metterle come in serbanza in un monasterio finche honoratamente sene pigli partito. Similmente alcuna volta o per assenti de mariti, o per altra ragionevole cagione, si è usato dare il medesimo di maritate. Ne' quali due casi si sono levati molti scandoli, et grandi, che sarebbe seguiti, et causatine infiniti beni, et tutto finalmente risulta in honor di Dio, et con gran quiete, et satisffatione dell'universale."

[112] Cohen, *Women's Asylums*, 105–8.

[113] Cohen, 88–9.

argued that Venetian *convertite* raised the art of earning one's dowry through work to new heights:

> The marriage market required that all prospective brides bring a dowry; this requirement paradoxically created the conditions for women to prostitute themselves temporarily in order to become wives later. The widespread practice of concubinage further undermined the distinctions in practice between marriage and this particular form of prostitution.[114]

Not only in Venice did young girls experience this jarring disjunction between "ideology" and practice. For Florence, Nicholas Terpstra has shown that among the herbs and pharmaceuticals that conservatory officials bought to minister to the health of girls in their charge, some are clearly identifiable as abortifacients.[115]

All of these institutions also struggled in their own ways with the inherent conflict between the need for personal and institutional patronage and the proper degree of separation between inmates and the outside world. It is hardly surprising that the placement of grilles and the visibility of work areas to the outside became such critical elements in the post-Tridentine debates over clausura. Family ties at the very least determined who got into such institutions and who was excluded. Once inside, girls made arrangements with inmates who were their blood relatives to solidify their family ties, making pacts among themselves, for example, to share the spoils of their common family inheritance. By paying a fee to the administrators of the *convertite*, for example, sisters could keep their portions of the spoils rather than have them automatically become the property of the institution itself.[116] When inmates of such institutions were disciplined, it was most often for coming to the grille to chat with outsiders. Even in the late seventeenth century, such outsiders were usually the inmate's relatives, and even at that late date, ecclesiastical authorities often found it easier to permit such contacts than to enforce complete seclusion.[117]

The history of the Hospital of the Mendicanti in Florence bears this out. During the plague of 1648, authorities interned two hundred poor of both sexes, of whom most were released in two years, with only twenty

---

[114] Laura Jane McGough, "'From the Devil's Jaws': A Convent for Repentant Prostitutes in Venice, 1520–1670" (Ph.D. Diss., Northwestern University, 1997), 23.

[115] Nicholas Terpstra, *Abandoned Children of the Italian Renaissance*, 139–40.

[116] Sherrill Cohen, "The Convertite and the Malmaritate: Women's Institutions, Prostitution, and the Family in Counter Reformation Florence" (Ph.D. diss., Princeton University, 1985), 142–4.

[117] This is abundantly clear not only in Italy but even in the Spanish Low Countries well into the seventeenth century. See Craig Harline, *The Burdens of Sister Margaret* (New York: Doubleday, 1994), 148–51.

remaining, who became administrators of the institution itself.[118] At least in Florence, attempts to intern great numbers of poor on a more permanent basis failed, and the large numbers of poor and abandoned girls who crowded such institutions testifies to the incapacity and unwillingness on the part of grand dukes to finance internment on a large scale. Given the matrix of values in which girls wandering the streets alone could automatically be presumed to be in danger of losing their honor and in which their families were unwilling or unable to take them in, the social control involved here was the preservation of lineage and the safeguarding of female honor, not the more ambitious goal of extending the technology and power of the state. Even so small a state as Tuscany of the grand dukes could not mobilize either the resources or the ingenuity to confine those girls for long periods of time.[119]

Thus, if this wide variety of institutions attempted to save the moral lives of young girls, placing the problematic of gender squarely within the context of the collective salvation of the city and the honor of successive grand dukes of Tuscany, one cannot with any great confidence proclaim their success at rescuing such girls from the margins of society. The monastic vision of discipline that would so successfully evolve into a self-disciplined society exacted a high toll as the workhouse model eclipsed the self-governing conventual model, leaving older women vulnerable to a much wider variety of exploitation than the mere dangers of *capitar male*. Unfortunately, institutions that assisted various strategies of patrician family preservation were always double-edged. Preserving the ideological vision of the lineage sometimes required the sacrifice of its most vulnerable members. Clearly, as Daniela Lombardi's study of the Hospital of the Mendicanti in the seventeenth century has so eloquently argued, the norms of lineage, order, and decorum could only assume coherence through the visible identification and eventual isolation of those who visibly threatened them.[120]

---

[118] Daniela Lombardi, *Povertà maschile, povertà femminile*, 138.

[119] This may help explain the discrepancy between the official figures counting the number of prostitutes in Florence and Rome and the accounts of travelers, whose estimates were much higher. On this discrepancy, see Fubini-Leuzzi, *Condurre a honore*, 34–5, and Tessa Storey, *Carnal Commerce in Counter-Reformation Rome* (Cambridge/New York: Cambridge University Press, 2008).

[120] Daniela Lombardi, *Povertà maschile, povertà femminile*, 183.

6

UNRULY NUNS: *CLAUSURA* AND CONFINEMENT

I F THE PREVIOUS CHAPTERS HAVE SUGGESTED SEVERAL EXPLANATIONS FOR the proliferation of institutions to house unmarried women during the sixteenth century, so far the argument has cited legal obstacles for women, obstacles tied to the transmission of property, and the tendency on the part of those families under Florentine jurisdiction to interpret laws concerning patrilineality with special harshness relative to other areas of Italy. In Venice, for example, women were much freer to dispose of property and thus enjoyed an enviable autonomy with respect to their Florentine counterparts. Yet the problems of conventual discipline and overpopulation, as well as the strains on states' efforts to regulate and confine unmarried women, afflicted Venice and her territories, as well as Milan, Bologna, and Genoa. Thus, to move the problem into a broader geographic context also requires the admission, ulti-mately, that specific problems with Florentine legal custom and inheritance practice must have been overshadowed by problems common to women and families across northern Italy.

In Florence, statistics bear out the strong association among dowry infla-tion, strategies of lineage preservation, and exponential increases in the num-ber of women taking monastic views. As Sharon Strocchia points out, in 1338, approximately 1 of every 220 Florentine residents was a nun. Through the late fourteenth and into the middle of the fifteenth century, the number of nuns remained approximately the same, but plague-related decreases in the city's population increased the ratio to 1 nun for every 141 inhabitants in 1384, and to 1 nun for every 72 inhabitants in the 1427 *catasto*. By 1480, the number of nuns had already doubled; by 1515, the number had doubled yet again to about 2,500. By 1552, there was 1 nun for every 19 inhabitants of the city.[1]

---

[1] Sharon Strocchia, *Nuns and Nunneries in Renaissance Florence* (Baltimore: Johns Hopkins University Press, 2009), 13, 28–38.

This chapter, then, examines convents as an institutional solution to these common problems and, in particular, what problems and opportunities conventual institutions generated in turn. Thus, if such conventual and quasi-conventual arrangements served the interests of family and lineage, patronage ties were bound to collide with efforts at reform. In the most extreme cases, as Gabriella Zarri points out, certain Venetian convents had reputations as brothels for the convenience of upper-class gentlemen. Fearing the scandal that would ensue from any real reform, the process of reformation was delayed until an epidemic left members of the patriciate even more worried that the intercessory powers of the prayers of nuns were no longer efficacious. Although describing convents as charitable institutions may seem to be stretching the boundaries of classification beyond ordinary credibility, the features that convents had in common with institutions more traditionally described as charitable warrants their inclusion in the larger discussion of solutions to social problems. First, in addition to providing alternatives for families concerned about dowry inflation, many families of lesser means sought positions for their daughters as conventual servants. Second, charitable institutions for wayward girls, repentant prostitutes, and maladjusted wives alike consciously and deliberately imitated conventual architecture, dress, daily routines, and intercessory prayers for benefactors. *Clausura*, for example, already important enough for defending the sexual honor of nuns old enough to protect themselves, loomed even larger in the minds of those administrators charged with the protection of very young and adolescent girls, whether or not their eventual intention was to become nuns.

Indeed, by extension, one might make the claim that *clausura*, or cloistering to protect female honor in convents, was one of those methods and objectives that prison borrowed from monastic life to control the moral laxity that post-Tridentine reformers might view as the cause of poverty and potentially criminal behavior. Yet to make such a claim would be to misread the practice of *clausura*, or even the process of church reform, discipline, and confessionalization in the sixteenth century, as exclusively aimed at the sexual behavior of the nuns within, however much in need of correction such behavior in fact might have been. For *clausura* was as much an issue of institutional control as social control, a matter of lineage and preservation of honor as much as internment.

Even in 1298, when Boniface VIII promulgated the bull establishing *clausura* and making it part of canon law, issues of sexual honor, conventual resources, and patronage converged. Addressing as "dangerous and detestable" the behavior of certain nuns who, "in defiance of the natural modesty of their sex, loosed the reins of honesty and frequently went about publicly in secular dress, and who also admitted suspect persons in to the convent, to the opprobrium of religion and the scandal of many,"[2] the decree ordered that all nuns, whether secretly or openly professed, be closed within their convents and admit no one without special permission, especially dishonest and otherwise suspect persons.[3]

As is often the case, the exceptions define the motivation more precisely than the rule. In addition to the clear issues of sexual honor, those who brought in provisions necessary for sustaining the convent were exempt from the ban on outside persons. Boniface VIII's decree also made an exception for prioresses and abbesses who held their convents of fiefs from an overlord, who could still freely leave the convent when necessary to render homage or fealty, providing that once they had done this, they speedily returned to the convent.[4] Similarly, prioresses, abbesses, and other nuns involved directly in conventual administration could, with express permission of the bishop, leave the convent to engage in negotiations or to appear in court on behalf of convents involved in lawsuits.

When, 250 years later, the Council of Trent renewed the specific provisions of this constitution, the language gave both more power and more discretion to the bishop:

> No nun shall after her profession be permitted to go out of the monastery, even for a brief period under any pretext whatever, except for a lawful reason to be approved by the bishop; any indults or privileges whatsoever notwithstanding. Neither shall anyone, of whatever birth or condition, sex, or age, be permitted, under penalty of excommunication to be incurred *ipso facto*, to enter the enclosure of a monastery without the written permission of the bishop or the superior. . . . And since monasteries of nuns situated outside the walls of a city or town are often without any protection exposed to the rapacity and other crimes of evil men, the bishops and other superiors shall make it their duty to remove, if they deem it expedient, the nuns from those places to new or old monasteries within cities or more populous towns.[5]

Yet the Tridentine decrees leave the mistaken impression that *clausura's* greatest enemies were rapacious men and lascivious women. Religious

---

[2] Boniface VIII, papal bull, *Periculoso* (anno 1298), cited in H. J. Schroeder, *Canons and Decrees of the Council of Trent* (St. Louis: Herder, 1941), 574–6.

[3] Ibid.

[4] Ibid. See also Elizabeth Makowski, *Canon Law and Cloistered Women: Periculoso and Its Commentators, 1298–1545.* Studies in Early Medieval and Canon Law, vol. 5 (Washington: Catholic University of America Press, 1997).

[5] Cited in H. J. Schroeder, *Canons and Decrees*, 221, Latin text, 488–9.

historians will understand the dynamics of *clausura* much more easily by reading the Tridentine decrees on patronage rather than relying exclusively on the sections concerning cloistering.[6]

The connection between patronage and *clausura* is evident even in pre-Tridentine attempts to enforce cloistering. Communal officials in Parma, for example, saw the reform of the city's convents from 1486 to 1525 as an issue of civic honor and in 1524 and 1525 sought to limit the factional potential of patronage by wresting control of the abbess's office from the powerful families in which it had previously been vested and placing it under a new magistracy known as the Deputati sulla Clausura. Several schemes attempted to place the city's major convent under communal control, including appointing abbesses for brief terms and alternating them. Nuns' constitutions in general attempted to regulate every word and gesture to support community and minimize factional conflicts inherent in patronage systems.[7] In Florence, at precisely the same time, convents evolved from "neighborhood enclaves" through family patronage to full-fledged civic institutions.[8]

Similar motivations were clearly at work in a series of decrees promulgated by the Patriarch of Venice, Pier Francesco Contarini, starting in 1555. These decrees forbade most of the nuns in Venetian convents to speak to any men whatsoever but attempted to respect the demands of patronage by establishing visiting hours for close relatives from terce until the sounding of the three o'clock bells. During those hours, nuns could receive at the *parlatorio* their mother, father, sisters, brothers, as well as the nuns' nieces and cousins related by blood or marriage.[9] None of these conversations would have been private, however, because when nuns received their relatives the sister assigned to the *parlatorio* had to be present to make sure that such conversations were fitting and proper to the religious life.[10] Unrelated outsiders who wished to speak to a particular nun had to apply to the abbess, who every Saturday had to send a list of such visitors to the patriarch. Moreover, the *parlatorio* was to be divided by gender in such a way that men and women could neither hear nor see each other.[11] In Florence, in 1567, when the archbishop's vicar, Ser Guido

---

[6] Ibid., 209–10, 230–1, 240–3.

[7] Letizia Arcangeli, "Ragioni politiche della disciplina monastica. Il caso di Parma tra quattro e cinquecento," in *Donna, Disciplina, Creanza Cristiana*, ed. Gabriella Zarri, 165–87.

[8] Sharon Strocchia, *Nuns and Nunneries*, 40–57. For a fuller history of *clausura* in Florentine nunneries over the course of the fifteenth century, and especially the close connection of *clausura* to patterns of patronage, see ibid., 152–95.

[9] Archivio Storico del Patriarcato di Venezia (ASPV), sezione antica, Liber Actorum Mandatorum Preceptorum 68 (1550–8) fol. 165r-v.

[10] Ibid.

[11] Ibid.

Serguidi, promulgated his printed summary of the Tridentine decrees on *clausura*, stipulations concerning relatives were explicit and absolute. Noting "not without great perturbation to our mind to what extent multiply and grow each day the disorders and scandals which cause an infinite number of persons to neglect their own salvation through inobservance of *clausura* established for nuns by the Holy Council of Trent," Serguidi sought to take away the occasions in the past "which have caused no little confusion." Serguidi commanded that

> in future no abbess, prior, minister, or superior of any convent in the city or Diocese of Florence shall desire or presume in any way nor under any pretext lodge, nor allow to ascend the stairs, or even admit inside their monastery, not even inside the first gate, any girl, married woman, or widow, whatever her age, status, grade, or condition, even if she be the mother or sister of the nuns, or related in any other way, unless she has first obtained permission from us in writing.[12]

Abbesses and other officials who violated these rules were to be suspended from office for two months for the first offense, indefinitely for the second offense, and permanently for the third. Nuns who violated *clausura* risked being deprived of their veils for a month for the first offense, jail for a month for the second offense, and, at a minimum, losing their right to participate in the business of the convent on the third offense.[13]

Initial resistance to Serguidi's interpretation of the Tridentine decrees was strong. Vincenzio Borghini proposed that Cosimo send a delegation consisting of Galeotto Rinieri and the Florentine ambassador to Pope Pius V himself, in hopes of modifying the harshness of the Tridentine decrees on *clausura*.[14] In a discourse that Cosimo I, grand duke of Florence composed, but which very much reflected Borghini's ideas and which Rinieri and the ambassador brought with them, Cosimo expressed his opposition to rigid

---

[12] Cf. Silvia Evangelisti, "'We do not have it and we do not want it': Women, Power and Convent Reform in Florence," *Sixteenth Century Journal* 34.3 (2003): 677–700, for an extended discussion of these issues. Cf. AOIF Estranei, V, unfoliated, 1 March 1566: "Comandiamo, et prohibendo ordiniamo che per l'auuenire niuna Badessa, Priora, Ministra, o Superiora di qual si voglia Monasterio della Città, et diocesi di Firenze Ardisca o presuma in modo alcuno, ne sotto alcuno quesito colore non solamente alloggiare, ne far' salire le scale, ma non pure intromettere dentro allor' Monasterio, ne ancora dentro alla prima porta, alcuna Fanciulla, Donna maritata, o Vedova di qual si voglia età, stato, grado, o conditioni si sia, se ben fussino Madre, o Sorelle, d'alcuna delle Monache, o per qual si voglia altro grado à loro congiunte, se prima non veggano la licentia ottenuta da noi in scriptis."

[13] Ibid.

[14] AOIF Estranei (CXLIV, V), n.p., n.d. This document, which is in Borghini's handwriting, comes in the codex immediately after a printed copy of Serguidi's decree. The argument that depriving nuns of the usual consolation of visits from their dear relatives threatened the patronage of convents is echoed quite specifically in Cosimo's document.

enforcement of the Tridentine decrees concerning *clausura* not only on the grounds that they threatened the crucial patronage lavished by nuns' relatives but also because *clausura* diminished the fervor and effectiveness of nuns' religious commitments.[15] Cosimo complained that restricting the access of nuns to their families and to the outside world dealt a double economic blow to convents: first, nuns could no longer sell the convent's products or earn money for their own keep by weaving and sewing, and, second, the alms of relatives constituted an important source of support. Indeed, in the poorest monasteries, nuns often depended on their relatives to bring them the basic necessities of daily living. More to the point, the grand duke argued that even those girls who were truly devout and sincerely interested in the religious life, once they saw the terrible poverty of these religious houses and contemplated being permanently separated from their mothers, would change their minds. This would "not only damage the fortunes of those religious houses" but also posed a potential threat "to their own honor."[16]

Such was Cosimo's concern that in the late autumn of 1570, he sent Galeotto Rinieri to Rome to plead the case before Pope Pius V. Rinieri's report, written on December 1, and addressed to Vincenzio Borghini, emphasized that opposition in Rome to *clausura* was foundering because "everyone knows the resolute determination of His Holiness, and no one can be found who has the will to oppose him, knowing through much experience that His Holiness means to see that the convents stay locked."[17] For more than three months, various persons had put off enacting *clausura* and only very fearfully had raised the issue with the pope, "only to encounter each time the rebuff of His Holiness."[18] Finally, wrote Rinieri, he was granted an audience with the ambassador, and given a good hour to reply to the pope. First, however, the pope reiterated his support of *clausura*, bringing up many arguments through which he expressed his intention that the convents should remain closed.

> He finished that part, and meant nothing other than that they should stay closed because that had been the rule from antiquity, and confirmed by the Council, and that to him had been granted by Divine Providence the task of executor of the Council's decrees. He said that whosoever placed his trust in God would never lack the necessities of human life, as the example

[15] AOIF Filze d'Archivio (LXII, 61), fol. 443r–445v, n.d.

[16] Ibid., fol. 443v: "et non senza estremo danno delle facultà delle case, et picolo del proprio honore."

[17] AOIF Estranei, V, n..p. 1 December 1570: Letter from Galeotto Rinieri, in Rome, to Vincenzio Borghini, in Florence: "perche conoscendo ogni persona la volonta resoluta di S[ua] S[antita] intende che a ogni modo le stieno serrate."

[18] Ibid.: "havendolo fatto circa 3 mesi fa che due n'hebbe quasi un rabuffo."

of Daniel and many others shows, and that nuns were not required to profess what they were unable to do. I did not fail to reply to His Holiness that these nuns were not saints that had God's grace in the same sense as the blessed fathers of whom there were so few. Rather, I said, there were nuns in sufficient number that they have to be helped, so that they do not perish from hunger and desperation. His Holiness replied that their relatives and the city should provide for them. Even though I remonstrated with him about the impracticality of his position, and the scandal that could follow, he returned my remonstrance by saying that everything had to be understood and provided for universally, and had to take place in common, or otherwise no one would take it seriously. When the ambassador and I had fought with him enough, we conceded that the convents must be closed provided that some way be found to provide the basic necessities of life, and that the responsibility for this should be given over to some person who could take care of it without bothering His Holiness. He responded that if some way were proposed to him that the convents could be closed and provide a living that he would gladly listen.[19]

Pius V further proposed that the petitioners persuade the grand duke to provide for the poverty of convents, but Rinieri pointed out to Borghini that this would involve more taxes, which Cosimo was clearly unwilling to impose, "much as this displeases me. And it seems to me that we have done all we can, there is little hope of gain at this point, nothing else can be done, and at this point, anything he will propose will have to have the approval of His Excellency."[20]

The response to Cosimo's discourse came not directly from the pope but from Monsignor Serguidi, who pointedly enclosed his original printed

---

[19] Ibid.: "Conclude che in questa parte, non intenderà altrimenti senon che stessino chiusi, che questo era ordine ab antico et confirmato dal concilio, et che alui era dato per divina providentia di far'essecutore et cosi intendeva dovessi essere giornalmente, onde sopra di questo n'haveva già detto l'animo suo al Signor Ambasciatore così ancora diceva a me, et disse che Chi confidava in dio non glo mancava da vivere, come detto per esempio di Daniello et altri, et che le monache non erano tenute a far professione di quello che non potevano osservare, non mancai di replicare le mie ragioni, et di dire a sua santita che queste non erano sante che havessino la gratia di dio come quelli beati padri che erano pochi, et queste in numero assai che era necessario s'aiutassino, et non si lasciassino morir' di fame et disperatione. Replicò che e parenti et la città provedessi, et sebene contradissi rimostrando l'incommodità, et lo scandolo che ne poteva succedere, tornò a dirmi che si facessi proveder nel'universale, et che tutti andassi in comune, et che altrimenti non l'intendina, et quando tra l'ambasciator et io l'haveamo combattuto assai ci gittamo abscender' che le sarebbano chiuse, purche il modo si trovasse del vitto loro, et che Sua Santità redessi la Cura a qualche persona che se ne potessi trattare senza fastidio di Sua Santità, ne rispose che v'era de' luoghi religiosi a quale avanzava di dare per l'amor di Dio, mi rispose che era bene avertiti che non avanzava loro, et che bisognia si provedessi altrimenti."

[20] Ibid.: "così cene torniamo a Casa con parere la Signor Ambasciatore che non si fara cosa alcuna et che lui di qua non proporrà cosa alcuna senza il consenso et ordine di S. A."

proclamation. Serguidi's arguments faithfully mirrored those the pope himself had made during his audience with Rinieri. Cosimo's arguments were
both specious and insignificant, Serguidi argued, by comparison to the
sweeping reform of the religious life promised both in Boniface VIII's original bull on *clausura* and the Council of Trent's reaffirmation of it. Boniface
VIII's bull and the Tridentine reforms, argued Serguidi, were much more
attuned than was Cosimo to what was appropriate for the religious life,
which required nuns to make a sacrifice, "or rather, a holocaust" of themselves to God. Moreover, the decrees of the Council were explicit and had
been accepted as "universal, holy, and good law" – not only for remedying
current abuses, but also for preventing those that might occur in the future.
Nuns could leave only when in danger of their lives from fire or plague,
and women and men could not enter except in cases permitted by the rules
observed by the convent's order. Did Cosimo not think, argued Serguidi,
that the Council of Trent, with its lengthy deliberations and extensive confirmation by Pius IV and the delegates, that the difficulties Cosimo brought
forward had not already been taken into consideration?[21]

As far as the poverty of religious houses was concerned, Pius V and
the delegates had already debated the issue and concluded that providing a
remedy was not particularly difficult. Surely the city's "shepherds" could encourage greater charitable giving, especially given that the highest merit
accrued to those who supported institutions embracing voluntary poverty,
in which the nuns were truly servants and brides of Christ. In response to
Cosimo's concern that labor shortages would result, Serguidi proposed that
professed nuns could and should do the same work equally well.[22]

Serguidi was most dismissive of Cosimo's concerns about the reliance of
convents on patronage, dismissing such doubts in a single sentence to the
effect that the visits of relatives usually damaged the spiritual lives of nuns and
distracted them with temporal concerns. Convents, Serguidi argued, were
intended not as vehicles for family preservation but to provide for the needs
of devout females. More broadly, he countered Cosimo's claim that *clausura*
was prejudicial to the city by pointing out the much greater good involved
when the city operated according to divine precept, especially because once
clausura was actually practiced, it would exclude those women who did not
have a gift for the religious life.[23]

---

[21] Ibid., unfoliated, n.d. Risposta al discorso mandato dal Signor duca di Firenze sopra la Clausura
delle monache.
[22] Ibid.
[23] Ibid.

To clinch the argument, Serguidi invoked the frailty of women. The dangers of leaving the convents open generated a much longer list of real dangers than closing them, because "without doubt women must be governed, and are not adept at governing themselves." If nuns are open, obedient, and honest, Serguidi argued, there should be no difficulty in smoothly implementing the Tridentine decrees. "Our efforts," wrote Serguidi, "should be directed toward implementing the decrees, not altering them."[24]

Serguidi's response did undoubtedly minimize the very real obstacle that the poverty of religious houses posed to the enforcement of *clausura*. The nuns of the convent of Santa Maria Nuova in Pescia, for example, petitioned the grand duke for funds to build the walls that would "assure *clausura*."[25] The officials of the Balìa of Siena wrote to Grand Duke Francesco I in the summer of 1575 that because most convents in the city of Siena had been built long before officious churchmen had given serious thought to *clausura*, such convents lacked every comfort, including rooms, oratories, water, courtyards, and many other things that strict enforcement of *clausura* would require. All these would cost anywhere from four thousand to six thousand scudi per institution. Because those sums represented double the annual revenues of such institutions, funds from other pious places and hospitals would have to be tapped. Further, the benefactors of those places had never intended their funds to be used for this purpose, and thus

> we do not see how this could benefit *clausura*, without very great confusion and prejudice to the normal stream of alms and good works. As Your Excellency is no doubt already aware, in the seven open convents of this city, there are more than 400 nuns of noble birth, very few of whom have brothers, fathers, or other relatives who could lend them some help.[26]

A quick and rough census of 1574, drawn up by Vincenzio Borghini for the purpose of estimating the amount of grain needed to feed the inhabitants of twenty-five convents, shows both the population and the financial need

[24] Ibid. "Ne io dubito che le Donne devono essere governate, et non sono habili a governarsi da se . . . essendoli concessa l'autorità del S. Iddio in edificatione, et non in destrutione, et per far osservar' le leggi, et non alterarle."

[25] ASF Segretario del Regio Diritto 4896, fol. 331, n.d.: "per assicurare clausura."

[26] ASF Mediceo del Principato 676, fol. 183r, 5 August 1575: "non vediamo che ne possa seguir tal effetto a benefitio delle clausure, senza grandissima confusione e pregiuditio delle solite limosine, e buone opere, essendo più della città così bisognosi, come li detti monasterii. Ella sappia ancora che nelli sette monasterii aperti di questa città, vi sono oltre à 400 suore di famiglie nobili senza quelle che vi sono per servitio loro, della quale pochissime hanno fratelli, padri, o altre persone che le possino prestare aiuto alcuno."

TABLE 6.1. *Population of some convents in 1574*

Convent or monastery	Bocche (mouths)
Murate	200
S. Orsola	130
S. Giorgio	120
S. Chiara	120
S. Clemente	130
S. Barnaba	130
Fuligno	130
S. Jacopo	110
Lapo	80
Boldrone	70
S. Maria degli Angeli	140
S. Caterina di Siena	140
S. Lucia	130
S. Joseph	65
Portico	80
S. Baldassare	70
S. Anna	70
S. Maria sul Prato	60
delle Poverine	75
Del Capitolo	50
Maiano	50
Angiol Raffaello	40
Bigallo	70
S. Monaca	120
Nunziatina	50
TOTAL	2,430

Source: AOIF Estranei V, n.p., 16 March 1573

of these convents to be substantial. The largest convent, the Murate, housed two hundred mouths. Of the remaining twenty-four convents, eleven had more than a hundred mouths to feed (see Table 6.1).

Not only the honor of women with a religious vocation was at stake. Cosimo also noted that enforcement of *clausura* would mean that orphaned and abandoned girls from the city's charitable institutions would no longer be allowed as servants in convents because they had not taken the permanent vows of the community. *Clausura*, he argued, deprived these girls of role models. Role modeling, however, was reciprocal: without the fear that their activities would be reported by these servant girls to the outside world, cloistered nuns would be more susceptible to the very abuses in discipline and behavior the new regulations had been designed to prevent. Cosimo's major issue, nonetheless, was a simple and humanitarian one: already these nuns suffered from the extreme misery of the insupportable poverty of convents. Why, then, deprive these nuns, he argued, "of that small and solitary consolation of being allowed to enjoy themselves with their sisters, mothers, and other close and dear relatives."[27]

Cosimo had much more than the consolation of nuns in mind. Some twenty years before sending this protest to Pius V, Cosimo had undertaken a wholesale reform (see Chapter 1) of religious and charitable institutions, centralizing the latter by reorganizing what had been two separate entities, the Buonomini di San Martino and the Bigallo, into a single supervisory board known as the Buonomini del Bigallo.[28] This reorganization had both a broad and narrow political context. The broad political context was to bring as many institutions as possible under Cosimo's direct control and patronage. The narrow context was to wrest control of these institutions away from the followers of Savonarola who had exercised tight control over Florence's charitable network in the early sixteenth century, a policy that culminated in the grand duke's ouster of the Dominicans at San Marco in 1545. Cosimo's embrace of the cause of religious reform well before the Council of Trent was not merely prescient but pragmatic.

In the same year that he ousted the Dominicans at San Marco, Cosimo also promulgated norms for the observance of the religious life. Through the Magistrato Supremo, Cosimo ordered that all those responsible for the spiritual life of nuns, by which he meant "those who say masses, hear confessions, and do other similar things," should be under the jurisdiction of the archbishops, bishops, and officials of their respective dioceses, both in regard to making appointments and terminating them. Everything else, however, Cosimo considered his legitimate territory, to be handled by the four Deputati sopra i Monasteri. In particular, the four commissioners were to consider what was most useful for monasteries, priests, or friars under their jurisdiction, making sure that the trustees of convents, who were appointed by Cosimo and the four commissioners for each convent, "be vigilant and precise in ensuring that said religious persons comport themselves well and

---

[27] AOIF Filze d'Archivio (LXII, 61), fol. 444v, n.d.: "ma privarsi anchora di quella poca et sola consolatione che elle havevano di ricrearsi talvolta con le loro sorelle, et madre, et altre strette, et care parenti, et questa contra ogni loro espettatione, et volontà."

[28] John Henderson, "Charity and Welfare," 63.

do their duty."[29] When this was lacking, the trustees had to notify the ecclesiastical authorities, and if the ecclesiastical authorities failed to act, they had to notify the grand duke himself.

Cosimo's legislation also barred from convents anyone who was not strictly a relative of the nuns, unless he or she had permission from ecclesiastical authorities. Conventual trustees, to protect the honor of convents, had to "begin construction, raise walls, close windows, secure gates and grilles, and wall up exits . . . to reduce the nuns to living in common."[30] If ecclesiastical authorities hired priests and confessors, the lay trustees "can and must hire and fire the service employees, such as doctors, workmen, servants, gardeners, and others, without the consent of the nuns."[31] The lay trustees also oversaw all the convents' financial transactions, including the buying and selling of real estate, none of which could be finalized without the consent of the ecclesiastical ordinary, the convent itself, and the four-man commission. To discourage overcrowding, no new nuns could be professed without the permission of the trustees. Finally, although Cosimo left the appointment of abbesses and the correction of abuses to the ecclesiastical ordinaries and to the various constitutions that governed each house, the trustees had to ensure that such norms were being followed.[32] In practice, the four commissioners, especially in the 1560s and 1570s, spent a considerable amount of time reviewing, renewing, and revising the statutes of convents and other charitable organizations.

At least some of that history was recapitulated in Vincenzio Borghini's original proposal to send Galeotto Rinieri and the Florentine ambassador to visit the pope. As Borghini pointed out, the office of the four commissioners had been founded "for the benefit and utility of your most happy State, from which follows the honor of God, the promotion of the Holy Religion, and the good government of the numerous religious women who are in your most happy state."[33] In particular, Cosimo had charged this office in 1544, with "reducing the entire range of necessities, occurrences and difficulties of the greatest importance" that convents had to face, and to provide for every "need, help, correction, or reformation" that these convents required, and

---

[29] ASF Magistrato Supremo, 10, fol. 19v, 12 April 1545, "Reformatio monasteriorum," cited in D'Addario, *Aspetti della controriforma*, 480–2.

[30] Ibid.

[31] Ibid., fol. 20r, cited in D'Addario, *Aspetti della controriforma*, 481.

[32] Ibid.

[33] AOIF Estranei (CXLIV, V), n.p., n.d.: "per benefitio et utile delle monache del suo felicissimo stato, accioche e ne segua l'honor di dio principalmente, et la conservatione et augmento della santa religione, et il buon governo di tante religiose che sono nello stato felicissimo di V. E. I."

to place themselves in consultation with and at the command of the grand duke in proposing, deliberating, and carrying out decisions.[34]

Borghini separated the issues involved into spiritual guidance and state supervision. Saying masses, hearing confessions, and disciplining nuns either by removing those who did not comport themselves appropriately or by changing their behavior according to need were functions to be carried out by the archbishops, bishops, and their vicars. Nonetheless, the spiritual government was so important that the four commissioners should supervise the convents and distinguish good spiritual government from bad, because "from the good or bad spiritual governance is born the good or bad existence of these convents."[35] More specifically, Cosimo had appointed four trustees for each convent, whose duties involved overseeing the well-being of their convent, reviewing the accounts, making sure that the convent was well governed and keeping an eye out that no disorder was taking place. The four trustees referred issues of major importance to the four commissioners, who then had to keep the grand duke well informed. The four commissioners, in turn, could make use of the services of the chancellor, whose labors were funded by ecclesiastical taxes.[36] The chancellor's role was balanced by an accountant (tavolaccino) who kept a written account of all the financial records and other transactions involving the four commissioners.

Cosimo, even with his new commissioners, found conventual reform a much more difficult task than he had initially envisioned. In a 1558 letter to Cardinal Ascanio Sforza, Cosimo complained that

> I have always had as one of my great thoughts in this world to preserve the honor of God as far as these convents are concerned. There are always some of evil reputation, but also an infinite number of very religious and holy ones. Because of the travails of war, I have not been able to attend to their care right away, with the result that some of those convents which were already freed, or which I myself freed from an evil life, have returned to the vomit.[37]

Even in those where he had directly enacted reforms, Cosimo complained, he had found that more than fifteen nuns had been violated and that priests

---

[34] Ibid.: "alla quale si havessino ridurre tutta la somma delle difficultà, occorrentie, casi di maggior importanza, che in detti monasteri occurrevano: ove fusse bisogno, ò aiuto, correttione, riforma, etc."

[35] Ibid.: "dal buono ò cattivo governo spirituale, nascerne questi sempre, il buono ò di cattivo essere di questi monasteri."

[36] Ibid. Borghini identified the holders of this office as Ser Giovanni Conti from Bucine and then, following his death, Ser Marco Segaloni.

[37] ASF Mediceo del Principato, 326, fol. 33r, 26 August 1558, cited in D'Addario, Aspetti, 484–5.

and friars were by and large the offenders. In trying to prosecute them, Cosimo had received no help from ecclesiastical authorities, who, unwilling to stir up the opposition of the friars, had not only been negligent but had obstructed his efforts to identify the guilty parties. As a result, Cosimo's prisons were filling up with laymen, priests, and friars alike.

> The friars are there because I will not lay a hand on them, nor would I, and because the vicars don't want to. I therefore beseech your Lordship to help me find a way that Christian justice can be done, since I wish to be thought of as a just and Christian prince, not so unjust and negligent that these men have to stay in prison for such a long time.[38]

Other worries of perceived negligence also surfaced. Borghini, in an undated memorandum, wrote.

> There is a lot of noise that [the nuns of the Paradise convent] are badly managed both in temporal and spiritual matters, and I suspect that this is not without cause. I don't quite remember whether something for the grille was ordered by the Visitor. It might be a good idea to make some kind of provision so that the Visitor doesn't accuse us of negligence, about which he would certainly be quite right.[39]

Even after the reforms of Trent presumably gave Cosimo and his son Francesco a stronger hand with which to pursue violations of *clausura*, problems still persisted elsewhere. In 1566, the archbishop's vicar, Guido Serguidi, notified Francesco that

> the morning of San Lorenzo [10 August], four friars of Santa Croce were arrested by an employee of the Bargello, who found them outside the convent of Santa Margarita in Arcetri without the permission of Your Excellency. When I examined them they claimed to have been sent there to celebrate mass, which they said they could do since the guardian sent them there, despite the fact that some of the friars have been warned several times not to go. I have denied them permission because their presence generates nothing but scandal. . . . These four, under pretext of saying divine offices, go to the convent for banquets and to consume what little substance the sisters have, and the rest of the day in pointless discussion at the grates. . . . Since I already had outstanding indictments against Calandro

---

[38] Ibid., fol. 33v.

[39] AOIF Estranei (CXLIV, V), n.p., n.d: "Monsignore Priore/Jesus/Monache del paradiso/E gran romor che elle sono mal menate, nel temporale al sicuro nello spirituale e sospetto non sine causa. Non mi ricorda bene, se intorno alle grille è ordinato cosa alcuna dal Visitatatore o intorno a' frati. Sarebbe bene farvi qualche provisione, al manco perche non pella dire á Ragione a Roma che Visitatore, che negligente etc. che in questo harebbe molta ragione."

and Granchi, I had their rooms searched and some lascivious sonnets were found.[40]

Moreover, one of the friars confessed that he had hidden a suspected murderer in the guardian's room overnight and then dressed him as a friar and hustled him outside the city gates.[41]

If Cosimo's reforms of institutions for nuns, wives, and prostitutes attempted to centralize his network of patronage, patronage nonetheless made *clausura* more difficult to enforce, especially if, as in the Sienese example, officials and benefactors perceived funds spent on *clausura* to be in direct competition with traditional forms of patronage. In this respect, institutions for unruly nuns, recalcitrant wives, and repentant prostitutes alike had to strike a delicate balance between complete separation of inmates from the outside world and dependence on the kindness of benefactors. In all three kinds of institutions, what bound the kindness of benefactors to particular institutions were family ties and family strategies. In France, the Guise family similarly used the convent of Saint Pierre in Reims as an instrument of dynastic advancement, strategically arranging important positions within the convent for their daughters as a base for distributing favors.[42]

When Cosimo openly spoke of the disciplinary problems of the cloister, his views were based on Vincenzio Borghini's long experience of visitations to Tuscan convents undertaken at Cosimo's behest from 1566 to 1570.[43] These visitations were meant not only to uncover instances of disorder but in particular to respond to allegations that rules of *clausura* were not being observed. In a 1571 complaint from the confessor of the convent of Santa Croce Val d'Arno to the bishop of Lucca, the work of the Deputati sopra i Monasteri played a vital role, even if their role in the subsequent investigation cannot be fully known. The formulation of the deposition only mentions that the witnesses were sworn before three officials: the vicar of the bishop of Lucca; a doctor of laws by the name of Rocco de' Nobili, also from

---

[40] ASF Carte Strozziane, I, 22, fol. 7r, 13 August 1566, Guido di Serguidi to Francesco de' Medici, cited in D'Addario, *Aspetti*, 486–7.

[41] Ibid.

[42] Joanne Baker, "Female Monasticism and Family Strategy: The Guises and Saint Pierre de Reims," *Sixteenth Century Journal* 28.4 (1997): 1091–1108.

[43] Records of the commissioners activities can be found not only in ASF, Segretaria del Regio Diritto, 4893 and 4896, but also those addressed to Borghini can be found in AOIF Estranei, V, passim. Another collection containing copies of such letters also exists in the Biblioteca Nazionale Centrale di Firenze (BNCF), fondo Magliabechiano, Serie VIII, 1393 and Fondo Nazionale II, X, 138. A smaller, neater version of Borghini's notes on the monasteries can be found in BNF, Fondo Nazionale, II, X, 73. For an impressive, although not exhaustive, inventory of Borghini's correspondence, see Francalanci and Pellegini, eds., *Vincenzio Borghini: Carteggio 1541–1580*.

Lucca; and the notary. At the very least, however, one commissioner saw the
notarized written record of the interrogation, and luckily for the historian,
this commissioner, Vincenzio Borghini, underlined parts of the testimony
and in some places in the text made marginal notes that left no doubt of his
reaction to the depositions.

In December 1570, a full eight months before depositions were taken
from the abbess and the nuns of the convent, Giovanbattista Altoviti, a priest
from Florence and a relative of the famous Florentine archbishop Antonio
Altoviti, was appointed chaplain at the convent of Santa Croce Val d'Arno, a
town in the floodplain of the Arno not too far east of Pisa. According to all
accounts, Giovanbattista's first month at the convent went quite smoothly.
Nonetheless, by the summer of 1571, the situation had deteriorated to the
point that the chaplain wrote to the bishop of Lucca complaining that *clausura*
was not being observed. On 31 July, the vicar of the bishop of Lucca, the
doctor of laws, and the notary, arrived at the convent and took the confessor's
deposition. In particular, not only was the abbess allowing the gardeners and
the carters to wander freely throughout the convent, but when one of the
nuns, Suor Vincenza, was at the point of death in late June, the abbess
permitted Suor Vincenza's aunt, ten-year-old brother, the father, and the
uncle to visit directly at her bedside. At Suor Vincenza's funeral, a number of
local women from the surrounding area were allowed to attend. In addition
to this, the abbess also allowed the gardener's wife to come and sleep several
nights within the convent, and allowed "notorious" women to come into
the convent, including the female servant of the gatekeeper. This servant,
according to the chaplain, was a woman of *mala fama et vita* who came to
visit Suor Jacopa and to eat at the convent.[44]

Moreover, the chaplain complained that divine offices were not being
said with any regularity, and that when they were said, even in church, a
group of nuns chatted and shouted so loud that they could be heard outside
the church in clear competition with the reading of the day's lesson. Indeed,
the commotion they caused had forced him on occasion to stop reading and
to have to begin again. When the nuns were not interrupting the divine
offices, they gravely disturbed the peace and quiet of the convent, breaking
the vow of silence so that often "many injurious and vituperative words,
as well as threats to choke someone were exchanged. Even though I spoke
to her about this, I did not punish anyone but I notified the bishop about
it."[45] Indeed, whatever might have been the truth of these allegations, there

---

[44] ASF Segretaria del Regio Diritto 4893, fol. 469v, 31 July 1571.

[45] Ibid., fol. 470r: "le altre et Suor Lucia ritirate in refettorio li fu detto molte parole ingiuriose et
vituperose et volato darli et minacciate di strozzarle come meglio loro sapranno dire. Et di questo

is no doubt from the subsequent interrogations that the convent was highly factionalized, and if some of the nuns are to be believed, factionalized along lines of patronage, that is, with the boundaries drawn between those nuns who were protégées and devotees (and in some cases, relatives) of the abbess and those who were outside her circle.

The interrogators, who are not identified individually, then had all fifty-seven professed nuns of the convent provide depositions. There were sixty-nine women in the convent altogether – the fifty-seven nuns, three *converse* and five others who were examined orally but whose responses were not written down, two girls who did not yet have the nun's habit because their dowries were not yet fully paid, and finally, the abbess's niece, who was not questioned. The first few were asked the same questions to address issues the chaplain had raised, but as each witness raised new issues, the subsequent witnesses would be interrogated about the new issues that had been raised as well. Finally the abbess herself was given an opportunity to respond to all the charges – and it is here that Borghini's marginal notes became copious, noting the abbess's responses, her inconsistencies, and even what he termed in one case her "outright lie."[46]

The interrogators began with the professed nuns who had been there the longest amount of time, worked their way through the ranks to the least experienced, and finally to the *converse* and undowered nuns. Among all these groups, the abbess clearly enjoyed the support of the majority, and a certain number of nuns were either nonaligned parties, or in some cases, had little good to say about any of the major players. The first witness, Suor Prudentia, was clearly nonaligned. When asked if the convent had any ills that needed correcting, she replied, "The greatest source of disorder is that the nuns speak very dishonestly and use words that would not sit well among prostitutes, never mind nuns." Nonetheless, she described the abbess as "a good woman," but also described the abbess's archenemy, the confessor, as "a good man," at least when he was not at the grate chatting with some of the nuns.[47]

---

non ne ho penitentiato alcuno, et di questo ne é stato avertito Monsignor Reverendissimo et io glene ho parlato."

[46] Ibid., fol. 509r.: "bugia manifesta."

[47] Ibid., fol. 471v: "Il maggior disordine che io cognoschi in questo nostro monistero è che le monache parlano molto dishonestamente et si dicano l'una ad altra parole brutte et dishoneste et che non stanno bene a' meretrice non che alle monache, et quanto alla Badessa io la ho sempre conosciuto donna da bene et utile per il governo della casa et quanto al confessore a me non ha mai satisfatto circa alla confessione et alla comunione, et mi dispiace il suo stare alla ruota a cicalare tanto ne i tempi della confessione quanto in altri tempi et in quanto al resto tengo che sia homo da bene."

Those who did not support the abbess, however, were vehement in their opposition. Suor Niesa, for example, complained that

> our convent has no fear of God or of superiors and for this reason it's like hell on earth as far as I am concerned. It's all because the abbess puts whomever she wants in the convent. A little while ago the abbess brought into the convent one of her nephews who was 16 or 18, and they played music and danced in the chapel near the garden. Later on, as the Ave Maria was being said, she brought her nephew and the gardener in to admire the new cell she had built above the convent. One nun, I didn't see who it was, told the gardener he was excommunicated and he replied, "Do you want me to tie my donkey where its master wants it?[48]

Another nun, Sister Stefana Buonchristiana, was quite partial to the confessor.

> Before he came we didn't live the common life in the refectory but now we do. The abbess's administration is bad and sometimes she favors one side so that we on the other side are very badly treated. She sends lots of gifts to her relatives in Florence and she keeps here a nine- or ten-year-old girl who is not a nun and who doesn't wear the habit, something that displeases the other nuns, who suffer in many respects, especially during the severe winter of the fire. . . . I have heard that the gardener pinched Suor Felice. I don't know whether to believe it but I believe that Suor Giulia, who said so, told the truth.[49]

The abbess also at various times, according to other witnesses, allowed her sister's servant with her three children to stay in the convent. When challenged on these points, several witnesses testified, the abbess claimed to have permission from the vicar and the archbishop to let in these groups of relatives, and apparently in her feistier moments claimed to have no superior, including the pope himself. At other times, her sense of authority was only slightly more circumspect, as when she told the confessor that she

[48] Ibid., fol. 472r-v: "et una monaca che non viddi chi fusse disse al'hortolano che era scomunicato et lui rispose che volete che io facci lego l'asino dove vuole il padrone?"

[49] Ibid., fol. 474r-v: "Dapoi che è venuto per confessore al governo di questo munistero prete Gio: batista habbiamo vissuto à comune in refettorio et ci viviamo et si legge mentre si mangia come è solito et avanti che lui venisse non si vivesse à comune in refettorio et da molti et molti anni in qua mentre che la nostra Badessa che hoggi è ancora ha governato siamo state molto mal trattate et siamo male d'accordo fra noi per il proceder' di lei che hoggi favorisce una parte et domani un'altra. e ho inteso che manda molti presenti a' suoi amici et parenti di Fiorenza et altrove et ha tenuto et tiene in munistero una sua nipote di 9 o X anni in circa et che non è monica [sic] ne ci è vestita da monica il che dispiace à molte monache che pateno in molte cose et particularmente la invernata del fuoco . . . et io ho inteso dire che [l'ortolano] de un pizzicotto à suor Felice impero io non lo so ma credo che Suor Giulia che lo disse dicesse il vero."

was accountable not to the bishop of Lucca but only to the grand duke of Tuscany.[50]

Suor Anna Ciccaporci from Florence complained that the abbess was partial. "Those to whom she is devoted she treats well and the others suffer in every way. And she has here a sister, four nieces and three cousins who have not brought any dowry with them. She is patron of everything."[51] In Suor Anna's view, the discords began when the confessor wanted to review the accounts. At that point, "he became her enemy and the enemy of all her relatives and friends. Now the poor man is assaulted at every turn by their character assassinations and threats."[52] Not to be outdone in the business of character assassination, Suor Anna remembered a certain Captain Borgiani, who had recently died, but while he was still alive maintained a friendship with the abbess. "She installed him in the convent and had him in her cell whenever she felt like it."[53]

The abbess's supporters, however, were themselves far from immune to the temptation toward slander and innuendo. Perhaps the mildest was the abbess's own sister, Suor Brigida, who meekly averred that although she was the abbess's sister, swore that what she was about to say was the truth.[54] Certainly among the abbess's more colorful supporters was Sister Eugenia Ghettini from Florence, who testified:

> according to my opinion I see no disorder other than some disagreements among us nuns deriving from the bad behavior of our confessor. He has friendships with particular nuns with whom he makes love, especially Suor Nannina and Suor Aurelia, who stay at the grate every day and talk to him with the cloth covering the grate raised. They murmur secretly to one another and give the confessor things to eat and drink. According to what I have seen them do I have expressed my disapproval and have gone to confession only reluctantly. Now I'm thinking of not going to confession at all, and I think that it would be a good idea to relieve him from his position, and the tranquillity of the convent will be restored.[55]

[50] Ibid., fol. 503r, fol. 510v.

[51] Ibid., fol. 481r: "et ci ha una sorella quattro nipoti et tre cugine le quali non hanno portato correde alcuno . . . è padrone d'ogni cosa."

[52] Ibid., fol. 481v: "ma perche lui ha voluto vedere i conti della Badessa è diventato inimico suo et delle suoi parenti et amiche di sorte che il povero homo tutta volta da loro assassinato et minacciato."

[53] Ibid., fol. 482r: "Item disse mentre che visse il Capitano Borgiani quale è morto molti anni fa essendo questa medema Badessa quale aveva amicitia con detto capitano lo metteva dentro in munistero et in cella sua quando li piaceva."

[54] Ibid., fol. 476r.

[55] Ibid., fol. 477v: "Hoggi nel nostro convento non ci vedo secondo il mio parere altro disordine che alcune discordie che sono fra noi monache nate dal mal procedere del nostro confessore quale

Indeed, many of the abbess's supporters ascribed the convent's disharmony to internal rivalries for the confessor's attentions. Suor Nannina's deposition failed to answer the question of whether she and the confessor had made love but provided only a partial admission that he "occasionally chats with the nuns at the grate but he only ate and drank there during carnival."[56]

Some twenty-five witnesses had their depositions recorded before Borghini's marginal notes begin. As though heartened to hear a dispassionate voice crying from the wilderness, he underlined Suor Fiammetta Centelli's deposition several times, especially where she said, "we remit ourselves into your arms and I pray Monsignor Reverendissimo and you commissioners that you do something about these disorders so we can live in the fear of God and as is proper for us."[57] Borghini was particularly interested in the nonobservance of *clausura* and in the charges that outsiders were allowed to wander freely through the convent. He was especially responsive to accusations that the abbess had no fear of God or superiors and was negligent in saying the divine offices.

The vicar and the doctor of laws worked with sufficient diligence that between 31 July and 2 August, they had deposed nearly sixty witnesses. Finally on 3 August, the abbess herself, Suor Ludovica di Ambrogia Batista had her day in court. In exemplary post-Tridentine spirit the interrogators queried the abbess concerning the frequency of divine offices. She replied, "divine offices are celebrated continuously in my church day and night and I participate when I am healthy and when I am not being called to the door," already a damaging admission of the proprietary stance she took ("mia chiesa"), as well as the frequency with which even divine offices were interrupted.[58] "Do the nuns always come to mass and to the refectory for

tiene amicitie di monache particulari con le quali per quanto posso conoscere per li andamenti fa l'amore et sono fra le altre Suor Nannina et Suor Aurelia le quali stanno ogni giorno alla grata a parlar' con detto confessore con il panno della grata alzato. Et fanno bisbigliamenti secreti et ivi li danno à detto confessore da bere et da mangiare. Segondo che io ho visto di che ho fatto et faccio cattivo giuditio et dopoi che ho visto tal cosa mi sono mal volentieri confessato da lui et così ho pensato di non mi voler mai più confessare da esso et però credo che sarà bene levarlo da questo governo et sarà la quiete di questo munistero."

[56] Ibid., fol. 486v: "Item interrogata disse fuori del tempo della confessione io non sono stata alla grata à ragionar' con il prete senon qualche volta essendo io rotaia et non havendo lui serva se li coceva il mangiar' in convento et io glelo porgevo et non so che sia stato à bere alle grate se non nei giorni di carnevale."

[57] Ibid., fol. 492v: "Noi ci rimettiamo nelle braccia vostre et prego Monsignore Reverendissimo et voi che provediate à questi disordini acciò possiamo vivere con il timor di Dio et come si conviene."

[58] Ibid., fol. 508r, 3 August 1571: "Item interrogata disse nella mia chiesa si celebrano continuamente li divinii offitii di dì et di notte alli quali continuamente intervengo quando sono et se io non sono *chiamata alla porta*" (underlining in original).

meals?" she was asked. "The majority come to hear mass in the church and the rest go to the oratory. Since I am always in church I can't oversee everything but in my judgment it would be better if they came to mass in the church so I could see them." As far as the refectory was concerned, "almost all the nuns come to the refectory but Suor Stefania and Suor Maddalena hardly ever come to meals and often miss mass and other divine offices."[59] Borghini's marginal comments were quick and furious: "This is her fault because she was supposed to chastise them or let the bishop know but she never did it . . . Why in all those years didn't she do something about it or advise the bishop? . . . It is too great a scandal to allow nuns to avoid hearing Mass."[60]

Much more serious was the matter of violation of *clausura* itself. When asked if she was aware of the decrees of 1560, she replied,

> I have always observed and now observe those decrees although it is true that I have allowed in some women with the vicar's permission and I have let in some others assuming that I could give that permission myself. On those grounds I let in my sister, my kinsman, and my nephew, who came to see their daughter who was ill. . . . I had permission for all these, although I think I got permission before the Council of Trent. I don't remember if I was made aware of the Council's 1564 decrees or not. I don't have a copy of them. In any case, after the council no one from outside has slept here except my sister and some children and a servant some nights and one night the gardener's wife. Another time, when Suor Vincenza was ill Suor Eugenia let four of her female relatives in and before she died she also let in Suor Maria Vincenzia's mother, father, and little brother who went to visit her at her bedside. And Sister Eugenia said she had the confessor's permission and if in this I have done wrong I beg your pardon.[61]

---

[59] Ibid.: "Item disse le monache la maggior parte vengano a udir' messa et un'altra parte vanno in oratorio che io non posso essendo io in chiesa veder' tutto per a mio giuditio sare[bbe] bene che tutte à udir' messa venissero in chiesa che io potessi vedere. Item interrogato disse la maggior parte et quasi tutte le monache vengano a mangiar' in refettorio ma Suor Stefania et Suor Maria Maddalena vengano poco in refettorio et molto manco alla messa et alli altri offitii."

[60] Ibid., "Questa è colpa sua perche doveva castigarle o avisarne il vescouo il che mai ha fatto. Perche in tanti anni non vi ha provisto ne avvisatene il vescouo? . . . Troppo grande scandalo sopportar che le monache non odino messa."

[61] Ibid., fol. 508r-v: "Item interrogata disse dopoi si è osservato et fatto osservare i deveti del 1560. Ma è ben vero che alle volte ho' intromiso alcune donne con licenza del vescovo foraneo et alcune altre ho intromiso pensando io di poterli dare licentia et ci ho intromissa mia sorella mia cugnato et mio nipote et mio cugnato venne a veder' sua figliuola che era malata . . . havemo licentia da Monsignor Reverendissimo ma tal licentia penso *che fusse avanti il concilio*, et se l'anno 1564 mi *fu intimato i decreti del concilio o non*, non mene ricordo et no ne ho copia alcuna. Et a dormir' nel munistero dopoi il concilio non ci è stato che *mia sorella et certi bambini et una serva alcune* notte et *una volta la moglie* del'hortolano la quale hebbe licenza dal prete et

Borghini's marginal comments were scathing. To the excuse that she had the vicar's permission, he wrote, "either she didn't have permission for the children or the vicar has also done wrong."[62] Borghini was especially harsh toward what he imagined to be the root of the problem. When the abbess thought she could give her own permission, that presumption showed that she wished to be accountable to no one.[63] Even harder to swallow was the excuse that she had the bishop's permission, for, in Borghini's words, "not only can no person be found except the doctor who ever had the bishop's permission, in all the bishop's letters to the abbess, chaplain and vicar, these visits are expressly prohibited."[64] Her inability to remember if she got copies of the decrees or not was "a very manifest sign of her small capacity for obedience and religion."[65] Indeed, in Borghini's view, the abbess's testimony so far had done her more harm than good, because she corroborated all the accusations the nuns had made against her. When it was her word against the confessor's, "the confessor is to be believed because when she asks our forgiveness she accuses herself."[66]

When asked if she had allowed the servant with a bad reputation and dishonest life to enter the convent, she said, "I didn't know about it but as soon as I found out she was never allowed in again," to which Borghini, clearly exasperated, wrote, "This is an outright lie because she never forbade the servant to come in and she saw her come in every day."[67]

Both the opponents and supporters of the abbess's administration inadvertently revealed two important issues. First, despite the attempts of the Tridentine decrees to seal off convents from the outside world, the influence of the outside world was everywhere and unavoidable. Alliances of kinship, friendship, and city did not by any means dissolve once nuns entered the convent. Indeed, several witnesses from the town of Santa Croce who had

dei licenzia a Suor Eugenia che intromettesse adì passati quando morse [sic] Suor Maria Vincenza quattro donne suo parente et prima che morisse havevo intromisso la madre et il padre et un fratellino piccolo che andorno a visitare al letto et l'inferma mi disse haver' hauto licenzia al confessore et hora se in questo ho fatto errore ne domando perdono a V. S." The underlining is from the original text.

[62] Ibid.: "O non si non a licenza che per fanciulle o el vicaro fiorentino et di questo ha fatto anco male."

[63] Ibid.: "Questa immaginativa è nata di non voler superiore."

[64] Ibid.: "Non solo non si troverà che alcuna persona habbia hauta licenza dal vescovo di entrare in munistero eccetto una cirugico [sic], ma si bene in tutte le lettere scritte dal vescovo all'Abbatessa Cappellano et al Vicario si ritruova expressamente prohibito."

[65] Ibid.: "segno manifestissimo della della [sic] poca obbedienza et religione che è in lei."

[66] Ibid.: "si verificano le depositioni delle monache . . . il confessore nega et se li debbe credere più che l'abbatessa domanda di ciò persino accusa se stessa."

[67] Ibid., 509r: "Questa è bugia manifesta perche sia mai ne le prohibito in la del continuo ogni giorno le l'ha vista."

only occasional contact with the convent were called on to testify that the misbehavior of the nuns was well known. Not only did the gossip of relatives keep townspeople informed, but when screaming and shouting reached an unbearable pitch, someone inside the convent would ring the convent's bells.

Within the convent as well, it is clear that at least one source of discontent among some of the nuns was that the abbess openly distributed favors of patronage and affection to her own relatives. Equally ruthlessly, at least if some of her detractors are to be believed, she appears to have excluded and even ill treated those nuns who were not part of her network. More than one nun complained that the abbess was "partial." It seems abundantly clear, then, that as was true with the Guise family in France, the abbess of Santa Croce Val d'Arno perceived that her obligations to her kin continued when she became abbess and that part of her obligation was certainly to secure places for her own relatives within the convent itself. So concerned was Lodovica d'Ambrogio to maintain her family ties that she did not hesitate to send her relatives in Florence, especially her sister's family and their children, presents from the revenues and produce of the convent. In the case of her sister's servant, the convent served as a convenient alternative to the foundling hospital, hiding the family shame a good distance away from Florence itself and making sure that mother and baby were reasonably well cared for.

Despite Borghini's harsh responses in the margins, the commissioners and the bishop's vicar took the high road, at least initially. Despite Borghini's comment, for example, that the gardener was both surly and profane and should be removed, no one suffered either removal or even a transfer. Instead, after calling all the parties together inside the convent's church, the archbishop's vicar admonished them that he had "found many disorders and discords and the nuns had to think along the lines of living in a different fashion, with greater fear of God and greater respect for religion than they had shown up to this point. They should have recourse to God and to pledge to Him that he guide them to live quietly and according to the precepts of their order."[68]

The vicar then had the notary attach to the church door a written notice and warned the nuns that whoever took it down would be excommunicated. This notice read that "the Vicar and the Bishop of Lucca command the

---

[68] Ibid., fol. 513v, 4 August 1571: "haveva trovato di molto disordini et discordie in esso munistero et che era di necessità providerci et che loro pensassero di haver' a viver ad un'altro modo et con più timore di Dio et da religione che non havevano fatte a qui et che ricorreseno à Dio et lo piegassono che le riducesse a vivere quietamente et secondo si conviene alla religion loro."

abbess that in future the nuns not presume to allow anyone into the convent without the written permission of the bishop" and that violators would be deprived of their office, excommunicated, and placed in jail "at the pleasure of the aforementioned Very Reverend Monsignor," with the exception of the confessor, the barber, the surgeon, the workers who brought materials to the convent, the mule drivers, the builders (when there is need for construction), and the gardener (only when there are no nuns inside and only in case of necessity).[69]

One would have thought that to escape so lightly would have encouraged the abbess to keep her silence, but on 19 August, only two weeks after the vicar, the notary, and the bishop had returned to Lucca, she wrote to the commissioners complaining of the "lies told about me by the chaplain." She also complained that the vicar of Lucca had embarked on a campaign of persistent persecution, "but it all in the end proceeds from the poisonous mouth of that confessor who already admitted in part that he made seventeen nuns his girlfriends and made them swear many false things." Hoping perhaps to capitalize on the Florentine origins of the commissioners, she wrote, "These nuns are all from Lucca and no better than bastards and the said nuns from Lucca are favorites in Lucca."[70] Indeed, in the depositions, one of her opponents, Suor Ilaria, claimed that the abbess and her nuns "chased me and with their fists in my face threatened to choke me, shouting, 'go back to Lucca where your protectors are.'" I answered, "all my relatives in Lucca are powerful but I didn't want to have recourse to them but to the bishop. And she answered me that she knew no other bishop than the grand duke himself and the four commissioners."[71] In any case, the abbess's letter to the commissioners made abundantly clear that she thought almost exclusively in terms of patronage ties and that she was confident, wrongly as it turned

[69] Ibid., fol. 513v–514r: "si comanda . . . che per l'advenire non ardischino ne presummino ne alcuna di loro ardisca o presumma intrometter' dentro all prima porta di esso munistero alcuna persona di che stato grado ò conditione si sia cosi maschio come femina grande ò piccola senza espressa licentia in scriptis di Monsignor Reverendissimo vescovo prefato."

[70] Ibid., fol. 467r-v, 19 August 1571: "qual cagione detto Monsignor mi perseguiti . . . ma tucto è nato dalla velenosa bocca di questo cappellano il quale a messo in parte in questo monastero per aver fatto 17 monache sue amiche. Fanno molte fede false le quale in parte lucchese et non sono di meglio et bastarde et dette Lucchese sono favorite in Luccha."

[71] Ibid., fol. 479r: "et mi è corsa adosso lei con altre monache con la pugnia sul viso et Suor Barbara conversa che era con seco mi minaccio di volermi strozzare dicendo contra di me sì la Badessa come le altre che erano seco molte parole ingiuriose dicendomi va à Lucca per i tuoi potenti et rispondendo gli io che con tutto che li miei a Lucca fussero potenti che io non volevo ricorrere à loro ma che bene volevo ricorrere al vescovo et lei mi rispuose che non conosceva altro vescovo che il Gran Duca et i quattro deputati."

out, that she could count on the grand duke and the four commissioners to break up what she thought was the unholy alliance between the confessor, the nuns from Lucca, and the bishop of Lucca himself.

Thus, when Cosimo I complained about the evils of *clausura*, and equally, when reforming bishops set out to remedy them, discipline involved much more than the control of individual behavior or the reduction of "disordine." It is noteworthy that only one question to the abbess even addressed the charge that she had supplied her relatives with gifts. She denied it, and Borghini made the notation that "all we need to do is review the accounts in detail and the truth will be found," and the interrogation moved on to a different topic.[72] It was equally clear that Borghini was more concerned about her flippancy toward authority and the violation of *clausura* than her propensity to allow in relatives. At the very least, then, one can say that the ties of patrons to convents often stood in the way of discipline. One might even venture the hypothesis that ecclesiastical reformers took on conventual reform precisely to remove this layer of control that stood between the ecclesiastical (as well as the temporal) hierarchy and the religious life itself. In any case, if nuns successfully forsook the world of kin and family for the purer religious air of the cloister, it was much more difficult for them to abandon the adage that "charity begins at home."

Issues of patronage did not always need to reflect tension between the lay and ecclesiastical worlds. In the case of the Florentine hospital of San Paolo, tensions existed also concerning its connections to the Franciscan order and the lay sisters, or *pinzochere,* who had traditionally cared for San Paolo's ever-dwindling census of patients. In 1531, a bull of Clement VII had given the *pinzochere* the patronage of the hospital, but they formed a religious order that devoted more of its energies, not to mention revenues from benefactors, to practices of personal piety, diverting these monies from their original purpose of care for the sick. In 1549, Cosimo I wrote to Paul III requesting reform of the situation, a reform finally ordered in 1570, which curbed the powers of the nuns to interfere in the hospital's administration.[73] The *deputati,* however, were already hard at work at least as early as 1568 on the case of San Paolo, ready to have a set of recommendations ready should Francesco ask for them.

In a letter of early 1568, Vincenzio Borghini, one of the four deputies, wrote to another of the deputies, Bartolomeo Carnesecchi, concerning the

[72] Ibid. 510v: "Se si rividessero i conti per il minuto si ritroverà la verità."
[73] D'Addario, *Aspetti,* 76–7.

proposed reforms for San Paolo. This letter was appended to some notes concerning ideas for reform, but Borghini confessed to omitting many

> particulars, complaints, and quarrels, which if they had all been placed there, would have made the report too long and perhaps bothersome to His Excellency. They are not really appropriate for the moment, because if later on His Excellency wants things to be put in good order, at that point we will lay everything out on the table to be considered, so that we can provide the necessary orders and rules, even if for the moment I have already hinted at what some of them will be.[74]

Borghini's approach was clearly cautious concerning whether control should be given to the Observants of San Francesco. He suggested that Carnesecchi should first see whether "some Monsignor or other might not first divine their intentions, so that we can explain them better to His Excellency, and so that they don't say one thing and then turn around and say something else completely," especially because only some, and not all, of the nuns had been polled concerning this change.[75] Borghini, having reviewed the accounts, described himself as "dissatisfied" with both the hospital of San Paolo and with the nuns, both over specific details and with the way in which the accounts had been kept. In particular, he cited unhealthy conditions and noxious odors arising from the hospital's proximity to its overcrowded burial ground. The stench was so overwhelming that it was nauseating for the nuns and the patients to hear mass, and the hospital's vines were being destroyed. Moreover, the conditions offended the dignity of sick patients who, already wracked by excruciating pain, also had to watch their roommates die and be buried.[76]

In August 1568, one of the nuns, clearly dissatisfied with the pace of reform, took the liberty of writing directly to the grand ducal commission

---

[74] AOIF Estranei V, n.p. 15 March 1567: Vincenzio Borghini to Bartolomeo Carnesecchi: "Io ho lasciato indietro molte particularità, lamente et querele, le quali se tutte si fussino poste, oltre che la faceano la cosa troppa lunga et forse fastidiosa a S. E. non erano anche à proposito per hora: perche se à S. E. I. piacerà che ci si metta qualche ordine buono, allora verranno tutta in campo, et si considereranno, et vi si potrà pigliare quegli ordini et regola che bisognerà, ancorche per talvolta ne ho accennato qualcuna."

[75] Ibid.: "considerate se è fusse bene in questo capo udirla di nuovo o vedere per qualche via di sapere l'intention loro, et di questo potreste un Monsignore havere qualche particular commodità: questo dico perche noi possiamo meglio esporre a S. E. I. la volontà loro, àciò non dicessino una cosa, et poi sene trovasse un'altra."

[76] Ibid.: The long litany of complaints can be found in ASF San Paolo 844 fol. 146r, nd, but sometime between 7 February 1568 and 1 May 1569. Attempts to address financial improprieties are recorded ibid., fol.147r, n.d.

appointed to oversee the reform of the institution. "I am certain," she wrote, "that my writing will be understood as presumption or nosiness. But you know that necessity obeys no law. We are here and we see everything concerning this matter."[77] Complaining that the abbess was a tyrant, who had only four of the most elderly nuns supporting her, the author of this letter argued that she and eighteen other nuns were "firm and constant," whereas the others were all volatile and needed to return to grace.

> I would like to die because I want to see this brought to an end and it is not possible to have to live in such confusion and faction. And I pray to you for the love of God and of San Francesco that you place an end to this confusion.[78]

In his notes concerning proposed statutes for San Paolo, Borghini clearly had worked out those areas in which ambiguities in language were likely to cause difficulty. For example, in leaving to the conscience of a particular administrator the choice of a guardian, Borghini wrote:

> We should consider whether this should be specified a little more tightly, so that if she develops a special affection or attachment to one particular guardian, or familiarity that we would want to remove, we should remove the opportunity. Otherwise every time a nun wants to argue a little, she will send for him, always invoking her conscience. Perhaps it would be better if the Visitor, or the guardian, should in this case be regular and superior, and thus be in a better position to institute and enforce order.[79]

Yet in other respects Borghini's comments reveal an extremely cautious side – in particular, where customs and rules had already been established, Borghini avoided unnecessary and disruptive changes. In regard to what habit the nuns of San Paolo should wear, for example, Borghini pointed out, "In this matter we have to consider what is appropriate and the disposition

---

[77] AOIF Estranei V, n. p., 8 August 1568: Suor Carità of San Paolo to Vincenzio Borghini: "Reverendissimo Monssignore: Certo chonosco lo scriver mio vi parra prosuttione per opera di churiosità. Ma ssapete che necessita non a legge noi sian qua e veggiano el tutto circha alla nostra faccenda."

[78] Ibid. "vorei morire perche juegho lachosa chondotta aun termine che sse ciritorna ssa a dire di noi per tutto el mondo perche none possibile avere a viver sempre in tanta chonfusione e parte io vi pregho per la amor de dio e Santo Francesco V[ostra] R[everentia] ponga fine a tantta chonfusione."

[79] Ibid., fol. 2r, n.d.: "Considerisi se è fussi bene legarla un po più stretta: per che se pure occorressi che è si pigliassi qualche affettione particulare, o familiarità o domestichezza che è quello che noi vorremo levar via, et levarne anche l'occasioni: ogni volta che si piacerà d'andarvi, et che una monaca per ragionare un poco: manderà per lui: sempre gliene dettera la coscientia: Pero forse sare' bene, che ò il visitatore, ò il guardiano gli sia in questo caso regola et superiore, con metter quell'ordine et quelle prohibitioni che convenghino."

of the Holy Council [of Trent], and use charity and discretion, never forcing them through too much severity to such desperation that it becomes a huge matter to change an old custom."[80] At the same time, however, he argued, presumably because of the factionalism at San Paolo, that the new *ministra*, or governor, should not be elected, but appointed.

> She has to be in charge of the women and to take responsibility for governing all of them in all matters spiritual. She shall proceed with the fear of God and in observance of our rules, and all other good orders and customs of that house. She shall be zealous in everything pertaining to the honor of God and the salvation of souls. She shall do everything to make sure that officials do their jobs, and to this purpose she shall visit their work spaces often... [she should] take care that the sick lack nothing; that she be especially watchful of the gate, and see who frequents it too often, and what quality of person they are. On letting the nuns speak at the grates she should be vigilant from beginning to end concerning the custody of her flock, keeping her eyes open, knowing that for everything scandalous that happens she is directly accountable to God.[81]

Borghini's recommendations concerning the common life demonstrate great concern for the ill effects of private property, and indirectly attack issues of patronage:

> What is more of a consideration, in my judgment, is that having one's own money and spending it is poisonous, even deadly to the religious life. And these nuns we have here have been accustomed to doing so for a long time. From this are many scandals born, and I understand that at someone's death a sum of money is often found, which is prejudicial not only to their souls, but is also the cause of infinite disorders in the common life. I would judge it the best medicine for every evil that there is to extirpate their private property, and not only property, but every opportunity [for acquiring it].

---

[80] Ibid., fol. 5r, n.d.: "Ma in questo noi habbiamo à considerare quel che conviene, et la dispositione del Santo Concilio pur sempre con carità et con discretione non le inducendo mai per troppa severità à disperatione che gran cosa è mutare una usanza vecchia."

[81] Ibid., fol. 2v-3r, undated: "Qui aggiugnerei un capitolo (a mio giuditio) necessario dell'ufitio et autorità della ministra che dichiarissi che ella ha da essere il capo delle donne et haver' cura à tutto il governo, et che così nelle cose spirtuali come nel [temporale crossed out] ordine... Si proceda col timor di Dio et con l'esservanza di questi nostri, et di tutti gli altri buoni ordini et consuetudini di quella casa. Sia zelante in ogni cosa dell'honor di Dio et salute dell'anime. Habbia l'occhio a tutto e' procuri che l'ofitiali faccino gli'ufitii loro diligentemente et sollecitamente et a questo effetto visiti l'officine loro spesso.... Habbia cura che agl'infermi non si manchi; habbia particular diligenzia alla porta: et vegga chi frequenta troppo, et che qualità di persone sono, et nel lasciare parlare alle ruote stia incipamente et finalmente vigili sopra la custodia detto gregio con gli occhi aperti, sapenda che tutto quello che succedesse del scandolo ha a render ragione a Dio."

I would want to do everything possible to make sure that all money goes into a common fund.[82]

Similarly, Borghini stressed the importance of having strict rule concerning under what conditions nuns could leave the premises. "If their superiors are old, and good, there is no danger, because they will keep a sharp eye out. But we have to make rules that will work no matter what quality of person is in charge . . . it being our office to provide not only for present needs, but also to remove any opportunity for disorders that might happen in the future."[83] Equally, it was important to make sure that the lay employees not mix in or become too familiar with the sisters and that they should be together only at previously designated times and in previously designated places.[84]

Despite Borghini's carefully worked out plans, and their implementation in 1570 by Grand Duke Francesco, it is clear that ten years later, San Paolo was still in considerable disorder. From a letter of early 1580 to the archbishop and his vicar, one can infer that the nuns of San Paolo had submitted to the ecclesiastical authorities a complaint about being mistreated. Borghini prefaced his reply with a short homily that one should take into consideration

human frailty, and especially of the feminine kind, weak by nature and in these poor little girls also by accident. . . . They feel mistreated, and they hate the Prior. As far as I'm concerned, the Prior is a gentleman. . . . With any Prior it would be the same dispute: that the girls are not in charge and can't have everything their own way. . . . Whenever the prior can do so with good conscience, he should treat them humanely and not exasperate them, but rather treat them with all charity and behave towards them as though they were children; we mean to say, as the sick with whom one must have much patience and discretion. As far as being ill-treated is concerned, they claim two things: that he mistreats them concerning their living, which

---

[82] Ibid., fol. 5r, n.d.: "Ma quell'che è piu considerabile (a mio giuditio) e che il tenere peculio et spendere in proprietà è il veleno anzi la morte delle religioni: et queste che noi habbiamo alle mani ci sono di lunga meno mal'avezze, e di qui son' nati di molti scandoli, et intendo che alla morte di qualcuna s'è trovato qualche somma di denari, cosa che non solo è in pregiuditio dell'anima loro, ma causa infiniti disordini nella vita comune: et io giudicherei ottima medicina per ogni male che ci è: stirpare la proprietà, et non solo la proprietà, ma ogni minima occasione et vorrei fare ogni opera che i denari venissino tutti nella cassa comune: et che non si serbassino in proprietà."

[83] Ibid., fol. 6r, n.d.: "Et se e'capi loro, cioè, le ministre, et quelle vecchie saranno buone, non ci sara pericolo, perche haranno molto ben l'occhio che accompagnature daranno: ma perche ogni caso che può nascere havendo noi a fare una regola che ha à servire per ogni tempo et per ogni qualità di persone."

[84] San Paolo's reforms are in ASF, San Paolo 912.

I don't believe; and that he does not consult with them at all about matters. This I do not understand, and they would need to supply details. When they were asked to do so by the trustees, and to put it on paper, they did not do a thing. . . . Their lack of devotion and spirituality does not keep to the humility of Father Saint Francis. Rather, on the contrary, they are full of pride, ambition, and property, and the cause of all this disorder. I wouldn't have the slightest idea where to turn for a remedy. The most humane and pious remedy would be to send them a good preacher – one of those reformers who could push them back onto the good path and to the humility of true religious women. The other harder way would be to take three or four of the most stubborn ones and give them back their dowries, and put them in a real convent of their order. And even though the hospital is poor, I think that for all they rob, consume, and send elsewhere, the hospital would be better off financially without them. And maybe showing them that we could get on quite well without them would put their brains back in their head. But whatever you judge most expedient in this case I will always approve and will be to my full satisfaction and contentment.[85]

---

[85] ASF Segretario del Regio Diritto 4896, fol. 558r–559r, n. d. but perhaps late 1579 or early 1580 judging by the letter following: "Considerando generalmente la fragilità humana et specialmente del genere femminile debole per natura et in queste poverelle anche per accidente . . . Par loro essere maltrate: et hanno in odio il Priore. Quanto al Priore io l'ho tanto per huomo da bene, ch'io non penserei punto a mutatione e tanto più che come diceva Donato Tornabuoni: con ogni Priore sarà la medesima disputa fin che elle non sieno padrone a fatto di fare assolutamente a modo loro: in modo che pre quello non si torrebbe il male ben vorrei (se bisgono facesse che non lo credo) che dove conviene et può salva la conscientia con parole et con fatti trattarle humanamente et non le esasperare che lo facesse con ogni carità et con loro come fanciugli o, vogliam dire infermi bisogna havere molta patientia et molta discretione. Dell'essere mal trattate, diccano in due cose, nel vivere, che nol credo punto: et che con loro non si conferiva cosa alcuna delle faccende: questa parte non intendo, et bisognerebbe che elle venissero a particulari, et di quelle furono ricerche da gli operai et che mettesino in carta et non hanno fatto nulla . . . Ma lor poca devotione e sprito [sic] et non ritener punti dell'humiltà del Padre San Francesco anzi pel contrario esser piene di superbia, d'ambitione, e di proprietà, e di tutti questi disordini cagione. Et per me non saprei dove volgermi pe' rimedii. Uno sarebbe il più pio e piu humano se per via di alcun buon predicatore come sarebbe di questi Riformati si potessi ridurre al buon camino et alla humiltà delle vere religiose. L'altra più dura ma alla quale un dì (e Dio voglia non sia profeta bisognera finalmente venire): di cavarne 3, or 4 delle più fiere e seditiose e rendendo loro la dote metterle in Monasterii del loro ordine: che avezze in tali agi quanto elle sono, parrà loro altro giuoco. E se bene lo spedale è povero, io credo che ha quel, che consumano e che le mandar male e che le rubano (che di loro guadagni non se ne vede mai nulla) che lo spedale ne farà molto meglio: e forse mostrando loro il viso e che si pensa a fare senza loro potrebbe rimittirle il cervello in capo. . . . Ma di tutto finalmente mi riporto al giuditio delle SS. VV. e di voi Monsignor Vicario specialmente di queste affari di religiose e per lunga pratica e per buon giuditio assai più di me intendente. E tutto quello che giudicheranno in questo caso espediente approverò sempre e sarà con piena mia sasifatione e contento."

This harsh opinion was one of the last things Borghini wrote. As he stated in a covering letter,

> I came here on my doctor's advice, thinking that with the benefit of the air I could free myself from the decline that has beset my entire person. Perhaps it will eventually happen, but now it seems the contrary, that everything is getting worse, and is failing little by little, so that for two days I have been unable to get out of bed, and I cannot move. Yet the business of the little crazy girls gives me cause for regret and requires an early resolution.[86]

Even in these last documents, the need for nuns to have property as the basis of patronage could not be extinguished. As Borghini had pointed out in his notes on the statutes, the nuns of San Paolo were always borrowing and lending things to each other. Even more telling was Borghini's suggested provision for two separate officials: one to handle the distribution of money, the other the distribution of material goods. Although the two officials should confer frequently so that their activities were coordinated, Borghini insisted on the necessity of two, undoubtedly to keep one official from monopolizing the distribution of goods and becoming a powerful center of patronage. In Borghini's view, keeping those two offices separate, "is of the utmost importance because in it is contained the recipe for peace or war in this house."[87]

Indeed, the most frequently cited motivations for getting poor girls off the streets into quasi-conventual institutions as well were more often linked to strategies of lineage and family preservation than to the danger they represented to the moral fabric of the community. Girls on the loose represented the danger of *capitar male* and lack of family support – the implication being that families were quite capable of guaranteeing the honor of their own charges, and only when the family was no longer in a position to do this did the state step in and make institutions fictive parents. Honor in this respect was a corollary of civic *bella figura*. Indeed, the very honor of the grand duke and the city was as much at risk as that of the girls themselves.

At the same time, however, the monastic model, even as it defined disciplinary strategies both within and outside the cloister, was essentially an

---

[86] Ibid., fol. 559r, 19 March 1579: "Io venni qui per consiglio del medico, pensando col benefitio dell'aria liberarmi di una scesa, che mi havea compresa la persona tutta, et fosse mi verrà fatto, ma fino ad hora mi pare il contrario, che tutta si è ridotta intorno a fianchi, et va da mano in mano calando e potrebbe volersene andare, pure già due giorni non sono uscito di letto, che non mi posso muovere. Et m'increscie perche la cosa di quelle povere pazzerelle vorrebbe prestezza et risolutione."

[87] AOIF Estranei (CXLIV, V), fol. 4r: "Questo cap[itol]o è importantissimo, perche in esso si contiene la pace et la guerra di casa."

Aristotelian and Machiavellian model of mixed government. One of the major benefits of restrictive admissions policies in all these institutions is that at least some women would prosper within the system to become its administrators. Because property was communal, ideally decision making was also. Thus, self-government and self-discipline consisted at least in part in submission to duly-constituted authority. As was the case with the Renaissance city, the discipline required of those confined within institutions bore a close relationship to architecture that deliberately furthered social and political goals. The convent of Le Murate, in Florence, for example, the architecture of which quite deliberately reflected the spiritual goals of its patrons and administrators, was spectacularly successful at balancing the conflicts of patronage and obedience, contemplation and service. In the 1570s, when the archbishop of Florence set severe limits on the size of convents in Florence and its immediately surrounding region, the Murate, even though it was the largest convent, because of its "reliable alms, its good works, its holiness and reputation, and because it has no debt, the numbers will be left as they are."[88]

Only one other institution of the sixty that Borghini surveyed achieved this distinction. Most others had their census targets dramatically reduced, and some, like the unruly and difficult nuns of the hospital of San Paolo, were ordered to stop investing novices altogether. More important, however, the sense of community that in the ideal monastic setting was made possible by self-government, and in quasi-monastic settings such as the Innocenti and the homes of the Pietà and the Ceppo, fostered cultures within such institutions that made possible considerable individual and collective accomplishment.

---

[88] BNCF, Magliabechiani, Cl. VIII, 1393, fol. 186v, n.d.: "Computato le limosine solite, et i lavori et atteso la santità e reputatione del Monastero, et che non hanno debito si lasciano sul numero che sono." On Le Murate, see Saundra Weddle, "Enclosing Le Murate: The Ideology of Enclosure and the Architecture of a Florentine Convent, 1390–1597 (Ph.D. diss., Cornell University, 1997), and idem, "Identity and Alliance: Urban Presence, Spatial Privilege and Florentine Renaissance Convents," in *Renaissance Florence: A Social History*, ed. Roger Crum and John Paoletti (Cambridge: Cambridge University Press, 2006), 394–414.

CONCLUSION: THE HONOR OF GOD, OF THE CITY, AND OF THEIR OWN HOUSES

T HE SELF-CONSCIOUS APPROPRIATION OF THE HUMANIST EDUCATIONAL program during the sixteenth century in the service of fashioning an aristocratic ruling class was absolutely crucial to the recasting of educational discipline, and therefore to the fortunes of both men and women.[1] What Manzoni described in the story of the nun of Monza, even if it exaggerated the coercive nature of the nun of Monza's monachation, certainly was historically accurate in its ascription of the count's motive: the preservation of the family's current standard of living. Yet it would still limit the scope of our inquiry to confine the discussion to class formation, because class formation was fundamentally about state formation. It is no accident that sixteenth-century treatises on the family so frequently are titled *Institutiones*. Humanist training, even – indeed especially – when it ended up in the hands of Jesuits, was directed toward political leadership. Thus, what from an economic point of view was an aristocratic response to the pressures of dowry inflation and the increasing urgency to put a lock on the safety of the family patrimony became an issue tied to charity and to social discipline. Just as the preservation of aristocratic status was tied to preservation of land and inheritance, so did humanist education and formation for leadership emphasize the importance of accentuating differences in hierarchy and status. The very process that Ginzburg describes in *The Cheese and the Worms* or that Bakhtin describes in his famous work on Rabelais bears out the notion that in the late Middle Ages, popular and learned culture could coexist more or less peacefully, but by the late sixteenth century, aristocratic self-definition

---

[1] The subtitle for the conclusion comes from "Editto di Mons. Illus. et Reverendiss. Card. d'Urbino Arcivescovo della S. Chiesa di Ravenna Sopra l'andare et entrare ne' Monasteri di monache della Città di Ravenna," cited in Serafina Maiola, *Vita della madre Felice Rasponi: scritta da una monaca nel MDLXX, e pubblicata da Corrado Ricci* (Bologna: Zanichelli, 1883), 209: "l'honor di Dio, della Città, et delle proprie case."

and public order merged to require the moderation of popular culture, the regulation of carnival, and ultimately the conscious degradation and scorn of popular culture by mainstream culture.[2] Discipline, in short, was the bond that connected noble status to a concern for public order and the need to confine and rationalize.

What role, then, did institutions for men and women play in the development of this status culture and the civilizing process? Did monastic institutions and asylums provide the formation of techniques for social control that Foucault claimed for them? At the center of these questions is an issue relatively unexplored by social and religious historians: what was *clausura*, precisely, in theory, and how and why did post-Tridentine reformers attempt to impose it in practice? *Clausura* in particular and charitable reform in general need, surely, to be situated within the matrix of confessional discipline, social discipline, and early modern state formation. Attempts to enforce *clausura* responded to institutional imperatives to discipline not the poor but the poor's benefactors by attempting to reorganize systems of patronage and clientage around the rulers of territorial states.

Certainly if Foucault's definition of modern penal practice encompasses a shift from violence perpetrated on the body to the rehabilitation of the soul or from botched executions and dismemberments to a precise specification of a daily timetable for the inmate, sixteenth-century institutions for orphans, men, and women would fall under the rubric of modernity. Foucault appears to have anticipated this possibility by seeing in monastic discipline the origins of the methods and objectives of the modern penitentiary: uniformity in architecture, clothing, and the distinction of inmates according to rank to produce a visible hierarchy.[3] Foucault has deliberately left vague the chronology of the development of such practices in institutions other than the prison, where he more precisely documents the change during the eighty years following 1757. Nonetheless, one can infer from Foucault's close reading of Philippe Ariès that monastic organization and humanist education, especially the latter as modified and transformed by the Jesuits, employed the models and strategies that the late eighteenth century would incorporate into the prison and then export as a system of political and social control.

The close attention that asylums of reformed prostitutes, orphanages, and shelters for wayward children paid to the organization of work and play in the wake of late Renaissance humanism and the Catholic and Protestant

---

[2] Ginzburg, *The Cheese and the Worms*, 126; Mikhail Bakhtin, *Rabelais and His World*, 116–19.

[3] Foucault, *Discipline and Punish*, 141–3.

reformations has produced a proliferation of works linking the discipline of such institutions to confessionalization, that is, the fusion of religious and patriotic discipline. Such internalized discipline formed the basis for the extension of the power and technology of the modern state and for the tacit consent that minimized resistance to authority's steady encroachments on individual space.[4] One need not argue, of course, that such self-discipline led only to totalitarian control. One might with equal force argue that political theories of democratic self-government and Enlightenment rationality might not have even been possible without the compliant individual that discipline created from classical and Renaissance abstractions of rational humanity.[5]

Although the extensions of the notion of discipline and confessionalization to the eventual rise of the modern state are themselves persuasive, they in fact rest on what I view as two major problems with Foucault's model. The first problem is that postmodern theorists neglect the contributions of the Renaissance revival of the classical tradition and its transformation into aristocratic codes of civility during the sixteenth century. If indeed hierarchical definition is essential to modernity, one cannot discount the importance of sixteenth-century neo-Aristotelian notions of decorum as the theoretical justification for social order.[6] An important aspect of this first problem is the tendency of such historians as Ariès and Foucault to imagine the medieval past as undifferentiated – from Ariès's contention that the Middle Ages had no concept of childhood to Foucault's portrayal of the integration of madness into mainstream medieval society. Both Ariès and Foucault, then, equated modernity with differentiation and repression, presenting a rather idealized portrait of medieval social life. Thus, all one requires for the theory to begin to unravel is to show that the Middle Ages did have a concept of childhood and that during the Middle Ages, the mad were incarcerated. In short, according to both authors, the severe repression of reason and order chased away the wild and joyous abandon of medieval *deraison*.

The second problem is directly related to the first. Just as Ariès and Foucault left medieval conceptions of childhood and madness deliberately undifferentiated, so, too, did they gather monasteries, convents, schools, orphanages, asylums, hospitals, and armies under the single rubric of total institutions. To swallow without criticism the argument that modern medicine and social assistance were little more than repressive systems of

---

[4] See, for example, the collection of essays, *Disciplina dell'anima, disciplina del corpo, e disciplina dello stato*, ed. Paolo Prodi.

[5] Cf. Chittolini, "Il privato, lo pubblico e lo stato," 565–6.

[6] See especially Gerhardt Oestreich, *Neo-stoicism and the Early Modern State*, Cambridge Studies in Early Modern History (Cambridge: Cambridge University Press, 1983).

social control masquerading as charity, kindness, and compassion is to blur important distinctions among all these institutions. Certainly such a cynical view of modernism and charity must have inspired the author of the "charity" article in the *New Catholic Encyclopedia* to shun the "debased" definition of charity in current use that equates it with nothing more than universal brotherhood and social work.[7]

Especially at issue is "the great confinement," the period between 1650 and 1790 in which, according to Foucault's thesis, criminals, the insane, the poor, and vagabonds, forced into institutions by economic necessity and stigmatized by the uncontrolled rise of merchant capitalism, became marginalized. Yet as the discussion of the organization of economic life among the boys and girls of the Innocenti has shown, as well as Thomas Safley's excellent book on charity and economy in the orphanages of Augsburg, far from being marginalized, the administration of orphanages and their incorporation into the economic schemes of early modern cities were at least in some cases the engine that drove capitalist expansion.[8]

Some historians, meanwhile, have viewed institutions for reformed prostitutes, the institutionalization of recalcitrant women, or even the regulation of order in the convent itself as a kind of anticipation of the great confinement. In this view, such institutions made of women an experimental group on whom secular authorities could try out techniques of confinement before extending them to other social categories.[9] Surely at issue, however, is an important difference between circumstances in which the state or some other authority forced inmates into institutions or whether economic or social necessity, or simple lack of alternatives, encouraged voluntary submission to institutional order. Equally important as a distinction, as in the case of reformed prostitutes, is that rehabilitation was a precondition of admission, not the goal of the institution. As Sandra Cavallo has pointed out, even in a relatively small state such as Turin, one cannot speak with any confidence of the coercive power of the state before the eighteenth century.[10]

In the case of Florence, at least, it is difficult to escape the conclusion that concern for girls was more directed to keeping up appearances than

---

[7] *New Catholic Encyclopedia* (New York: McGraw-Hill, 1967), s.v. "Charity." The 2003 edition (Detroit: Gale, 2003) moderated this language only slightly: "the word has gone down in the world and is applied to an active benevolence toward those in need and sometimes to a dutiful or even a patronizing regard for those one finds socially and psychologically taxing."

[8] Gavitt, "Charity and State Building," 260–2; Thomas Max Safley, *Charity and Economy in the Orphanages of Early Modern Augsburg*, Studies in Central European Histories. (Atlantic Highlands, NJ: Humanities Press, 1996), 11–13.

[9] Cohen, *The Evolution of Women's Asylums*, 5.

[10] Cavallo, *Charity and Power*, 251–2.

to effective strategies of relief. The strange career of Vincenzio Borghini as superintendent of the Ospedale degli Innocenti demonstrates a constant concern for the honor of the Innocenti's female charges, including both their separation from wet nurses and the expansion of the hospital's dormitories to accommodate the steadily increasing influx of girls. Yet the two volumes of *suppliche* in the Innocenti's archive do not suggest that Cosimo's administration was particularly responsive to the urgency of Borghini's requests, and once the reins of government had been passed to Francesco, the urgency of Borghini's pleas increased in direct proportion to the apparent decrease of Francesco's interest in providing anything but the most basic support for the honor of the Innocenti's women.

This lack of support certainly had its consequences. Even in the best years of the 1530s, over half of infants admitted to the Innocenti died before reaching their first birthdays. If Richard Trexler's work on the Innocenti is unreliable for the hospital's opening years, a century later the grim portrait of institutionalized infanticide rings true. Certainly girls made up the majority of admissions to the Innocenti, although once there, the death rate of female children is only slightly higher than that of boys, and for some years, infant and child mortality was greater among boys, reflecting their greater biological vulnerability during the first year of life. During years of acute crisis, boys were as likely to be abandoned as girls; when economic pressures relaxed slightly, Florentines once again abandoned more girls. Acute crises of subsistence also tended to equalize death rates between the sexes.

After the famine of 1539, in particular, Cosimo I addressed reforms of charitable institutions, especially the centralization of the city's charity under the magistracy of the Bigallo, to children between the ages of three and ten. In a parallel and undoubtedly related development, the years after the famine also saw the proliferation of private efforts to open small conservatories and orphanages, a development chronicled in Nicholas Terpstra's excellent comparative study of Florence and Bologna.[11] The most important thrust of Cosimo's reforms, however, was the lumping together of the city's charitable efforts into a more coherent system of religious discipline. Cosimo successfully exercised his patronage over ecclesiastical institutions, consulting with Vincenzio Borghini concerning nominations for various ecclesiastical posts but retaining the rights to final decisions concerning appointments. The Florentine state even occasionally sponsored visits by preachers known to be eloquent voices in support of both ecclesiastical and personal reform. Not only did the new combined magistracy of the Bigallo and the Buonomini

---

[11] Terpstra, *Abandoned Children*, 28–63.

di San Martino centralize the city's charity, but Cosimo also took under his wing the city's youth confraternities.[12]

Two magistracies, the Conservatori della Legge and the Magistrato dei Pupilli, oversaw legal and administrative issues related to the abandonment of children and the honor of girls. The first oversaw cases concerning the restitution of dowries to their rightful recipients; the second not only oversaw the administration of estates for orphaned children but, when appropriate, appointed mothers the guardians of their children's estates after the death of the father.

In 1478, the Magistrato dei Pupilli enacted statutes that allowed unmarried girls over age eighteen to enter their protection to help them marry and prevent their natal families from keeping them out of the marriage market to avoid paying their dowries. The reforms of the 1530s and 1560s specifically extended the protection of this magistracy to widows and to the recovery of their dowries. Not surprisingly, the proliferation of such magistracies attuned to the problems of unmarried girls and widows led more to confusion than to centralization, despite the attempts of successive Medici governments to clarify problems of overlapping jurisdiction. By 1565, for example, the Magistrato dei Pupilli was supervising more than 20,000 inheritances and had such large amounts of wealth entrusted to it that continuing safeguards had to be put in place to curb the temptations of its officials to misappropriate its funds.

Complicating still further the situation of such large charitable institutions as the Innocenti, Santa Maria Nuova, and even the Monte di Pietà was the tendency of Grand Dukes Cosimo and Francesco, as well as private investors, to use them as depositories for wealth. Certainly the use of such institutions as banks cemented the centrality of charity to the concerns of the grand duchy and, along with artistic patronage, consolidated the link between the honor of the state and the honor of children. The introduction of tapestry manufacture further consolidates this link between the city's prestige as benefactor, its artistic legacy, and its attempt to attain greater economic prominence by using cheap labor to manufacture products for everyday elite consumption.

For private investors, the relative safety of charitable institutions provided a number of advantages. Depositors could use their property, for example, as security for their pledges to underwrite their children's institutionalization

---

[12] Indeed, this practice seems to have been widespread throughout northern and central Italy. In Chioggia, for example, the *podestà* and the council chose preachers to preach in the cathedral on Sundays during Lent. Cf. Archivio Comunale di Chioggia, 31 (Consigli IX, 1540–1560), fol. 37v, 6 February 1547.

and could even use the revenues from those properties as support. Women often used such depositories as the Innocenti as a base from which they could exert more control over their financial lives. Florentine families also used such deposit accounts as a way to accumulate money for dowries. In all three instances, charitable institutions such as the Innocenti, as well as the much smaller and more exclusive conservatories and orphanages that proliferated during the sixteenth century, showed that such institutions were a crucial element in the family strategies of elites. They could be used not only to preserve the honor of girls and as temporary placement for children who otherwise might constitute an intolerable familial burden but also to accumulate dowries and support family honor both for institutionalized girls and girls who never even entered the institution's doors. In short, charitable institutions were not so much places where one could dump inconvenient children and promptly forget them but places where children appeared, disappeared, and reappeared according to the differing needs and capacities of each family in various stages of the life cycle.

Although the studies of anthropologists of the Mediterranean region have provided an invaluable conceptual structure for the axis of honor and shame around which the world of the late Middle Ages revolved in Italian cities, certain features of so-called gender ideology do not adequately describe how women and families actually behaved. In traditional accounts of gender ideology, for example, the dowry allegedly functioned as a guarantee of a woman's honor and, more specifically, her virginity. Yet Laura McGough's brilliant dissertation has turned up evidence that in Venice at least, young concubines expected that their patrons would provide dowries for them before they passed beyond marriageable age.[13] For Florence as well, Maria Fubini-Leuzzi has suggested that in the sixteenth century, domestic servitude may have veiled what were in some cases actually relationships of concubinage, a conclusion based on the reduced numbers of female servants in Florentine households after anticoncubinage laws were put into effect.[14] Moreover, before the standardization of marriage practices decreed at the Council of Trent, the rituals of courtship and marriage in many Italian provincial towns, complained Bishop Nacchianti of Chioggia, amounted to little more than legalized fornication.[15]

These developments both drove and in turn were driven by the development of a status culture of consumption that redefined the development

---

[13] Laura Jane McGough. "'From the Devil's Jaws': A convent for repentant prostitutes in Venice, 1520–1670" (Ph.D. diss., Northwestern University, 1997), 23.

[14] Fubini-Leuzzi, *Condurre a honore*, 47–9.

[15] Chioggia, Archivio Storico Diocesano, Vescovi, 3, fol. 185v, 22 May 1567.

of aristocratic, noble culture. Insofar as these developments can be tied to any particular historical crisis, the Italian wars of 1494–1530 seem to have increased the pressure on aristocratic families to preserve patrimony through patrilineality, a development that led both to intense competition of landed resources and to dowry inflation.

These developments were not caused by the Italian wars; rather, the Italian wars accelerated trends that predated even the Black Death: the spread of Roman law throughout the Italian communes, as well as the increasing incorporation of Roman law into communal statutes and, in the case of Florence, in a way that elites consciously attempted to exclude women from direct inheritance. Yet in Venice, where such exclusion was not widespread, the same problems of dowry inflation and overcrowding of convents and charitable institutions continued to take place. This suggests also that these developments were not strictly tied to issues of gender but to issues of lineage.

The appropriation of the classical tradition in the service of rationalizing these developments, although it led to a relatively uniform interpretation of the importance of family and lineage to the state, by no means led to a uniform interpretation of gender roles. Two distinct traditions represented a split concerning the proper place of women in this domestic economy. One followed Aristotelian and pseudo-Aristotelian arguments based on medicine and nature that emphasized the physical and mental inferiority of the female sex. Another tradition followed Plato and Xenophon in emphasizing that the weakness was physical only – and that in companionate marriage the physical deficiencies were offset by their ability to act as conservators of household wealth. Indeed, given the importance of the conservation of wealth to this newly emerging status culture of consumption, the role of women in conserving patrimony became acknowledged by sixteenth-century *trattatisti* as central. In other words, considerations of gender were certainly important but ultimately subservient to concerns for the preservation of lineage and, by extension, the patrimony of the lineage. Moreover, as the chapter on law and practice shows, both sons and daughters who got in the way of lineage ideology were disposable. Even that seemingly and outrageously misogynistic portion of Alberti's *Della famiglia*, so beloved as an example of why women allegedly had no Renaissance, has been shown by John Najemy to be so divergent from Alberti's own views that it should rather be seen as a parody and a critique of the emerging status culture that in the name of patrilineality put unreasonable demands on even noble families.[16] As we have seen, this was an intensely personal issue for Alberti as

---

[16] Najemy, "Giannozzo and His Elders," 57–8.

well, because his status as a "figlio naturale" ran up against the unwillingness of his biological father to purse his legitimation and make him part of the *famiglia* about which he wrote with such desperate eloquence.[17]

Sixteenth-century treatises, especially those that form part of the *querelle des femmes*, show that not only did most sixteenth-century authors argue in favor of the companionate model of marriage, they further emphasized the moral equality of men and women. In many cases as well, debates that focused on the physical qualities of women sought to impart neo-Platonic wisdom concerning the philosophical importance of beauty and to understand better the nature of the good. Indeed, one could argue that the recognition of women as intellectually capable creatures was a necessary step in the transition to the post-Tridentine treatises that placed the family and the education of children as central not only to the success of noble and aristocratic culture but also more largely to the success of the fully disciplined Christian state. Discipline involved a certain readiness to understand the connections between the family and the state, for which reason women had to be able to read at the very least the examples of female sanctity that they were to emulate in the government of the household.

Lineage ideology had its limitations and weaknesses, however, especially as a blueprint for everyday life. If its goal extended beyond the preservation of patrimony to the preservation of the family and to preserving the resemblance of the family to the unified state, lineage ideology seems conspicuously unsuccessful reaching that goal, which in turn might help explain the lack of success of state formation until at least the eighteenth century. To codify lineage ideology into communal statutes and legal rules for inheritance was one thing. Making those work in the service of the preservation of family and patrimony was quite another, more laborious, and, frankly, quixotic undertaking.

Stronger than the laws of inheritance were the laws of unintended consequences. As families, Florentine families in particular, but not exclusively, attempted to fit the needs of family honor to the strategies of family preservation, their stories consist largely of how they coped with the unintended consequences of early modern lineage ideology. Critical to those strategies were convents and charitable institutions. Indeed, Richard Trexler argued that historians needed to understand that charitable institutions served not only the spiritual but also the material needs of their wealthy and powerful benefactors.[18]

---

[17] Kuehn, *Law, Family, and Women*, 157–75.
[18] Trexler, "Charity and the Defense of Elites in the Italian Communes," 77–8.

In particular, the single most important demographic factor that patrilineal inheritance strategy failed to take into account was the difference in age of marriage between men and women. Widows were numerous as a result of this difference; the more dependence women had on fathers and husbands for their material support, the more vulnerable they were at their husband's death. Where this vulnerability had the most devastating effect, as Klapisch-Zuber has shown, was on a woman's children from the first marriage.[19] Yet this vulnerability was not exclusive to women. Those men who outlived several wives, as did Andrea Nacchianti, found themselves under constant pressure to support children from previous marriages, and even children from wives' previous marriages. Even if the law left such children little or no recourse, their mothers could be strong advocates that some provision be made for them, as in the case of Andrea Nacchianti's fourth wife, Maddalena.

Indeed, the pressures of dowry inflation, and the economic and social consequences of those pressures, pressed post-Tridentine moralists to ever harsher critiques of placing dowry at the center of family marriage strategy. Commentators who were not moralists were just as eager to point out the flaws in sixteenth-century systems of family and inheritance.[20] The Venetian noblewoman Moderata Fonte in her dialogue *The Worth of Women* not only pointed out the devastating effects of these strategies on young women, but also pointed out that different fathers responded in different ways to the problems dowries and dowry inflation created.[21]

Although convents and charitable institutions were certainly one important solution for a large number of families, one must also take into account the importance of informal networks of charity. As Nicholas Terpstra so eloquently wrote, "nowadays we say that you can't choose your family, but in the Renaissance you could, and indeed would have been foolish not to."[22] The *ricordanze* of Andrea Nacchianti showed clearly that despite his wishes and better judgment, he became the reluctant source of support for a number of family members who otherwise would have had few resources to fall back on. Even if this example were unrepresentative, it was far more common to see neighbors and business associates who could afford it to provide dowry funds for girls from other families, often as a supplement

---

[19] Klapisch-Zuber, *Women, Family and Ritual*, 125–6.

[20] I wish to thank Professor William Wallace for pointing out to me that Michelangelo's marriage advice to his nephew Leonardo urged the latter to treat dowry as a secondary consideration in the choice of a spouse.

[21] Moderata Fonte, *The Worth of Women: Wherein Is Clearly Revealed Their Nobility and Superiority to Men,* trans. Virginia Cox. The Other Voice in Early Modern Europe (Chicago: University of Chicago Press, 1997), 62.

[22] Terpstra, *Abandoned Children*, 2.

to augment the family's existing dowry. Moreover, the high frequency of fostering out children for various periods of time, especially for household service and apprenticeships, became a little-recognized but widespread form of charity in which labor services were exchanged for food, clothing, and shelter.

As in the case of Tommaso Banchozzi and his sister Francesca, siblings helped each other out, reducing expenses by living together for brief periods of time. Moreover, families used charitable institutions as ways to make provision for younger sons and daughters. Family lands could be and often were donated to charitable institutions in exchange for using the income from those lands to support children placed under the tutelage of orphanages and hospitals. Most important, evidence from the Ospedale degli Innocenti in Florence makes clear that wealthy families used charitable institutions as saving banks, not as substitutes for inheritance but as part of comprehensive family strategies that transferred wealth from richer to poorer members of the same lineage.

When these strategies supported the conservation of material wealth, they certainly benefited the lineage as a whole. Clever as these strategies were, however, they did tend to undermine the very lineage solidarity they were meant to maintain. Perhaps more important, not all families possessed both the resources and the ingenuity to pursue contradictory goals. Nonetheless, the actual experience of boys and girls in charitable institutions suggests that such institutions attempted to impose the cultural and disciplinary expectations required of young family members. Although Nicholas Terpstra, among others, has cast doubt on whether the guardians of such institutions actually read the moralistic literature that set out in such detail how to produce well-disciplined Christian subjects, both the precepts of moralists and the rules governing behavior in charitable and conventual institutions show such a high degree of congruence that it is difficult to ignore a kind of consensus on the general outlines, even when details (to use corporal punishment or not, for example) often differed.

Equally clear in the moralistic literature is a shift in emphasis from the close link between child rearing and the classical tradition to a post-Tridentine emphasis on confessionalization and discipline. Ser Silvano Razzi argued that the totality of classical antiquity could hardly equal either the scriptures or Christian tradition when it came to formulating precepts for child rearing, whereas the physician from Colle Val d'Elsa, Francesco Tommasi, emphasized that "Christian" upbringing meant orthodox Catholic upbringing.[23]

---

[23] Silvano Razzi, *Della economica Christiana e civile di Don Silvani Razzi: I dve primi libri* Ne i quali da vna nobile brigata di Donne e huomini si ragiona della cura, e governo famigliare: secondo

The sources for such discipline, especially for boys, were neither the "civilizing process" related to the self-definition and articulation of a "new" noble elite nor solely the product of post-Tridentine reform. Rather, the model for the discipline of education and the discipline of society was a much older monastic model, enriched, certainly, by the classical tradition and Renaissance humanism and applied to the discipline of lay society.

The practice of pedagogy at the Ospedale degli Innocenti in Florence was clearly informed both by the classical tradition and by sixteenth-century developments outlined in the treatises of moralists. Central to this pedagogy was close supervision and observation of boys by their masters, with good behavior enforced by rituals of public guilt and reconciliation. The centrality of prayer and other forms of devotion to the daily routine reflected the practices of both the *scuole pie* and the Jesuit schools, as did the insistence, at least for boys, on retaining Latin and other staples of the humanist curriculum, despite opposition from some quarters that argued that training of poor boys in Latin and the classical tradition encouraged subversive social mobility. Downward social mobility, nonetheless, dominated the concern of the statutes that boys refrain from contact with the seedier characters who frequented the loggia and the streets near the hospital. As moralistic treatises encouraged the segregation of both boys and girls in the home from maids, laborers, and wet nurses, so, too, were boys in the Innocenti forbidden to wander about in vaults and cellars.

Although the preoccupation with both prayer and matters of cleanliness of the body suggests the strong religious and disciplinary focus of such institutions as these, the modern reader of these statutes runs the risk of losing sight of the relationship of both these issues to family patronage. If such institutions as the Innocenti and the Ospedale degli Abbandonati in Florence provided solutions to the economic anxieties of families, so much more did they reflect the preoccupation of the social anxieties of elites. The prayers that boys and girls were expected to say for the institutions' benefactors cemented the place of those institutions in the networks of patronage that both worked cooperatively for the salvation of the city and competitively for the advancement in the standing of individual families. Well-behaved, well-educated, and well-disciplined children were living proof of the righteousness of both the donor and the institutions receiving the support.

The Innocenti's statutes of 1618 make clear that as much as the Innocenti made distinctions of class among its children, it also made distinctions based on close observation of children's inclinations and abilities. In particular, the

---

la legge Christiana, e vita Ciuile (Florence: Bartolomeo Sermartelli, 1568), 214–15. Francesco Tommasi, *Reggimento del padre di famiglia* (Florence: Giorgio Marescotti, 1580), 138.

Innocenti's close connections to post-Savonarolan reformers resulted in close ties between the hospital's management and the Dominicans at San Marco. At least two of the Innocenti's boys, Giovanbattista Nacchianti and Costantino Antinori, pursued distinguished clerical careers partly as a result of this connection, and both received doctorates in theology, a distinction that Nacchianti carried with him in every official document from the bishop's palace in Chioggia, where he always included the phrase "sacrae theologiae professor."

The latter was a protégé of one of the Innocenti's most energetic superintendents, Vincenzio Borghini, who as part of the grand duke's program to combine artistic patronage with the patronage of charitable institutions, brought the hospital into the orbit of the cultural life of Florence, including a flourishing musical life, the introduction to tapestry manufacture, and instruction in drawing. In 1563, the Innocenti itself held the first exhibitions put on by the Accademia del Disegno, and artists of the caliber of Pontormo and Vasari served as mentors to the most talented boy foundlings, including Battista Naldini and Ulivo di Vincenzo Ulivieri. The rug and tapestry workshops of the Innocenti not only redounded to the cultural glory of the grand dukes but also provided Florence's ruling family with a supply of cheap labor and a laboratory for experiments in state economic planning.

Officials at the Innocenti were acutely aware that the upbringing of girls was a far more arduous and demanding task than the upbringing of boys, if only because there were more girls and because they stayed longer within the walls of the institution. The dangers of girls falling victim to prostitution was a preoccupation never far from the minds of officials in charge of charitable institutions, and the organization of care both at the Innocenti and in quasi-conventual institutions took great pains to keep vulnerable girls cloistered as far away from potential predators as possible.

Particular to the discipline of girls was attention given to the body, not only in the instructions that girls should keep their eyes lowered but also should avoid gestures with the hands or allowing hands to touch any part of the body. Advice for girls stressed the importance of appearance – that modesty required dignity and decorum in every activity, even in the presence of one's own family; to walk and behave, in short, like virgins and not like streetwalkers. The author of the 1471 treatise known as the *Decor Puellarum* even went so far as to suggest that girls use their apparently abundant free time to construct and pray before an altar in their own rooms.[24]

---

[24] Giovanni di Dio da Venezia (attr.), *Decor puellarum: zoe honore de la donzelle la quale da regola, forma, e modo al stato de le honeste* (Venezia: Magistrum Nicolaum Jenson, 1471), 44r.

Sewing and weaving were considered, on the basis of models from Greek literature and Latin moralizing, appropriate forms of manual labor for young girls. Indeed, sewing, weaving, and honor were so closely intertwined that weaving undertaken by girls in charitable institutions not only supported the economic ambitions of the grand duchy but also symbolized the honor of female inmates and the honor of the institutions themselves. Sewing and honor were also connected through dowries, because at Florentine institutions, at least, officials kept track of what girls were accumulating through their earnings toward a modest dowry. This practice also reflected what young household servants could expect from their household and family employers, who withheld earnings for girls until they were old enough for marriage or the convent. Finally, the girls who worked in the Innocenti's tapestry workshops, especially under the good-humored tutelage of Ventura di Vincenzo Ulivieri between 1581 and 1585, also contributed through their industrial and artistic production to the cultural life of the grand ducal court, and even to Grand Duke Francesco I's penchant for economic and scientific experimentation.[25]

Although Nicholas Terpstra's excellent studies comparing Florentine and Bolognese institutions draw a distinction between the small-scale, exclusionary world of the orphanage or conservatory and the large-scale, workhouse atmosphere of such mega-hospitals as the Innocenti in Florence and the Esposti in Bologna,[26] the Innocenti did not consign all its female inmates to the business of supplying cheap labor to support grand ducal economic ambitions. True, more than 80 percent (484) of the hospital's 586 girls in 1581 were engaged in cloth production of some sort, but among the remaining 20 percent, girls were learning to become pharmacists, physicians, nurses, and administrators, and even though we have no female equivalents for Bishop Nacchianti and Battista Naldini, many women became prioresses either at the Innocenti or at neighboring hospitals and conservatories, viewed with sufficient respect to have their elaborate funeral rites recorded affectionately, if formulaically, in great detail.[27]

As Maria Fubini-Leuzzi has so astutely pointed out, although this wide variety of institutions for girls ostensibly sought to solve or at least ameliorate the problems of prostitution, one has to ask why, with all the private and governmental commitment to conservatories and hospitals, were these efforts so spectacularly unsuccessful. If one looks at the number of prostitutes

---

[25] For a detailed description of the activities of this workshop, see Gavitt, "An Experimental Culture."

[26] Terpstra, *Abandoned Children*, 19–20.

[27] Cf. Gavitt, "Charity and Statebuilding," 257–9.

registered with the Ufficiali dell'Onestà in 1560, the figure of 150 seems surprisingly low by comparison to the estimate of the English traveler Robert Dallington of some 8,000 prostitutes in Florence.[28]

In this sense charitable institutions such as the Ospedale degli Innocenti in Florence, as well as the conservatories and orphanages with more restrictive admissions, served family strategies of honor in much the same ways as convents. As the previous chapter has shown, the patronage of convents was contested territory in which families and even the grand ducal state fought for the extension of control. To be patron of a convent was not merely to emblazon the family honor with a connection to a religious institution but was also to use that institution as part of larger family strategies of influence and control. Certainly the abbess of the convent of Santa Croce Val d'Arno viewed the church of that convent as her personal possession and the privileges of novices and nuns alike as hers to extend or withdraw. Similarly, the Guise family in France used its influence over convents as part of a larger strategy of aggrandizement of extended family ties.

Thus, when ecclesiastical and civil authorities pursued sometimes parallel, sometimes converging strategies of discipline and social control, gender ideology, although hardly negligible, was much less important in shaping the history and function of both convents and charitable institutions than civic pride and family strategy. Indeed, in sixteenth- and seventeenth-century Florence, civic pride and family strategy were still inseparable. Consequently, the process of ecclesiastical reform was far from straightforward. Insofar as *clausura* attempted to disrupt the ties between families and the conventual institutions that depended on them, ecclesiastical officials could only ignore the threats to institutional survival this disruption implies by suggesting, as Pius V did to Cosimo and Francesco, that the state had the responsibility to ameliorate the economic conditions of convents and their charges. Although such single-minded devotion to the process of ecclesiastical reform might be commendable in the abstract, in practical terms, such suggestions only worked to intensify the competition of families over charitable spoils as much as over other perquisites administered by state power. Only, as in the case of Parma, when states understood the connection between the honor of the city and the maintenance of order in convents, might civic authorities

---

[28] Fubini-Leuzzi, *Condurre a onore*, 34–5. In Rome, as she points out, the official figures counted 800; Cardinal Rusticucci, "who wished to rid the city of their scandalous presence, spoke of 13,000 prostitutes." On prostitution in early modern Rome, see now Tessa Storey, *Carnal Commerce in Counter-Reformation Rome* (Cambridge: Cambridge University Press, 2008). For Rome, cf. also BAV, Vat. Lat. 9729, fol. 104r–107v "Riforma del habitar de le meretrici publici a Roma" and Vat. Lat. 9435, fol. 143r–147r.

work to reduce rather than amplify the hold of patronage that families had over convents traditionally associated with them. Even in the case of Parma, such attempts at reform as overseeing the appointment of abbesses tended to shift the players in conflicts rather than reducing disorder itself.[29] Conventual disorder had much less to do with the rigors of conventual life living in close quarters and much more to do with the extended involvement of convents in the outside world of their patrons. Even in convents that were hardly wealthy enough to attract benefactors, nuns within the walls brought their vision of corporatism and factionalism in the outside world into the cloister with them. Distinctions of social status continued – a frequent source of contention among nuns was how many servants were allotted to each nun and to what extent individual nuns could claim servants as entirely their own.

Yet the inability to separate charitable institutions and convents from the grip of familial patrons could bring honor both to their charges and to the state. The great achievements of High Renaissance and baroque art and music often took place in the context of orphanages, conservatories, and convents. From the connection between the Ospedale degli Innocenti to the development of Florentine mannerism in the visual arts, to the more celebrated eighteenth-century connection of such musicians as Vivaldi to the hospital of the Pietà in Venice, and the culture of motets and madrigals associated with convents all over northern Italy, the cultural riches associated with charitable patronage hardly foreshadow the great impersonal Dickensian institutions of the nineteenth century. Nor did such institutions herald the birth of the clinic and the prison. Although one might see in refuges for battered wives or shelters for reformed prostitutes attempts at totalitarian social control, early modern states and their aristocracies in northern Italy thought of these institutions quite literally in more familiar terms. Charity attempted to extend the discipline of the family to reach those members of the family, primarily women and girls, whom strategies of so-called family and lineage preservation had displaced. Yet such displacement was in some cases only temporary, and a last resort after other measures, including reliance on the charity of extended family and neighbors, had failed.

[29] Letizia Arcangeli, "Ragioni politiche della disciplina monastica," 165–87.

BIBLIOGRAPHY

ARCHIVAL AND MANUSCRIPT SOURCES

Arezzo
  Archivio di Stato (ASA)
    Archivio Vasari
Chioggia
  Archivio Comunale (ACC)
    31 Consigli (IX 1540–1560)
  Archivio Storico Diocesano
    Vescovi, 3
Florence
  Archivio di Stato (ASF)
    Archivio Mediceo del Principato
    Arte della Seta
    Bigallo
    Corporazioni Religiose Soppresse dal Governo Francese
      112, Società dello Spedale di Pietà 78: Libro Segreto A
    Magistrato dei Pupilli et Adulti Avanti il Principato
    Magistrato dei pupilli et Adulti del Principato
    Manoscritti 129, Memorie Fiorentine di Francesco Settimanni
    Mediceo del Principato
    Monastero di S. Maria e S. Niccolò del Ceppo
      Capitoli MS 1bis
      MS 59
    Monastero di S. Caterina
      7: Capitoli, et Ordinationi delle Fanciulle Abbandonate di Santa Caterina
      Martire della città di Firenze (1590)
    Provvisioni Registri
    Pratica Segreta
    Segretario del Regio diritto
    Senato del Quarantotto
    Archivio notarile antecosiminiano
    Carte Strozziane

Diplomatico (Spedale degli Innocenti)
Diplomatico (Bigallo)
Archivio dell'Ospedale degli Innocenti (AOIF)
    Balie e Bambini
    Entrata e Uscita
    Suppliche e Sovrani Rescritti
    Estranei
    Debitori, Creditori, e Richordi
    Filze d'Archivio
    Fabbrica di San Pietro in Roma (CXXX, filze 1–11), 1560–1692.
    Ricordanze
    Giornale
Archivio del Capitolo di San Lorenzo (ACSL)
    2299 Libro dei Partiti del Capitolo di San Lorenzo (1544–62)
    1673 Registro Lettere (1560–1613)
Biblioteca Moreniana, Florence (BMF)
    Fondo Bigazzo 61
    Fondo Bigazzi 168
    Fondo Palagi 246
Bibiloteca Nazionale Centrale di Firenze (BNCF)
    cod. Magliabechiana, II, I, 399
    Cl. VIII, 1393
    II.X. 138
Ravenna
    Biblioteca Comunale
Rome
    Biblioteca Vallicelliana codex G43
Vatican City
    Biblioteca Apostolica Vaticana (BAV)
        Barb. Lat. 3724
        Barb. Lat. 3956
        Ottob. Lat. 3004
Venice
    Archivio Storico del Patriarcato di Venezia (ASPV), sezione antica,
    Liber Actorum Mandatorum Preceptorum 68 (1550–1558)

PRINTED PRIMARY SOURCES

Alberti, Leon Battista. *Opere volgari*, ed. Cecil Grayson. 3 vols. Bari: Laterza, 1960.
———. *Della Famiglia*, trans. R. N. Watkins as *The Family in Renaissance Florence*. Columbia: University of South Carolina Press, 1969.
Antoniano, Silvio. *Dell'educatione cristiana de' figliuoli libri III*. Verona: Sebastiano delle Donne, 1584.
———. *Dell'educatione cristiana de' figliuoli libri III*. Cremona: C. Diaconi, 1609.
Aquinas, Thomas. *Summa Theologica*, trans. Fathers of the English Dominican Province. London: R. T. Washburne, 1918.
Aretino, Pietro. *Ragionamenti*, ed. Paolo Procaccioli. Milan: Garzanti, 1984.

Aristotle. *Aristoteles' Politik*, ed. Alois Dreizehnter. Studia et Testimonia Antiqua, vol. 7. Munich: Wilhelm Fink Verlag, 1970.

————. *The Politics and the Constitution of Athens*, ed. Stephen Everson. Cambridge Texts in the History of Political Thought. Cambridge: Cambridge University Press, 1996.

Beatrice del Sera. *Amor di virtù: Commedia in cinque atti*, ed. Elissa B. Weaver. Ravenna: Longo, 1990.

Belmonte, Pietro. *Institution del la sposa del caualier Pietro Belmonte ariminese, fatta principlamente per madonna Laudomia*. Rome: Heredi di Giouanni Osmarino Gigliotto, 1587.

Benedetto da Mantova. *Il beneficio di Cristo*, ed. S. Caponetto. De Kalb: Northern Illinois University Press, 1972.

Borghini, Rafaello. *Il riposo*. Florence: G. Marescotti, 1584.

Borghini, Vincenzio. *Considerationi sopra l'allogare le donne delli Innocenti fuora del maritare o monacare*, ed. Gaetano Bruscoli. Florence: E. Ariani, 1904.

————. *Il Carteggio di Vincenzio Borghini*, ed. Daniela Francalanci, Franca Pellegrini, and Eliana Carrara. Florence: Società per Edizioni Scelte, 2001.

Buonarotti, Michelangelo. *Il Carteggio di Michelangelo*, ed. P. Barocchi and R. Ristori. 5 vols. Florence: Studio per Edizioni Scelte, 1965–83.

Cantini, Lorenzo, comp. *Legislazione toscana raccolta e illustrata*, 32 vols. Florence: Pietro Fantosini, 1800–8.

Castiglione, Baldassare. *The Book of the Courtier*, trans. George Bull. London: Penguin, 1967, repr. 1976.

Concilium Tridentinum: Diarorum, Actorum, Epistularum, Tractatuum nova collectio, ed. Societas Goerresianae. Fribourg: Herder, 1901.

Dominici, Giovanni. *Regola del governo di cura familiare*. Florence: A. Garinei, 1860, trans. and abridged by A. B. Coté as *On the Education of Children*. Washington, DC: Catholic University of America Press, 1927.

Erasmus, Desiderius. *Desiderii Erasmi Roterodami opera omnia*, ed. J. Le Clerc. Leiden: Pieter van der Aa, 1703–6.

————. *A Book Called in Latin Enchiridion Milites Christiani*. London: Methuen, 1905.

————. *Colloquies*, trans. and annotated by Craig R. Thompson. Toronto: University of Toronto Press, 1997, 1: 88–108.

Fara, Giovanni Francesco. *Tractatus de essentia infantis, proximi infanti, & proximi pubertati*. Florence: apud Juntas, 1567.

Ferrari, Ognibene. *De arte medica infantium, libri quatuor*. Brescia: apud Petrum Mariam Marchetti, 1598.

Firenzuola, Agnolo. *On the Beauty of Women*, ed. and trans. Konrad Eisenbichler and Jacqueline Murray. Philadelphia: University of Pennsylvania Press, 1992.

Firpo, Massimo, and Marcatto, Dario, eds. *Il processo inquisitoriale del cardinal Giovanni Morone*. Rome: Istituto storico italiano per l'età moderna e contemporenea, 1981–9.

Flaminio, Giovanni Antonio. *Dialogus de education liberorum ac institutione*. Bologna: G. de Benedetti, 1523.

Folco, Giulio, comp. *Effetti mirabili de la limosina. Le sentenze degne di memoria appartenenti ad essa*. Rome: Zanetti, 1586.

Fonte, Moderata. *The Worth of Women: Wherein Is Clearly Revealed Their Nobility and Superiority to Men*, trans. Virginia Cox. The Other Voice in Early Modern Europe. Chicago: University of Chicago Press, 1997.

Frey, Karl. *Der litterarische Nachlass Giorgio Vasaris.* Munich: G. Müller, 1923.

Gaye, Johann, ed. *Carteggio inedito d'artisti de secoli XIV, XIV, XVI.* Florence: Giuseppe Molini, 1839.

Giovanni di Dio da Venezia. *Decor puellarum: zoe honore de la donzelle la quale da regola, forma, e modo al stato de le honeste.* Venezia: Magistrum Nicolaum Jenson, 1471.

Giovanni Gherardi da Prato, *Il Paradiso degli Alberti,* ed. A. Lanza. Rome: Salerno, 1975.

Giuliano de'Ricci. *Cronaca (1532–1606),* ed. G. Sapori. Milan/Naples: Riccardo Ricciardi, 1972.

Griffiths, G., Hankins, F., and Thompson, D., eds. *The Humanism of Leonardo Bruni: Selected Texts.* Binghamton, NY: Medieval and Renaissance Texts and Studies, 1987, 311.

Jerome. *Lettera a Leta o dell'educazione della figliuola,* trans. F. Bocchi. Modena: G. Ferraguti, 1930.

King, Margaret, and Rabil, Albert, eds. *Her Immaculate Hand.* Binghamton, NY: Medieval and Renaissance Texts and Studies, 1983.

Landucci, Luca. *Diario fiorentino dal 1450 al 1516, continuato da un Anonimo fino al 1542.* Florence: G. C. Sansoni, 1883.

Livy. *History of Rome,* trans. B. O. Foster. Cambridge: Loeb Classical Editions of Harvard University Press, 1976.

Lombardelli, Orazio. *Degli uffizi e costumi de' giovani, libri III.* Florence: G. Marescotti, 1579.

Machiavelli, Niccolò. *Opere,* ed. M. Bonfantini. La letteratura italiana: storia e testi, vol. 29. Milano, R. Ricciardi, 1954.

———. *The Prince,* ed. Daniel Donno. New York: Bantam, 1966.

Maiola, Serafina. *Vita della madre Felice Rasponi: scritta da una monaca nel MDLXX, e pubblicata da Corrado Ricci.* Bologna: Zanichelli, 1883.

Memmo, Giovanni Maria. *Dialogo del magn. caualiere M. Gio. Maria Memmo, nel quale dopo aclune filosofiche dispute si forma un perfetto Principe, et una perfetta Republica, e parimente in Senatore, un Cittadino, un soldato et un Mercante.* Venice: Gabriel Giolito di Ferrari, 1563.

Morandini, Francesca. "Statuti e Ordinamenti dell'Ufficio dei pupilli et adulti nel periodo della Repubblica fiorentina (1388–1534)." *Archivio Storico Italiano* 113 (1955): 522–51, 114 (1956): 92–117, and 115 (1957): 87–104.

Morelli, Giovanni di Pagolo. *Ricordi,* ed. Vittorio Branca. Florence: Le Monnier, 1956.

Nacchianti, Iacopo. *Tractatus de episcoporum residentia: ex divinis literis* Venice [s.n.], 1554.

———. *Enarrationes piae, doctae, et catholicae, in Epistolam Pauli ad Ephesios . . . per R. P. et D. Iacobum Naclantum Episcopum Clugiensem* Venice: apud Iosephum Vincentinum, 1557.

———. *Enarratio Maximi Pontificatus, Maximive Sacerdotii: Necnon augustissimi ac Felicissimi Regni Iesu Christi Servatoris nostri* Venice: [s.n.], 1557.

———. *Opus doctum ac resolutum in quatuor tractatus, seu quaestiones dissectum: In quo ex naturali lumine et peripatetico fonte, eorum Philosophorum revincuntur errores, qui asserunt ex philosophie principiis, haberi non posse, creationem rerum, immortalitatem animae, contingentiam in universo, et vigorem in infinitum, in primo principio.* Venice: apud Iosephum Vincentinum, 1557.

———. *Scripturae Medulla.* Venice: [s.n.], 1561.

————. *De episcoporum residentia ad sanctissimos Patres in Concilio.. Enarratio seu tractatio compendiaria habita in generali congregatione,* Venice: [s.n.], 1562.

————. *De Papae ac Concilii potestate compendiaria enarratio tractatiove.* Venice: Lucantonio Giunti Heredi, 1562.

————. *Iacobi Naclanti Clugiensis Episcopi Operum tomus primus [-secundus] . . . omnia nunc ex sacrae paginae fonte eruta, & ad piae atque orthodoxae fidei veritatem conscripta.* Venice: apud Iuntas, 1567.

Palmieri, Matteo. *Della vita civile.* Biblioteca scelta di opere Italiane antiche e moderne, vol. 160. Milan: G. Silvestri, 1825.

Piccolomini, Alessandro. *De la institutione di tutta la vita de l'homo nato nobile e in citta libera, libri X. in lingua toscana: dove e peripateticamente e Platonicame[n]te, intorno à le cose de l'etica, iconomica, e parte de la politica, è raccolta la somma di quanto principalmente può concorrere à la perfetta e felice uita di quello.* Florence: apud Hieronymum Scotum, 1543.

————. *Diaologo de la bella creanza de le donne,* in *Trattati del cinquecento sulla donna,* ed. Giuseppe Zonta. Bari: Laterza, 1913.

Plato. *Platon, Ouevres completes,* ed. E. Chambry. Paris: Les Belles Lettres, 1967.

————. *Republic,* trans. G. M. A. Grube, rev. C. D. C. Reeve. Indianapolis: Hackett, 1992.

Ragionamento sopra le pompe della citta di Bologna; nel quale anco si discorre sopra le perle, i banchetti, et corsi che si fanno per la città. Bologna: S. Mamolo, 1568.

Razzi, Serafino. *Istoria de gli uomini illustri così nelle prelature Come nelle Dottrine, del Sacro ordine degli Predicatori. Scritta da F. Serafino Razzi dell'istesso ordine, e Dottore Theologo, della Prouincia Romana.* Lucca: Per il Busdrago, 1596.

Razzi, Silvano. *Della economica Christiana e civile di Don Silvani Razzi: I dve primi libri Ne i quali da vna nobile brigata di Donne e huomini si ragiona della cura, e governo famigliare: secondo la legge Christiana, e vita Ciuile.* Florence: Bartolomeo Sermartelli, 1568.

————. *Trattato dell'opere di misericordia, e corporali, e spirituali. Del padre don Siluano Razzi monaco camaldolense.* Florence: Bartolomeo Sermartelli, 1576.

Riforma delli statuti degli Uficiali de' Pupilli, fatta il di 20 d'Agosto 1565. Con l'aggiunte sino al presente anno 1575. Florence: Giunti, 1575.

Rousseau, Jean-Jacques. *Reveries of a Solitary Walker,* trans. Charles E. Butterworth. Indianapolis: Hackett Publishing, 1992.

Schroeder, H. J., ed. *Canons and Decrees of the Council of Trent.* St. Louis: Herder, 1941.

Statuta populi et communis Florentiae: publica auctoritate, collecta, castigata et praeposita anno salutis MCCCCXV, Fribourg: Michaelem Kluch, [1778]–83.

Tasso, Torquato. *Dialoghi,* ed. Ezio Raimondi. Florence: G. C. Sansoni, 1958.

Tommasi, Francesco. *Reggimento del padre di famiglia.* Florence: Giorgio Marescotti, 1580.

Varchi, Benedetto. *Opere di Benedetto Varchi.* 2 vols. Trieste: Lloyd Austriaco, 1858.

Vasari, Giorgio. *Le vite de' piu eccellenti pittori, scultori, e architettori.* Florence: Tipografia Giunta, 1568.

Vives, Juan Luis, *De institutione foeminae Christianae.* Antwerp/Cologne: Apud Michaelem Hillenium Hoochstratanum, 1524.

————. *De la institution de la femina Christiana, vergine maritata, o vedova.* Venice: appresso Vincenzo Vaugris, 1546.

————. *The Education of a Christian Woman,* ed. and trans. Charles Fantazzi. The Other Voice in Early Modern Europe. Chicago: University of Chicago Press, 2000.

Xenophon, *La Economica di Xenofonte, tradotta da lingua greca in lingua toscana, dal S. Alessan-dro Piccolmini, altrimenti lo Stordito Intronato*, trans. Alessandro Piccolomini. Venice: Comin dal Trino, 1540.

———. *Oeconomicus: A Social and Historical Commentary*, trans. Sarah B. Pomeroy. Oxford: Clarendon Press, 1994.

Zonta, Giuseppe, ed. *Trattati del cinquecento sulla donna*. Bari: Laterza, 1913.

SECONDARY SOURCES

Adelson, Candace. "Cosimo I and the Foundation of Tapestry Production in Florence." In *Firenze e la Toscana dei Medici nell'Europa del Cinquecento*, ed. Gian Carlo Garfagnini. Florence: Leo S. Olschki, 1983, 3: 899–924.

Arcangeli, Letizia. "Ragioni politiche della disciplina monastica. Il caso di Parma tra quattro e cinquecento." In *Donna, disciplina, creanza cristiana*, ed. Gabriella Zarri. Rome: Edizioni di Storia e Letteratura, 1996, 165–87.

Ariès, Philippe. *Centuries of Childhood: A Social History of Family Life*. New York: Vintage, 1962.

Arru, Angela. "Il matrimonio tardivo dei servi e delle serve." *Quaderni Storici* 23 (1988): 469–96.

Assirelli, Marco, et al. *San Lorenzo: i documenti e i tesori nascosti*. Venice: Marsilio, 1993.

Baker, Joanne. "Female Monasticism and Family Strategy: The Guises and Saint Pierre de Reims." *Sixteenth Century Journal 28.4*, 1997: 1091–108.

Banker, James. *The Culture of San Sepolcro during the Youth of Piero della Francesca*. Ann Arbor: University of Michigan Press, 2003.

Barrochi, Paola. "Appunti su Francesco Morandini." *Mitteilungen des Kunsthistorischen Institutes in Florenz*, 11 (1964): 117–48.

Barzman, Karen-edis. *The Florentine Academy and the Early Modern State: The Discipline of Disegno*. Cambridge: Cambridge University Press, 2000.

Baskins, Cristelle. *Cassone Painting, Humanism, and Gender, in Early Modern Italy*. Cambridge: Cambridge University Press, 1998.

Baxandall, Michael, *Painting and Experience in Fifteenth-Century Italy*. Oxford: Clarendon Press, 1970.

Becker, Marvin. "Aspects of Lay Piety in Early Renaissance Florence." In *The Pursuit of Holiness in Late Medieval and Renaissance Religion*, ed. C. Trinkaus and H. Oberman. Leiden: E.J. Brill, 1974, 177–99.

———. *Civility and Society in Western Europe,1300–1600*. Bloomington: Indiana University Press, 1989.

———. *The Emergence of Civil Society in the Eighteenth Century: A Privileged Moment in the History of England, Scotland, and France*. Bloomington: Indiana University Press, 1994.

Belloni, Gino, Drusi, Riccardo, and Calcagni-Abrami, Artemisia, eds. *Vincenzio Borghini: filologia e invenzione nella Firenze di Cosimo I*. Florence: Leo S. Olschki, 2002.

Benadusi, Giovanna. *A Provincial Elite in Early Modern Tuscany: Family and Power in the Creation of the State*. Baltimore/London: Johns Hopkins University Press, 1996.

Berengo, Marino. "Un agronomo tocscano del cinquecento: Francesco Tommasi da Colle val d'Elsa." In *Studi di storia medievale e moderna per Ernesto Sestan*. 2 vols. Florence: Leo S. Olschki, 1980, 2: 500–7.

Bizzochi, Roberto. "Stato e/o potere: Una lettera a Giorgio Chittolini." *Storia e politica*, 3 (1990): 55–64.

Black, Robert. "The Curriculum of Italian Elementary and Grammar Schools." In *The Shapes of Knowledge from the Renaissance to the Enlightenment*, ed. Donald Kelley and Richard Popkin. Archives Internationales d'Histoire des Idèes, vol. 124. Dordrecht/Boston/London: Kluwer Academic, 1991, 137–64.

———. *Studio e scuola in Arezzo durante il medioevo e il rinascimento: i documenti d'archivio fino al 1530*. Florence: Leo S. Olschki, 1996.

Blok, Anton. "Notes on the Concept of Virginity in Mediterranean Societies." In *Women and Men in Spiritual Culture, XIV–XVII Centuries: A Meeting of North and South*, ed. Elisja Schulte van Kessel. The Hague: Netherlands Government Printing Office, 1986, 27–33.

Blum, Rudolf. *La biblioteca della Badia fiorentina e i codici di Antonio Corbinelli*. Studi e Testi, vol. 155. Vatican City: Biblioteca Apostolica Vaticana, 1951.

Bornstein, Daniel. "Giovanni Dominici, the Bianchi and Venice: Symbolic Action and Interpretive Grids." *Journal of Medieval and Renaissance Studies* 23 (1993): 143–71.

———. "Le donne di Giovanni Dominici: un caso nella recezione e trasmissione dei messaggi religiosi." *Studi medievali* 36 (1995) 355 61.

Bourdieu, Pierre. "Les stratégies matrimoniales dans le système de reproduction." *Annales: Economies, Sociétés, Civilisations* 22 (1972): 1105–27.

———. *Outline of a Theory of Practice*, trans. Richard Nice. Cambridge Studies in Social Anthropology, vol. 16. Cambridge: Cambridge University Press, 1977.

Branca, Vittorio. *Linee d'una storia della critica al Decamerón*. Florence: Società anonima editrice Dante Alighieri, 1939.

Braudel, Fernand. *The Mediterranean and the Mediterranean World in the Age of Philip II*, trans. Sian Reynolds. 2 vols. New York: Harper and Row, 1972.

Brown, Judith. "Concepts of Political Economy: Cosimo I de' Medici in a Comparative European Context." In *Firenze e la Toscana dei Medici nell'Europa del Cinquecento*, ed. C. Garfagnini. 3 vols. Florence: Leo S. Olschki, 1983, 1: 279–93.

———. "Monache a Firenze all'inizio dell'età moderna. Un analisi comparata," *Quaderni Storici* 85 (1994) 117–52.

Bruscoli, Gaetano. *Lo Spedale di Santa Maria degli Innocenti dall sua fondazione ai nostri giorni*. Florence: E. Ariani, 1900.

———. *L'archivio del regio spedale di Santa Maria degli Innocenti*. Florence: Società Colombaria, 1911.

Bulman, Louisa M. "Artistic Patronage at SS. Annunziata, ca. 1440–1520." Ph.D diss., University of London, 1971.

Burke, Peter. *A Historical Anthropology of Early Modern Italy*. Cambridge: Cambridge University Press, 1987.

———. *The Fortunes of the Courtier: The European Reception of Castiglione's Cortegiano*. Cambridge: Cambridge University Press, 1995.

Buschbell, Gottfried. *Reformation und Inquisition in Italien um die Mitte des 16 Jahrunderts Quellen und forschungen aus dem gebeite der geschichte*. Paderborn: F. Schöning, 1910.

Calvi, Giulia. *Il contratto morale: Madre e figli nella Toscana moderna*. Bari: Laterza, 1994.

Carcereri, Luigi. "Fra Giacomo Nacchianti vescovo di Chioggia e fra Girolamo da Siena inquisiti per eresia." *Nuovo Archivio Veneto* 21 (1911): 468–89.

Cavallo, Sandra, and Cerruti, Simona. "Onore femminile e controllo sociale della riproduzione in Piemonte tra Sei e Settecento." *Quaderni Storici* 44 (1980): 346–83. Repr. and trans. in *Sex and Gender in Historical Perspective*, ed. G. Ruggiero and E. Muir. Baltimore: Johns Hopkins University Press, 1990, 73–109.

———. "Bambini abbandonati e bambini 'in deposito' a Torino nel settecento." In *Enfance abandonnée et société en Europe, XIVe–XXe siècle*. Collection de l'Ecole Française de Rome, no. 140. Rome: Ecole Française de Rome, 1991, 341–75.

———. *Charity and Power in Early Modern Italy: Benefactors and Their Motives in Turin, 1541–1789*. Cambridge: Cambridge University Press, 1995.

Cavazzini, Laura. "Dipinti e sculture nelle chiese dell'Ospedale." In *Gli Innocenti e Firenze nei secoli: un ospedale, un archivio, una città*, ed. Lucia Sandri. Florence: Studio per Edizioni Scelte, 1996, 113–50.

Cecchi, Alessandro. "Borghini, Vasari, Naldini e la 'Giuditta' del 1564." *Paragone* 28 (1977): 100–7.

Cerreto, Florindo. *Alessandro Piccolomini: letterato e filosofo senese del Cinquecento*. Siena: Accademia Senese degli Intronati, 1960.

Chabot, Isabelle. "Widowhood and Poverty in Late Medieval Florence." *Continuity and Change* 3 (1988): 291–311.

———. "La dette des familles: femmes, lignages, et patrimonies à Florence aux XIVe et XVe siècles." Ph.D. diss., European University Institute, Florence, 1995.

———, and Fornasari, Massimo. *L'economica della carità*. Bologna: Il Mulino, 1997.

Chiecchi, Giuseppe. *"Dolcemente Dissimulando": Cartelle Laurenziane e ≪Decameron≫ censurato (1573)*. Padua: Antenore, 1992.

Chittolini, Giorgio. "Il privato, lo pubblico e lo stato." In *Origini dello stato: Processi di formazione statale in Italia fra medioevo ed età moderna*, ed. G. Chittolini, A. Molho, and P. Schiera. Bologna: Il Mulino, 1994, 553–90.

Chittolini, G., Molho, A., and Schiera, P., eds. *Origini dello stato: Processi di formazione statale in Italia fra medioevo ed età moderna*. Bologna: Il Mulino, 1994.

Chojnacki, Stanley. "Dowries and Kinsmen in Early Renaissance Venice." *Journal of Interdisciplinary History* 5 (1975): 571–600. Repr. in *Women in Medieval Society*, ed. Susan M. Stuard. Philadelphia: University of Pennsylvania Press, 1976, 173–98.

Cipolla, Carlo. *Money in Sixteenth-Century Florence*. Berkeley/Los Angeles/London: University of California Press, 1989.

La civiltà del torneo (sec. XII–XVII): Giostre e Tornei fra medioevo ed età moderna, Atti del VII convegno (Narni, 14–16.10.1988). Narni: Centro studi storici di Narni, 1990.

Clover, Catherine. "Documentation on Naldini's Ascension for S. Maria del Carmine in Florence." *The Burlington Magazine* 141 (1999): 615–17.

Cochrane, Eric. *Florence in the Forgotten Centuries, 1527–1800*. Chicago/London: University of Chicago Press, 1973.

———. *Historians and Historiography in the Italian Renaissance*. Chicago: University of Chicago Press, 1981.

Cohen, Sherrill. *"The Convertite and the Malmaritate: Women's Institutions, Prostitution, and the Family in Counter Reformation Florence."* Ph.D. diss., Princeton University, 1985.

———. *The Evolution of Women's Asylums Since 1600: From Refuges for Ex-Prostitutes to Shelters for Battered Women*. New York/Oxford: Oxford University Press, 1992.

Cohn, Samuel, K. *Death and Property in Siena, 1205–1800: Strategies for the Afterlife*. Baltimore: Johns Hopkins University Press, 1988.

———. "Donne e controriforma a Siena: autorità e proprietà nella famiglia." *Studi Storici* 29.1 (1989): 203–24.

———. *The Cult of Remembrance and the Black Death: Six Renaissance Cities in Central Italy*. Baltimore: Johns Hopkins University Press, 1992.

Corsini, Carlo. "'Era piovuto dal cielo e la terra l'aveva raccolto': il destino del trovatello." In *Enfance Abandonee et Societe, XIVe–XXe siècle: Actes du colloque international*. Collection de l'École Française de Rome 140. Rome: École Française de Rome, 1991, 81–119.

Covi, Dario. "A Documented Altarpiece by Cosimo Rosselli." *The Art Bulletin* 53.2 (1971): 236–8.

Cox, Virginia. "The Single Self: Feminist Thought and the Marriage Market in Early-Modern Venice." *Renaissance Quarterly* 48.3 (1995): 513–81.

———. *Women's Writing in Italy, 1400–1650*. Baltimore: Johns Hopkins University Press, 2008.

Crabb, Ann. *The Strozzi of Florence: Widowhood and Family Solidarity in the Renaissance*. Ann Arbor: University of Michigan Press, 2000.

Cracco, Giorgio. *Dizionario biografico degli italiani 5: 657 667*, s.v. 'Banchini, Giovanni di Domenico.'

D'Addario, Arnaldo. *Aspetti della controriforma a Firenze*. Rome: Ministero dell'Interno, 1972.

———. *La formazione dello stato moderno in Toscana*. Lecce: Adriatica editrice salentina, 1976.

D'Amelia, M. "La conquista di una dote: Regole del gioco e scambi femminili alla confraternità dell'Annunziata (sec. XVII–XVIII)." In *Ragnatele di rapporti. Patronage e reti di realzioni nella storia delle donne*, ed. L. Ferrante, M. Palazzi, and G. Pomata. Turin: Rosenberg and Sellier, 1988, 305–43.

Davis, Natalie Zemon. "Poor Relief, Humanism, and Heresy: The Case of Lyons." *Studies in Medieval and Renaissance History* 5 (1968): 217–69.

———. "Printing and the People." In Natalie Zemon Davis, *Society and Culture in Early Modern France: Eight Essays*. Stanford: Stanford University Press, 1975.

———. *Society and Culture in Early Modern France: Eight Essays*. Stanford: Stanford University Press, 1975.

Davis, Robert. *Shipbuilders in the Venetian Arsenal: Workers and Workplace in the Preindustrial City. Johns Hopkins University Studies in Historical and Political Science*, 109th series, no. 1. Baltimore: Johns Hopkins University Press, 1991.

De'Antoni, Dino. "A proposito di Erasmo e Nacchianti." *Chioggia: Rivista di studi e ricerche* 3.4 (1990): 176–9.

Debby, Nirit Ben-Aryeh. *Renaissance Florence in the Rhetoric of Two Popular Preachers: Giovanni Dominici (1356–1419) and Bernardino da Siena (1380–1444)*. Late Medieval and Early Modern Studies, vol. 4. Turnhout: Brepols, 2001.

de Pace Anna. *Encyclopedia of the Renaissance*, vol. 5, s.v. "Alessandro Piccolomini."

di Agresti, Domenico. *Sviluppi della riforma monastica Savonaroliana*. Florence: L. S. Olschki, 1980

Duerr, Hans-Peter. *Nacktheit und Scham*, vol. 1 of *Der Mythos vom Zivilisationsprozeß*. Frankfurt-am-Mein: Suhrkamp, 1988–2002.

Eisenbichler, Konrad. *The Boys of the Archangel Raphael*. Toronto: University of Toronto Press, 1998.

Eisenstein, Elizabeth. "The Advent of Printing and the Problem of the Renaissance." *Past and Present* 45 (1969): 19–89.

———. *The Printing Press as an Agent of Change*. 2 vols. Cambridge: Cambridge University Press, 1979.

Elias, Norbert. *The Civilizing Process: The History of Manners*, trans. Edmund Jephcott. Oxford: Blackwell, 1994.

Enfance Abandonee et Societe, XIVe–XXe siècle: Actes du colloque international. Collection de l'École Française de Rome 140. Rome: École Française de Rome, 1991.

Epstein, S. R. "Cities, Regions and the Late Medieval Crisis." *Past and Present* 109 (1991): 3–50.

Esposito, Anna. "Le confraternite del matrimonio, carità, devozione, e bisogni sociali a Roma nel tardo Quattrocento." In *Un'idea di Roma, Società, arte, e cultura tra Umanesimo e Rinasimento*, ed. Laura Fortini, Roma nel Rinascimento. Rome: Vechiarelli, 1993, 7–51.

———. "Town and Country: Economy and Institutions in Late Medieval Italy." *Economic History Review* 46 (1993): 453–77.

Evangelisti, Silvia. "'We do not have it and we do not want it': Women, Power and Convent Reform in Florence." *Sixteenth Century Journal* 34.3 (2003): 677–700.

Fasano-Guarini, Elena, ed. *Un microcosmo in movimento (1494–1815)*. Vol. 2 of *Prato: Storia di una città*. Florence: Le Monnier for the Comune di Prato, 1986.

———. "Centro e periferia, accentramento e particolarismo: dicotomia o sustanza degli stati in età moderna." In *Origini dello stato*, ed. G. Chittolini, A. Molho, and P. Schiera. 147–76.

Ferraro, Joanne. *Marriage Wars in Late Renaissance Venice*. Studies in the History of Sexuality. Oxford: Oxford University Press, 2001.

Findlen, Paula. *Possessing Nature: Museums, Collecting, and Scientific Culture in Early Modern Italy*. Berkeley/Los Angeles: University of California Press, 1994.

Fischer, Colomban. "Jacques Nacchianti, O. P., évêque du Chioggia (Chiozza) + 1569 et sa théologie de la Primautè absolue du Christ." *La France Franciscaine* 20 (1937): 97–174.

Fisher, Caroline. "The State as Surrogate Father: State Guardianship in Renaissance Florence, 1368–1532." Ph.D diss., Brandeis University, 2003.

Foucault, Michel. *Madness and Civilization: A History of Insanity in the Age of Reason*, trans. R. Howard. New York: Vintage, 1961, repr. London/New York: Routledge, 2001.

———. *Discipline and Punish: The Birth of the Prison*, trans. A. Sheridan. New York: Pantheon Books, 1977.

Frajese, Vittorio. *Il popolo fanciullo: Silvio Antoniano e il sistema disciplinare della controriforma*. Milan: F. Angeli, 1987.

Francalanci, Daniela, and Pellegrini, Franca, eds. *Vincenzio Borghini, Carteggio 1541–1580: Censimento*. Florence: Accademia della Crusca, 1993.

Frigo, Daniele. *Il padre di famiglia: governo della casa e governo civile nella tradizione dell'«Economica» fra Cinque e Seicento*. Rome: Bulzoni, 1985.

Fubini-Leuzzi, Maria. "Vita Coniugale e vita familiare nei trattati Italiani fra XVI e XVII secolo." In *Donna, Disciplina, Creanza Cristiana*, ed. Gabriella Zarri. Rome: Edizioni di Storia e Letteratura, 1996, 253–67.

———. *Condurre a onore: famiglia, matrimonio, e assistenza dotale a Firenze in Età moderna*. Florence: Leo S. Olschki, 1999.

———. "Le ricevute di Francesco de' Medici a Vincenzio Borghini. La contabilità separata dello spedalingo degli Innocenti." *Archivio Storico Italiano* 140 (2002): 353–68.

Garfagnini, Carlo, ed. *Firenze e la Toscana dei Medici nell'Europa del '500*. 3 vols. Florence: Leo S. Olschki, 1983.

————. *Giorgio Vasari: tra decorazione ambientale e storiografia artistica. Convegno di studi (Arezzo, 8–10 ottobre 1981)*. Florence: Leo S. Olschki, 1985.

Gavitt, Philip. *Charity and Children in Renaissance Florence: The Ospedale degli Innocenti, 1410–1536*. Ann Arbor: University of Michigan Press, 1990.

————. "'Perchè non avea chi lo ghovernasse': Cultural Values, Family Resources and Abandonment in the Florence of Lorenzo de' Medici, 1467–85." In *Poor Women and Poor Children in the European Past*, ed. J. Henderson and R. Wall. London: Routledge, 1994, 65–93.

————. "Charity and State Building in Cinquecento Florence: Vincenzio Borghini as Administrator of the Ospedale degli Innocenti." *Journal of Modern History* 21 (1997): 230–70.

————. "An Experimental Culture: The Art of the Economy and the Economy of Art under Cosimo I and Francesco I." In *The Cultural Politics of Duke Cosimo de' Medici*, ed. Konrad Eisenbichler. Aldershot: Ashgate, 2001, 205–22.

————. "From *putte* to *puttane*: Female Foundlings and Charitable Institutions in Northern Italy, 1530–1630." In *At the Margins: Minority Groups in Premodern Italy*, ed. Stephen J. Milner. Minneapolis: University of Minnesota Press, 2005, 111–29.

————. "Corporate Beneficence and Historical Narratives of Communal Well-Being." In *Renaissance Florence: A Social History*, ed. Roger Crum and John Paoletti. Cambridge: Cambridge University Press, 2006, 138–60.

————. *A Moral Art: Grammar, Society, and Culture in Trecento Florence*. Ithaca: Cornell University Press, 1993.

Gehl, Paul F. "Libri per donne. Le monache clienti del libraio fiorentino Piero Morosi (1588–1607)." In *Donna, disciplina, creanza cristiana*, ed. Gabriella Zarri. Rome: Edizioni di Storia e Letteratura, 1996, 67–82.

Geiger, Gail L. *Filippino Lippi's Carafa Chapel: Renaissance Art in Rome. Sixteenth-Century Essays and Studies*, vol. 5. Kirksville: Sixteenth Century Journal, 1986.

Gibson, Craig, and Newton, Francis. "Pandulf of Capua's *De Calculatione*: An Illustrated Abacus Treatise and Some Evidence for the Hindu-Arabic Numerals in Eleventh-Century South Italy." *Medieval Studies* 57 (1995): 293–335.

Gilmore, David, ed. *Honor and Shame and the Unity of the Mediterranean*. Washington, DC: American Anthropological Association, 1987.

Ginzburg, Carlo. *The Cheese and the Worms: The Cosmos of a Sixteenth-Century Miller*. New York: Viking Penguin, 1982.

Giovanetti, Alessandra. *Francesco Morandini detto il Poppi*. Florence: EDIFIR, 1995.

Goldthwaite, Richard. "Schools and Teachers of Commercial Arithmetic in Renaissance Florence." *Journal of European Economic History* 1 (1972): 418–33.

————. *The Building of Renaissance Florence: An Economic and Social History*. Baltimore: Johns Hopkins University Press, 1980.

————. "Banking in Florence at the End of the Sixteenth Century." *Journal of European Economic History* 27.3 (1998): 471–536.

————. *The Economy of Renaissance Florence*. Baltimore: Johns Hopkins University Press, 2009.

————, and Rearick, W. Roger. "Michelozzo and the Ospedale di San Paolo in Florence." *Mitteilungen des Kunsthisorischen Institutes in Florenz* 21 (1977): 221–306.

Goody, J., and Tambiah, S. *Bridewealth and Dowry*. Cambridge: Cambridge University Press, 1973.

Grell, O. P., Cunningham, A., and Arrizabalaga J., eds. *Health Care and Poor Relief in Counter-Reformation Europe*. London/New York: Routledge, 1999.

Grendi, Edoardo. "Ideologia della carità e società indisciplinata: la costruzione del sistema assitenziale genovese (1470–1670)." In *Timore e carità: i poveri nell'Italia moderna*, ed. G. Politi, M. Rosa, and F. della Paruta. Atti del convegno "Pauperismo e assistenza negli antichi stati italiani," Cremona, 28–30 marzo 1980. Cremona: Libreria del Convegno Editrice, 1982, 59–75.

Grendler, Paul. *Schooling in Renaissance Italy: Literacy and Learning, 1300–1600*. Baltimore: Johns Hopkins University Press, 1989.

Hale, J. R. *Florence and the Medici: The Pattern of Control*. London: Thames and Hudson, 1977.

Hamburgh, Harvey. "Naldini's *Allegory of Dreams* in the Studiolo of Francesco de' Medici." *Sixteenth Century Journal* 27.3 (1996): 679–704.

Harline, Craig. *The Burdens of Sister Margaret*. New York: Doubleday, 1994.

Härter, Karl. "Disciplinamento sociale e ordinanze di polizia nella prima età moderna." In *Disciplina dell'anima, disciplina del corpo, e disciplina della società tra medioevo, ed età moderna*, ed. Paolo Prodi. Annali dell'Istituto storico italo-germanico di Trento, vol. 40. Bologna: Il Mulino, 1994, 635–58.

Henderson, John. "Charity and Welfare in Early Modern Tuscany." In *Health Care and Poor Relief in Counter-Reformation Europe*, ed. O. P. Grell, A. Cunningham, and J. Arrizabalaga. London/New York: Routledge, 1999, 56–86.

Hudon, William. *Marcello Cervini and Ecclesiastical Government*. De Kalb: Northern Illinois University Press, 1990.

Hughes, Diane. "From Brideprice to Dowry in Mediterranean Europe." *Journal of Family History* 3 (1978): 262–96.

Huizinga, J. *The Autumn of the Middle Ages*, trans. Rodney Payton and Ulrich Mammitzsch. Chicago: University of Chicago Press, 1996.

Jaher, Frederick, ed. *The Rich, the Well Born, and the Powerful*. Champaign: University of Illinois Press, 1964.

Jedin, Hubert. *A History of the Council of Trent*, trans. E. Graf. 2 vols. London: Thomas Nelson and Sons, 1961.

Jordan, Constance. *Renaissance Feminism: Literary Texts and Political Models*. Ithaca: Cornell University Press, 1990.

Kelley, Donald, and Popkin, Richard, eds. *The Shapes of Knowledge from the Renaissance to the Enlightenment*. Archives Internationales d'Histoire des Idèes, vol. 124. Dordrecht/Boston/London: Kluwer Academic, 1991.

Kendrick, Robert L. *Celestial Sirens: Nuns and Their Music in Early Modern Milan*. Oxford: Clarendon Press/New York: Oxford University Press, 1996.

Kent, F. W. "A Proposal by Savonarola for the Self-Reform of Florentine Women (March 1496)." *Memorie Domenicane* 14 (1983): 334–41.

Kertzer, David, and Saller, Richard, eds. *The Family in Italy from Antiquity to the Present*. New Haven: Yale University Press, 1991.

Kirshner, Julius. *Pursuing Honor while Avoiding Sin*. Milan: A. Giuffrè, 1978.

———. "Materials for a Gilded Cage: Non-Dotal Assets in Florence, 1300–1500." In *The Family in Italy from Antiquity to the Present*, ed. D. Kertzer and R. Saller. New Haven: Yale University Press, 1991, 184–207.

Klapisch-Zuber, C. *Women, Family, and Ritual in Renaissance Italy*, trans. Lydia Cochrane. Chicago: University of Chicago Press, 1985.

————. "Blood Parents and Milk Parents: Wet Nursing in Florence, 1300–1530." In *Women, Family, and Ritual in Renaissance Italy*, trans. Lydia Cochrane. Chicago: University of Chicago Press, 1985, 132–64.

————. "Holy Dolls: Play and Piety in Florence in the Quattrocento." In *Women, Family and Ritual in Renaissance Italy*, trans. Lydia Cochrane. Chicago: University of Chicago Press, 1985, 310–29.

————. "Women Servants in Florence." In *Women and Work in Pre-industrial Europe*, ed. Barbara Hanawalt. Bloomington: Indiana University Press, 1986, 56–80.

Knox, Dilwyn. "Disciplina: The Monastic and Clerical Origin of European Civility." In *Renaissance Society and Culture: Essays in Honor of Eugene F. Rice, Jr.*, ed. John Monfasani and Ronald G. Musto. New York: Italica Press, 1991, 107–35.

Kuehn, Thomas. *Emancipation in Late Medieval Florence*. New Brunswick, NJ: Rutgers University Press, 1982.

————. "Some Ambiguities of Female Inheritance Ideology in the Renaissance." *Continuity and Change* 2 (1987): 11–36. Reprinted in T. Kuehn, *Law, Family and Women: Toward a Legal Anthropology of Renaissance Italy*, Chicago/London: University of Chicago Press, 1991, 238–57.

————. "Women, Family, and *Patria Potestas* in Late Medieval Florence." *Tijdschrift voor Rechtsgeshiedenis* 49 (1981): 127–47. Reprinted in T. Kuehn, *Law Family and Women: Toward a Legal Anthropology of Renaissance Italy*. Chicago/London: University of Chicago Press, 1997, 197–211.

————. "Person and Gender in the Laws." In *Gender and Society in Renaissance Italy*, ed. Judith Brown and Robert C. Davis. London/New York: Longman, 1998, 86–107.

————. *Illegitimacy in Renaissance Florence*. Ann Arbor: University of Michigan Press, 2002.

Lansing, Carol. *The Florentine Magnates: Lineage and Faction in a Medieval Commune*. Princeton: Princeton University Press, 1991.

————. *Power and Purity: The Cathar Heresy in Medieval Italy*. Oxford/New York: Oxford University Press, 1998.

Lastri, Marco. *Ricerche sull'antica e moderna popolazione della città di Firenze per mezzi dei registri del battistero di San Giovanni dal 1451 al 1774*. Florence: Gaetano Cambiagi, 1775; repr. Florence: Le Lettere, 2001.

Legrenzi, A. *Vincenzo Borghini studio critico*. 2 vols. Udine: Tip. D. del Bianco, 1910.

Lesca, G. "Vincenzo Borghini e il Decameròn." *Miscellenea storica della Val d'Elsa* 21 (1913): 246–63.

Lesnick, Daniel. "Civic Preaching in the Early Renaissance: Dominici's Florentine sermons." In *Christianity in the Renaissance*, ed. John Henderson and Timothy Verdon. Syracuse: Syracuse University Press, 1990, 208–25.

Liebrich A. K. "Piarist Education in the Seventeenth Century." *Studi Secenteschi* 26 (1985): 225–77; 27 (1986): 57–88.

Litchfield, R. Burr. *Emergence of a Bureaucracy: The Florentine Patriciate, 1530–1790*. Princeton: Princeton University Press, 1986.

Lloyd, Genevieve. *The Man of Reason: "Male" and "Female" in Western Philosophy*. Minneapolis: University of Minnesota Press, 1984. 2nd ed. London: Routledge, 1993.

Lombardi, Daniela. "Poveri a Firenze: Programmi e realizzazioni della politica assistenziale dei Medici tra cinque e seicento." In *Timore e carità: i poveri nell'Italia moderna*, ed. G. Politi, M. Rosa, and F. della Paruta. Atti del convegno "Pauperismo e assistenza negli antichi stati italiani," Cremona, 28–30 marzo 1980. Cremona: Libreria del Convegno Editrice, 1982, 165–84.

————. *Povertà maschile, povertà femminile: L'Ospedale dei Mendicanti nella Firenze dei Medici*. Bologna: Il Mulino, 1988.

Lovett, A. W. "The Castilian Bankruptcy of 1575." *Historical Journal* 23 (1980): 899–911.

MacLean, Ian. *The Renaissance Notion of Woman*. Cambridge: Cambridge University Press, 1980.

Maddalena, A., and Kellenbenz, H., eds. *Finanze e ragion di stato in Italia e Germania nella prima età moderna*. Bologna: Il Mulino, 1984.

Mahfouz, Naguib. *Palace Walk*, trans. W. M. Hutchins and O. E. Kenny. New York: Anchor Books, 1991.

Majorana, Bernadette. "Finzioni, Initazioni, Azioni: Donne e Teatro." In *Donna, disciplina, creanza cristiana*, ed. Gabriella Zarri. Rome: Edizioni di Storia e letteraura, 1996, 121–39.

Makowski, Elizabeth. *Canon Law and Cloistered Women: Periculoso and Its Commentators, 1298–1545. Studies in Early Medieval and Canon Law*, vol. 5. Washington, DC: Catholic University of America Press, 1997.

Manno Tolu, Rosalia. "Ricordanze delle abbandonate fiorentine di Santa Maria e San Niccolo del Ceppo nei secoli XVII–XVIII." In *Studi in onore di Arnaldo d'Addario*, ed. L. Borgia. Lecce: Conte Editore, 1995, 3: 1007–24.

————. "Echi Savonaroliani nella Compagnia e nel conservatorio del Ceppo nei secoli XVII-XVIII." In *Savonarola e la politica*, ed. G. C. Garfagnini. Firenze: Edizioni del Galluzzo, 1997, 209–24.

Martin, John J. *Myths of Renaissance Individualism*. New York: Palgrave, 2006.

Martines, Lauro. *Lawyers and Statecraft in Renaissance Florence*. Princeton: Princeton University Press, 1968.

Matteini, Anna Maria Testaverde. "La biblioteca erudita di Don Vincenzo Borghini." In *Firenze e la Toscana dei Medici nell'Europa del Cinquecento*. 3 vols. Florence: Leo S. Olschki, 1983, 2: 611–43.

McGough, Laura Jane. "'From the Devil's Jaws': A Convent for Repentant Prostitutes in Venice, 1520–1670." Ph.D. diss., Northwestern University, 1997.

Meloni-Trkulja, Silvia. *I fiorentini nel 1562: descritione delle bocche della citttà et stato di Fiorenza fatto l'anno 1562*. Florence: Bruschi, 1991.

Menning, Carol Bresnahan. "Loans and Favors, Kin and Clients: Cosimo de' Medici and the Monte di Pietà." *Journal of Modern History* 61 (1989): 487–511.

————. *Charity and State in Late Renaissance Italy: The Monte di Pietà of Florence*. Ithaca/London: Cornell University Press, 1993.

Mitterauer, M., and Sieder, R. "The Reconstruction of the Family Life Course: Theoretical Problems and Empirical Results. In *Family Forms in Historic Europe*, ed. R. Wall, J. Robin, and P. Laslett. Cambridge: Cambridge University Press, 1983, 309–46.

Molà, Luca. "Artigiani e brevetti nella Firenze del Cinquecento." In *La grande storia dell'artigianato: vol. 3. Il Cinquecento*, ed. Franco Franceschi and Gloria Fossi. Florence: Giunti, 2000, 57–79.

Molho, Anthony. "Deception and Marriage Strategy in Renaissance Florence: The Case of Women's Ages." *Renaissance Quarterly* 41 (1988): 193–217.

————. "Lo Stato e la finanza pubblica. Un'ipotesi basata sulla storia tardo mediovale di Firenze." In *Origini dello stato: Processi di formazione statale in Italia fra medioevo ed età moderna*, ed. G. Chittolini, A. Molho, and P. Schiera. Bologna: Il Mulino, 1994, 225–80.

————. *Marriage Alliance in Late Renaissance Florence*. Cambridge: Harvard University Press, 1994.

Monfasani, John, and Musto, Ronald G. eds. *Renaissance Society and Culture: Essays in Honor of Eugene F. Rice, Jr.* New York: Italica Press, 1991.

Monson, Craig. "Elena Malvezzi's Keyboard Manuscript: A New Sixteenth-Century Source." *Early Music History* 9 (1989): 73–128.

————. *Disembodied Voices: Music and Culture in an Early Modern Italian Convent*. Berkeley/ Los Angeles: University of California Press, 1995.

Morelli, Roberta. *La seta fiorentina nel cinquecento*. Milan: A. Giuffrè 1976.

Mozzato, Pietro Jacopo Nacchianti: un vescovo riformatore (Chioggia 1544–1569)*. Chioggia: Edizioni Nuova Scintilla, 1993.

Najemy, John. "Giannozzo and His Elders Alberti's Critique of Renaissance Patriarchy." In *Society and Individual in Renaissance Florence*, ed. William J. Connell. Berkeley and Los Angeles: University of California Press, 2002, 51–78.

Navarrini, Roberto, and Belfanti, Carlo Marco, "Il Problema della povertà nel ducato di Mantova: Aspetti istituzionali e problemi sociali" (secoli XIV–XVI). In *Timore e carità: i poveri nell'Italia moderna*. Atti del convegno "Pauperismo e assistenza negli antichi stati italiani," Cremona, 28–30 marzo 1980, ed. G. Politi, M. Rosa, and F. della Paruta. Cremona: Libreria del Convegno Editrice, 1982, 121–36.

Niccolai, Franco. *La formazione del diritto successorio negli statui comunali del territorio lombardo-tosco*. Milan: A. Giuffrè, 1940.

Niccoli, Ottavia. *Il seme della violenza: putti, fanciulli, e mammoli nell'Italia tra cinque e seicento*. Bari: Laterza, 1995.

Noonan, John T. *The Scholastic Analysis of Usury*. Cambridge: Harvard University Press, 1957.

Oestreich, Gerhardt. *Neostoicism and the early Modern State. Cambridge Studies in Early Modern History*. Cambridge: Cambridge University Press, 1983.

O'Malley, John W. "Some Renaissance Panegyrics of Aquinas." *Renaissance Quarterly* 27.2 (1974): 174–92.

————. *The First Jesuits*. Cambridge/London: Harvard University Press, 1993.

Ong, Walter. *Ramus, Method, and the Decay of Dialogue: From the Art of Discourse to the Art of Reason*. Cambridge, MA: Harvard University Press, 1958, repr. 1983.

Ortner, Sherry "The Virgin and the State," *Feminist Studies* 4.3 (1978): 19–35.

Pansini, Giuseppe. "I conservatori di leggi e la difesa dei poveri nelle cause civili durante il Principato Mediceo." In *Studi di storia medievale e moderna per Ernesto Sestan*. 2 vols. Florence: Leo S. Olschki, 1980, 2: 529–70.

Parker, Charles H. "The Moral Agency and Moral Autonomy of Church Folk in Post-Reformation Delft, 1520–1620." *Journal of Ecclesiastical History* 48 (1997): 44–70

Partridge, Loren, and Starn, Randolph. *Arts of Power: Three Halls of State in Renaissance Italy*. Berkeley: University of California Press, 1992.

Passerini, Luigi. *Storia degli stabilmenti di beneficenza ed istruzione elementare gratuita della città di Firenze*. Florence: LeMonnier, 1853.

Pierattini, Giovanna. "Suor Fiammetta Frescobaldi: cronista del monastero di Sant'Iacopo a Ripoli in Firenze (1523–1586)." *Memorie Domenicane* 56 (1939): 101–268.

Pilliod, Elizabeth. *Pontormo, Bronzino, Allori: A Genealogy of Florentine Art.* New Haven/London: Yale University Press, 2001.

Plebani, Tiziana. "Nascita e caratteristiche del pubblico di lettrici tra medioevo e prima età moderna." In *Donna, disciplina, creanza cristiana,* ed. Gabriella Zarri. Rome: Edizioni di Storia e letteratura, 1996, 23–44.

Politi, G., Rosa, M., and della Paruta, F., eds. *Timore e carità: i poveri nell'Italia moderna.* Atti del convegno "Pauperismo e assistenza negli antichi stati italiani," Cremona, 28–30 marzo 1980. Cremona: Libreria del Convegno Editrice, 1982.

Polizzotto Lorenzo. *The Elect Nation: The Savonarolan Movement in Florence 1494–1545.* Oxford: Clarendon Press, 1994.

———. *Children of the Promise: The Confraternity of the Purification and the Socialization of Youths in Florence 1427–1785.* Oxford-Warburg Studies. New York: Oxford University Press, 2004.

Pomeroy, Sarah. *Goddesses, Whores, Wives and Slaves: Women in Classical Antiquity.* New York: Schocken Books, 1975.

Pozzi, Mario. *Lingua e cultura del Cinquecento: Dolce, Aretino, Machiavelli, Guicciardini, Sarpi, Borghini.* Padua: Liviana, 1975.

Prodi, Paolo ed., *Disciplina dell'anima, disciplina del corpo, e disciplina della società tra medioevo, ed età moderna.* Annali dell'Istituto storico italo-germanico di Trento, vol. 40. Bologna: Il Mulino, 1994.

Pullan, Brian. *The Jews and the Inquisition of Venice.* London: I. B. Tauris, 1983.

Pullapilly, Cyriac K. "Agostino Valier and the Conceptual Basis of the Catholic Reformation." *Harvard Theological Review* 85.3 (1992): 307–33.

Queller, Donald, and Madden, Thomas F. "Father of the Bride: Fathers, Daughters, and Dowries in Late Medieval and Early Renaissance Venice." *Renaissance Quarterly* 46 (1993): 685–711.

Reinhard, Wolfgang. "Disciplinamento sociale, confessionalizzazione, modernizzazione: Un discorso storiographico." In *Disciplina dell'anima, disciplina del corpo, e disciplina della società tra medioevo, ed età moderna,* ed. Paolo Prodi. Annali dell'Istituto storico italo-germanico di Trento, vol. 40. Bologna: Il Mulino, 1994, 101–23.

Rocke, Michael. *Forbidden Friendships: Homosexuality and Male Culture in Renaissance Florence.* Oxford: Oxford University Press, 1996.

———. "Gender and Sexual Culture in Renaissance Italy." In *Gender and Society in Renaissance Italy,* ed. Judith Brown and Robert Davis. New York/London: Longman, 1998, 150–170.

Romanello, Marina. "Essere bambine cel Cinquecento: modelli educativi tra continuità e innovazione." In *Le bambine nella storia dell'educazione,* ed. Simonetta Ulivieri. Rome/Bari: Editori Laterza, 1999, 111–47.

Rose, Mary Beth, ed. *Women in the Middle Ages and the Renaissance: Literary and Historical Perspectives.* Syracuse: Syracuse University Press, 1986.

Rosselli, John. *Singers of Italian Opera: The History of a Profession.* Cambridge: Cambridge University Press, 1995.

Rubin, Patricia. *Giorgio Vasari: Art and History.* New Haven: Yale University Press, 1995.

Safley, Thomas Max. *Charity and Economy in the Orphanages of Early Modern Augsburg. Studies in Central European History.* Atlantic Highlands, NJ: Humanities Press, 1996.

The Saint Louis Art Museum Handbook of the Collections. St. Louis: The Museum, 1991.

Saller, Richard P. "Roman Heirship Strategies. In Principle and in Practice." In *The Family in Italy from Antiquity to the Present,* ed. D. Kertzer and R. Saller. New Haven: Yale University Press, 1991, 26–47.

Sandri, Lucia. "L'assistenza nei primi due secoli di attività." In *Gli Innocenti e Firenze nei secoli: Un'ospedale un archivio, una città,* ed. Lucia Sandri. Florence: Studio per Edizioni Scelte, 1996.

―――. "L'attività di Banco di deposito dell'ospedale degli Innocenti di Firenze: don Vincenzio Borghini e la 'bancarotta' del 1579." In *L'uso del denaro: Patrimoni e amministrazione nei luoghi pii e negli enti ecclesiastici in Italia (secoli XV–XVIII),* ed. Marina Garbelotti and Alessandro Pastore. Bologna: Il Mulino, 2001, 153–78.

Sarton, George. "Incunabula Wrongly Dated. Fifteen Examples with Eighteen Illustrations." *Isis* 40.3 (August 1949): 227–40.

Schilling, Heinz. "Chiese confessionali e disciplinamento sociale: Un bilancio provvisorio della ricerca storica." In *Disciplina dell'anima, disciplina del corpo, e disciplina della società tra medioevo, ed età moderna,* ed. Paolo Prodi. Annali dell'Istituto storico italo-germanico di Trento, vol. 40. Bologna: Il Mulino, 1994, 125–60.

Schneider, Jane. "Of Vigilance and Virgins: Honour, Shame and Access to Resources in Mediterranean societies" *Ethnology* 9 (1971): 1–24.

Schutte, Anne Jacobson. "Legal Remedies for Forced Monachation in Early Modern Italy." In *Heresy, Culture, and Religion in Early Modern Italy,* ed. John Jeffries Martin. Kirksville: Truman State University Press, 2006, 231–44.

Scorza, Rick. "Vincenzo Borghini's Collection of Paintings, Drawings and Wax Models: New Evidence from Manuscript Sources." *Journal of the Warburg and Courtauld Institutes* 66 (2003): 63–122.

Sebregondi-Fiorentini, Ludovica. *Tre confraternite fiorentine: Santa Maria della Pietà, detta ≪Buca≫ di San Girolamo, San Filippo Benizi, San Francesco Poverino.* Florence: Salimbene, 1991.

Seidel-Menchi, Silvana. *Erasmo in Italia 1520–1580.* Turin: Bollati Boringheri, 1987.

Simoncelli, Paolo. "Note sul sistema assistenziale a Roma nel XVI secolo." In *Timore e carità: i poveri nell'Italia moderna.* Atti del convegno "Pauperismo e assistenza negli antichi stati italiani," Cremona, 28–30 marzo 1980, ed. G. Politi, M. Rosa, and F. della Paruta. Cremona: Libreria del Convegno Editrice, 1982, 137–56.

Soudek, Josef. "Leonardo Bruni and His Public: A Statistical and Interpretive Study of His Annotated Latin Version of the ps.-Aristotelian Economics." *Studies in Medieval and Renaissance History* 5 (1968), 51–136.

Sperling, Jutta. *Convents and the Body Politic in Late Renaissance Venice.* Chicago/London: University of Chicago Press, 1999.

―――. "The Paradox of Perfection: Reproducing the Body Politic in Late Renaissance Venice." *Comparative Studies in Society and History* 41 (1999): 3–32.

Storey, Tessa. *Carnal Commerce in Counter-Reformation Rome.* New Studies in European History. Cambridge: Cambridge University Press, 2008.

Strasser, Ulrike. *State of Virginity: Gender, Religion, and Politics in an Early Modern Catholic State.* Ann Arbor: University of Michigan Press, 2004.

Strocchia, Sharon. *Death and Ritual in Renaissance Florence.* Baltimore/London: Johns Hopkins University Press, 1992.

————. "Taken into Custody: Girls and Convent Guardianship in Renaissance Florence." *Renaissance Studies* 17 (2003): 177–200.

————. *Nuns and Nunneries in Renaissance Florence.* Baltimore: Johns Hopkins University Press, 2009.

Stuard, Susan M. *Women in Medieval Society.* Philadelphia: University of Pennsylvania Press, 1976.

Stumpo, Enrico. "Finanze e ragion di stato nella prima Età moderna: due modelli diversi: Piemonte e Toscana, Savoia e Medici." In *Finanze e ragion di Stato in Italia e Germania nella prima Età moderna,* ed. A. Maddalena and H. Kellenbenz. Bologna: Il Mulino, 1984.

Taddei, Ilaria. *Fanciulli e giovani: crescere a Firenze nel Rinascimento.* Biblioteca Storica Toscana a cura della Deputazione di storia patria per la Toscana, vol. 40. Florence: Leo S. Olschki, 2001.

Takahashi, Tomoko. "I bambini e i genitori-≪espositori≫ dello spedale di Santa Maria degli Innocenti di Firenze nel XV secolo." *Annuario dell'Istituto Giapponese di Cultura* 25 (1991–92): 35–75.

————. *Il Rinascimento dei trovatelli: il brefotrofio, la città e le campagne nella Toscana del XV secolo.* Rome: Edizioni di Storia e Letteratura, 2003.

Teicher, Anna. "Politics and Finance in the Age of Cosimo I: The Public and Private Face of Credit." In *Firenze e la Toscana de' Medici nell'Europa del Cinquecento.* 3 vols. Florence: Leo S. Olschki, 1983, 2: 343–62.

Terpstra, Nicholas. "In loco parentis: Confraternities and Abandoned Children in Florence and Bologna." In *The Politics of Ritual Kinship: Confraternities and Social Order in Early Modern Italy,* ed. Nicholas Terpstra. Cambridge: Cambridge University Press 1999, 114–31.

————. *Abandoned Children of the Italian Renaissance: Orphan Care in Florence and Bologna.* Baltimore: Johns Hopkins University Press, 2005.

————. *Lost Girls: Sex and Death in Renaissance Florence.* Baltimore: Johns Hopkins University Press, 2010.

Thiem, Christle. *Das römische Reiseskizzenbuch des Florentiners Giovanni Battista Naldini 1560/61.* Munich/Berlin: Deutscher Kunstverlag, 2002.

Thomas, Yan. "The Division of the Sexes in Roman Law." In *From Ancient Goddesses to Christian Saints,* ed. Pauline Schmitt Pantel, vol. 1 of *A History of Women in the West,* ed. Georges Duby and Michele Perrot. Cambridge/London: Belknap Press of Harvard University Press, 1992: 83–137.

Trexler, Richard. "Charity and the Defense of Urban Elites in the Italian Communes." In *The Rich, the Well Born, and the Powerful,* ed. F. Jaher. Urbana: University of Illinois Press, 1973, 64–109.

————. "Adolescence and Salvation in the Renaissance." In *The Pursuit of Holiness in Late Medieval and Renaissance Religion,* ed. C. Trinkaus and H. Oberman. Leiden: E. J. Brill, 1974, 200–64.

————. "A Widow's Asylum of the Renaissance: The Orbatello of Florence." In *Old Age in Pre-Industrial Society,* ed. Peter Stearns. New York: Holmes and Meier, 1982, 119–49.

van Egmond, Warren. "The Commercial Revolution and the Beginnings of Western Mathematics in Renaissance Florence, 1300–1500." Ph.D. diss., Indiana University, 1976.

————. *Practical Mathematics in the Italian Renaissance: A Catalog of Italian Manuscripts and Printed Books to 1600*. Florence: Istituto e Museo di Storia della Scienza, 1981.

Wallace, William E. *Michelangelo at San Lorenzo: The Genius as Entrepreneur*. Cambridge: Cambridge University Press, 1994.

————. "'*The Greatest Ass in the World*': Michelangelo as Writer." 2006 Geske Lecture University of Nebraska – Lincoln. Lincoln, NE: Hixson-Lied College of Fine and Performing Arts, 2006.

Wazbinski, Zygmunt. "La prima mostra dell'Accademia del Disegno a Firenze." *Prospettiva* 14 (1978): 47–57.

————. "La Cappella dei Medici e l'origine dell'Accademia del Disegno." In *Firenze e la Toscana dei Medici nell'Europa del Cinquecento*, ed. G.C Garfagini. 3 vols. Florence: Leo S. Olschki, 1983, 1: 54–69.

————. "Giorgio Vasari e Vincenzo Borghini come maestri accademici: il caso di G. B. Naldini." In G. C. Garfagnini, ed. *Giorgio Vasari: tra decorazione ambientale e storiografia artistica. Convegno di studi (Arezzo, 8–10 ottobre 1981)*, 285–99. Florence: Leo S. Olschki, 1985.

Weaver, Elissa B. "Spiritual Fun: A Study of Sixteenth-Century Tuscan Convent Theatre." In *Women in the Middle Ages*, ed. Mary Beth Rose. Syracuse: Syracuse University Press, 1986, 173–206.

————. "Suor Maria Clemente Ruoti, Playwright and Academician." In *Creative Women in Medieval and Early Modern Italy: A Religious and Artistic Renaissance*, ed. E. A. Matter and J. Coakley. Philadelphia: University of Pennsylvania Press, 1994, 281–96.

Weber, Max. *Economy and Society: An Outline of Interpretive Sociology*, ed. Guenther Roth and Claus Wittich; trans. Ephraim Fischoff. Berkeley: University of California Press, 1978.

Weil, Mark. "The Devotion of the Forty Hours and Roman Baroque Illusions." *Journal of the Warburg and Courtauld Institutes* 37 (1974): 218–48.

Weinstein, Donald. *Savonarola and Florence: Prophecy and Patriotism in the Renaissance*. Princeton: Princeton University Press, 1970.

Williams, Robert. "Vincenzo Borghini and Vasari's 'Lives.'" Ph.D. diss., Princeton University, 1988.

Wittkower, Rudolph, and Wittkower, Margot. *The Divine Michelangelo: The Florentine Academy's Homage on His Death in 1564*. London: Phaidon Press, 1964.

Woodhouse J. R. "Borghini's Theory of the Decay of Tuscan." *Studi Settecenteschi* 13 (1971): 100–15.

————. "Per un'edizione critica dei Pensieri e annotazioni di Vincenzio Borghini." *Lingua Nostra* 33 (1972): 39–45.

————. "Il Borghini e la rassettatura del ≪Decameron≫ del 1573: Un documento inedito." *Studi sul Boccaccio* 7 (1973): 303–15.

————. "Vincenzio Borghini's view of Charlemagne's Empire." *Viator* 19 (1988): 355–75.

Zarri, Gabriella. "Monasteri femminili e città (secoli XV–XVIII)." In *La chiesa e il potere politico dal Medioevo all'età contemporanea*, ed. Giorgio Chittolini and Giovanni Miccioli. Vol. 9 of *Storia d'Italia*. Turin: G. Einaudi, 1986, 357–429.

————. "Disciplina regolare e pratica di coscienza: le virtù grave; e i comportamenti sociali in comunità femminili (secoli XVI–XVIII)." In *Disciplina dell'anima, disciplina del corpo, e disciplina della società tra medioevo, ed età moderna*, ed. Paolo Prodi. Annali dell'Istituto storico italo-germanico di Trento, vol. 40. Bologna: Il Mulino, 1994, 257–78.

————. "Ursula and Catherine: The Marriage of Virgins in the Sixteenth Century." In *Creative Women in Medieval and Early Modern Italy*, ed. E. A. Matter and John Coakley, Philadelphia: University of Pennsylvania Press, 1994, 237–78.

————, ed. *Donna, disciplina, creanza cristiana.* Rome: Edizioni di Storia e letteratura, 1996.

Zecher, Carla. "The Gendering of the Lute in Sixteenth-Century French Love Poetry." *Renaissance Quarterly* 53.3 (2000):769–91.

Zorzi, Andrea. "Contrôle social, ordre public et répression judiciare à Florence à l'epoque communale: éléments et problèmes." *Annales: Économies, Sociétés, Civilisations* 5 (1990): 1169–88.

Zupko, Ronald. *Italian Weights and Measures from the Middle Ages to the Nineteenth Century.* Philadelphia: American Philosophical Society, 1981.

INDEX